Prejudice and Christian Beginnings

Prejudice and Christian Beginnings

Investigating Race, Gender,
and Ethnicity in Early Christian Studies

Edited by

Laura Nasrallah and Elisabeth Schüssler Fiorenza

Fortress Press
Minneapolis

PREJUDICE AND CHRISTIAN BEGINNINGS
Investigating Race, Gender, and Ethnicity in Early Christian Studies

Cover design: Ivy Palmer Skrade
Book design: PerfecType, Nashville, TN

Library of Congress Cataloging-in-Publication Data
Prejudice and Christian beginnings : investigating race, gender, and ethnicity in early Christian studies / edited by Laura Nasrallah and Elisabeth Schüssler Fiorenza.
    p. cm.
  Discussions of a small symposium held at Harvard University Divinity School in spring 2007.
  ISBN 978-0-8006-6340-7 (alk. paper)
  1. Discrimination—Religious aspects—Christianity. 2. Prejudices—History. 3. Church history—Primitive and early church, ca. 30-600. 4. Racism—Religious aspects—Christianity. 5. Sexism—Religious aspects—Christianity. 6. Ethnocentrism. I. Nasrallah, Laura Salah, 1969- II. Schüssler Fiorenza, Elisabeth, 1938-
  BT745.P74 2009
  270.108—dc22
                          2009017615

The paper used in this publication meets the minimum requirements of American National Standard for Information Sciences — Permanence of Paper for Printed Library Materials, ANSI Z329.48-1984.

Printed in Canada

13 12 11 10 09 1 2 3 4 5 6 7 8 9 10

Contents

Preface

The explorations of this volume have their roots in the discussions of a small symposium on the same topic held at Harvard University Divinity School in Spring 2007. This conference was made possible by a faculty grant from the Center for the Study of World Religions at Harvard. We want to thank its director, Donald Swearer, and its faculty committee for supporting our work with this grant. We are also grateful to Susan Lloyd McGarry and Charles Anderson at the Center for their help in bringing the symposium to fruition. Many others also helped us, mounting websites and facilitating other activities. Felicia Share was invaluable in organizing information and coordinating our various needs. We are deeply grateful.

We want to thank as well those colleagues who responded to papers in the context of the symposium; their voices are reflected in the improvements that each chapter saw: Wallace Best, Bernadette Brooten, Elizabeth Castelli, Caroline Johnson Hodge, Richard Horsley, Melanie Johnson-DeBaufre, and Jennifer Wright Knust, as well as our students, Cavan Concannon, Katherine Shaner, and Justine Smith. We are also grateful to Clarice Martin, who presented an important paper at the original symposium but was unable to offer an essay for this volume.

We are especially grateful to our very able doctoral students, without whose work neither this book nor the symposium would have been possible. Taylor Petrey adeptly assisted us in the organization of the conference itself and tirelessly contacted speakers and vendors.

Michal Beth Dinkler and Margaret Leslie Butterfield very competently contacted the contributors to this volume and expertly pre-edited the individual essays. Without their work we would not have been able to undertake this volume. We are deeply grateful to them and hope that the work on the symposium and the book will fructify their own scholarly work.

We are grateful to Neil Elliott and Susan Johnson of Fortress Press for encouraging this publication and to Andrew DeYoung for carefully shepherding it through the publication process.

Contributors

Cynthia M. Baker is Associate Professor of Religion at Bates College in Lewiston, Maine. Her publications include *Rebuilding the House of Israel: Architectures of Gender in Jewish Antiquity* (Stanford: Stanford University Press, 2002) and "When Jews Were Women," *History of Religions* 45:2 (2005). She is presently at work on an extended history of the term "Jew."

Denise Kimber Buell is Associate Professor and Chair of the Department of Religion at Williams College. She is author of *Why This New Race? Ethnic Reasoning in Early Christianity* (New York: Columbia University Press, 2005) and *Making Christians: Clement of Alexandria and the Rhetoric of Legitimacy* (Princeton: Princeton University Press).

Gabriella Gelardini is Senior Research Associate at the University of Basel, Switzerland. Her publications include an acclaimed study of the Book of Hebrews, *"Verhärtet eure Herzen nicht": Der Hebräer, eine Synagogenhomilie zu Tischa be-Aw* (Leiden: Brill, 2007). Her forthcoming book explores the role of ethnicity and religion in the New Testament in shaping a collective Christian identity.

Shelley P. Haley is Professor of Classics and Africana Studies at Hamilton College and contributor to the *African American Women Writers Series, 1910–1940*. She has lectured nationally and internationally on reshaping the discipline of Classics from a black feminist perspective and on her research concerning the role of a classical education in the lives and careers of nineteenth-century college-educated Black women.

Susannah Heschel is Eli Black Professor in Jewish studies in the Department of Religion at Dartmouth College. Her scholarship focuses on Jewish-Christian relations in Germany during the nineteenth and twentieth centuries. Her monograph *Abraham Geiger and the Jewish Jesus* (Chicago: University of Chicago Press) won a National Jewish Book Award, and her new book is *The Aryan Jesus: Christian Theologians and the Bible in Nazi Germany* (Princeton: Princeton University Press, 2008). She has edited a classic collection, *On Being a Jewish Feminist.*

Shawn Kelley is a professor at Daemen College, where he chairs the Department of Religion and Philosophy. He is a Research Associate in the Institute for Signifying (on) Scriptures and is the author of *Racializing Jesus: Race, Ideology and the Formation of Modern Biblical Scholarship* (London: Routledge, 2002). He is currently researching the intersection of race, religion, gender, and genocide.

Joseph A. Marchal is Assistant Professor of Religious Studies, teaching in the areas of Bible and critical theory, at Ball State University. His scholarship attends to the intersections of gender, sexuality, ethnicity, and empire through a strategic combination of feminist, postcolonial, and queer approaches. His dissertation *Hierarchy, Unity, and Imitation* was published in 2006 (from the Society of Biblical Literature and Brill) and a second work, which includes elaborations on his contribution to this volume and is titled *The Politics of Heaven: Women, Gender, and Empire in the Study of Paul,* was published in the fall of 2008 by Fortress Press.

Laura Nasrallah is Associate Professor of New Testament and Early Christianity at Harvard Divinity School. Her most recent book, *Christian Responses to Roman Art and Architecture: The Second-Century Church in the Spaces of Empire,* is forthcoming from Cambridge University Press. Her *An Ecstasy of Folly: Prophecy and Authority in Early Christianity* (Cambridge, Mass.: Harvard University Press, 2004) focuses on 1 Corinthians and on materials from the second- and third-century controversies over prophecy and the nature of the soul. She is writing a commentary on 1 Corinthians for the Hermeneia series through Fortress Press and co-editing a volume emerging from a conference she organized with colleagues from Greece and the United States: "From Roman to Early Christian Thessalonikē: A Conference in Religion and Archaeology."

Elisabeth Schüssler Fiorenza is Krister Stendahl Professor of Scripture and Interpretation at Harvard Divinity School. Her teaching and research focus on questions of biblical and theological epistemology, hermeneutics, rhetoric, and the politics of interpretation. Her many published works include *In Memory of Her: A Feminist Theological Reconstruction of Christian Origins* (New York: Crossroad, 1983, subsequently translated into fourteen languages); *Revelation: Vision of a Just World*, rev. ed. (Minneapolis: Fortress, 1991); *But She Said: Feminist Practices of Biblical Interpretation* (New York: Beacon, 1993); *Discipleship of Equals: A Critical Feminist Ekklesia-ology of Liberation* (London: SCM, 1993); *Jesus: Miriam's Child, Sophia's Prophet* (New York: Continuum, 1995); *Bread Not Stone: The Challenge of Feminist Biblical Interpretation* (New York: Beacon, 1995); (ed.) *The Power of Naming: A Concilium Reader in Feminist Liberation Theology* (London: SCM, 1996); *Sharing Her Word: Feminist Biblical Interpretation in Context* (New York: Continuum, 1998); *Jesus and the Politics of Interpretation* (New York: Continuum, 2000); *Wisdom Ways: Introducing Feminist Biblical Interpretation* (Maryknoll: Orbis, 2001); *The Power of the Word: Scripture and the Rhetoric of Empire* (Minneapolis: Fortress, 2007); her most recent book, *Democratizing Biblical Studies: Toward an Emancipatory Educational Space*, will be published by Westminster John Knox in Fall 2009.

Fernando F. Segovia is Oberlin Graduate Professor of New Testament and Early Christianity at Vanderbilt University and author of *Decolonizing Biblical Studies: A View From the Margins* (Maryknoll: Orbis, 2000). He is the editor of *Postcolonial Biblical Criticism: Interdisciplinary Intersections* (New York: Continuum, 2007), and co-editor of *Teaching the Bible: The Discourses and Politics of Biblical Pedagogy* (Maryknoll: Orbis, 1998).

Sze-kar Wan is Professor of New Testament at Perkins School of Theology and author of *Power in Weakness: Conflict and Rhetorics in Paul's Second Letter to the Corinthians* (New York: Continuum, 2000).

Vincent L. Wimbush is Professor of Religion and Director of the Institute for Signifying Scriptures at Claremont Graduate University in California. Among his most recent publications are *Theorizing Scriptures: New Critical Orientations to a Cultural Phenomenon* (New Brunswick: Rutgers University Press, 2008); *The Bible and African Americans: A Brief History* (Minneapolis: Fortress Press, 2003); and editor, with the assistance of R. Rodman, of *African Americans and the Bible: Sacred Texts and Social Textures* (New York: Continuum, 2001).

Abbreviations

Modern Sources

ABD	*The Anchor Bible Dictionary*
BibInt	*Biblical Interpretation*
CBQ	*Catholic Biblical Quarterly*
CIL	*Corpus Inscriptionum Latinarum*
DNP	*Der Neue Pauly*
JBL	*Journal of Biblical Literature*
JECS	*Journal of Early Christian Studies*
JFSR	*Journal of Feminist Studies in Religion*
JJS	*Journal of Jewish Studies*
JRA	*Journal of Roman Archeology*
JRS	*Journal of Roman Studies*
JSJ	*Journal for the Study of Judaism*
JSNT	*Journal for the Study of the New Testament*
HR	*History of Religions*
HTR	*Harvard Theological Review*
LCL	*Loeb Classical Library*
MMLA	*Bulletin of the Midwest Modern Language Association*
OCT	*Oxford Classical Texts/Scriptorum classicorum bibliotheca oxoniensis*
Rend.	Atti della Accademia nazionale dei Lincei. *Rendiconti Classe di Scienze Morali Storiche e Filologiche*

SBL	Society of Biblical Literature
SBLDS	*Society of Biblical Literature Dissertation Series*
ScrHier	*Scripta hierosolymitana*
SPhilo	*Studio Philonica*
TRE	*Theologische Realenzyklopädie*

Introduction

Exploring the Intersections of Race, Gender, Status, and Ethnicity in Early Christian Studies

Elisabeth Schüssler Fiorenza

Prejudice and Christian Beginnings brings together the critical and constructive explorations of leading scholars who have already made significant contributions either to the study of the intersection of race,[1] ethnicity,[2] and critical feminist theory[3] with Early Christian Studies or

---

1. See the collected essays in Philomena Essed and David Theo Goldberg, ed., *Race Critical Theories: Text and Context* (Malden, Mass.: Blackwell Publishing, 2000).

2. Cf. John Hutchinson and Anthony D. Smith, ed., *Ethnicity* (New York: Oxford University Press, 1996), and Steve Fenton, *Ethnicity* (Malden, Mass.: Polity, 2003).

3. Among the vast literature, I have found especially helpful Jacqui Alexander and Chandra Talpade Mohanti, *Feminist Genealogies, Colonial Legacies, Democratic Futures* (New York: Routledge, 1997); Patricia Hill Collins, *Fighting Words: Black Women and the Search for Justice* (Minneapolis: University of Minnesota Press, 1998); France Winddance Twine and Kathleen M. Blee, ed., *Feminism and Antiracism: International Struggles for Justice* (New York: New York University Press, 2001).

to the investigation of how race, gender, ethnicity, and empire[4] shaped early Christian or classical texts. It explores how Early Christian Studies can benefit not only from the diverse methodological approaches already developed within the field, but also from interactions with insights from classics, from the history of antiquity, from the study of religion and the*logy,[5] and from critical theory—especially critical race, feminist, and postcolonial theories.

Recently, scholars of classical antiquity as well as of canonical and postcanonical Early Christian literatures have turned their attention to ethnicity in the ancient world. They have been slow, however, to engage this research with critical theories of gender, on the one hand, and critical race theory, on the other. Hence, this interdisciplinary volume brings together the work of important scholars in the fields of Christian Testament Studies, Classics, early Christian history, and Jewish Studies.

By proposing the study of race, gender, empire, and ethnicity as an entry point or theoretical lens, these essays make great contributions to rethinking how we read ancient texts, including the Christian Scriptures, as well as to reconceptualizing the field of Early Christian Studies. The chapters address topics such as gender, ethnicity, and race under the Roman Empire; the crucible of nineteenth-century thinking about race, gender, and empire that has shaped Classics as well as Early Christian Studies; and the theoretical frameworks and methods by which such studies can best proceed in their analysis of race, gender, and ethnicity in the ancient worlds.

Scholars for some time have discussed ethnic constructions of Jews, Barbarians, and Greeks, how religion and gender shaped these

---

4. For a discussion of empire and Early Christian Studies, see my book, *The Power of the Word: Scripture and the Rhetoric of Empire* (Minneapolis: Fortress Press, 2007).

5. In order to indicate the brokenness and inadequacy of human language to name the Divine, I switched in my book, *Jesus: Miriam's Child, Sophia's Prophet: Critical Issues in Feminist Christology* (New York: Continuum, 1994), from the orthodox Jewish writing of G-d, which I had adopted in *But She Said: Feminist Practices of Biblical Interpretation* (Boston: Beacon Press, 1992) and *Discipleship of Equals: A Critical Feminist Ekklesia-logy of Liberation* (New York: Crossroad, 1993), to this spelling of G*d, which seeks to avoid the conservative malestream association which the writing of G-d has for Jewish feminists. Since the*logy means speaking about G*d or G*d-talk, I write it in the same way.

identity constructions, and how Roman imperialism has produced or sustained these ideological structures of domination. In recent years, classicists have turned with great energy to the topic of race and ethnicity (for example, Jonathan Hall,[6] Edith Hall,[7] Benjamin Isaac,[8] Siän Jones[9]) and have continued to research the topic of gender in Mediterranean antiquity. While scholarship on the topic of ethnicity has swelled, longstanding arguments that "race" (and especially racism) and "gender" (hetero-sexism) are modern categories not applicable to an analysis of the ancient worlds have compelled some scholars of antiquity to shy away from using the terms "race" or "gender" in discussions of the ancient worlds. Recently, classicists such as Benjamin Isaacs, however, have begun to utilize race as a critical category of analysis in the investigation of ancient sources.

In the study of Christianity in antiquity, too, scholars like Mark G. Brett,[10] Denise Buell,[11] Judith Lieu,[12] Shaye Cohen,[13] and Gay Byron[14] have done path-breaking work in identifying the way in which early Christian writers construct race, gender, sexuality, and ethnicity. While the topic of race, gender, and ethnicity in the ancient world has begun to be addressed, scholars such as R. S. Sugirtharajah[15] and

---

6. Jonathan M. Hall, *Ethnic Identity in Greek Antiquity* (New York: Cambridge University Press, 1997).

7. Edith Hall, *Inventing the Barbarian: Greek Self-Definition through Tragedy* (Oxford: University Press, 1991).

8. Benjamin Isaac, *The Invention of Racism in Classical Antiquity* (Princeton: Princeton University Press, 2004).

9. Siän Jones, *The Archeology of Ethnicity: Constructing Identities in the Past and in the Present* (New York: Routledge, 1997).

10. Mark G. Brett, ed., *Ethnicity and the Bible* (Boston: Brill Academic Publishers, 2002).

11. Denise Kimber Buell, *Why This New Race? Ethnic Reasoning in Early Christianity* (New York: Columbia University Press, 2005).

12. Judith M. Lieu, *Christian Identity in the Jewish and Graeco-Roman World* (New York: Oxford University Press, 2004).

13. Shaye J. D. Cohen, *Why Aren't Jewish Women Circumcised? Gender and Covenant in Judaism* (Berkeley: University of California Press, 2005).

14. Gay L. Byron, *Symbolic Blackness and Ethnic Difference in Early Christian Literature* (New York: Routledge, 2002).

15. Among his many publications, see R.S. Sugirtharajah, *The Bible and Empire: Postcolonial Explorations* (New York: Cambridge University Press, 2005).

the contributors to this volume have embarked on the exploration as to how racial and ethnic theories of modernity have affected the origins and practices of Early Christian Studies themselves.

With "prejudice and domination" as its primary theoretical lens, this collection of essays seeks to continue the conversation begun at a conference on "Race, Gender, and Ethnicity" held at Harvard University Divinity School in 2007. It explores a number of significant avenues of inquiry that push scholarship forward in several directions. First, it seeks to further the theoretical discussion on critical race theory and the intersection of race with class, gender, and empire in the study of religion in general and in that of early Christianity in particular. Second, while classicists have investigated race and ethnicity in antiquity, there has been less scholarship specifically directed toward the intersections of race, gender, ethnicity, and empire in Early Christian Studies. This study seeks to address that gap.

Third, the volume engages in explicit conversation about the theoretical frameworks and methodologies by which Early Christian and Early Jewish Studies might proceed in the analysis of race, gender, and ethnicity. Early Christian Studies are caught between the longstanding authority of the historical critical method, which insists that such inquiry be limited to the first centuries C.E., on the one hand, and critical theory, hermeneutics, epistemology, cultural studies, ethnicity studies, and literary studies, on the other, which insist that all interpretations and readings are shaped by contemporary intellectual frameworks and sociopolitical locations. Work investigating race, gender, or colonialism in the Christian Testament is often marginalized, and students who want to address the topic of race, gender, or domination often do double or triple work as they must "master" a set of scholarly tools that does not allow them to investigate the problems that initially drew them to the field.

Finally, the significant analytics of feminist, postcolonial, and critical race theories have developed alongside each other but have not been integrated to accomplish an intersectional analysis of early Christian literature and history. While scholars of early Christianity have quickly embraced the study of ethnicity or empire in antiquity, including the important question of how ethnicity and empire shape religion and religious practices, they have been slower to address the question of how race and gender are involved in social and ideological constructions of Christianity. This is more than surprising, since a rich body of critical feminist work on the intersectionality of race, gender, class, ethnicity, and empire has existed for quite some time.[16]

I. Toward an Intersectional Social Analytic in Early Christian Studies

The term intersectionality was coined by the legal scholar Kimberly Crenshaw and entails "the notion that subjectivity is constituted by mutually multiplicative vectors of race, gender, class, sexuality, and imperialism." It has emerged as a key theoretical tool in critical feminist and race studies for subverting race/gender and other binaries of domination. Some have criticized "identity politics" for eliding intra-group differences; intersectionality seeks to address that criticism while still recognizing the necessity of group politics. "Finally, inter-sectionality invites scholars to come to terms with the legacy of the exclusions of multiply marginalized subjects from feminist and antira-cist work," and "to draw on the ostensibly unique epistemological posi-tion of marginalized subjects to fashion a vision of equality."[17] Hence, I suggest, intersectionality can provide a critical framework and lens for the critical explorations of race, gender, ethnicity, and empire in Early Christian Studies undertaken in the essays of this book.

Bonnie Thornton Dill studied this emerging method of social analysis in 2001 and saw it as "in the process of being created."[18] According to Dill, intersectional scholarship is grounded in the experi-ence of those whose identities are constructed at the intersections of

16. See however now Randall C. Bailey, Tat-siong Benny Liew, Fernando F. Segovia, eds., *They Were All Together in One Place. Toward Minority Biblical Criti-cism* (Atlanta: SBL, 2009).

17. Jennifer C. Nash, "Rethinking Intersectionality," *Feminist Review* 89, no. 1 (2008) 3.

18. Bonnie Thornton Dill, "Work in the Intersections of Race, Gender, Eth-nicity and Other Dimensions of Difference in Higher Education," *Newsletter of the Consortium on Race, Gender, and Ethnicity of the University of Maryland* (Fall 2002) 5–7. Accessed on 8/23/2008 at http://www.crge.umd.edu/publications/news.pdf. See also, Patricia Hill Collins, Fighting Words, 201–29.

race, gender, and ethnicity. The goal of this work "at the intersections" is to contribute to a more just world. The theory of intersectionality has been articulated as a theory of marginalized subjectivity, as a theory of identity, and as a theory of the matrix of oppressions. In the first iteration, intersectional theory refers only to multiply marginalized subjects; in its second iteration, the theory seeks to illuminate how identity is constructed at the intersections of race, gender, class, sexuality, and imperialism; the third iteration stresses intersectional theory as a theory of structures and sites of oppression. Race, sex, gender, class, and imperialism are seen as vectors of dominating power that create coconstitutive social processes which engender the differential simultaneity of dominations and subordinations.

Leslie McCall in turn describes three methodological approaches to intersectionality which are defined primarily "in terms of . . . how they understand and use categories to explore the complexity of intersectionality in social life."[19] She calls the first approach "anticategorical complexity," which deconstructs the analytical categories of race, gender, class, sexuality, and imperialism. She terms the second approach "intracategorical complexity" because scholars working in this mode focus on "people whose identity crosses the boundaries of traditionally constructed groups."[20] The third approach, termed "intercategorical complexity," requires that scholars adopt "existing analytical categories" to analyze "the relationships of inequality among social groups."[21] Whereas the first approach renders categories of analysis suspect because they have no foundations in reality, the third seeks to use them strategically. The first approach deploys postmodernist discourse, which "attempts to move beyond essentialism by pluralizing and dissolving the stability and analytic utility of the categories of race, class, gender, sexuality," whereas the third holds "the relations of domination and subordination that are named and articulated through the processes of racism and racialization still exist and they still require analytic and political specification and engagement."[22]

---

19. Leslie McCall, "The Complexity of Intersectionality," *Signs* 30, no. 3 (2005) 1773.

20. Thornton Dill, *Intersections*, 5.

21. McCall, *Complexity*, 1773.

22. Alexander and Mohanti, *Feminist Genealogies*, xvii.

In sum, it is important to pay attention to the material and discursive significance of categories in order to analyze how they are "produced, experienced, reproduced, and resisted in everyday life."[23] The interactive complexity of the social and discursive relations of inequality within and across analytical categories is at the heart of an intersectional analytics.

In attempting to define the categories of race and gender as well as their intersectionality, Sally Hasslanger[24] has pointed out that in such an intersectional analysis, the definition of gender or race in terms of social relations of dominance is decisive. Gender and race categories are defined in terms of one's social position. They are hierarchically— or, as I would say, kyriarchically[25]—structured, and bodily differences function as physical markers to socially distinguish and locate people in the pyramid of dominations.

Hasslanger distinguishes between race and ethnicity in the following way:

> One's ethnicity concerns one's ancestral links to a certain geographical region (perhaps together with participation in the cultural practices of that region); often ethnicity is associated with characteristic physical features. For our purposes, however, it might be useful to employ the notion of "ethnicity" for those groups that are like races . . . except that they do not experience systematic subordination or privilege in the context in question. . . . In short, we can distinguish between grouping individuals on the basis of their (assumed) origins, and grouping them *hierarchically* on the basis of their (assumed) origins, and the contrast between race and ethnicity might be a useful way to capture this distinction.[26]

With such a theorization, Hasslanger joins the ranks of First World materialist feminists, as well as of Two-Thirds World feminists who

---

23. McCall, *Complexity*, 1783.
24. Sally Hasslanger, "Gender and Race: (What) Are They? (What) Do We Want Them To Be?" *Nous* 34, no. 1 (2000) 31–55.
25. See pages 6–13 below, where I discuss this term.
26. Hasslanger, *Gender and Race*, 45.

have problematized the interpretation of wo/men's[27] oppression solely in terms of gender or racial dualism. They have pointed out, on the one hand, that wo/men are oppressed not only by heterosexism, but also by racism, classism, and colonialism. On the other hand, they have rejected an essentializing definition of gender and patriarchy which holds that all men are oppressors and all wo/men are their victims. The same critique of dualistic essentializing constructions applies to race, class, and postcolonial theories.

Instead, critical intersectional theorists have argued consistently that wo/men of subordinated races, nations, and classes are often more oppressed by elite white wo/men than by the men of their own class, race, culture, or religion. As a result of this contradiction in wo/men's lives, the interconnection between the exclusion of wo/men and all other "subordinates" from citizenship has not been given sufficient attention. The same is true for its ideological justifications in the form of reified "natural" sexual/racial/class/cultural differences. Hence, intersectional theorists usually conceptualize such social and ideological structures of domination as *hierarchical*, in order to map and make visible the complex interstructuring of the conflicting status positions of different wo/men.

---

27. In order to lift into consciousness the linguistic violence of so-called generic male-centered language, I write the term wo/men with a slash, in order to use the term "wo/men" and not "men" in an inclusive way. I suggest that whenever you read "wo/men," you need to understand it in the generic sense. Wo/man includes man, she includes he, and female includes male. Feminist Studies of language have elaborated that Western, kyriocentric, that is, master, lord, father, male-centered language systems, understand language as both generic and as gender specific. Wo/men always must think at least twice, if not three times, and adjudicate whether we are meant or not by so-called generic terms such as "men, humans, Americans, or professors." To use "wo/men" as an inclusive generic term invites male readers to learn how to "think twice" and to experience what it means not to be addressed explicitly. Since wo/men always must arbitrate whether we are meant or not, I consider it a good spiritual exercise for men to acquire the same sophistication and to learn how to engage in the same hermeneutical process of "thinking twice" and of asking whether they are meant when I speak of wo/men. Since, according to Wittgenstein, the limits of our language are the limits of our world, such a change of language patterns is a very important step toward the realization of a new feminist consciousness.

II. Naming Intersectional Structures of Domination: Kyriarchy

I believe that the label "hierarchy" for such a pyramidal system is a misnomer, since it only targets one specific, religiously sanctioned form of domination. Hence, I have proposed to replace the category of "hierarchy" with the neologism *kyriarchy*, which is derived from the Greek words *kyrios* (lord, slave master, father, husband, elite propertied educated man) and *archein* (to rule, dominate).[28]

In classical antiquity, the rule of the emperor, lord, slave master, husband, or the elite freeborn, propertied, educated gentleman to whom disenfranchised men and all wo/men were subordinated is best characterized as *kyriarchy*. In antiquity, the social system of kyriarchy was institutionalized either in empire or as a democratic political form of ruling. Kyriarchy is best theorized as a complex pyramidal system of intersecting multiplicative social and religious structures of superordination and subordination, of ruling and oppression. Kyriarchal relations of domination are built on elite male property rights as well as on the exploitation, dependency, inferiority, and obedience of wo/men who signify all those subordinated. Such kyriarchal relations are still today at work in the multiplicative intersectionality of class, race, gender, ethnicity, empire, and other structures of discrimination.

Kyriarchy is constituted as a sociocultural and religious system of dominations by intersecting multiplicative structures of oppression. The different sets of relations of domination shift historically and produce a different constellation of oppression in different times and cultures. The structural positions of subordination that have been fashioned by kyriarchal relations stand in tension with those required by radical democracy.

Rather than identifying kyriarchy with the binary male over female, white over black, Western over colonialized peoples, it is best to understand this term in the classical sense of antiquity. Modern democracies are still structured as complex pyramidal political systems of superiority and inferiority, of dominance and subordination.

---

28. For the first development of this concept, see my book *But She Said*, 103–32.

As kyriarchal democracies, they are stratified by gender, race, class, religion, heterosexualism, and age; these are *structural positions* that are assigned to us more or less by birth. However, how people live these structural kyriarchal positions is conditioned not simply by these structural positions themselves, but also by the subject positions through which we live our structural kyriarchal positions. Whereas an essentialist approach assigns to people an "authentic" identity that is derived from our structural position, our subject position becomes coherent and compelling through political discourse, interpretive frameworks, and the development of theoretical horizons regarding domination.

Thus, a critical intersectional analytic does not understand kyriarchy as an essentialist ahistorical system. Instead, it articulates kyriarchy as a heuristic (derived from the Greek, meaning "to find") concept, or as a diagnostic, analytic instrument that enables investigation into the multiplicative interdependence of gender, race, class, and imperial stratifications, as well as into their discursive inscriptions and ideological reproductions. Moreover, it highlights that people inhabit several structural positions of race, sex, gender, class, and ethnicity. If one position becomes privileged, it constitutes a nodal point. While in any particular historical moment class may be the primary modality through which one experiences gender and race, in other circumstances gender may be the privileged position through which one experiences sexuality, race, and class.

Rather than trace the different historical formations of kyriarchy in Western societies and biblical religions, I discuss here the classic and modern forms of democratic kyriarchy and its legitimating discourses. *Greek kyriarchal democracy* constituted itself by excluding the "others" who did not have a share in the land, but whose labor sustained society. It measured freedom and citizenship over and against slavery, but also in terms of gender. Moreover, the socioeconomic realities in the Greek city-state were such that only a few select freeborn, propertied, elite, male heads of households actually exercised democratic government. According to the theoretical vision—but not the historical realization—of democracy, all those living in the *polis*, the city-state, should be equal citizens, able to participate in government. In theory, all citizens share equal rights, speech, and power. As the assembly or congress (in Greek, *ekklēsia*) of free citizens, people were to deliberate and decide together the best ways to pursue their own well-being and the welfare of all citizens. In practice, however, democratic government excluded most inhabitants of the city-state.

This classic Greek form of kyriarchal democracy was both kyriocentric and ethnocentric. It drew its boundaries in terms of dualistic polarities and analogies between gods/humans, Greeks/Barbarians, male/female, human/beast, culture/nature, civilized/uncivilized world. Civilization, war, and marriage constituted the boundaries of citizenship. The structuring dividing lines run between men who owned property and those who were owned, between rulers and those who were ruled, between those who, as superiors, commanded and those who, as subordinates, had to obey, between those who, free from manual labor, had leisure for philosophy and politics, and those who were economically dependent, whose labor was exploited.

This mapping of ancient kyriarchy as an overarching system of domination, however, must not be misconstrued as a universal ahistorical "master paradigm." Rather, it is best understood as a particular reflection of the sociopolitical situation and common good of the Athenian city-state. Nevertheless, in its uses of ancient Greek democracy, which systemically excluded slaves, wo/men, and foreigners, Western political philosophy has justified such structures of exclusion. The political discourses of subordination that shape the subject positions of domination have decisively determined modern forms of democracy.

Roman kyriarchal imperialism is exemplified by a monarchical pyramid[29] of intersecting structures of domination that incorporates elements of traditional democratic practices (for example, the Senate). At its apex stood the emperor, who is called *pater patrum* or the "father of all fathers," and who is divinized and acclaimed as "God of Gods and Lord of Lords." Roman imperial power was seen as *Pax*

---

29. For a similar construction of the social pyramid of the Roman Empire, but without taking gender into account, see G. Alföldi, *The Social History of Rome* (Totowa, N.J.: Barnes & Noble, 1985), as well as Ekkehard Stegemann and Wolfgang Stegemann, *The Jesus Movement: A Social History of Its First Century* (Minneapolis: Fortress Press, 1999).

Romana, a beneficial system of peace for all conquered peoples. Its harsh and exploitative rule is symbolically indicted in the Book of Revelation.[30]

Neo-Aristotelian philosophy legitimated this Roman kyriarchal model of imperial power and entered into the Christian Scriptures in the form of kyriarchal injunctions to submission. The First Epistle of Peter, for instance, admonishes Christian servants to be submissive even to harsh and brutal masters (2:18–25) and instructs freeborn wives to subordinate themselves to their husbands, even those who are not Christians (3:1–6). Simultaneously, it entreats Christians to be subject to and honor the emperor as supreme (2:13–17). In the United States today, this kyriarchal scriptural ethos funds the political Right's discourses on marriage and family values.

The *modern (American) form of democratic kyriarchy or kyriarchal democracy*, like ancient Greek democracy, also initially excluded freeborn wo/men, as well as immigrant, poor, and slave wo/men, from democratic rights. "Property" and elite male status by birth and education, not simply biological-cultural masculinity, entitled a few men to govern over the many. Modern liberal democracy thus continued many of the ideological practices found in ancient democratic kyriarchy, insofar as it claims that its citizens have equal rights and are entitled to "liberty and the pursuit of happiness," while simultaneously retaining allegedly "natural" kyriarchal, economic, socio-political stratifications.

Hence, modern political philosophy continues to assume that the propertied, educated, elite Western Man is defined by reason, self-determination, and full citizenship, whereas freeborn wo/men and other subordinated peoples are characterized by emotion, service,

---

30. For this debate, see for instance Elisabeth Schüssler Fiorenza, *The Book of Revelation: Justice and Judgment*, 2nd edition with a new epilogue (Philadelphia: Fortress Press, 1998). See especially also the classic work of W. M. Ramsay, *The Letters to the Seven Churches*. Updated Edition by Mark W. Wilson (Peabody: Hendrickson, 2001), which appeared first in 1904. For the more recent discussion, see Steven J. Friesen, *Imperial Cults and the Apocalypse of John: Reading Revelation in the Ruins* (Oxford: Oxford University Press, 2001); Nelson Kraybill, *Imperial Cult and Commerce in John's Apocalypse* (Sheffield: Sheffield Academic, 1996); Leonard J. Thompson, *The Book of Revelation: Apocalypse and Empire* (Oxford: Oxford University Press, 1990), argued for no persecution at all.

and dependence. They are seen not as rational and responsible adult subjects, but as emotional, helpless, and child-like, subject to exploitation. Emancipatory biblical studies such as postcolonial studies or liberation theologies have done well to expose this model. But insofar as they have developed their analytic without considering explicitly the status position of multiply oppressed wo/men, they perpetuate the ideologies of kyriocentrism, despite their intentions.

Furthermore, modern political philosophy elaborates two aspects of kyriarchal power, one seeking to secure species reproduction, the other sexual gratification. The first sustains the kyriarchal order by wielding control over wives, children, slaves, servants, and wealth. The second articulates kyriarchal power as masculine-phallic power that controls those it desires. Kyriarchal power operates along the axes of gender, race, class, culture, nation, and religion. Its "politics" of dominations fashions ideological "subject positions" around which notions of discrimination and domination are constructed.

In light of this analysis, it becomes clear that the universalist kyriocentric rhetoric of Euro-American elite men does not simply reinforce the dominance of the male sex, but it legitimates the imperial "White Father" or, in black idiom, the enslaving "Boss-Man" as the universal subject. By implication, any critical theory—be it critical race, feminist, liberationist, or Marxist theory—that articulates gender, class, or race difference as a primary and originary difference masks the complex interstructuring of kyriarchal dominations inscribed *in* the subject positions of individual wo/men and in the status positions of dominance and subordination *between* wo/men. It also masks the participation of white elite wo/men, or better "ladies," and of Christian religion in kyriarchal oppression, insofar as both have served as civilizing colonialist conduits of kyriarchal knowledges, values, and culture.

Since modern liberal democracies are modeled after the classical ideal of kyriarchal democracy, they continue the contradiction between kyriarchal practices and democratic self-understandings inscribed in the discourses of democracy in antiquity. It must not be overlooked, however, that this institutionalized contradiction between the ideals of radical emancipatory democracies and their historical kyriarchal actualizations has also engendered emancipatory movements seeking full self-determining citizenship.

In conclusion, I want to stress the following structural aspects of kyriarchy:

- Kyriarchy is a complex pyramidal system of dominations that works through the violence of economic exploitation and lived subordination. However, this kyriarchal pyramid must not be seen as static, but as an always-changing net of relations of domination.

- Kyriarchy is realized differently in different historical contexts. Democratic kyriarchy or kyriarchal democracy was articulated differently in antiquity than in modernity. It is different in Greece, Hellenism, Rome, Asia Minor, Europe, America, Japan, or India; it is different in Judaism, Islam, or Catholicism.

- Not only a gender system, but also the stratification systems of race, class, colonialism, and heterosexism structure and determine this kyriarchal system. These structures intersect with each other in a pyramidal fashion; they are not parallel but multiplicative. The full power of kyriarchal oppression comes to the fore in the lives of wo/men living on the bottom of the kyriarchal pyramid.

- To function, kyriarchal cultures need a servant class, a servant race, a servant gender, a servant people. Such a servant class is maintained through the ideologies of kyriocentrism, which are internalized through education, socialization, and brute violence, and rationalized by malestream scholarship. Kyriarchy is sustained by the belief that members of a servant class of people are naturally or by divine decree inferior to those whom they serve.

- Both in Western modernity and in Greco-Roman antiquity, kyriarchy stands in tension with a democratic ethos and social system of equality and freedom. In a radical democratic system, power is not exercised through "power over" or through violence and subordination, but through the human capacities for respect, responsibility, self-determination, and self-esteem. This radical democratic ethos has repeatedly engendered emancipatory movements that insisted on equal freedom, dignity, and justice for all.

- Feminist political theorists have shown that the classical Greek philosophers Aristotle and Plato articulated in different ways a theory of kyriarchal democracy, in order to justify the exclusion of certain people, such as freeborn wo/men or slave wo/men and men, from participation in democratic government. These people were not fit to govern, the philosophers argued, because of their deficient natural powers of reasoning. Such explicit ideological justifications need to be developed at a point in history when it becomes increasingly obvious that those who are excluded from the political life of the *polis*, such as freeborn wo/men, educated slaves, wealthy *metics* (alien residents), and traveling mercenaries, are actually indispensable to it. Philosophical rationalizations of the exclusion of diverse people from citizenship and government are engendered by the contradiction between the democratic vision of the city-state and its actual practices.

- This contradiction between the logic of democracy and historical sociopolitical kyriarchal practices has produced the kyriocentric logic of identity as the assertion of "natural differences" between elite men and wo/men, freeborn and slaves, property owners and farmers or artisans, Athenian-born citizens and other residents, Greeks and Barbarians, the civilized and uncivilized world. A similar process of ideological kyriocentrism is inscribed in Christian Scriptures in and through the so-called (household) codes of submission. It is found in modern societies in the form of the family as nucleus of the kyriarchal state.[31]

III. Changing Kyriarchal Relations of Domination

In the past centuries, emancipatory struggles for equal rights as citizens have gained voting and civil rights for all adult citizens in many

---

31. See the excellent intersectional analysis of Patricia Hill Collins, "It's all in the Family: Intersections of Gender, Race, and Nation," *Hypatia* 13, no. 3 (1998) 62–82.

parts of the world. Since these movements, however, could not completely overcome the kyriarchal stratifications that continue to determine modern liberal representative democracies, they seem to have made the democratic circle merely coextensive with the kyriarchal pyramid, thereby reinscribing the contradiction between democratic vision and political kyriarchal practice and in turn spawning new movements of emancipation. Such an analysis helps us to understand the work of emancipatory scholarship and education to be an integral part of social radical democratic movements for change.

In and through cultural, political, and religious discourses, the social structures in which we are positioned are interpreted. Since scholars cannot stand outside of interpretive frameworks available in our society and time, we "make sense" out of texts and life with their help. If we always have to resort to existing interpretive discourses for making sense of our lives or of biblical texts, then the importance of critical theories and social movements for justice becomes obvious.

Since malestream hegemonic discourses provide the frameworks in which we "make meaning," emancipatory discourses must provide analyses of "common sense" assumptions that illuminate not only the choreography of oppression but also the possibilities for a radical democratic society and religion. Emancipatory discourses, however, are able to articulate a self- and world-understanding of justice only within the context of radical democratic movements that shape theories that help to exploit the contradictions that exist between the diverse sociohegemonic discourses.

Consequently, adherents to emancipatory Early Christian Studies need to equip its practitioners to become skilled in analyzing the kyriarchal and kyriocentric inscriptions of today as well as those at work in the biblical text. We need to learn how to produce and teach knowledge of Early Christian texts not simply for the sake of knowledge or just for mediating understanding, but rather for the sake of conscientization and the production of critical knowledge. In such a social analytic of dominations, I have argued here, a *status* rather than an *identity* model of social organization is appropriate. A kyriarchal status model of social analysis is able to examine the institutionalized structures and value patterns of domination for their effects on the relative status of social actors in a given society, even if these are inscribed in literary texts. If such status inscriptions constitute persons as peers, capable of participating on a par with each other, then we can speak of status equality or grassroots democracy; if they do not do so, then we speak of domination.

Here, the distinction between a person's *structural position* and her *subject position* becomes important. Every individual is *structurally* positioned within social, cultural, economic, political, and religious systems by virtue of birth. No one chooses to be born white, black, Asian, European, multiracial, poor, healthy, male, or female. Persons find themselves always already positioned by and within kyriarchal structures of domination, which limit the chances they get in life.

In contrast, a *subject position* is variable, open to intervention and changeable, but also limited by hegemonic structures of domination. According to the theorists Ernest Laclau and Chantal Mouffé, "A 'subject position' refers to the ensemble of beliefs through which an individual interprets and responds to her structural positions within a social formation. In this sense, an individual becomes a social agent insofar as she lives her structural positions through an ensemble of subject positions."[32]

The relationship between a *subject position* and a *structural position* is quite complex since our self-understandings are always already determined by our *structural position* with its rewards and pressures. Thus, a person theoretically might be able to live her structural positions through a wide range of subject positions, but practically might be restricted to a rigidly defined and closed set of available interpretive frameworks. Hence, the importance of emancipatory movements and the different interpretive frameworks they engender.

Feminist critical theory has made a range of such interpretive frameworks and categories available for analyzing structural dominations that are shaping people's *subject positions*. It has provided various social analytics for diagnosing and changing wo/men's structural positions in and through the articulation of different *subject positions*. Readings of canonical texts or reconstructions of Christian beginnings

---

32. Anna Marie Smith, *Laclau and Mouffé: The Radical Democratic Imaginary* (New York: Routledge, 1998), 58–59.

can either sustain the status quo or can contribute to the articulation of different subject positions. Key analytic concepts and categories with which to read in a critical fashion have been developed either as reverse discourse to the binary intellectual framework of systemic dualisms or in a critical liberationist intersectional frame.

IV. Exploring the Intersections of Race, Gender, Status, and Ethnicity in Early Christian Studies

The essays in this volume engage in an intersectional analysis and thus seek to fashion Early Christian Studies as a discipline capable of articulating knowledge that does not reproduce the intersecting structures of domination but critically interrogates them. After this introductory essay, the first section of the book opens with an article by classics scholar Shelley P. Haley, who explores the reception and interaction of critical race theory in Classical Studies. Critical race theory had its beginnings in the scholarship of jurisprudence and in the sociological theory of social construction that developed in the 1970s as a response to the backlash and rollbacks of civil rights legislation. The application of such a theory to the study of the ancient world is justified, she argues, because the interpreters of ancient societies were or are intellectuals of nineteenth through twenty-first centuries and so have internalized (consciously or not) the values, structures, and behaviors that foster the need for critical race theory. Moreover, Roman society at the time of Augustus was multi-layered and complexly multicultural. As we discover the extent of that complexity, critical race theory can be useful in unlayering the intersectionality of the constructs of ancient Roman society.

Laura Nasrallah's essay unfolds the gendered and racial discourse in the "social life" of the statue of the Aphrodite of Knidos. Although scholars have long recognized that it is worth discussing the ancient Knidia's gender, this essay argues that it is also necessary to address her race. Early Christians, among others, critiqued images of the Aphrodite of Knidos not only by using the sexual invective of the day, but also by entering into a debate about the differential valuations of race in the ancient world.

Ancient writers recognized a world of ethnoracial diversity among the Jews of their era, Cynthia Baker argues. Yet, the notion of Jewish ethnic multiplicity remains foreign and virtually unexplored in popular and scholarly cultures that still labor under the weight of racialized discourses of Jewish "particularity" crafted as counterpoint to narratives of Christian "universalism." This essay investigates the varieties of "ethnic reasoning" brought to bear on imagining and constructing Jewishness within the multiethnic or multiracial community of Jews in antiquity.

The last two essays of the first section analyze texts and interpretations of Paul. Joseph Marchal investigates the frequency and the centrality of the rhetoric of "imitation" in Paul's letters. He suggests that Homi Bhabha's work on mimicry as a strategy in the negotiation of identity in postcolonial contexts could be a resource in recognizing and interrogating these rhetorics. Yet Bhabha's importance must be reassessed in light of the contributions of others such as Rey Chow and Meyda Yegenoglu. Marchal works toward a multiaxial analysis that includes gender, class, ethnicity, and empire, and thus provides a richer picture of historical possibilities in ancient Corinth, on the one hand, and tools for ongoing readings of the rhetoric of imitation within the letter on the other.

Since ethnicity is a construct, Sze-kar Wan suggests that Paul in Romans attempts to construct the Jewish *ethnos* by subverting and redefining prevailing ethnic categories used by his Roman audience. While Paul in Romans addresses Gentile converts, he incorporates them through code-switching into this expanded Jewish *ethnos*, changing their ethnic division "Greeks and Barbarians" into his own "Jews and Greeks" by focusing on circumcision as the central symbol of Jewishness. However, Paul defines Judaism in the exclusive terms of the male body. Thus, in deploying the arsenal he acquires under the empire for his construction of Jewish universalism, he also runs the risk of re-erecting an ideological *kyriarchal* edifice. On the surface, Paul could claim to have overcome the problem by his thoroughgoing allegorization, which enables him to distance Jewishness from the physical rite itself, but his final formulation of genuine faith cannot escape his male limitations.

The essays in the second part of the book focus on the capability of Early Christian Studies as a discipline to deploy an intersectional analytic of race, gender, and ethnicity. The contribution of Denise Kimber Buell suggests that haunting and inheritance are figures that can contribute to ethically engaged forms of New Testament and Early Christian Studies. Haunting offers readers a way to negotiate the insistence on situational particularity (for example, the widespread view that "race" is a "modern" construct, but also that "race," "ethnicity," and "gender" have only context-specific meanings), while also allowing us to consider the evidence for the "afterlives" of ancient texts and ideas. Inside and outside the canon, texts survive that presume that humans can be classified in terms of kinds of difference, including differences in *genos*, *ethnos*, and *laos*, as well as differences in gender, status, forms of religious worship, age, wealth, and other factors. Claims of peoplehood in texts *re-membered* as Christian are resources from which hegemonic religious, ethnic, national, and racial belonging have been constructed. But they also have been used to challenge and transform dominant meanings of race and ethnicity.

Shawn Kelley's essay in turn maintains that through aesthetic ideology, the racialization of much formative, historical-critical New Testament scholarship has taken place. While aesthetic ideology informs much of formative, historical-critical New Testament scholarship, its presence can be felt most acutely in parable scholarship. Parable scholarship became the gateway through which racialized aesthetics entered historical-critical biblical scholarship. Parable scholarship was the single aspect of historical criticism that maintained its appeal to those scholars who rejected historical criticism on methodological grounds. As a result, the methodological innovations of the past two decades simultaneously reinscribe aspects of parabolic-racialized discourse in new scholarly terrain (by embracing a parabolic aesthetic) and provide critical space for challenging racialized discourse within the discipline by developing alternative reading strategies and interpretive goals.

Susannah Heschel's essay provocatively asks: "Was Jesus a Nazi?" and argues that during the Third Reich, German Protestant theologians, motivated by racism and tapping into traditional Christian anti-Semitism, redefined Jesus as an Aryan and Christianity as a religion at war with Judaism. In 1939, these theologians established the Institute for the Study and Eradication of Jewish Influence on German Religious Life. The surprisingly large number of distinguished professors, younger scholars, and students who became involved in the effort to synthesize Nazism and Christianity should be seen, she argues, not simply as a response to political developments, nor simply as an outgrowth of struggles within the field of Christian theology. Rather, the Institute reflects underlying affinities between racist ideology and Protestant Christian theology. In tracing the work of the Institute, its funding, publications, and membership activities, the emergence of a Nazi Christianity comes to light.

Gabriella Gelardini continues this inquiry by arguing that German-speaking Protestant historical Jesus research was caught in a real dilemma. From its very beginnings with Reimarus, such research had to grapple with the fact that Jesus was a Jew, which suited neither orthodox dogma nor modern Protestant theology's arrangement with historical criticism. In order to exercise theological control, scholars had to establish a conflictive tension between Jesus' "religion" and his "ethnicity" (or "nationality"). This was done in two distinct ways. First, Jesus was construed as a figure whose religion conflicted with or transcended his (Jewish) ethnicity or nationality, rendering negligible the latter aspect of his identity as merely external or formal. Second, when, in the late-nineteenth and early-twentieth centuries, the non-dissoluble cohesion of Jesus' ancient ethnoreligious Jewish identity had to be acknowledged, the pattern shifted to (Christian) transethnic religion versus (Jewish) ethnoreligion (including the historical Jesus). Only a modern concept of individualism, Gelardini argues, was able to construct a historical Jesus along lines in which the nature of his "religion" could be distinguished or even separated from his "ethnicity."

Vincent L. Wimbush's essay in turn focuses on racism in the context of the United States. He aims to show how inextricably nationalization, Scriptures, and race as a modern world phenomena and dynamics are woven together and what problems, challenges, and consequences they hold for critical scholarship (including but going beyond scholarship on the Bible). With the United States as primary context and point of reference, the rhetorics as well as the ideological and political orientation of Frederick Douglass is the special focus. Wimbush uses as an analytical wedge and discursive site a speech Douglass delivered in Washington, D.C., in 1883, in which he confronted the country with Lincoln's challenge to decide whether it would tolerate a society half slave and half free.

Drawing upon a number of philosophical and civic texts, religious exhortations, and exegetical treatises as well as the Bible, Douglass argued that the nation can and should be rebuilt, but only through serious and honest grappling with the poison of slavery and the racialism that is associated with it, and only if it is recognized that there is "no modern Joshua" to take the onus from the people of interpreting, deciding, and acting for themselves. Douglass's nationalization ideology suggests the challenge of a mode of discussion located in the public square and focused on the Bible precisely because the latter is the discursive site in relationship to which the most sensitive, even haunting, public policy issues can be addressed.

Fernando F. Segovia's study concludes the argument of the book for an intersectional analytic by highlighting, classifying, and explaining the poetics and rhetorics at work in minority biblical criticism within the United States of America. The study begins with a critical exposition of its own theoretical-methodological framework. Subsequently, it advances a working repertoire of minority rhetorical dynamics in which primary strategies (interpretive contextualization, border transgressionism, interruptive stock-taking, as well as intercultural engagement) and respective secondary tactics are identified and theorized. Segovia's study closes with both a critical vision regarding future lines of development for minority rhetorics and a return to the question of the ideological agenda behind the quest for a poetics of minority criticism.

The volume as a whole contributes to a rhetoric of inquiry and an ethic of interpretation[33] that seeks not only to deconstruct the kyriarchal structures of racism, heterosexism, ethnocentrism, and imperialism inscribed in early Christian writings and modern Early Christian

---

33. For elaboration and discussion of a rhetoric of inquiry and an ethic of interpretation, see my book *Rhetoric and Ethic: The Politics of Biblical Studies*. Minneapolis: Fortress Press, 1999.

Studies but also to find religious memories, resources, and visions for a more just world. With *Prejudice and Christian Beginnings*, we hope to open up an intellectual space for further exploration and inquiry not only into the kyriarchal intersections and prejudices inscribed in early Christian writings and beginnings but also in the possibilities for articulating elements of an early Christian and a scholarly ethos that fosters appreciation, tolerance, and justice.

PART I

Race, Gender, and Ethnicity in Early Christianity

Theorizing the Field of Inquiry

CHAPTER 1

Be Not Afraid of the Dark
Critical Race Theory
and Classical Studies

Shelley P. Haley

Critical race theory, which began in the scholarship of jurisprudence and the theory of social construction in the 1970s, was a response to the backlash against civil rights legislation. Its oppositional stance and its use of storytelling to challenge negative portrayals of people of color hold attraction in particular for people of African descent. The justification for using a theory focused on modern phenomena like "race" and "racism" to analyze ancient Greek and Roman society is that modern interpreters of those ancient societies have internalized the modern values, structures, and behaviors that are the object of critical race theory.

In light of literary evidence from the first centuries B.C.E. and C.E., it is plausible that the Romans were aware of skin-color difference and that it played a role, among other factors, in the social construction of *difference*. Given the simultaneity of other factors as well, it is important to examine the Roman construction of difference with particular attention to color, gender, class, and culture using a symmetrical mode of analysis. The Romans in Augustus's day were more keenly aware of different cultural practices—especially those of African societies—than we have given them credit for up to now, as Vergil's *Aeneid* and the Psuedo-Vergilian *Moretum* illustrate.

Introduction

Critical race theory had its beginnings in the scholarship of jurisprudence and in the sociological theory of social construction that developed in the 1970s as a response to the backlash and rollbacks of civil rights legislation. To me, as a Classical Studies scholar who is simultaneously a woman of African descent, critical race theory is appealing because of its oppositional stance and its use of storytelling to challenge negative portrayals of all people of color, but particularly people of African descent.

Critical race theory has found its way into the academy with the publication of Ladson-Billings and Tate's article, "Towards a Critical Theory of Education."[1] In addition, critical race theory has nurtured critical race feminism, which centers on the experiential knowledge of women of color and challenges white liberal feminism and essentialist feminism. I would argue that critical race theory has also found its way into literary criticism, most notably in Toni Morrison's *Playing in the Dark*.[2]

Admittedly, this all sounds very twentieth and twenty-first century. How can a classicist justify using a theory so closely aligned with modern phenomena like "race," "racism," and "systemic oppression" to analyze the vanished societies of ancient Greece and ancient Rome? I hope to show in this chapter that my justification abides in the fact that the interpreters of these ancient societies were or are intellectuals of the nineteenth through twentieth-first centuries, and so have internalized (consciously or not) the values, structures, and behaviors that foster the need for critical race theory.

It is important to remember that critical race theory challenges the experience of whites as the norm while at the same time it centers its conceptual framework in the experiences of people of color. In its broadest possible framing, critical race theory demonstrates that there are multiple levels of meaning of race and difference and that these levels are experienced simultaneously.

---

1. G. Ladson-Billings and W. Tate, "Towards a Critical Theory of Education," *Teachers College Report* 97 (1995): 4–68.
2. Toni Morrison, *Playing in the Dark: Whiteness and the Literary Imagination* (Cambridge, Mass: Harvard University Press, 1992).

According to George J. Sefa Dei, "There is a social, political, cultural, and intellectual meaning of race and difference. . . . Race and
racisms also work differently for groups depending on history, geography, culture, class, and gender."[3] Before we can even attempt an
integrated analysis of these factors on the ancient construction of race,
we must interrogate the extent to which we bring our modern "social,
political, cultural, and intellectual meaning of race and difference"[4] to
our analyses of the ancient world. Only by acknowledging the presence of this meaning can we begin to pull back the layers in order to
arrive at the ancient construct of race. It certainly is not easy. However, I shall present here my attempts to apply a critical race theory to
begin this unlayering process.

Defining Race and Color in the Ancient Mediterranean World

In 1996, a reporter for the *Chronicle of Higher Education* called me.
She was reviewing a book by a notoriously vitriolic critic of Afrocentric interpretations of "classical" history.[5] The reporter called me
because the author mentions my defense of the position that Cleopatra was "black."[6] After my explanation that Cleopatra symbolizes
the treatment we have received at the hands of Eurocentric patriarchy, and that it is in this light that we embrace Cleopatra as a "sister," the reporter asked, "Symbolic construction aside, what do you
tell your students regarding Cleopatra's race?" I explained that this
is a very complex question when one can ask it about Cleopatra or
any ancient—or modern—historical figure. "Race" as the social and

---

3. George J. Sefa Dei, "Recasting Anti-Racism and the Axis of Difference:
Beyond the Question of Theory," *Race, Class and Gender* 7, no.2 (2000): 38–48.
This particular quote is taken from the *ProQuest* version, 3.
4. Ibid., 4.
5. Ellen Coughlin, "Not out of Africa," review of *Not Out of Africa: How
Afrocentrism Became an Excuse to Teach Myth as History,* by Mary Lefkowitz, *The
Chronicle of Higher Education* 16 (February 1996): A6–7.
6. Shelley P. Haley, "Black Feminist Thought and Classics: Re-membering,
Re-claiming, Re-empowering," in Nancy Sorkin Rabinowitz and Amy Richlin,
eds., *Feminist Theory and the Classics* (New York: Routledge, 1993), 23–43,
especially 27–30.

ideological construct that we understand in the late twentieth century in the United States of America clearly had not been formulated in the first-century B.C.E. Mediterranean.

So my answer to the reporter and to my students and to colleagues—whether Afrocentric or Eurocentric in standpoint—is that Cleopatra, and indeed, the people of "the ancient world," had a "race," but that it is anachronistic to insist that she or they had a race as we understand it. Instead, we must search out and analyze *their* construct of race. So, my caveat to readers of this chapter is the same. Do not read our construct of race into ancient cultures. Did the Romans conceptualize a phenomenon such as "racial difference"? Yes. Did the Romans notice skin-color differences? Yes. Did they attach a value to skin-color differences? That question is not answered so easily. In any society's value system, individuals are aggregates of multiple differences; judgments are then made according to the combination. The Romans did react strongly, even prejudicially, to difference; however, one cannot point just to Roman reactions to skin color, but must take into account class, gender, culture, and sexuality as well. In this chapter, I hope to demonstrate that, based on literary evidence from the first centuries B.C.E. and C.E., it is plausible (we can *never* know for sure) that the Romans were aware of skin color difference and that skin color was a factor in their formulation of a social construction of *difference*. But it was one of many factors. The simultaneity of these factors is crucial to my analysis; it is, therefore, important to examine the Roman construct of difference with particular attention to color, gender, class, and culture using a symmetrical, nonlinear mode of thinking. The texts on which I shall concentrate are Vergil's *Aeneid*, particularly Book Four, with its familiar story of Queen Dido of Carthage, and the Pseudo-Vergilian *Moretum*.

Before beginning to discuss difference as constructed by the Romans, we need to establish the "norm." Just as in the United States, when Americans say "African Americans," they mean black men, and when they say "Americans," they mean white men, so for the Romans, *Romani* meant Roman men. Roman masculinity (a social construct in and of itself) was the norm in each of the texts we shall examine. Roman society was patriarchal and androcentric; the fact that the authors of the texts under examination are mostly all male reflects that.[7] Gender difference is filtered through a male lens, which is the framework for gender difference.

What color did the Romans see themselves? Was there a skin-color "norm" in Roman society? There was, in fact, a range of skin hues, and this is reflected in the skin color terminology. *Albus, ater, candidus, fuscus,* and *niger* are all used by Roman authors to describe the skin color of peoples with whom they came in contact.[8] However, it is equally important to note that there are many contexts where skin color is not mentioned at all. For example, there is no skin color given for Aeneas, Dido, or Iarbas, three central characters in Book Four of the *Aeneid.* In these contexts, character—or characterization—was not dependent on skin color, an attitude that ironically was Martin Luther King Jr.'s dream. When the Romans did apply a skin color descriptor to themselves it was *albus.* What did *albus* mean to a Roman?

Nineteenth-century lexicographers render *albus* as "white," and *candidus* as "shiny or glistening white." The opposite of *albus* is *ater,* "black" ("lusterless black"), and opposite to *candidus* is *niger,* "black" ("shiny or glistening black"). Lloyd Thompson, in *Romans and Blacks,* persuasively argues against the reference point of "white," which for the modern reader in the United States connotes a Nordic or northern European coloring. As Thompson says, "no concept of 'white' people as a meaningful socio-cultural category could arise in Roman society. . . . The 'developed world' of the Roman world view was definitely the world of pale-brown Mediterraneans."[9]

If, then, the reference point for *albus* is pale-brown, not the white of a Nordic consciousness, interpretations and reading of the other skin color terminology are transformed. *Ater, candidus, fuscus,* and *niger* become degrees of brownness. For me, *candidus* is reminiscent of Gwendolyn Brooks's use of the term "brights" for the lighter shades of brown associated with mixed-race (African-European) Americans. She says,

---

7. There is an outside chance that a woman authored the *Moretum.* However, given that there is very little surviving Roman literature authored by women, female authorship of this text is highly unlikely.

8. I am using the masculine morpheme of the adjectives, because this is the form that is traditionally listed first in lexicons and dictionaries. Feminine forms would be *alba, atra, candida, fusca,* and *nigra.*

9. Lloyd Thompson, *Romans and Blacks* (Norman, Okla.: University of Oklahoma Press, 1989), 10–11.

One of the first "world"-truths revealed to me when I at last became a member of SCHOOL was that, to be socially successful, a little girl must be Bright (of skin). It was better if your hair was curly too—or at least Good Grade (Good Grade implied, usually, no involvement with the Hot Comb)—but Bright you marvelously *needed* to be.[10]

Fuscus, ater, and *niger* then become deeper shades of brown until the shade *niger,* which was associated with the ancient Africans. Scybale, the African woman in the *Moretum,* is described as being "of a deep brown color" (*fusca colore,* 1.33).[11] This skin coloring is given as one of several traits, each reinforcing her African descent (*Afra genus,* 1.32). Cypassis, the sexually exploited hairdresser in Ovid's *Amores* 2.7 and 2.8, is addressed as *fusca Cypassi* (2.8.22), which, given the pale-brown reference point for Ovid, should be rendered as "deep-brown Cypassis."[12] *Albus* is often contrasted by *ater* as, for example, when Cicero in *Philippics* 2.16 says to Marc Antony:

> vide quam te amarit is qui albus aterne fuerit ignoras. Fratris filium praeterit. [13]

Haley: See, how much that man loved you, a man about whom you do not know whether he was pale brown or dark brown. He passed over his nephew.

Or as in *Catullus* 93:

> Nil nimium studeo, Caesar, tibi velle placere,
> nec scire utrum sis albus an ater homo.[14]

---

10. Gwendolyn Brooks, *Report from Part One: The Autobiography of Gwendolyn Brooks* (Detroit: Broadside, 1972), 37.

11. Latin text from W.V. Clausen et al., eds. *Appendix Vergiliana* (OCT; Oxford: Clarendon, 1966).

12. Latin text from Ovid, *Amores; Medicamina faciei feminae; Ars amatoria; Remedia amoris* (ed. E.J. Kenney; OCT; Oxford: Clarendon, 1994).

13. Latin text from Cicero, *Orationes* vol. 6 ed. A.C. Clark (OCT; Oxford: Clarendon,1900).

14. Latin text from Catullus, *Carmina* ed. R. A. B. Mynors (OCT; Oxford: Clarendon, 1958).

Haley: I'm not terribly eager to please you, Caesar, nor do I care to know if you are pale-brown or dark brown.

Albus and *ater* connote a matte-like quality, whereas *candidus* and *niger* imply luster and brightness. Consequently, a graffito contrasts a *candida* (a "bright brown woman") and a *nigra* (a "bright black woman"):

> candida me docuit nigras
> odisse puellas . . . (*CIL* 4.1520)[15]

Haley: A bright brown girl taught me to hate bright black girls.[16]

Based on these examples, it is plausible to assume that pale-brown was the reference point for the Roman evaluation of skin-color differences, and that skin color was one of many factors—not necessarily the most important one—in the Roman construction of difference.

As I noted before, often skin color is not mentioned, and thus was not the chief component in the construction of difference. For example, in Book Four of Vergil's *Aeneid*, in the character of Dido, gender, culture, and geographical location, rather than the somatic trait of skin color, are the factors construing difference. Here, we meet the Semitic queen Dido, who founds a new city, Carthage, on the northeastern shores of Africa. By so doing, she brings together in one character all the fears of Roman ruling class men: a foreign woman with political power in a geopolitical area that, historically, produced Rome's most tenacious and feared rivals: Hannibal (whose coming is prayed for by Dido at 4.625–30), and Cleopatra. Dido, through conflation with Cleopatra, represents the Roman male fear of the power of the "Other." At the same time, Dido provides Vergil with an opportunity for moral didacticism. By having Aeneas abandon Dido, Vergil crafts an Aeneas who demonstrates the moral supremacy of what will be known to Vergil's contemporaries as "old-fashioned" Roman virtues.

---

15. Karl Friedrich Wilhelm Zangemeister, ed., *Inscriptiones Parietariae Pompeianae, Herculanenses, Stabianae* (vol. 4 of *CIL*; Berlin: G. Reimerus, 1871). No date is given; the following contextual information is provided: "Nunc Neapoli in museo; inter duos limites quibus rubrum tectorium distinctum est" (97).

16. The author clearly is referring to sexually mature women; he may be referring to women who are prostitutes. By labeling them "girls," he infantilizes and devalues them further.

This moral supremacy stands in stark contrast to Marc Antony, who—according to the propaganda—surrendered to the wiles of a foreign seductress and enmeshed Rome in a messy war.

Vergil was not the only author of the Augustan age to promote a moral agenda by employing the image of the foreign seductress.[17] Livy also articulates the dangers of beautiful, foreign women, most noticeably in the case of the Carthaginian princess Sophoniba. Once again, there are parallels with both the historical and literary Cleopatra: a beautiful passionate woman of Africa who distracts a Roman—or in this case, the Roman surrogate Massinissa—from his duty to Rome.[18] Through such characters, Augustan authors reinforced the need for patriarchal control of female sexuality, whether domestic or foreign. Without it, women are destructive and suspect.

Reconsidering Race and Vergil's Dido

Vergil reinforces this position towards female sexuality through his development of Dido's character. When first we meet her, she is the model *univira*—a "one-man woman"—having taken a vow of celibacy and fidelity to her dead husband.[19] She sublimates her sexuality, diverting her energy to the founding of a city for her people. In the beginning, she embodies the solid moral and asexual character of a Roman *matrona*. Furthermore, like Livy's Lucretia, she works hard for the welfare of those dependent on her. In this way, Dido recalls the one positive category of women illustrated in Semonides' *Catalogue of Women*. Vergil (1.430) reinforces the parallel by using a metaphor of bees to describe the activity of the city builders. Before Aeneas arrived, Dido had rejected an offer of a marriage/political alliance from the native African prince Iarbas: she could remain sexually controlled and true to her vow to her deceased husband.

---

17. For an explanation of how a controlling image differs from a stereotype, see Patricia Hill Collins, *Black Feminist Thought: Knowledge, Consciousness, and the Politics of Empowerment* (Boston: Unwin Hyman, 1990), 67–90.

18. Shelley P. Haley, "Livy's Sophoniba," *Classica et Mediaevalia* 40 (1989): 171–81.

19. Readers do not actually learn about this vow until the beginning of book four.

Clearly, Dido had to change. At the beginning of the episode, she represents the ideal Roman woman. Within the frame of a misogynistic lens, what destroys the moral fabric of women, even seemingly good women? What is the *essence* of foreign women that makes them especially alien to Romans? The answer, of course, is passion and control of their sexuality. Passion was a cultural stereotype projected upon Africans by Romans and Greeks.[20] Vergil moves Dido further away from Rome and closer to Africa by implicating her in the flaw of passion. In Vergil's depiction, the emotional stress of coping with the eruption of her repressed sexuality and the moral pressure of breaking a sacred vow drives Dido toward madness. This, in turn, deepens her "Otherness," distancing Dido from the ideal Roman woman. As her madness grows, she is drawn towards indigenous African cultural practices, which bring her comfort. By rejecting Roman and Tyrian religious rituals, she alienates herself further from the Roman male audience.

There are two fascinating elements in Vergil's development of this progression. First, he reveals an awareness of African rituals and cultural values, and second, nearly all interpreters of the *Aeneid* have ignored or dismissed this awareness. They tend to follow the paradigm that Toni Morrison discusses in *Playing in the Dark* by reading Vergil's "Africanism"[21] out of his epic.

For example, in many precolonial, West African societies, women did not achieve any significant status until they became mothers. Through motherhood, women gained political, social, and economic power. Among ancient African societies, and especially in ancient Egypt, motherhood was also highly valued, conferring political and religious power upon women. While it is true that under Augustus motherhood was touted as the most valuable role for Roman women, no political or economic power accrued to them because of it. Certainly, mothers of the elite class had social and even political *influence*, but not power. Viewed from the African cultural valuation of motherhood, Dido's wish for a "little Aeneas" takes on further

---

20. Shelley P. Haley, "Livy, Passion, and Cultural Stereotypes," *Historia* 39 (1990): 375–81.

21. Morrison, *Playing in the Dark*, 6–10.

significance. The following lines are usually read as a last desperate attempt by a frantic, spurned lover to keep her faithless lover with her just long enough to leave her with a token reminder of the love they shared:

> Saltem si qua mihi de te suscepta fuisset
> ante fugam suboles, si quis mihi parvulus aula
> luderet Aeneas, qui te tamen ore referret,
> non equidem omnino capta ac deserta viderer. (*Aen.*
> 4.327–330)

Haley: If only I had conceived a child by you before your flight, if some small Aeneas played in my courtyard who, despite everything, resembles you in looks, then I'd feel less like one taken and discarded.

This futile plea is viewed as another indication of Dido's deteriorating mental state: no successful, sane woman-ruler would *want* to be a mother. Such an interpretation comes from a social theoretical stance that devalues motherhood and discredits matrifocality.[22] But from an Afrocentric perspective, Dido's lines can be read not only as a wish but also as a need: to come into her fullest power both as a ruler and as a human—Dido must be a mother. This interpretation is reinforced further by the encouragement Dido's sister Anna gives her to pursue a relationship with Aeneas:

---

22. Matrifocality, especially as a trait of African or African-descended societies, has been pathologized and bestialized by white men. For an example of this in Classical studies, see Thomas Fleming's review of Judith P. Hallett, *Fathers and Daughters in Rome: Women and the Elite Family* in *The Classical Journal* 82, no.1 (1986):

> The term matrifocal was coined to describe the situation of Caribbean Black societies in which women are often abandoned by their husbands or lovers and find themselves compelled to exercise a sort of matriarchal authority over their family. . . . (Some primatologists use matrifocal to describe the life of chimpanzees, whose only enduring bonds are based on maternity.) It is completely illegitimate to take a term of social pathology and apply it to the ordinary conditions of Roman life—unless Hallett means to suggest that Roman society was organized matricentrically like that of the chimpanzee. (p. 77)

solane perpetua maerens carpere iuventa,
nec dulcis natos, Veneris nec praemia noris? (*Aen.*
4.32–33)

Haley: Why, alone, do you squander your youth always—grieving
without sweet sons or the gifts of love?

The "sweet sons" would confer status and a mother's power upon her,
as well as provide companions and heirs. Taken this way, Dido has
not yet totally abrogated her sense of self to her love of Aeneas. This
is not to discount the desperation of her pleas; that is certainly there.
However, the motivation for the desperation varies depending on the
reader's perspective.

It is important to note that mention of skin color is absent. In the
character of Dido, gender, culture, and geographical location, rather
than the somatic trait of skin color, are factors in construing difference. If Dido had belonged to the gene pool for which "having fair
hair and skin and usually light eyes"[23] is the norm, then it seems to
me that Vergil, whose reference point is *candidus* (pale brown), would
have found that remarkable and would have mentioned it when we
first encounter Dido. However, he does not describe her physically at
all, making it all the more plausible that Vergil conceived of Dido as
what I call the "beautiful norm": southern Mediterranean and Semitic
women who were *candidae*, with black hair, pale-brown skin, and dark
eyes.[24]

Therefore, why then does Vergil describe Dido as having "yellow
hair" (*flaventis abscissa comas*, 4.590; and *nondum illi flavum Proserpina
crinem/abstulerat Stygioque caput damnaverat Orco*, 4.698–99)? Let us
review what has taken place: (1) Dido has fallen in lust with Aeneas,
perhaps under the influence of Venus; (2) She has consummated what

---

23. William Morris, ed., *The American Heritage Dictionary*, New College
Edition (Boston: Houghton Mifflin, 1978), 142 (under the entry for "blond").

24. After all, Dido is, in Vergil's vision, Semitic. Of course, we must not forget that Dido is a fictional character, a product of Vergil's imagination. What is
the plausibility that blondes (or redheads, for that matter) were so deeply embedded in Vergil's consciousness as standards of beauty, that they would enter his
fantasy? Dido is not believable as anything other than the beautiful norm mentioned above.

she believes is a marriage with Aeneas; (3) She catches him being, in the words of Tina Turner, a typical male: he's about to abandon and jilt her. She does not want Aeneas to go, and she wants a child. Using that desire explicitly, she pleads with Aeneas to stay long enough to make her pregnant.

When it is clear that personal appeals have no effect on Aeneas's resolve, Dido turns not to Greek or Roman religious rites, but rather to indigenous religious practices. The usual interpretation of Dido's consultation with an African priestess and her subsequent augury ritual is that they are further indications of Dido's deepening descent into madness and irrationality. As far as I know, no commentator has considered that these rituals may have been more familiar or more comforting to Dido. None has considered the parallels between traditional African religions (and their permutations in the Diaspora) and the advice and rituals delineated in Book Four. Vergil describes the priestess as a member of the "Massylian people" (*Massylae gentis*, 1.483); her home is the "westernmost boundary of the Ethiopians" (*ultimus Aethiopum locus est*, 1.481); before Dido notices her, she was guardian of the temple of the Hesperides, and she was minister to the "serpent" (*draconi*, 1.484). I would like to suggest that this priestess was from an ethnic group that might have been the ancestors of the Maasai. Migration would account for the current home of the Maasai in east Africa. Furthermore, I would suggest that this African woman was a priestess of a religion with strong parallels to the traditional African religions, especially as practiced by the Yoruba, and that the serpent is the symbolic representation of a major divinity of this religion.[25]

The advice that the unnamed priestess gives Dido follows the charms and spells of vodoun, santeria, and other African-derived religions. One important aspect of ritual in some traditional African religions involves dousing the worshippers and presiders with a yellow mud made from ochre. I suggest also that Dido has been doused

---

25. The connection between the serpent and the divinity is clearest in voudoun, where one of the chief spirits, Damballah, comes in the form of a serpent or snake. Vodoun is a variation of Yoruba religion. Both religions employ priestesses as well as priests.

with a similar mud, hence the description of her as having yellow hair (*flaventis abscissa comas*, 1.590). Translators render *flaventis* as "golden" or "yellow," but the word is a participial adjective from the verb *flaveo*, "to be yellow," so that in line 590 there is a sense that Dido's hair has just become yellow. Furthermore, the adjective *flavus* can refer to the coloring that comes from the "puzzolan earth" associated with the Tiber River. (Vergil uses *flavus* in this way in 7.31, *Tiberinus . . . multa flavus harena*). It is crucial to keep in mind that since Dido is Semitic and has been described as "beautiful" by a poet whose reference point for skin color is pale brown, it is highly unlikely that Dido's natural or even usual hair color is "golden" or "yellow." *Flaventis* seems to refer to an action; given the context of the ritual in which she has participated, and which was performed by an African priestess with connections to traditional African practices, it is plausible that Dido's hair has become yellow because of a ritualistic dousing of ochre mud.

Vergil reveals his knowledge not only of the different ethnic and linguistic groups in Italy (book twelve), but also those in Africa. Near the beginning of book four, Anna lists the geographical neighbors of Dido's newly founded city. For each, there is a cultural or national stereotype: the Gaetulians are "invincible in war" (*genus insuperabile bello*); the Numidians are "unbridled" (*infreni*), an epithet which conjures up their cultural stereotype of being passionate and oversexed; and finally the nomads of Barca are perceived as "wild" (*furentes*).[26] Most important for our purposes, however, is the introduction of a specific suitor who was rejected by Dido: Iarbas, the Gaetulian. Iarbas here is presented as one of several leaders "whom Africa—rich and proud—nourished" (*quos Africa terra triumphis divis alit*, 1.36), but whom Dido still rejected.

According to Vergil, Iarbas[27] is the product of the rape of a Garamantine nymph by the northern African god Ammon who, in the syncretism with Greco-Roman religious tradition, became associated with Zeus/Jupiter. There was a shrine to Zeus Ammon at Dodona,

26. See again Haley, "Livy, Passion", 375–81.
27. The name Iarbas occurs at three places in Roman literature: Vergil, *Aeneid*, 4.36; Ovid, *Fasti*, 3.552; and Juvenal, *The Satires*, 5.45; italics added.

which was, like Delphi, an oracular shrine. Iarbas is credited with introducing the worship of Ammon to the Numidians.

Vergil gives no physical description of Iarbas; what is important to Vergil's intentions is how Iarbas will move the story along. Consequently, he is described in terms of Dido's actions. He is scorned (*despectus*), even though he is the child of a divine parent and a rich and powerful ruler. Dido rejects Iarbas not because he is African per se, nor because he is inferior in terms of class. Succinctly put, Iarbas is scorned because he is a man. By accepting his proposal—and Vergil implies that it was one of the first that Dido received—Dido would violate her sacred vow of heterosexual celibacy. Iarbas can accept her decision as long as she rejects all men. However, when she accepts the proposal of, or rather does the proposing to, a man inferior in nearly every way to Iarbas, he, relying on parental loyalty, berates Jupiter for allowing this to happen and seeks redress.

However, in the Roman construction of the foreign woman, Dido's vow and her strict observance of it, or of any vow, is unnatural. It is only a matter of time before she reveals her natural, perfidious character. She becomes what all women would be without the strict reins of patriarchy: mad, out of control, and destructive. Dido, in a sense, foreshadows later stereotypes of women of color, particularly of black women. While I am not arguing here that Dido was the definitive antecedent for the stereotype of the foreign seductress, I am interested in what happens when readers and interpreters of the ancient texts come out of intellectual traditions and societal constructions that acquiesce to these stereotypes. Wole Soyinka is quoted as saying:

> We black Africans have been blandly invited to submit ourselves to a second epoch of colonialism—this time by a universal humanoid abstraction defined and conducted by individuals whose theories and prescriptions are derived from the apprehension of *their world, and their history, and their social neuroses, and their value systems.*[28]

---

28. Ketu H. Katrak, "Decolonizing Culture: Toward a Theory for Post-colonial Women's Texts," in Bill Ashcroft, Gareth Griffiths, and Helen Tiffin, eds., *The Post-Colonial Studies Reader* (London: Routledge, 1995), 256; italics added.

I would argue that this recolonizing occurs in Classical studies.

Race and Gender in Pseudo-Vergil's *Moretum*

Images of black womanhood are part of a generalized ideology of domination. The ability to form and control images of black womanhood—that is, the authority to define these symbols—is a major instrument of power. In order to exercise power, elite white men and their representatives must be in a position to manipulate appropriate symbols concerning black women. They may do so by exploiting already existing symbols. I would like to suggest that this manipulation of symbols occurs even when such symbols are encountered in ancient texts. The ancient text then becomes the validation of a stereotype that is, in fact, alien—"other"—to the ancient society. This is particularly true of the physical stereotype of black women.

As seen from the foregoing discussion, I do not imply that no cultural or social stereotypes existed for women, whether African, Greek, or Roman, in the ancient world. One can see that, from Roman literature, Dido has come to represent the most persistent cultural stereotype for foreign women: the seductress, or "Jezebel." She is the sultry enticer who disrupts the social and moral order with her sexuality. Nevertheless, I suggest that our understandings of the life experiences and images of ancient African women need revision, since scholars who have studied them were and are operating under the influence of physical and sexual stereotypes prevalent today.

Nowhere in Roman literature is the intersection of color, ethnic origin, gender, and class better represented than in the pseudo-Vergilian *Moretum*. This poem of 123 dactylic hexameters gives a detailed physical description of an African woman of the peasant class. Most scholarly attention has centered on the authorship of the piece, and once its attribution to Vergil was deemed implausible, it was forgotten and received little attention. However, in recent times, with renewed interest in the somatic and cultural diversity of the ancient Mediterranean world, Scybale, the African woman in question, has attracted more attention. Frank Snowden praises the author of the *Moretum* for the congruence of his or her description with the racial characteristics delineated by modern physical anthropologists. He remarks, "The author of the *Moretum* who described Scybale would be rated today as a competent anthropologist."[29]

I provide the Latin and my translation of the description of Scybale. It is important to note that most translations of this piece have been done by men influenced by stereotypical descriptions of the physique of African women. Consequently, I have deliberately made my rendering as sensitive to black-feminist and female-empowering concerns as the Latin will allow:

> Erat unica custos,
> Afra genus, tota patriam testante figura,
> torta comam, labroque tumens et fusca colore,
> pectore lata, iacens mammis, compressior alvo,
> cruribus exilis, spatiosa prodiga planta. (*Moretum* 31–35)

Haley: She was his only companion, African in her race, her whole form a testimony to her country: her hair twisted into dreads, her lips full, her color dark, her chest broad, her breasts flat, her stomach flat and firm, her legs slender, her feet broad and ample.

Needless to say, the *Moretum* is not now part of the Classical canon, but recently whenever the racial composition of ancient Greece or Rome is discussed, scholars always find it. Once again, men have overanalyzed this passage, and although I have respect for the conclusions reached by Lloyd Thompson, in particular, in his book *Romans and Blacks*, he, like other male scholars both black and white, has been imprinted with the physical and sexual stereotypes of black women. As a point of comparison with my translation, here are the translations of Snowden and Thompson, two black male scholars:

Snowden: African in her race, her whole figure proof of her
country—
her hair tightly curled, lips thick, color dark,

---

29. Frank M. Snowden, *Blacks in Antiquity* (Cambridge, Mass.: Harvard University Press, 1970), 9. Most contemporary physical anthropologists reject both the ideology and the determinants of "scientific races."

chest broad, breasts pendulous, belly somewhat
   pinched,
legs thin, and feet broad and ample.[30]

Thompson: She was his only help.
            She was African in stock, and all her physical
               features gave testimony of her land of origin:
            tightly-curled hair, swollen lips, dusky complexion,
            broad chest with low-swinging breasts, belly rather
               pinched,
            thin legs, broad and ample feet.[31]

For our purposes, this passage illustrates one very crucial point. Whoever the author of the *Moretum* was, she or he had detailed physical knowledge of Africans, in particular African women. The author also assumes that her/his audience has had enough contact with Africans to appreciate how Scybale's physical traits testify to her being of African descent (*Afra genus*). We can make the important inference that Africans were not a rare spectacle for at least some portion of the Roman populace. If such intimacy of physical contact existed, then detailed knowledge of cultural and ritualistic practices becomes even more plausible. While Scybale is a fictional character—and it is important to remember that—I believe that she is sympathetically drawn.[32]

   Despite this, Scybale has not fared well at the hands of most classical scholars. The last two translations cited above have been influenced by the stereotypical descriptions of the physique of black women. Snowden's "pendulous breasts" and Thompson's "low-swinging" ones

---

30. Ibid., 6.
31. Thompson, *Romans and Blacks*, 31.
32. Every indication is that Scybale is the equal of the peasant Simylus, with whom she lives and for whom she cares. Others disagree. Thompson thinks the author is mocking Scybale, ibid., 136. Jehan Desanges thinks the name is a play on the Greek word for "dung" and so it suggests "rubbish," "shit," or "riff-raff," and as such is, perhaps, a commentary on her color. Jehan Desanges, "l'Afrique noire et le monde mediterraneen dans l'antiquite: Ethiopiens et Greco-romains," in *The Image of the Black in Western Art, Volume I, From the Pharaohs to the Fall of the Roman Empire (Menil Foundation)*, ed. Jean Devisse, Jean Marie Courtes, Ladislas Bugner (Cambridge, Mass.: Harvard University Press, 1983), 409–11.

are reminiscent of a description from 1837 of a "Hottentot" woman.[33] Many white male observers and scholars seem to have had a curious preoccupation with black women's breasts. Francis Moore, who first published his travelogue of Africa in 1738, included this description of Gambian women: "large breasts, thick lips and broad nostrils, are esteemed extreamly [sic] beautiful. One breast is generally larger than the other."[34]

In the treatment of ancient texts, modern scholars have assumed that ancient Romans would have found the breasts of African women "disgusting." David Wiesen comments upon Juvenal 13.162–63 (quis tumidum guttur miratur in Alpibus aut quis/in Meroe crasso maiorem infante mamillam?[35]) that, "a huge-breasted African woman nursing her fat child would have been an amazing, perhaps disgusting sight to a Roman viewer."[36] Thompson agrees with Wiesen on this point, stating, "According to a widely held Roman view, the somatic 'defects' of the Aethiops somatic type comprised colour, hair, facial shape, and over-large breasts in the female of the genus."[37] When scholars cite these lines as "evidence" for the physical characteristics of African women, they seem to forget that Juvenal is writing satire, a genre which requires the poetic device of hyperbole. He, like Lucretius before him,[38] is listing the varieties of the human condition and observing that there is nothing surprising about any of them in their own context.

---

33. J.J. Virey, *Histoire Naturelle du Genre Humane* (Paris: 1810) [*Natural History of the Negro Race*], J. H. Guenbault, trans. (Charleston, S.C.: D. J. Dowling, 1837), 13: "[Hottentot women] can suckle a child on their back, by throwing the breast over their shoulders."

34. Francis Moore, *Travels into the Inland Parts of Africa* (London: Edward Cave, 1738). Online: http://people.uvawise.edu/runaways/lit/moore.html; this edition was published in 1767.

35. "Who is amazed by a throat goiter in the Alps or who is amazed by a breast larger than a chubby baby in Meroe?"

36. David S. Weisen, "Juvenal and the Blacks," *Classica et Mediaevalia* 31 (1970): 145.

37. Thompson, *Romans and Blacks*, 35.

38. Lucretius, *De Rerum Natura*, 4.1160–69, especially 1168: *at tumida et mammosa 'Ceres' est 'ipsa ab Iaccho.'* (But the plump and busty one is "Ceres herself [being suckled] by Bacchus.") Lucretius is speaking of how love transforms blemishes into beauty marks in the eyes of the lover.

So, he says, there is nothing surprising about throat goiters in the Alps, Germans with their hair twisted into greasy horns, or Meroetic women with breasts larger than their fat babies. It is clear that Juvenal is exaggerating to make his point. No one now believes that throat goiters are an ethnic characteristic of the French and Swiss; no one travels to Germany expecting to see people with their hair twisted into greasy horns. Why, then, does the leading commentator on Juvenal, Edward Courtney, remark on Juvenal 13.163, "Large pendulous breasts are common in negro women"?[39] Furthermore, Wiesen's comment on this line (cited earlier) takes Juvenal's hyperbole as a point of fact. Juvenal's point is that large breasts on *any* woman would have been surprising to a Roman. Incidentally, it is a flaw of the male-centered perspective of these scholars that none notes the fact that in these examples, the women are lactating. Lactating women of all races have fuller, larger breasts than when they are not lactating.

Because Scybale's depiction is part of a text that today is decidedly marginal, Classical scholars sometimes turn to handbooks to read a general description of the work. How does Scybale fare in these reference works? In *A Literary History of Rome from the Origins to the Close of the Golden Age* (1910), J. Wight Duff describes Scybale as "the ugly, old, negress who is his [the peasant Simylus's] housekeeper."[40] H. J. Rose describes her in *A Handbook of Latin Literature* (1936) as, "an old negress who comprises his entire household."[41] Paul Harvey comments in the 1937 edition of the *Oxford Companion to Classical Literature*, "[The *Moretum*] vividly describes a peasant rising . . . and preparing his meal with the help of his old negress servant."[42] M. C. Howatson's 1989 edition of the same reference work renders Scybale invisible: "It [the *Moretum*] vividly describes

39. Edward Courtney, *A Commentary on the Satires of Juvenal* (London: Athlone, 1980), 554.

40. J. Wight Duff, *A Literary History of Rome from the Origins to the Close of the Golden Age* (London: T. F. Unwin, 1910), 358.

41. H. J. Rose, *A Handbook of Latin Literature: From the Earliest Times to the Death of St. Augustine* (London: Methuen & Co., 1936), 265.

42. Paul Harvey, *The Oxford Companion to Classical Literature* (Oxford: Clarendon, 1937), 280.

the farmer rising early on a winter morning . . . and preparing his meal, then starting his day's work at the plough."[43] Thompson (1989) describes Scybale as "the slave and sole house companion of a simple peasant."[44] I have searched these lines and the remaining hexameters of the poem. There are no indications that she is old or ugly or a slave. She only becomes ugly if the beholder has been socialized to believe that African physiognomy is ugly. No commentator raises the possibility that the peasant Simylus and Scybale might be companions out of mutual affection.[45] It is also clear that Scybale is not sexualized the way that Dido or the black and pale-brown women of Pompeian graffiti are. Rather, she is asexual and in this regard she resembles the controlling image of the mammy/Aunt Jemima figure in the United States.

What other examples are there of modern stereotypes intruding upon the analysis of ancient women? I found it fascinating that when we have evidence that ancient men from Italy or Greece love women of color, many male scholars assume that the women are prostitutes. There are two inscriptions from Pompeii that deal with such relationships.

> Candida me doCvit nigras
> OdIsse Pvellas; odero; sepotero; sed non InvItvs
> Amabo;
> SCripsit Venus; FisiCa; Pompeiana. (*CIL* 4.1520)

Haley: A bright pale-brown woman taught me to hate bright
           black women
         I would hate them if I could; but not unwilling
         I will love them.[46]

---

43. M. C. Howatson, *The Oxford Companion to Classical Literature* (Oxford: Oxford University Press, 1989), 45.

44. Thompson, Ibid., 30.

45. Could the Anglo-American fear of miscegenation be lurking behind the omission of this possibility?

46. Cf. Ovid, *Amores*, 3.11b.35:
Luctantur pectusque leve in contraria tendunt
hac amor hac odium, sed, puto, vincit amor.
odero, si potero; si non, invitus amabo. (Italics added.)
Haley's translation:

The second is strikingly reminiscent of the Sable Venus Ode;[47] with my translation, it reads:

> Quisquis amat nigra(m) nigris carbonibus ardet.
> Nigra(m) cum video mora libenter ed<e>o. (CIL
>   4.6892)

Haley: Whoever loves a bright black woman burns with black
                coals.
            When I see a bright black woman, I gladly eat
                blackberries.

Compare the following translations:

Thompson: Any man who loves a black girl is set on fire by hot
                    charcoal flames;
                when I see a black girl I am ready and willing to eat
                    that blackberry.[48]

Wick (an epigrapher and commentator on this inscription):

> . . . se . . . nigras omnino timere et adversus eas mora
>   edere
> solere tamquam amuletum fassus est.[49]

Love and hate struggle over my fickle heart and pull it—Love in one direc-tion, Hate in the other—but Love, I think, is winning. *I would hate if I could; if not, I will love unwilling.* (Italics added.)

47. *The Sable Venus Ode* (circa 1777), in Bryan Edwards, *The History, Civil and Commercial, of the British Colonies in the West Indies*, vol. 2, 3rd ed. (1801): 32–38:

Next comes a warmer race, from sable sprung,
To love each thought, to lust each nerve is strung;
The Samboe dark, and Mullattoe brown,
The Mestize fair, the well-limb'd Quaderoon,
And jetty Afric, from no spurious sire,
Warm as her soil, and as her sun—on fire.
These sooty dames, well vers'd in Venus' school,
Make love an art, and boast they kiss by rule.

48. Thompson, *Romans and Blacks*, 108.

Haley: He confesses that he really fears black girls and usually eats blackberries as a protection against them.

Note that *quisquis* can be either feminine or masculine, but both Thompson and Wick assume it refers to a man.

Thompson assumes that the bright-black women ("girls," as he puts it) in both these inscriptions are prostitutes. In his note on 6892, he elaborates as follows:

> The author may have been a slave; *nigra* in the context of a group of prostitutes in a brothel, as in this particular case, can hardly refer to any but an exotic or rare type of physical appearance: the scribbler's sentiments presuppose such a rare type as distinct from a merely dark-skinned girl or a brunette, and so the graffito should be taken as alluding either to black prostitutes in general or to a particular black prostitute. But in any case it clearly exudes sexual curiosity and emphasizes the exoticism of one or more black prostitutes (probably slave girls) as sex objects offering a *rare* experience in Pompeian brothels.[50]

It is important to note that Thompson is the same commentator who interprets Scybale as a slave. For him, a black woman must be a slave; if she is loved, she must be a prostitute. But there is nothing in inscription 6892 to indicate this; there is no way to know the ethnicity of the authors of 6892 or 1520. The author of 1520 might well have been a black man. Is there any textual evidence to support prostitution in either of these cases? The attribution of *Venus Fisica* in 1520 might arguably indicate a brothel, and the physical context of the inscription cannot be firmly determined. The inscriptions apparently were not found on the walls of brothels.[51] In all probability, there were some black women who were prostitutes. But to read all black women from an ancient context as prostitutes is indicative of racist and sexist attitudes not of the ancient society, but of the modern reader.

---

49. *CIL* 4.6892, 721.
50. Thompson, *Romans and Blacks*, 210–11.
51. The only commentary on 6892 regards orthography: *litteris cursivis magnis et pulchris.*

Conclusions

In conclusion, there is evidence in the Roman literature of the Augustan age and later that the Romans were acute observers of color, gender, and class difference. For instance, there is evidence that ancient Roman men feared female sexuality, but that sexuality is not necessarily colorized. Indeed, all women arouse such fear. In morally didactic texts like those of Vergil and Livy, the foreign woman with political power offers the greatest threat, but once she is subsumed into the domestic sphere, like Scybale, she becomes asexual and less of a threat. However, powerful foreign women distract the Roman man/hero (or his representative) from his *virtus* ("manly virtue") and *officium* ("duty") with their exotic sexuality.

Clearly, each of these differences carried varying value, and their intersection and simultaneity carried yet another value. It is too simplistic to assume that the Romans had no skin color prejudice; it is equally simplistic to assume that all women were perceived as Roman women. The Romans were more keenly aware of different cultural practices—especially those of African societies—than we have previously recognized. This should not be surprising, since Roman society at the time of Augustus was multilayered and complexly multicultural. As we discover the extent of that complexity, critical race theory can help to unlayer the intersectionality of the constructs of ancient Roman society.

CHAPTER 2

The Knidian Aphrodite in the Roman Empire and Hiram Powers's *Greek Slave*

On Ethnicity, Gender, and Desire

Laura Nasrallah

🔳🔳🔳🔳🔳🔳🔳🔳🔳🔳🔳

Although we may not know the original form of the statue of the Aphrodite of Knidos, she was replicated across time and space from the second-century Roman world to late-eighteenth-century discussions of history and aesthetics to twentieth- and twenty-first-century art historical debates. In crafting his *Greek Slave* out of white marble, the mid-nineteenth century artist Hiram Powers replicated the form of the Knidian Aphrodite. His work was an object of debate in abolitionist and pro-slavery circles in the U.S. Similarly, nineteenth- and twentieth-century art historical discussions of the Knidia had gendered and racial dimensions.

Scholars have long discussed the ancient Knidia's gender; it is also necessary to address her race. Early Christians, among others, critiqued images of the Aphrodite of Knidos not only by using the sexual invective of the day, but also by engaging contemporaneous valuations of race. In the second-century Roman world and nineteenth-century U.S. society alike, race and gender function together in literary and imagistic interpretations of this famous statue. Early Christians, among others, used the Aphrodite of Knidos—which was simultaneously woman, goddess, and thing, a material object for trade, just like a slave—to think with, organizing around it their rhetoric of race and gender.

⑤⑤⑤⑤⑤⑤⑤⑤⑤⑤⑤⑤⑤⑤

Introduction

Between 1842 and 1869, American sculptor Hiram Powers completed at least six versions of the *Greek Slave* (figure 1). First rendered in plaster in 1842 and later in marble, these statues stood life-sized; Powers's agent, the painter Miner Kellogg, describes one version as 5 feet, 6.5 inches and carved from a "single piece of Serravezza marble."[1] The *Greek Slave* was popular not only in European exhibitions, but also

Figure 1. Hiram Powers, Greek Slave. *Yale University Art Gallery. Photo: Yale University Art Gallery/Art Resource, NY.*

---

1. Miner K. Kellogg, "Introduction: The Greek Slave," in *Powers' Statue of the Greek Slave* (New York: R. Craighead, 1847), 5. This book is a collection of favorable reviews of the statue, part of Kellogg's promotion of the statue, which helped to lead to its enormous popular and financial success, according to Charmaine A. Nelson, *The Color of Stone: Sculpting the Black Female Subject in Nineteenth-Century America* (Minneapolis and London: University of Minnesota Press, 2007), 75.

in America, where it toured from 1847 to 1851.[2] She was also replicated and distributed in miniatures; as Henry James puts it, she is "so
undressed, yet so refined, even so pensive, in sugar-white alabaster,
exposed under little domed glass covers in such American homes as
could bring themselves to think such things right."[3]

Powers's *Greek Slave* has perhaps unexpected links to issues
regarding ethnicity, religion, gender, and desire in the ancient world.
In crafting his *Greek Slave*, Powers replicates the form of the Knidian Aphrodite. The turned head, the shielded genitals, the pedestal,
drape, and nudity echo Praxiteles' long-lost Aphrodite of Knidos,
which from the Hellenistic period on was often replicated in various
sizes and media.[4] Scholarly discussions of the statue of the Aphrodite
of Knidos and her ongoing role in antiquity frequently treat issues
of gender, but not those of race.[5] But as Charmaine Nelson argues

---

2. Nelson, *Color of Stone*, 78; a slaveholder from South Carolina was an early
patron (94).

3. The quotation occurs in the context of a description of his time among
American sculptors in Florence. Henry James, *William Wetmore Story and His
Friends*, 2 vols. (Boston: Houghton, Mifflin Co., 1903), 1:114–15. See discussion
of the phenomenon of reproduction in Nelson, *Color of Stone*, 78; replicas "included
smaller full-length figures, busts, and even Parian ware and ceramic 'souvenirs'." On
Phryne (Praxiteles' rumored courtesan model for the statue) and the popularity of
her story and the rampant replication of forms of the Knidia in nineteenth-century
France, see Edouard Papet, "Praxitèle: Un Mythe au XIXe siècle?" in Alain Pas-
quier and Jean-Luc Martinez, *Praxitèle* (Paris: Musée du Louvre, 2007), 362–415.

4. The *Greek Slave* was not the only image that evoked issues of race and gender in the nineteenth century, drawing the black woman together with Venus:
there was also the famous image of the "Sable Venus," which drew from Bot-
ticelli's Venus emerging from a shell in the sea, and the "Hottentot Venus." For
the latter, see Stephen Jay Gould, "The Hottentot Venus," in *The Flamingo's Smile*
(New York: W. W. Norton and Company, 1985), 291–305. For the ways in which
Powers understood his sculpture to be better than ancient models, such as the
Medici Venus, see Charles Colbert, " 'Each Little Hillock Hath a Tongue'—Phrenology and the Art of Hiram Powers," *The Art Bulletin* 68, no. 2 (1986): 290.

5. In this essay I use the terms "race" and "ethnicity" interchangeably, especially with regard to the ancient world. I have been influenced by Denise Kimber
Buell's arguments about why the use of the term "race" is relevant for the ancient
world, even if there is no one semantic match for it in Greek or Latin. My readings of assertions of Greek *paideia* as a racialized discourse, and Christian invective against them as similarly racialized, are largely due to her work. See esp.
Why This New Race? Ethnic Reasoning in Early Christianity (New York: Columbia
University Press, 2005), x–xi.

regarding the nineteenth-century *Greek Slave* and similar works, "the sexualization of the body can never be separated from the body's racial identifications."[6] My project begins with nineteenth-century America and moves to the second-century Roman world to highlight how race and gender function together in literary and imagistic interpretations of this famous statue that is simultaneously woman, goddess, and thing—a material object for trade, just like a slave. In doing so, I show how early Christians among others organize their rhetoric of race and gender around the Aphrodite of Knidos.

Hiram Powers's *Greek Slave*

The nineteenth-century sculpture depicts a young woman, her head turned in profile, looking to her left, and her hair neatly gathered into a bun at the nape. She stands naked beside a pedestal on which is draped a cloth, a locket, and a cross. Her chained or manacled hands (depending on the version) are bound before her, concealing her genitalia. According to the sculptor, this image depicts a Greek Christian woman being sold into slavery by Turks in the markets of Constantinople during the Greek War of Independence. In Powers's words,

> as there should be a moral in every work of art, I have given to the expression of the Greek Slave what trust there could still be in a Divine Providence for a future state of existence, with utter despair for the present mingled with somewhat of scorn for all around her. She is too deeply concerned to be aware of her nakedness. It is not her person but her spirit that stands exposed, and she bears it all as Christians only can.[7]

In the years of her great popularity, the *Greek Slave* presented at least two problems for viewers: her female nakedness and her color. The two are connected, since the nakedness of a black woman's body

---

6. Nelson, *Color of Stone*, 102.

7. Hiram Powers to Edwin W. Stoughton, 29 November 1829, Hiram Powers Papers, Archives of American Art, Smithsonian Institution, quoted and cited in Vivien Green, "Hiram Powers' 'Greek Slave': Emblem of Freedom," *American Art Journal* 14, no. 1 (1982): 32.

would not be as shocking. A black woman could be seen naked at slave market; a white lady retained the privilege of "modesty." The sculpture is usually studied "primarily for its singular position in the history of American art as the first female nude to be accepted by the public."[8] Her nakedness was much discussed and disavowed in this Victorian age; the sculptor himself tried to frame her nakedness as unselfconscious, and even in terms of a paradisiacal Eve.[9] Others argued similarly. "She stands not bare—Another robe, of purity, is there," poeticized James Freeman Clarke.[10] "To the pure all things are pure," insisted an anonymous writer in *The National Era*. Writers sought to frame or control the embarrassing and arousing potential of a woman's nude body.

The *Greek Slave*'s color was also discussed. That this marble is "finer and harder than that of Carrara, and more free from blemishes,"[11] and that it is a pure white is not incidental to the image's importance and popularity. The irony of a "sugar-white" and unblemished slave—especially a slave woman, who was subject to sexual use in the master's household—was not lost on some American and British writers. An unsigned editorial from 1847 begins with a description of the statue, and the issue of its purity or lack thereof, and then cajoles her admirers:

> But, alas! in the midst of the pleasing emotions excited by this admirable work of art, there came sad thoughts of the wondrous hardness of that nature which can weep at sight of an insensate piece of marble which images a helpless virgin chained in the market-place of brutal lust, and still more brutal cupidity, and yet listens unmoved to the awful story of the American slave!
>
> There were fair breasts, that heaved with genuine sympathy beneath the magic power of the great artist, that have never yet

---

8. Green, "*'Greek Slave'*", 31.

9. For discussion of this, see Nelson, *Color of Stone*, 79–80. This irony is also discussed in Green, Ibid., 31–32. For a satire of prudish viewers and the *Greek Slave*, see Unsigned, "Correspondence of the Era. New York Correspondence. Powers' Statue of the Greek Slave. New York August 30, 1847," *The National Era* (Washington, D.C.), 2 September 1847, 3.

10. Cited in Green, "*'Greek Slave'*", 32.

11. Kellogg, "'Greek Slave'", 5.

breathed a sigh for the sable sisterhood of the South! . . . Waste not your sympathies on the senseless marble, but reserve some tears for the helpless humanity which lies quivering beneath the lash of *American freemen.*[12]

The *Greek Slave*, in her nakedness and whiteness, could confuse the viewer. On the one hand, to gaze on her was (potentially) to take the viewpoint of the dark, male Turkish captor or buyer of the pure white woman.[13] As Nelson discusses, the sculpture reverses the race of master and slave as it was known in nineteenth-century America: the master becomes dark, the slave white.[14] The viewer, presumably white and elite, identified with and enjoyed watching her plight, primed by the Orientalism of the day that spawned sexualized texts and images that horrified and titillated with the idea of white female bodies subject to and serving the darker Arabs.

On the other hand, the *Greek Slave* caused some viewers to recognize the tragedy of American slavery, even if that tragedy was still sometimes framed in terms of a color scale: that is, the tragedy of the nearly white who was enslaved.[15] Powers himself, while waffling regarding abolitionism, shifted the statue's iconography from chains to "a more realistic and historically specific manacle" which evoked American slavery.[16] As Vivien Green has shown, the *Greek Slave* fits into the *topos* not of the black slave, but of the "tragic octoroon" in the mid-nineteenth century. Such a figure, discussed in abolitionist literature, is sometimes depicted as the daughter of the slave master and his mulatto mistress, who passes and is educated as white.[17] An

---

12. Unsigned, "Correspondence of the Era. New York Correspondence. Powers' Statue of the Greek Slave. New York August 30, 1847," *The National Era* (Washington, D.C.), 2 September 1847, 3. Italics original. The same page of this issue of *The National Era* contains articles titled "The Slave Trade" and "The First Anti-Slavery Meeting in the United States."

13. See Green, " 'Greek Slave' ", 35–36.

14. Nelson, *Color of Stone*, 80–84; see also 98–105 on contemporaneous images of white women captured by Native Americans.

15. Green, " 'Greek Slave' ", 34–39; Nelson, *Color of Stone*, 93–97.

16. Nelson, *Color of Stone*, 78–79; 105–12. See also her discussion of Powers' own shifting political positions and his statue *America* and its relation to slavery (87–93).

17. Green, " 'Greek Slave' ", 36.

article in the *Christian Inquirer,* a Unitarian publication, demonstrates the tension between asserting that the *Greek Slave* has meaning for the situation of American slavery, on the one hand, and a distancing of such political critique from sympathy for the "darkest" among slaves, on the other. The article insists that there is nothing wrong in viewing the *Greek Slave;* "the very best of our countrymen travelling in Europe" see such objects frequently; thus, the writer positions the viewer in relation to certain elite cultural practices, coded as European. The article insists that the statue is "an impersonation of Slavery," but then begs the reader not to "keep down the natural promptings of his indication by the notion of woolly heads and black skins." Rather, the writer evokes sympathy by foregrounding—calling to the front of the slave market, in a way—those slaves who are whiter. "Let him not ignore the fact that white skins, fair hair, delicate beauty, often enhance the market value of his countrywomen thus exposed for sale."[18]

Charmaine Nelson puts it well: "It was through the identification of the white Negroes, the 'daughters of white men' whose bodies bore the symbolic signs of white female identity, 'white skins, fair hair, delicate beauty,' that the antislavery message of the Greek Slave was most widely deployed."[19] Such color prejudice was mocked and exposed in print and image; implicitly, so too were white American concerns about "passing" or about being racially misidentified. In a cartoon in England, a drawing of a statue echoed the *Greek Slave,* but presented the woman as black, standing next to a short pillar draped with the American flag, and standing atop a pedestal decorated with whips and chains and the inscription *e pluribus unum.* The caption read "The Virginian Slave. Intended as a companion to Power's [*sic*] 'Greek Slave'."[20] In print, we find an essay that claims to be written by a viewer of the *Greek Slave* as it toured St. Louis. The writer "records" the words of one spectator who addresses the statue:

Thou, woman in marble, hast been brought from a land we call heathen, to show us Christians how much more pure and humane

---

18. Unsigned, "The Greek Slave," *Christian Inquirer,* 9 October 1847, 207.
19. Nelson, *Color of Stone,* 97.
20. Discussed in Green, "'Greek Slave'", 37.

are our ways than theirs. We are in thy presence reminded that no divine image of humanity wrought as thou hast been in white can here be chained and worked like mere animals. By thee we are reminded that in our Christian land no Turk can lay his trafficking hand upon a skin that is white and say, *mine, for I have paid my money.* . . . With the spread of the Gospel slavery shall no more put its chain around a white wrist; but that, under the benignant sway of Christianity, this doom shall be confined to black people.

The statue turns and answers him:

I was carved from Parian [marble], rather than from Ebony, that I might more effectually appeal to perverted justice and partial sympathy; but I am the representation of the captive and the forsaken everywhere, and whatever sympathy I may secure for my enslaved sisters in Turkey, are due to my sisters of another hue in the land throughout which I am making my pilgrimage. . . . Cease your sympathy for a slave in Constantinople, and go show kindness and justice to those over whom you have power.

The writer then echoes the gospel story of the rich young man, and thus places the *Greek Slave* in the role of Jesus: the spectator leaves, grieved and chastened by the statue, because he owns many slaves.[21]

The *Greek Slave* was enormously popular, and Hiram Powers was even called an American "Phidias or Michael Angelo."[22] Even if this demonstrates an ignorance of the history of this statue's form, which

---

21. Unsigned, "Powers' Greek Slave in Saint Louis," *The National Era* (Washington, D.C.), 16 January 1851, 9–10.

22. *Boston Daily Advertiser*, 27 June 1848 and the New York *Literary World*, 18 December 1847; cited in Green, "'Greek Slave'", 33. See also discussion of Anna Lewis's 1855 review of the statue (*Graham's Magazine*) in Nelson, *Color of Stone*, 78; Lewis relates the *Greek Slave* to "treasured ancient sculptures." One of the essays collected by Miner Kellogg explicitly discusses the biography of Powers and his role alongside ancient artists, but does not include mention of the ancient Venuses on which Powers modeled his work: Edward Everett, "American Sculptors in Italy" (from the *Boston Miscellany* for February 1841) collected in Kellogg, "Greek Slave", 6–11.

derives from traditions regarding the sculpture of Praxiteles, not Phidias, it shows an understanding that this statue has a long place within history. More importantly, it signals recognition of the statue's ethnic genealogy: the *Greek Slave*'s Greekness derives not only from the fact that she is said to represent modern-day Greeks under the Ottoman Empire, but from a long history associating her form with the best of ancient Greek *paideia* (culture or education). And more ominously in terms of race and bodies, Powers's *Greek Slave* was not only inspired by the phrenology of his age, but also became an embodiment of phrenological ideals; the *Greek Slave*'s head came to be understood as quintessentially American—but an American woman of a certain sort, raced as white, balanced, modern.[23]

The Aphrodite of Knidos among Art Historians

In the second and nineteenth centuries, the Aphrodite of Knidos was a form in which one could invest one's own meaning with regard to race, gender, and religion. In nineteenth-century antebellum America, as we have seen, the *Greek Slave*, modeled after the Knidia, can be read as white, as octoroon, and even as standing in for her phenotypical opposite (in the logic of the day): one of those with "woolly heads and black skins."[24] The complicated politics of sex and race in Powers's *Greek Slave* mirror the popularity of the Aphrodite of Knidos in the second century. At that time, she represented an aesthetic of the Greek female/goddess that was a commodity on the Roman market. To draw the analogy more directly, in a period of Greek idealization and sometimes enslavement in the Roman Empire, the Aphrodite of Knidos is bought and sold, duplicated and reduplicated in the markets of the empire.[25] She even becomes a funerary monument; the naked,

---

23. Colbert, "Phrenology", 298; see 288–92 especially regarding phrenology and discerning a woman's characteristics. On physiognomy, craniometry, and theories of race, see Robert J. C. Young, *Colonial Desire: Hybridity in Theory, Culture and Race* (New York: Routledge, 1995), esp. ch. 3.

24. Unsigned, "The Greek Slave," *Christian Inquirer*, 9 October 1847, 207.

25. We should understand these Roman productions of the Knidia not as imitative or derivative; see discussion of Johann Winckelmann below. Recently, art historians have avoided terminology of "copying" for that of emulation or

rounded bodies of otherwise presumably modest Roman matrons were surmounted by the matrons' own portrait heads, some with strained faces and aging skin, even in marble.[26] Christians and others also discuss her; she is a magnet for criticisms that deal with her sexualized form, her blurring of the boundaries between human and divine, her role as a Greek object desired by Roman connoisseurs. The Knidia and her second-century multiplications, as well as the *Greek Slave* and her sugar-white replications, are *things*, yet things with biographies or "social lives," to use Arjun Appadurai's terminology.[27]

Turning to Roman art historians' discussion of the elusive "original" from which second-century CE sculptures and Powers's *Greek Slave* derive, we learn much about race and gender in the evaluation of statuary and aesthetics in the nineteenth and twentieth centuries.[28] No one today has seen Praxiteles' fourth-century BCE sculpture, which was installed at a temple for Aphrodite at the city of Knidos. Yet her original form is much debated; the Aphrodite of Knidos, like the historical Jesus, is an ever-vanishing point on the horizon. We know much about the Knidia from her profusion in literature and image, especially in the second century CE. The Capitoline Venus, a second-century piece in Parian marble, provides an example of a version of

interpretation. See, for example, Miranda Marvin, *The Language of the Muses: The Dialogue between Roman and Greek Sculpture* (Los Angeles: Getty Museum, 2008); Ellen Perry, *The Aesthetics of Emulation in the Visual Arts of Ancient Rome* (Cambridge, UK, and New York: Cambridge University Press, 2005); Elaine K. Gazda, *The Ancient Art of Emulation: Studies in Artistic Originality and Tradition from the Present to Classical Antiquity* (Ann Arbor, Mich.: Published for the American Academy in Rome by University of Michigan Press, 2002). See the review discussion by Christopher Hallett, "The Romanization of Late Hellenistic Sculpture," in *JRA* 15, no. 2 (2002): 393–96.

26. See esp. Eve D'Ambra, "The Calculus of Venus: Nude Portraits of Roman Matrons," in Natalie Boymel Kampen, ed., *Sexuality in Ancient Art: Near East, Egypt, Greece, and Italy* (New York: Cambridge University Press, 1996), 219–32.

27. Arjun Appadurai, ed., *The Social Life of Things: Commodities in Cultural Perspective* (Cambridge: Cambridge University Press, 1986); see especially the introduction by Appadurai, "Introduction: Commodities and the Politics of Value" (3–63), and Igor Kopytoff, "The Cultural Biography of Things: Commoditization as Process" (64–91).

28. On aesthetics and race, see Shawn Kelley's chapter in this volume, 191–209.

Figure 2. Capitoline Venus.
Musei Capitolini, Rome, Italy.
Photo: Scala/Art Resource, NY.

the Knidia that one might have encountered in the Roman world (figure 2).[29] Another example is found in the over–life-size, second-century Campo Iemini Aphrodite in the British Museum (figure 3). The Knidia's image multiplied in forms small and large, in painting, coinage, and sculpture across the Roman Empire.[30]

---

29. Kristen Seaman offers a catalogue of 200 representations of the Knidia, and these are limited to images that conform to "the statue's main features as depicted on Knidian coinage . . . : a naked woman who covers her *aidos* with one hand and holds drapery that reaches to a pot in the other" ("Retrieving the Original Aphrodite of Knidos," *Rend.* 9, no. 15 [2004]: 531–32, 534–35 [quotation at the latter]). See also Wiltrud Neumer-Pfau, "Die Nackte Liebesgöttin: Aphroditestatuen als Verkörperung des Weihlichkeitsideals in der griechisch-hellenistischen Welt," in Hans G. Kippenberg, *Approaches to Iconology, Visible Religion, V. 4–5* (Leiden: E. J. Brill, 1985), 208, and her fuller discussion of the Capitoline Aphrodite in *Studien zur Ikonographie und Gesellschaftlichen Funktion Hellenistischer Aphrodite-Statuen* (Bonn: R. Habelt, 1982), 62–116.

30. See especially Seaman, "Aphrodite of Knidos", 531–94; also Christine Havelock, *The Aphrodite of Knidos and Her Successors* (Ann Arbor: University of Michigan Press, 1995), 74; *LIMC* II.1.52.

Figure 3. Campo Iemeni Venus. British Museum, London. © The Trustees of the Britsh Museum.

Nearly everyone agrees that the Greek sculptor Praxiteles' Aphrodite of Knidos was new and powerful in the mid-fourth century BCE;[31] in fact, art historians generally date the origins of the female monumental nude to Praxiteles. Art historians' debates over the meaning of this modestly nude or shamefully naked statue, whether it represents Aphrodite or women as Aphrodite (what, really, is the difference, after all), exemplify the complicated gender and racial politics of interpreting the Knidia not only in the second century, but also today.

Johann Winckelmann's 1764 *History of the Art of Antiquity* (*Geschichte der Kunst des Altertums*) framed much of the debate about ancient sculpture and aesthetics in the years since; even if art historians have rejected his categories and his periodization, they still cope implicitly and explicitly with his evaluations. Winckelmann set forth four stages of art.[32] The first style, that of the Archaic period, was

---

31. Havelock, "Aphrodite of Knidos", 1–2.
32. Johann Joachim Winckelmann, *History of the Art of Antiquity* trans. Harry Francis Mallgrave (Los Angeles: Getty Research Institute, 2006), 232–38.

straight and hard. Then, "at the time when full enlightenment and freedom appeared in Greece, art likewise became freer and more elevated," and the second phase, the "grand style," began. Art formed its own nature, and the artist improved nature's hard edges into a beautiful, flowing style. In Winckelmann's third or "beautiful" phase, commenced by Praxiteles, the remaining angularity of the high style came to flow;[33] "grace" was its main characteristic. This grace was formed from the marriage of what Winckelmann calls the "heavenly Venus" of the high style, with the earthly Venus who "willingly descends from her elevated state and reveals herself with benevolence, without degradation, to those who cast their eyes on her."[34] Winckelmann links this grace to Ionian artists (Parrhasios and Apelles) and thus ethnically situates this style in the Greek East and in colonies of Athens. The fourth phase is characterized by imitation; with the rise of the Romans, the genius of the past "cramp[ed] the spirit" and led to a mechanistic and derivative art; this imitation was characterized not only by timidity and diligence, but also by a "[decline] into the effeminate."[35]

Following Winckelmann's powerful assessment, those involved in the antiquities market were motivated to date objects to the grand or beautiful periods; Roman copies of earlier sculptures were seen as inferior, mechanical, not embodying the "Greek" spirit.[36] Ethnicity already functions in the evaluation of sculptures of antiquity, and Greekness was valued more than Romanness not only because of its greater antiquity,[37] but also, and even more, because it evoked what were perceived as key Western values regarding democracy and the beauty and value of the human form.

---

33. Ibid., 234.

34. Ibid., 235–36.

35. Ibid., 238. On how modern-day aesthetics and racism affect scholars' approaches to ancient literature and translations of ancient stories about African women, see Shelley Haley's essay in this volume, 27–49.

36. Winckelmann, *History*, 232: "Those who, like Montfaucon, believe that no works by Greek sculptors have survived except those made after Greece came under the rule of Rome likewise have much to learn." See discussions of art historical discourses of Greek authenticity and Roman "copying," for example, in Marvin, *Language of the Muses*.

37. Winckelmann's model seems to assume the erasure of Greeks under the Roman period, or the subsuming of Greek identity to Roman at that time.

Let me give an example of the social life of one articulation of the Knidia and how Winckelmann's periodization functions in her valuation.[38] The Campo Iemini Venus (see again figure 3) was once highly valued; after it was unearthed in 1794 in an excavation headed in part by Prince Augustus of Britain, the Prince of Wales wanted to expropriate it and was very afraid when he heard that it had been lost in a shipwreck. Napoleon conquered Rome, taking the Capitoline Venus back to Paris and waiting, too, to take the Medici Venus, another quotation of the Knidia, back to France. Italy was in danger of being entirely bereft of famous Venuses. The Campo Iemini Venus's status suddenly elevated; now she was desired not only by the Prince of Wales, but also by the Roman scholars who had previously considered her good enough, but not quite as lovely as the Medici Venus. The Romans could not keep the promised Campo Iemini Venus away from the Prince of Wales, and they were left only with plaster casts of her and of the Capitoline Venus. Yet the Campo Iemini Venus was later consigned to the basement of the British Museum by the power of Winckelmann's sort of assessment of statuary; she was seen as a Roman copy, derivative, lacking the authenticity and essence of Greekness.

Ethnicity was a factor in Winckelmann's assessment of ancient statuary; so too was gender and desire. This latter theme was articulated in relation to sculptures themselves, as in Winckelmann's assessment of the Medici Venus, herself an emulation of the Knidia: "The Medici Venus in Florence—like a rose that after a beautiful dawn, unfolds at sunrise—steps from the age that, like fruit not fully ripened, is hard and slightly tart, as shown in her breasts," he writes.[39] Perhaps more significantly, desire and gender are figured at the end of the *History of the Art of Antiquity*, where Winckelmann figures himself and the connoisseur viewer as feminized, gazing after the masculinized sculptures of the past:

> I have in this history of art already gone beyond its set bounds,
> and although contemplating the collapse of art has driven me

---

38. I summarize the story from Ilaria Bignamini, "The 'Campo Iemini Venus' Rediscovered," *The Burlington Magazine* 136, no. 1097 (Aug., 1994), 548–52; see also Papet, Ibid., 362–415.

nearly to despair, still, like someone who, in writing the history of his native land, must touch upon the destruction that he himself has witnessed, I could not keep myself from gazing after the fate of works of art as far as my eye could see. Just as a beloved stands on the seashore and follows with tearful eyes her departing sweetheart, with no hope of seeing him again, and believes she can glimpse even in the distant sail the image of her lover— so we, like the lover, have as it were only a shadowy outline of the subject of our desires remaining. But this arouses so much the greater longing for what is lost, and we examine the copies we have with greater attention than we would if we were in full possession of the originals. In this, we are often like individuals who wish to converse with spirits and believe they can see something where nothing exists.[40]

Winckelmann presents himself as haunted by the ideal art of the past, which, even if the object itself is female, is simultaneously marked by gender and ethnicity.[41] It is male; it is embodied by the Greek.

Winckelmann's ideas inform more recent art historical interpretations of Praxiteles' Knidian Aphrodite. One example is Andrew Stewart, who argues that whereas previous Greek sculptors took the male form as canon and imaged females as mutated men, Praxiteles took seriously female bodies and thereby inaugurated a "new representational orthodoxy."[42] Stewart assumes both that Praxiteles sculpted Aphrodite using his courtesan lover Phryne as the model and that the elite male viewer—better, the connoisseur of both art and the female body—is the intended audience for such a piece.

Kenneth Clark's famous 1956 *The Nude: A Study of Ideal Form* influenced Stewart's interpretation. Clark reads the Knidian Aphrodite as a rejection of the "bulging body" and a turn to "geometrical

---

39. Winckelmann, *History*, 203.

40. Ibid., 351.

41. For a fruitful possibility for reading this language of haunting, or to think about how the racial ideologies of antiquity haunted the eighteenth and nineteenth centuries, see Denise Buell's contribution in this volume, 159–190.

42. Andrew Stewart, *Art, Desire, and the Body in Ancient Greece* (Cambridge and New York: Cambridge University Press, 1997), 104.

discipline."[43] We learn about the type of female body of which Clark was a connoisseur: "Although the *Capitoline* is more carnally realistic than the *Knidian* [for which he admits we have no original form], and the action of her right hand does nothing to conceal her magnificent breasts, a formal analysis shows that the title [Venus Pudica, Venus of Modesty] has some justification."[44] Clark's aesthetic criteria derive from and echo the responses of ancient writers, and connoisseurship can be seen merely as one art historian's preference for a certain kind of female object. Moreover, art historians subsequent to Clark still must grapple with the same categories of nakedness (which marks shame) and nudity (an ideal type), with such questions as whether a certain form of the Knidia has a modest or shameful glance.[45] Clark's writing, like those of the second-century writers whom we will encounter shortly, seems to emerge from and to evoke desire for a particular kind of female body.

If on the one side of the Knidia's interpretive divide we have scholars like Stewart and Clark, who interpreted the Knidia as the height of female beauty,[46] on the other we find Nancy Salomon, for example, who argues that while the monumentality and nudity of Praxiteles' mid-fourth-century Knidian Aphrodite was an innovation, it is not coincidental that she is the first to have her hand over her *pubes* in the *"pudica* or so called modest pose." In investigating the political meaning of the Knidia, she asserts that Praxiteles' "configuration" of the Knidia gives form to "the continued and incessant idealization of

---

43. Clark's evaluation is founded in uninvestigated criteria connected to his notions of status and sex: one statue of a woman is a "stocky little peasant"; another painting of female bodies is "almost comically unideal." Kenneth Clark, *The Nude: A Study of Ideal Art* (London: J. Murray, 1956), 115, 112.

44. Ibid., 130.

45. Clark's distinction between nakedness and nudity has influenced scholars of Roman art like Andrew Stewart and Christopher Hallett, even as some have attempted to reverse the terms, rendering nakedness into truth and authenticity and nudity into convention and posturing. See also Lynda Nead, *The Female Nude: Art, Obscenity, and Sexuality* (London and New York: Routledge, 1992), 14–15.

46. See also Havelock's apologia for the Knidia: "One is justified in writing rhapsodies about the Doryphoros' marvelous equilibrium. But the Knidia deserves no less" (*Aphrodite of Knidos*, 18; see also 21).

female humiliation in the Western tradition from ca. 340 BCE to the present."[47]

For both art historical sides of the coin—Stewart and Clark on the one side, and Salomon on the other, in my examples—there is an inchoate attempt to deal with the eroticism of the Knidia. In Stewart and Salomon, and indeed, as we shall see in ancient texts, the debate over the Knidia is longstanding. What is she meant to *do* to you? And what has been done to her? Sexual arousal is usually seen as an improper response to art; to use Lynda Nead's words, it is a "transgression of and deviation from the norms of public viewing" that "lacks the elevated intent demanded by high culture," where "the image is responded to in terms of its content, rather than its formal qualities."[48] Yet the Knidia is an object not only of replication, but also of the stimulation of desire. This is also true in second-century literary discussions.

The Aphrodite of Knidos in the Second Century

Those who wrote about Praxiteles' sculpture in the second century, whether Christian or non-Christian, often accuse Praxiteles of lacking propriety or refer to the sleight of hand whereby the slatternly Phryne, Praxiteles' rumored courtesan/model (*hetaira*), becomes Aphrodite.[49] The perhaps second-century epistolary inventions of Alciphron

---

47. Salomon admits that "each reiteration of the *pudica* pose"—and there were many iterations in the ancient world, and into the Renaissance and the present—has a meaning specific to its context. But she also thinks that there is an "accrued force of their collective strength." Nanette Salomon, "Making a World of Difference: Gender, Asymmetry, and the Greek Nude," in *Naked Truths: Women, Sexuality, and Gender in Classical Art and Archaeology*, ed. Ann Olga Koloski-Ostrow and Claire L. Lyons (London and New York: Routledge, 1997), 197–99.

48. Nead, *Female Nude*, 88.

49. See especially Havelock, *Aphrodite of Knidos*, 50–51. The literary rumor-mongering started as early as the Hellenistic period, when we find epigrams that allude to the story that Praxiteles' model for the statue was his *hetaira*, Phryne. Her very name describes what she is, since this name was used for prostitutes in Athens from the classical period on. Havelock, ibid., 43, who cites Aristophanes *Ecclesiazusae*. For a summary of some of the texts regarding Phryne, see 42–49.

include a letter that Phryne writes to Praxiteles; in it, she toys with the theological implications of Praxiteles' creation.[50]

> [D]o not fear. For you have achieved such an all-beautiful thing [*chrēma*, a term used for products or goods], such as no one, indeed, has ever yet seen of all things worked by (human) hands; you have set up your very own *hetaira* in a sacred precinct. For I stand in the midst, by Aphrodite and Eros, both yours. Do not begrudge me the honor. For those who gaze at me sing praises to Praxiteles.

Phryne continues, we can imagine, in breathy tones: "One thing is yet lacking in your gift: that you come to me, so that we may lie with each other in the sacred precinct. For we may not defile the gods whom we ourselves have created."[51] In the Roman period, Phryne is depicted as using sexuality and as being available for sexual use.

---

50. Alciphron claims that her naked breasts transformed the opinion of an Athenian jury in her favor. In these invented letters, Bacchis writes to Phryne, "Please now, dearest, do not prejudice the case of us courtesans . . . and when people tell you that, if you hadn't torn open your shift and shown the judges your breasts, your advocate would have been of no avail, don't believe them" (English translation: *The Letters of Alciphron, Aelian, and Philostratus*, LCL; trans. Allen Rogers Benner and Francis H. Fobes [Cambridge, Mass.: Harvard University Press, 1949], 259). On the date and relation of these "letters" to Lucian, including the question of who borrowed from whom, see 6–18. The early-third-century writer Athenaios tells the story of her walking naked into the sea at the Eleusinian festival; from this image of her loosening her hair, Apelles painted his Aphrodite Anadyomene (13.590). Athenaios 13.591; Alciphron, *Letters of the Courtesans* 4.

51. Alciphron, *Letters of the Courtesans* 2; my translation. Clement among others would shudder at this blatant joking about the imperceptible slide between human and divine in statuary of the Roman period: he himself combines these themes and the connection of Aphrodite with a prostitute near the beginning of the *Protreptikos*: "For the Cypriot islander Kinyras may never persuade me, he who dared to transfer the lewd orgies for Aphrodite from night to day, because he was ambitious to deify a prostitute of his city" (II 13.4). See also Pliny, *Nat. hist.* 35.37.119 (LCL 9.349): "A little before the period of his late lamented Majesty Augustus, Arellius also was in high esteem at Rome, had he not prostituted his art by a notorious outrage, by always paying court to any woman he happened to fall in love with, and consequently painting goddesses, but in the likeness of his mistresses; and so his pictures included a number of portraits of harlots."

This idea of sexual use of the statue's model extends to the famous (and facetious) story in (Pseudo) Lucian's *Amores*: in it, an admirer more or less rapes the statue of the Aphrodite. He wrote on walls and scratched into trees messages of love for Aphrodite; and "he honored Praxiteles as equal to Zeus" (*Amores* 16). This goddess-stalker dedicated everything in his home to the Knidia. One "night that cannot be spoken of" (ἀρρήτου νυκτός), he slipped into the chamber and had his chance. He left a stain of semen on her thigh, and then threw himself into the sea, whence Aphrodite had come.[52] The statue, it seems, provoked the young man's passionate love and lustful deed. Yet the story reveals not only the power of the beautiful goddess, but also her material vulnerability, her enslavement to stone and her gendered subjection.[53] As Pseudo-Lucian says, the artisan triumphed over the hard stone (*Amores* 12) in producing the Knidia, and of course, Aphrodite punishes mortals mortally for seeing her statuary body naked and soft. Yet, she is also vulnerable. Praxiteles and those after him offered a challenging, provocative theological message.[54]

In the second century, the Knidia is thus discussed in gendered language that highlights her connection with flagrant sexuality on the one hand and her sexual vulnerability on the other. She is also understood in terms of ethnicity. The Aphrodite of Knidos is such a synecdoche for high Greek culture that she, among others, represents the emperor's Greek mistress in Lucian's *Eikones* or "Essays in Portraiture." The speaker, Lykinos, says that, seeing her, he was practically turned to stone, "more motionless than statues" (1). The play between

---

52. *Amores* continues with Charikles' and Kallikratidas's prayerful speeches to Aphrodite, in which one justifies love between men and women, and the other love between men. There are also allusions to the story of a young man who fell in love with the Knidia in such texts as Lucian, *Eikones* 4 and Pliny, *Nat. Hist.* 36.4.21.

53. Nicole Loraux writes, "Aphrodite incarnates the immediacy of realized desire, the very image of 'love made flesh.'" Nicole Loraux, *The Experiences of Tiresias: The Feminine and the Greek Man* (Princeton, N.J.: Princeton University Press, 1995), 197.

54. Consider the blindness of Tiresias, effected by Zeus when Tiresias saw Aphrodite naked, or the myth of Actaeon, the hunter who was torn apart by his own dogs after he accidentally stumbled upon Artemis bathing naked in a pool. Stewart (Ibid., 100) discusses the general theme of the danger of seeing the gods.

statues and people continues as the Greek mistress is described in terms of various famous statues:

> "Have you ever travelled to Knidos, Polystratos?"
> "Yes, certainly!"
> "So then you saw their Aphrodite, no doubt?"
> "Yes, by Zeus, the most beautiful of Praxiteles' creations."
> "But have you also heard the story which the inhabitants tell about her, how someone fell in love with the statue, and, unnoticed, was left in the temple and had sexual intercourse with the statue, as much as that was possible?" (*Eikones* 4)

Lykinos hints at the famous story of the Knidia's violation, and he and Polystratos flaunt their connoisseurship and *paideia*; they have been tourists or worshippers in Knidos.

After bantering sophisticatedly about other statuary, Lycinus and Polystratos return to the topic at hand: how to describe the Greek mistress. Lykinos describes the woman in terms of statues:

> [H]e takes the head alone from the Knidia, for nothing else is needed, since the body is naked. Around the hair, and the forehead and the well-drawn brows, will be just as Praxiteles made them, and the softness of the eyes together with their brightness and graciousness. . . . The apple-cheeks and such front parts of the face by Alkamenes will be taken also from her in the Gardens, and besides the surfaces of the hands and the proportion of the wrists and the ease of the fingers in their fine tapering: also these things [will be] from the Lady in the gardens. (*Eikones* 6)

Through this portrait, Polystratos finally realizes whom Lykinos describes: "It is the emperor's consort!" (*Eikones* 10).

The description of the woman in terms of multiple severed bits of famous sculpture is deliberately Frankensteinish. Lucian satirizes the cultural pretentions of the day; the Roman emperor has fallen for Greekness.[55] The satire continues when Polystratos describes the

---

55. This is part of a long discourse in the ancient world. As Horace famously wrote even in the first century BCE, "Captive Greece conquered her savage captor" (*Graecia capta ferum victorem cepit.* Horace, *Epistles* 2.1.156). Internal critique

fine qualities of the emperor's mistress in terms drawn from Homer, from stories of Orpheus and Amphion—from all of Greek culture. Polystratos's interest in the purity of her ethnicity becomes clear.

> For this precision of language and Ionic purity, and that she is able to engage in social discourse with chattering and much Attic loveliness: this is nothing to marvel at. For it is her inheritance and ancestry (πάτριον γὰρ αὐτῇ καὶ προγονικόν), nor does she share in anything other than Athenian qualities, on account of the colony [which they planted in Ionia]. Nor again should I be amazed if she delights in poetry and converses much in it, she who is a countryman of Homer. (*Eikones* 15)

Her experience in statecraft is like that of Perikles' consort (17); she is even like Socrates' Diotima (18). Through the emperor's mistress, Lucian satirizes the many ways in which Greekness can be inherited and acquired.[56] The emperor's garrulous consort is Greek by inheritance; she is literarily crafted as a composite of Greek literary references and language on the one hand and a composite of bits and pieces of classical and Hellenistic Greek statuary on the other.[57]

---

of Roman decadence often implicated Greece as a corruptor of solid Latin, or even barbarian, values. See also Margaret M. Miles, *Art as Plunder: The Ancient Origins of Debate about Cultural Property* (Cambridge: Cambridge University Press, 2008); Susan Alcock, *Graecia Capta: The Landscapes of Roman Greece* (Cambridge: Cambridge University Press, 1993); Jeremy Tanner, *The Invention of Art History in Ancient Greece: Religion, Society, and Artistic Rationalisation* (Cambridge: Cambridge University Press, 2006), ch. 5–6.

56. On different strategies for articulating ethnicity (such as inheritance, birth, affiliation), see discussions in Buell, *Why This New Race*, and Caroline Johnson Hodge, *If Sons, Then Heirs: A Study of Kinship and Ethnicity in the Letters of Paul* (New York: Oxford University Press, 2007). See also discussions in Jonathan Hall, *Hellenicity: Between Ethnicity and Culture* (Chicago: University of Chicago Press, 2002); Benjamin Isaac, *The Invention of Racism in Classical Antiquity* (Princeton, N.J.: Princeton University Press, 2004); Emma Dench, *Romulus' Asylum: On Roman Identities from the Age of Alexander to the Age of Hadrian* (New York: Oxford University Press, 2005); Greg Woolf, *Becoming Roman: The Origins of Provincial Civilization in Gaul* (Cambridge: Cambridge University Press, 2000).

57. On the fragmented nature of Greek language, despite claims to its purity, see Tatian, *To the Greeks* 1.

Alciphron, as well as both texts under Lucian's name, reveal a second-century debate about Roman-period connoisseurship of Greek objects, about the value of Greek ethnicity under Rome. These objects include not only the mix of statuary that constitutes the emperor's consort, but even the consort herself, whom Lucian satirically describes as a model of ethnic Greekness.

The Knidia among Second-Century Christians

Early Christians, too, discuss the Knidia and her ethnicity. When early Christians write against images, their invective is usually understood as a product of aniconism and cultural marginalization. Instead, we can understand contemporaneous Christian texts to be engaged in a similar ethnocultural critique, reacting to the proliferation of statuary in their day and to the satirical stories that their "pagan" interlocutors told about the questionable morality of those statues' origins and use.

The second-century Tatian is usually understood as a bitter Syrian, offering a barbarian brand of Christianity over and against mainstream protoorthodoxy, and opposing the dominant strains of Greco-Roman culture.[58] He not only states that there is no unity to Greek language (*To the Greeks* 1) and insists that his interlocutors "stop your triumphal procession of another's words; stop decorating yourselves with feathers that aren't your own, as if you're a jackdaw!" (26.1). He also proudly takes up a barbarian identity (42) and so seems to reject all things Greek, including many items of cultural capital in the Roman Empire. Yet in the second-century context, where ethnicity was marketable and where someone with a Syrian accent could "pass" and be hired as a Greek teacher (see Lucian *Nigrinus*), we should read at least parts of his *To the Greeks* as satire. Like Pseudo-Lucian and Alciphron,

---

58. For only one example, see Simon Swain's discussion of Atticism in "Polemon's *Physiognomy*," in Simon Swain, ed., *Seeing the Face, Seeing the Soul: Polemon's Physiognomy from Classical Antiquity to Medieval Islam* (Oxford and New York: Oxford University Press, 2007), 142; see also J. N. Adams, Mark Janse, and Simon Swain, eds., *Bilingualism in Ancient Society: Language Contact and the Written Text* (Oxford and New York: Oxford University Press, 2002). For Tatian's context, see my "Mapping the World: Justin, Tatian, Lucian, and the Second Sophistic," *HTR* 98, no. 3 (2005): 283–314.

Tatian is a cultural critic, and part of his criticism engages the folly of connoisseurship of Greek statuary under Rome.

Tatian puts a knife into the gut of Greek pride by offering a long list of statues that he claims to have seen in Rome: Greek cultural booty confiscated and displayed elsewhere, in the long tradition that we know from Cicero and others.[59] Moreover, the list of ancient Greek sculptures available from Tatian's own, guaranteed eyewitness shows that Greek *paideia*, particularly as represented in women and statuary of women, is not so fancy and admirable, but is actually monstrous.

> Why is Glaukippe brought forward by you as a sacred object, who bore a monstrous child as her image (εἰκών) shows, which is cast in bronze by Nikeratos son of Euktemonos, an Athenian by race? For if she was pregnant with an elephant, what cause was there for Glaukippe to enjoy public honor? Praxiteles and Herodotos made Phryne the courtesan for you, and Euthykrates wrought Panteuxida in bronze after she was seized by a rapist. (33.3–4)

The list[60] winds its way to Ares seducing Aphrodite and various prostitutes memorialized in art, concluding: "Why on account of Leochares have you honored Ganymede the man-woman, as if you had

---

59. "Therefore I set these observations down not from second-hand knowledge, but I haunted much of the earth and played the sophist, toying with your goods. I set this forth having met with much arts and ideas, but finally I spent time in the city of the Romans and learned thoroughly the varieties of statues which they retrieved from you as theirs. For I did not try, as is the custom of the majority, to empower myself with foreign opinions, but I wished to put in order a record of all these things I myself have made from direct apprehension" (Tatian, *To the Greeks* 35.1).

60. For a possible source for Tatian or a common tradition, see Pliny, *Nat. hist.* 7.3.34: "Pompey the Great among the decorations of his theatre placed images of celebrated marvels, made with special elaboration for the purpose by the talent of eminent artists; among them we read of Eutychis who at Tralles was carried to her funeral pyre by twenty children and who had given birth 30 times, and Alcippe who gave birth to an elephant" (Pliny, *Nat. hist.*, LCL; 10 vols.; trans. H. Rackham [Cambridge, Mass.: Harvard University Press, 1942], 2:529). On similar rhetoric regarding women's bodies at another time period, including an account of a woman who prolifically produced rabbits rather than children, see Lisa Forman Cody, *Birthing the Nation: Sex, Science, and the Conception of Eighteenth-Century Britons* (New York: Oxford University Press, 2005).

a worthwhile possession, and also a certain armleted woman that Praxiteles made?" (34.3). Thus, Tatian highlights two images charged with great power in the Roman Empire: Ganymede (often associated with the emperor Hadrian's lover, Antinoos),[61] and the Knidian Aphrodite.

Tatian is coy; if you do not know the discussions of his day you miss his unnamed Knidia and his sharp rhetorical jab at famous statuary. Tatian alludes to the Knidia twice, referring once to Phryne, Praxiteles' model, and once to an "armleted woman," thus doubly denying the statue's divinity: she is a courtesan model, and only a woman with jewelry. For Tatian, "your women"—that is, women valued by Greek culture and prized by Romans—are monstrous and shameful compared to Christian women's modesty: When Tatian urges, "Hear the nonsense of matters done by the Greeks!" (33.1), he speaks not only of Christian difference, but also criticizes Roman-period valuations of Greek objects and Greek ethnicity.

Clement of Alexandria does not go so far as to trumpet a barbarian identity, but his second-century *Protreptikos* is launched to (and against) Greeks, even as it employs excellent Greek and proudly displays great cultural sophistication. Yet, like Tatian, Clement argues that statues of the gods are the product of lustful desire, since tawdry artisans use their tawdry lovers as models for divine bodies. Those who make statues, says Clement, do so out of shameful impulses, crafting their own lovers into the form of the gods or leaving upon the body of the god some memorial of their lovers. "On the finger of the Olympian Zeus, Phidias the Athenian inscribed, 'Pantarkes is beautiful,'" writes Clement, and, he sardonically continues, Pantarkes is not an epithet of Zeus, but is the name of Phidias's beloved.[62] So also, according to Clement, Praxiteles' lover is the model of his Knidian Aphrodite,

---

61. Ganymede and Zeus also feature in Plato, *Phaedrus* 255b in a discussion of erotic love and the "route to self-knowledge" (Shadi Bartsch, *The Mirror of the Self: Sexuality, Self-knowledge, and the Gaze in the Early Roman Empire* [Chicago: University of Chicago Press, 2006], 80).

62. Clement, *Prot.* IV 53.4. The Greek edition is Clément d'Alexandrie, *Le Protreptique*, ed. and trans. Claude Mondésert (Sources chrétiennes; Paris: Cerf, 1949). The Roman numeral refers to traditional book divisions within the *Protreptikos*; the Arabic numbers to section and subsection. Regarding Pantarkes see Pausanias, *Elis* I, 5.XI.2

and Phryne, the Thespian *hetaira*, is depicted as Aphrodite in many paintings of her time (IV 53.5–6). Clement challenges the reader to decide "if you want to worship courtesans" (IV 54.6; εἰ βούλει καὶ τὰς ἑταίρας προσκυνεῖν).[63]

Clement repeats the rumors of his day:

> Thus that Kypriot, Pygmalion, loved an ivory statue. It was the *agalma* of Aphrodite and it was naked.[64] The Kypriot is conquered by its form and he has sexual intercourse with the statue, and Philostephanos tells this story. Another Aphrodite in Knidos was stone and was beautiful; another man loved her and commingled with the stone. Poseidippos tells [this]. . . . *Technē* has power to deceive such a man; it leads humans who are amorous into ruin. Now craftsmanship is efficacious, but such things should not deceive the rational person nor those who have lived according to reason. (*Prot.* X 98.1–3)[65]

Clement uses the story of Pygmalion[66] and a rapid reference to the Knidia in order to support his idea that statues (*agalmata*) are inextricably linked to error and questionable sexual morals. We recall the many protests that Powers's *Greek Slave* should not produce lust in the viewer, that her nakedness was pure. Here, Clement argues that

63. Elsewhere, Clement compares Aphrodite herself to a prostitute when he claims that "the initiates carry a coin in to the goddess, as lovers to a prostitute." *Prot.* II 14.2. On Aphrodite, see also *Prot.* II 33.7–9.

64. It is significant, of course, that Venus/Aphrodite enlivens the ivory statue. The goddess of love enlivens the sculpture and thus grants the sculptor the strange pleasure of marital and sexual relations with his own creation, and then a son who is another product of desire (*Met.* 10.280–97).

65. The passage continues: "They say a girl loved an image (*eikōn*) and a beautiful boy the statue (*agalma*) of the Knidia, but the eyes of the beholders were deceived by art (*technē*). For no one would embrace a goddess, nor would someone have been buried together with a female corpse, nor would a sober-minded person have fallen in love with a *daimōn* and stone."

66. See Ovid, *Metamorphoses*. 10.238–97. Regarding Ovid's Pygmalion and other examples of the blurring of humans and statuary in the Roman period, see Deborah Steiner, *Images in Mind: Statues in Archaic and Classical Greek Literature and Thought* (Princeton: Princeton University Press, 2001), Ch. 4; Caroline Vout, *Power and Eroticism in Imperial Rome* (Cambridge: Cambridge University Press, 2007), 27–31.

technē—image-making and, particularly, the prestige of the Greek culture of image-making—results in theological and moral crisis. It produces a mash of desire and stone, a confusion of the human and the goddess, a transgression of the line between thingness and person-hood: the social lives of these valued Greek things, Clement argues, lead to perversion.[67]

Clement goes on to challenge the talents of celebrated artisans whose craft confuses the thing and the person, and the person and the divine:

> Stone-stupid artisans and worshippers of stones (ἠλίθιοι τῶν
> λίθων δημιουργοί τε καὶ προσκυνηταί)![68] Let your Phidias
> and Polykleitos come; Praxiteles and Apelles too and as many
> as seek after the vulgar arts (ὅσοι τὰς βαναύσους μετέρχον-
> ται τέχνας), who are earthly workers of earth. . . . None of
> them anyway has ever fashioned an in-breathed image, nor ever
> softened supple flesh from the earth. Who melted the marrow,
> and who fastened together bones? Who stretched out the nerves,
> and who grew forth the veins? . . . Only the creator of all, the
> "best artisan father," has formed such an in-breathed statue as
> the human. But *your* Olympian [Zeus], an image of an image,
> some great dissonance with the truth, is a mute work of Attic
> hands. (*Prot.* X 98.1–3)

Clement weaves in the concept of the human as God's image, by which of course he does not mean Praxiteles' courtesan in Aphrodite's image or Phidias's Pantarkes in Zeus's image. The famed artisans of the classical and Hellenistic period could not animate a real human,

---

67. Later in the passage Clement introduces a desiring female viewer—it is rare to meet such a reference in this time period—and Tatian mentions daughters at spectacle. Regarding female desire, we have an example perhaps in the Corinthian girl mentioned by Pliny (*Nat. hist.* 35.43.151) and referenced in Athenagoras (*Leg.* 17.3); perhaps the phrase "a girl loved an image" refers to this. See Natalie Boymen Kampen, "Epilogue: Gender and Desire," 268, in Ann Olga Koloski-Ostrow and Claire L. Lyons, *Naked Truths: Women, Sexuality, and Gender in Classical Art and Archaeology* (London and New York: Routledge, 1997), on imagining women as "desiring beings" and agents.

68. ἠλίθιοι (foolish, senseless) puns nicely with λίθων (stones); thus my free translation.

no matter the marketability of their objects and pure Greekness in the Roman period. Moreover, those who value their images are deluded, whether they value them for worship or even more as objects which are replicated, bought, sold, and displayed as evidence of a connoisseur's cultured status in the Roman period.[69]

Conclusions

In antiquity and beyond, the Knidian Aphrodite has served as a paradigm or form in which the intersections of gender, race, ethnicity, and sexuality are culturally and religiously negotiated. In the second and third centuries, Roman matrons were memorialized as Aphrodite/ Venus in death, "wearing" the Knidia's body, to use Larissa Bonfante's terminology.[70] As we have seen, other Knidias proliferated then too, in

---

69. For more discussion of Clement, see Laura Nasrallah, "The Earthen Human, the Breathing Statue: The Sculptor God, Greco-Roman Statuary, and Clement of Alexandria," in Konrad Schmid, ed., *Beyond Eden: The Biblical Story of Paradise [Genesis 2–3] and Its Reception History*, Forschungen zum Alten Testament II (Tübingen: Mohr Siebeck, 2008) and my forthcoming *Christian Responses to Roman Art and Architecture: The Second-Century Church Amid the Spaces of Empire* (New York: Cambridge University Press, 2010).

70. It is unusual to find Roman matrons depicted in the nude and portrait heads placed on the nude bodies of Aphrodite. Despite the many nude goddesses and other figures of the time, Christopher Hallett (*The Roman Nude: Heroic Portrait Statuary 200 BC to AD 300* [Oxford: Oxford University Press, 2005], 219) counts sixteen surviving nude portraits of women, compared to 320 known examples of portraits of men in heroic or divine costume. Moreover, the statues that have been found are associated mostly with funerary contexts and mostly around Rome. Nevertheless, we know from literary sources that women were depicted not only as the nude Aphrodite, but also in other forms in their funerary monuments, and sometimes in multiple forms. The tomb of Priscilla, wife of T. Flavius Abascantus, a minister and imperial freedman of Domitian, was adorned with statues depicting her as the goddesses Ceres, Diana, Maia, and Venus; the latter is defined as *non improba*, "not immodest," probably indicating that Priscilla was depicted nude or semi-nude, with the gesture of the hand over the *pubes* understood as an act of modesty (Statius, *Silvae* 5.1.222–24; D'Ambra, "Calculus of Venus", 222). The tomb of Claudia Semne, wife of imperial freedman M. Ulpius Crotonensis, was discovered along the Via Appia and dates to the 130s. She was depicted as Fortuna, Spes, and Venus there. Hallett, *Fathers and Daughters*, 209–12; Henning Wrede, "Das Mausoleum der Claudia Semne und die bürgerliche Plastik der Kaiserzeit," *Mitteilungen des Deutschen Archaeologischen Instituts. Römische Abteilung* 78, no. 2 (1971): 125–66.

literary and sculptural form: the Capitoline Venus, the Campo Iemini Venus, comments about the emperor's consort, Christian and non-Christian stories about the statue and her model, the *hetaira* Phryne.

The Knidia's story does not stop in antiquity. As Henry James said of replicas of Powers's *Greek Slave*, it was "exposed under little domed glass covers in such American homes as could bring themselves to think such things right"; who supported such exposure, and who thought such things right, was an issue of debate over time. The vulnerable femaleness of emulations of the Knidia, as well as her quintessential Greekness, are key to Winckelmann's periodization of ancient art; they are key matters of debate among art historians today. The form of the Knidia also becomes the model for Hiram Powers's *Greek Slave*. Charmaine Nelson unites gender and race in her comment: "but it was also the racial specificity of Powers's female slave, her signification as a white woman, that simultaneously ensured the sweeping sentimentalism and the paternalistic moral concern with which she was greeted, inasmuch as it disavowed the immediacy and horrors of American and transatlantic slavery and the specific oppression of black female slaves."[71] The Knidia's many sculpted forms are things—sculptures in marble, usually—with biographies and shifting value as they are bought, sold, traded, and passed through various hands. Of course, the irony is that slaves in antiquity and in antebellum America, like statues, have the status of things: they too have social lives, are bought, sold, traded, passed along.

This essay has highlighted the gendered and racial discourse around a famous art object, the ever elusive Aphrodite of Knidos. Although her original form remains unknown, she replicates across time and space, finding her way from the second-century Roman world to late-eighteenth-century discussions of history and aesthetics to twentieth- and twenty-first-century art historical debates. Although scholars have long recognized that the ancient Knidia's gender is worth discussing, this essay has argued that is it also necessary to address her race or ethnicity. Christians, among others, critiqued images of the Aphrodite of Knidos not only by using the sexual invective of the day, but also by debating the differential valuations of race in the ancient world.

71. Nelson, *Color of Stone*, 80.

CHAPTER 3

"From Every Nation under Heaven"

Jewish Ethnicities in the Greco-Roman World[1]

Cynthia M. Baker

Ancient writers recognized a world of ethnoracial diversity among the Jews of their era. Yet the notion of Jewish ethnic multiplicity remains foreign and virtually unexplored in popular and scholarly cultures that still labor under the weight of racialized discourses of Jewish "particularity" crafted as counterpoint to narratives of Christian "universalism." Recent work examining the "ethnic reasoning" at play in numerous early Christian texts, however, has challenged traditional claims that Christian "universalism" was conceived beyond and in opposition to concepts of race and ethnicity. Indeed, discursive constructs of race and ethnicity function as important constitutive elements in the rhetoric of the early Christian community, where multiethnic constituencies are taken for granted. This essay

1. I would like to thank Lisa Maurizio, Margaret Imber, Catherine Murphy, Deepti Shenoy, Hayim Lapin, and Seth Mirsky, who offered valuable feedback on various drafts of this essay.

represents a parallel investigation into the varieties of "ethnic reasoning" brought to bear on imagining and constructing Jewishness within
the multiethnic/multiracial community of Jews in antiquity. Through
an examination of two familiar (albeit widely misread) first-century
texts, Philo's In Flaccum 46 (and the closely related Legatio ad Gaium
281–4) and Acts 2, traditional histories of scholarly interpretation
that have long served to obscure and downplay images of Jewish ethnic diversity are highlighted for critical analysis.

Introduction

In the present day and age, we are all likely familiar with the widespread characterization of Jews as a particular "race" or "ethnic group."
At the same time, anyone who has even minimal knowledge of, or
acquaintance with, the global Jewish community (or even the relatively tiny Israeli Jewish community) is also aware of the real variety
among Jews, a variety encompassing distinctions that would themselves commonly fall under the rubrics of "race" and "ethnicity." One
need only invoke such terms as "Sephardi," "Ashkenazi," "Ethiopian/
Beta Israel," "Mizrahi," and their myriad subcategories or point to
prominent Latin American or Russian or North African writers, artists, and teachers who are Jews to illustrate this phenomenon. We
might be tempted to assume that such multiplicity is a function of
modern nationalisms or contemporary globalization, yet a trip to the
Renaissance-era ghetto of Venice, with its several ethnically discrete
synagogues (crammed cheek-by-jowl in that restricted space), would
demonstrate the error of that assumption.

But are the distinctions represented, for example, in Venice's
ghetto properly "ethnic" distinctions? Did Venice's Jews treat them as
such? What is at stake—and for whom—in determining how difference is imagined and labeled? To the originators of the ghetto, all Jews,
it seems, were merely Jews (a pedigree that *conversos* to Christianity could not always escape), whereas among the ghetto's Jews, other
"ethnic" categories evidently held fundamental significance. How far
back in history do we find such "multiethnicity" to be characteristic

of Jews? Do Jews characterize themselves as multiethnic in antiquity? Do others do so?

In this essay, I consider the ways in which ancient Jewish and non-Jewish writers do, indeed, depict Jews as a multiethnic or multiracial people whose individual members, from earliest antiquity, are imagined to embody multiple (often dual) lineages of birth, land, history, and culture. At the same time, these ancient writers, Jewish and non-Jewish alike, employ a strong rhetoric of Jewish unity that has all but occluded Jewish diversity. The contexts and strategic aims for which images of Jewish ethnic diversity and ethnic unity are mobilized vary among different authors and even within the work of a single author. Ultimately, both kinds of images—of diversity and of unity—proved useful, and neither appears to have precluded the other. Nonetheless, since antiquity, we find ourselves heirs to a legacy of widespread, common, and often racialized discourses of Jewish "particularity" presented as counterpoint to evolutionary projects of humane "universalism," including Hellenism, Christianity, modernity, philosophy, and the like. Given the persistent harms authorized by appeal to these discourses of ethnoracial particularism versus enlightened universalism, our legacy calls us to careful consideration of what it is we have inherited.[2]

We might begin such consideration by examining the concepts of "ethnicity" and "race" in their ancient and modern forms. A number of scholars of Greco-Roman antiquity have, in recent years, offered excellent, if diverse, working definitions of "ethnicity" by which to sift and interpret the ancient evidence. Among these, Jonathan M. Hall's is perhaps the most narrow and concise. For Hall, "the definitional criteria or 'core elements' which determine group membership in an ethnic group—and distinguish the ethnic group from other social collectivities—are a putative subscription to a myth of common descent and kinship, an association with a specific territory, and a sense of shared history."[3] Hall, importantly, emphasizes the "fictive" quality

<hr/>

2. For related conversations, please see the articles by Shawn Kelley (191–209), Susannah Heschel (211–234), and Denise Buell (159–190) in this volume.
3. Jonathan M. Hall, *Hellenicity* (Chicago: University of Chicago Press, 2002), 9.

of origin, descent, and kinship accounts as well as the socially constructed nature of "race" as a close ideological cousin to "ethnicity." As for applying the admittedly modern category and definition of "ethnicity" to his ancient Greek subjects, Hall observes that "in attributing the social solidarity of an *ethnos* ["class of beings"] to *genos* (birth) and *syngeneia* (kinship), the Greeks came about as close as they could to our concept of ethnicity."[4]

Many, myself included, will find Hall's definition restrictive, while other, broader definitions—ones that include elements like language and dialect; food, clothing, and cultic practices; cultural taboos; and the like—are more apt for some purposes. Nonetheless, the minimalism and stringency of this definition will serve as a useful reference point in what follows, as will Hall's important reminder that "ethnic identity is *socially constructed and subjectively perceived.*"[5] By Hall's definition, then, we might ask, are ancient *Ioudaioi* and *Yehudim* properly understood as an ethnic group? And are ethnic identifications exclusive, or might individuals and groups subjectively perceive their own or another's simultaneous membership in more than one ethnic group?

The most sustained attention to what might be termed "Jewish ethnicity" in antiquity is found in Shaye Cohen's *Beginnings of*

---

4. Ibid., 17–18. My use of the terms "ethnicity" and "race" in this essay takes seriously Hall's observations about their close ideological kinship; hence, the two terms are not intended to signify discrete or separable concepts, especially as employed in interpretations of ancient texts. Denise Buell makes a case for highlighting the leakage between these concepts by choosing to "deliberately use the terms 'race' and 'ethnicity' interchangeably." She observes that "neither term has a one-to-one counterpart in antiquity and . . . neither term can be neatly distinguished from the other even in modern parlance" (Buell, "Rethinking the Relevance of Race for Early Christian Self-Definition," *HTR* 94, no. 4 [2001]: 449–76, 450 n.3). See also Anthony Saldarini's important exploration of "ethnicity" and the terms *ethnos* and *ethnikoi* in antiquity in "The Social World of Christian Jews and Jewish Christians," in *Religious and Ethnic Communities in Later Roman Palestine*, ed. Hayim Lapin (Bethesda: University Press of Maryland, 1998). Saldarini aptly notes that "the boundaries among groups and between them and the culture of the eastern empire shifted often. The terms for the 'other' were not stable or all-encompassing" (124).

5. Jonathan M. Hall, *Ethnic Identity in Greek Antiquity* (Cambridge: Cambridge University Press, 2000), 19; italics in the original.

Jewishness.[6] Cohen's study, despite often problematic classifications
and distinctions, is noteworthy for its implicit acknowledgement of
the multiethnic character of ancient Judaism. Under the Hasmoneans
(late-second century BCE), according to Cohen, "Judaism became like
Hellenism, a citizenship and a way of life open to people of diverse
origins. . . . Thus, even as they were becoming more 'nationalistic'
and 'particularistic,' the Judeans/Jews were becoming more 'universalistic.'"[7] Hence, from earliest Jewish/Judean history (the era of the
Hasmoneans, according to Cohen; earlier, by others' measures), it is
clear that "one could be a Macedonian and a Jew, a Syrian and a Jew, a
Cappadocian and a Jew,"[8] and that one could find oneself in the company of countless others of similarly dual "ethnicity."[9]

In fact, the identification of Jews by diverse ethnic-geographic
signifiers occurs in all manner of Greek and Semitic (Hebrew and
Aramaic) writings by Jews in the Hellenistic and Roman periods. For
example, among the writings of Josephus and the earliest rabbinic

---

6. Shaye Cohen, *Beginnings of Jewishness* (Berkeley: University of California
Press, 1999).

7. Ibid., 138.

8. Ibid., 135.

9. Although the concept of "ethnicity" is key to Cohen's formulations and
arguments, his primary conceptual categories are "Jewishness" and "Judaeaness,"
terms around which he clusters a number of variations on the theme of ethnicity.
(Cohen avoids entirely any engagement with the category "race.") In a chapter
entitled "From *Ethnos* to Ethno-religion," Cohen argues for a pre-Hasmonean
"Judaeaness" that is:

> a function of birth and geography; *Ioudaioi* belonged to the ethnos of
> Judaeans in Judea. Even when Judaeans left their homeland to live in
> the diaspora, they maintained themselves as ethnic associations. Eth-
> nic (or ethnic-geographic) identity is immutable; non-Judaeans cannot
> become Judaeans any more than non-Egyptians can become Egyptians,
> or non-Syrians can become Syrians. (109)

By contrast, argues Cohen,

> The Hasmonean period witnesses for the first time in the history of
> Judaism the establishment of processes by which outsiders can become
> insiders, non-Judaeans can become Judaeans, and non-Jews can become
> Jews. . . . Ethnicity is closed, immutable, an ascribed characteristic
> based on birth. But by investing Judaean identity with political or cul-
> tural (religious) content, the Hasmoneans were able to give outsiders an
> opportunity to attain membership in Judaean society. (136)

texts, we find Jews identified as Arabs/Nabateans, Persians/Medes, Idumeans, Itureans, Adiabenes, Cyprians, Syrians, Antiochenes, Alexandrians, Judeans, Galileans, and Babylonians, among others. The early rabbinic texts employ such ethnic signifiers alone—without a "Jewish modifier"—when distinguishing among those with whom the rabbis identify. In other words, rabbinic traditions refer to "Medes," "Arabians," "Alexandrians," and the like when referring to various Jews or Jewish communities.[10] Indeed, as others and I have noted elsewhere, uses of the term "Jew" itself in rabbinic (as well as in epigraphic) sources often give the impression of a juridically constructed or socially complicated ethnicity, in contradistinction to some more certain kind. That is, the designation "Jew" might show up only when the status or identity of the subject in question might be in doubt. A striking number of such instances involve women.[11]

In this and other respects, "Jews" as an identity category in antiquity shares a good deal in common with "women" when it comes to race and ethnicity. In the case of both "Jews" and "women," their "difference" (on the order of "race" or even "species") from a dominant "norm" seems often to preempt or destabilize any identification of them as members of particular ethnic communities. Jews are often disregarded or unacknowledged as bearers or transmitters of other

---

While Cohen here charts a profoundly significant historical shift in elite Judean political practices, his categorizations, arguments, and conclusions are, nonetheless, deeply problematic. They are particularly so with regard to implied assumptions about the universality of early diasporic "ethnic associations" (for which we have only limited evidence), claims of ethnic-geographic immutability (despite the obvious example of marriage, among other ways, for entering the pre-Hasmonean *ethnos*), and clear evidence for both cultural/religious and political content to the identity term *Ioudaioi* prior to the Hasmonean revolution. The intractable complexity and mutability of *Ioudaios*—"Judean" or "Jew"—as an identity category that resists all attempts at neat distinctions is perhaps most clearly conveyed by Cohen's repeated resort to compound formulations like "ethnic-geographic" versus "ethnoreligion" to characterize its variable content.

10. See, for example, *t. Ketubbot* 4:9; *m. Shabbat* 6:6.

11. Cynthia M. Baker, "When Jews Were Women," *HR* 45, no. 2 (2005): 114–34; Ross Shepard Kraemer, "On the Meaning of the Term 'Jew' in Greco-Roman Inscriptions," *HTR* 82, no. 1 (1989): 35–53, and "Jewish Tuna and Christian Fish: Identifying Religious Affiliation in Epigraphic Sources," *HTR* 84, no. 2 (1991): 141–62.

ethnic identities,[12] on the one hand, while, on the other, the extent to which women function as carriers or transmitters of ethnic identity is often a matter of debate or uncertainty in any number of patrilineal cultural contexts and time periods.[13]

In the Greek and Hebrew literature of the Hellenistic, Roman, and Byzantine periods, these phenomena combine and transmute in a fascinating manner. Particular Moabite, Ethiopian, and Egyptian characters are transformed into proper Jewish ancestors while retaining these other ethnic designations; all are women. Hagar the Egyptian gets a calculated makeover from Philo;[14] Ruth the "Moabitess" receives the same from the later rabbinic midrashists (for whom the feminine form of the ethnic term is crucial),[15] as does Moses'

---

12. Neil Silberman observes, for example, of Jews and Muslims that "it could be argued that no two other groups of 'outsiders,' if we call them that, have left such a deep material record and were so deeply involved in the formation of European civilization and identity" while being largely disregarded in modern, nation-based historiographic reconstructions. "Jewish and Muslim Heritage in Europe: The Role of Archaeology in Defending Cultural Diversity," in *The Archaeology of Difference: Gender, Ethnicity, Class and the "Other" in Antiquity: Studies in Honor of Eric M. Meyers*, ed. Douglas R. Edwards and C. Thomas McCollough (Boston: American Schools of Oriental Research, 2007), 13–16.

13. In a very few cultures, mothers are singled out as determining the social status (if not always the "ethnicity") of their offspring from "mixed" unions, a phenomenon that begins to gain currency in Jewish texts composed under Roman rule (although the expulsion of "foreign" wives and children enjoined in Ezra 9–10 is a possible precursor). The so-called matrilineal principle came into being in rabbinic Judaism (and, arguably, in Philo), under Roman rule; it did not exist prior to this, and patrilineality is assumed in writings from the Bible and the Ptolemaic period. Even in the Roman period matrilineality was not by any means universally recognized. The reasons for the development of the matrilineal principle among Jews are obscure but likely have a good deal to do with mimicry of Roman tax laws. See Cohen, *Beginnings*, 263–307; Maren Niehoff, *Philo on Jewish Identity and Culture* (Tübingen: Mohr-Siebeck, 2001), 17–24.

14. Philo, *Abraham*, 250–51. See Niehoff, *Philo*, 24–32, for an extended discussion of Philo on Hagar and Tamar.

15. *Ruth Rabbah*, see esp. IV.I, which glosses the Deuteronomic (23:4) perpetual exclusions from Israel of the "Ammonite but not the Ammonitess, Moabite but not the Moabitess." The gender distinction drawn by the rabbis in these instances nicely illustrates the easy separability of women from a corporate ethnic identity; women, in this case, are not subject to the ethnic exclusion applied to the men of "their" ethnic group: a "Moabitess" is *not* a Moabite nor is an "Ammonitess" to be counted as an Ammonite.

Ethiopian wife;[16] while Joseph's Egyptian priestess wife, Aseneth, is reconceived as a Jew by conversion and marriage in an anonymous Hellenistic romance.[17] As "Jews," these women continue to be identified as "Moabitess," "Egyptian," and "Ethiopian," respectively.

We begin to perceive throughout some ancient literatures, then, a pervasive but largely unexamined notion of Jewish ethnic multiplicity that calls for further, careful and nuanced, study. The scope of such a study is well beyond what can be accomplished in the present context. What is offered here, instead, is more modest: a close examination of two key texts, two discrete (and familiar) articulations of Jewish multiethnicity from the first century CE, one by a Jew, the other by a non-Jew, along with a look at some of the history of interpretation that has rendered these otherwise illuminating texts obscure.

Philo of Alexandria

The first-century Jewish writer Philo of Alexandria not only recognized multiple Jewish ethnic identifications; he insisted on them as an essential attribute of Jews:[18]

> For so populous are the Jews that no one country can contain them, and therefore they dwell in many of the most prosperous countries in Europe and Asia both in the islands and on the mainland, and while they hold the Holy City where stands the sacred Temple of the most high God to be their mother city (*metropolis*), yet those which are theirs by inheritance from their fathers,

---

16. On this theme, see Tessa Rajak, "Moses in Ethiopia: Legend and Literature," *JJS* 29 (1978): 111–22; Avigdor Shinan, "Moses and the Ethiopian Woman," in *Studies in Hebrew Narrative Arts*, ed. Joseph Heinemann and Shmuel Werses (Scrhier; Jerusalem: Magnes, 1978), 27:66–78; and Cohen, *Beginnings*, 270.

17. On Joseph and Asenath, see Ross Shepard Kraemer, *When Aseneth Met Joseph: A Late Antique Tale of the Biblical Patriarch and his Egyptian Wife, Reconsidered* (New York: Oxford University Press, 1998); and Gideon Bohak, *Joseph and Aseneth and the Jewish Temple in Heliopolis* (Atlanta: Society of Biblical Literature, 1996).

18. The monikers assigned to Philo throughout history are wonderfully emblematic of the subject explored in my essay: in present, scholarly usage, the man is most often identified as "Philo of Alexandria" or *Philo Alexandrinus*; in other (primarily church-related) contexts, he is called *Philo Judaeus*.

grandfathers, and ancestors even farther back, are in each case accounted by them to be their fatherland (*patridas*) in which they were born and reared (*egennēthēsan kai etraphēsan*), while to some of them they have come at the very time of their foundation as colonists as a favor to the founders. (*Flaccus* 46)[19]

In this oft-quoted passage from a treatise composed in response to "ethnic" attacks and rivalries in Roman Alexandria, Philo sets out to formulate explicit and universal claims about the nature of Jewish "ethnicity." It is in this context that he asserts that, although Jews (ought to) bear an attitude of fond piety for what he terms (adapting the ancient Greek colonial concept) their "mother city"—a certain unnamed "Holy City where stands the sacred Temple of the most high God"—their claims of ancestry, birth, kinship, and inheritance are appropriately reserved for the myriad "fatherlands" around the world where they have dwelt from time immemorial. The dual and gendered parentage constructed through the two "genealogical" elements of Jews' identities ("fatherland" and "mother city") signals the relative import of each (fatherland is primary), even as it affirms the significance of both.[20] The insistence that "no one country" can be associated with all Jews, coupled with the abstracted reference to a distant cult center, serves to counter any attribution of "resident alien" or "immi-

---

19. My translation, largely following that of F. H. Colson in *Philo*, vol. 9, (LCL; Cambridge, Mass: Harvard University Press, 1967).

20. As is the case in all patriarchal and patrilocal cultures, the ancient Mediterranean and Near Eastern cultures at issue here assigned far greater authority, weight, compulsion, and demand for fidelity to ideals and matters associated with "fathers" than to those associated with "mothers." Philo's juxtaposition of the two gendered terms here conveys precisely this hierarchy of allegiance. Further evidence for Philo's insistence on the "fatherland's" priority over the "mother city" may be found in other writings of his wherein he affirms that the locales that "colonists" found "become their native land *instead of the mother city*" (*Confusion* 78; italics added). Niehoff argues that Philo's references to the "mother city" indicate a sudden reversal of the traditional gender hierarchy (and hence the priority of the unnamed "mother city" over all "fatherlands" in determining primary ethnic identity) under the influence of shifts in the legal significance of maternal descent in Roman class/tax codes in the early first century (*Philo*, 33–44). Regardless of which gendered term is taken to indicate priority, Philo's appeal to both suggests a fundamentally dual conception of Jewish ethnicity.

grant" status to Jews by non-Jews in each *patris*, each common nation or ancestral homeland shared by non-Jews and Jews.

In the corresponding passage in *Embassy*, Philo likewise affirms that any good will and benefit bestowed on the "mother city" would benefit myriad other cities and countries through the Jewish native sons of such places as:

> Egypt, Phoenicia, the part of Syria called the Hollow and the rest as well and the lands lying far apart, Pamphylia, Cilicia, most of Asia up to Bithynia and the corners of Pontus . . . Europe, Thessaly, Boeotia, Macedonia, Aetolia, Attica, Argos, Corinth, and most of the best parts of the Peleponnese . . . Euboea, Cyprus, Crete . . . and the countries beyond the Euphrates . . . (Philo, *Embassy*, 281–84)[21]

The speaker to whom Philo attributes these words is Agrippa, who, in his petition as king of Judea to the emperor Gaius, is very careful to distinguish between *his own* (Agrippa's) *patris*—that is, native holy city and native country—of Judea, on the one hand, and the native cities and countries of most of the world's Jews, on the other. Judea is not *their patris*, nor are Judeans like Agrippa their countrymen. Philo's Judean king speaks of his homeland in the singular possessive; for him, it is "my" homeland, never "ours." Even the "mother city" is not "our" mother city; rather, she is the mother city of "Judea" and of "most other countries," countries that have their own peoples, their own local *ethnē*, a number of whom are Jews.

Like all proclamations of ethnic identity, ancient and modern, these by Philo serve the particular rhetorical purposes for which they were fashioned. As such, they both resonate with and diverge from other such proclamations, some of them by Philo himself, crafted for other contexts. Nonetheless, the conformity of these particular assertions to Hall's narrow "definitional criteria or 'core elements' which determine group membership in an ethnic group and distinguish the ethnic group from other social collectivities" is secured in the claims put forth in Philo's *Flaccus* passage. To wit, Jews, in their many,

---

21. *Philo*, Vol. 10, trans. F. H. Colson (LCL; Cambridge, Mass.: Harvard University Press, 1971).

disparate fatherlands, subscribe to narratives of "descent and kin-ship" associated with each ancestral fatherland or "specific territory" and that territory's "sense of shared history," often back to its very foundation. At the same time, this diverse array of Jews of diverse fatherlands nevertheless shares with other Jews a sense of cultic piety toward a Holy City, broad patterns of worship, and other ancient cus-toms. Hall himself remarks on the intriguing variety or peculiarity of ancient Jews' ethnic identifications as expressed in documents predat-ing Philo's by centuries:

> In some respects they were barely distinguishable from Hel-lenes, especially with regard to language, and some Jews appear as "Hellenes" in third-century fiscal registers from the Arsinoite village of Trikomia. In others—notably religious profession and the preservation of specific customs . . . they maintained a fairly distinct identity. What is interesting is how rarely the "children of Israel" [Hall's term, not found in the texts he cites] in this [Hellenistic] period appeal to a properly "ethnic" basis of self-identification through genealogy; when they do, it is to promote an affiliation with the Spartans rather than proclaim their own distinctiveness. . . . In fact, the term "Hebraioi" which writers of the period often employ to designate the historical population of Israel is rarely applied to contemporary Jews.[22]

Hall is struck by *how rarely* surviving evidence shows Jews embrac-ing what could properly be termed a distinctive, much less exclusive, "Judean/Jewish" or "Hebrew" ethnic identity from at least the third century BCE. through the Roman conquest of the eastern Mediterra-nean and North Africa. Indeed, the few identifiable Jews among the "Hellenes" of Trikomia or the "Alexandrians" of later periods indicate the likely presence of many more unidentified Jews among such "eth-nic groups," as the self-identification by "Hellenos, an Alexandrian," later emended to "Hellenos, a Jew of Alexandria," clearly suggests.[23]

---

22. Hall, *Hellenicity*, 223.

23. Gideon Bohak makes a similar point (while offering a slightly different interpretation of the *Flaccus* passage analyzed in the present essay) in "Ethnic Continuity in the Jewish Diaspora in Antiquity," in *Jews in the Hellenistic and*

In these same periods, Jewish writers appear to demonstrate a striking flexibility in asserting genealogical membership among Abraham's
descendents by other "ethnic groups" and individuals.

My readings of these Philo texts conflict with a dominant view
that understands Philo, in these passages, to be asserting an expressly,
even exclusively, "Jewish/Judean" ethnicity through his use of the
Greek colonial concept of "mother city."[24] The standard interpretation
is difficult to account for, however, in a treatise (*Flaccus*) that presents itself as a rebuttal to violent, officially sanctioned actions taken
by a segment of the Alexandrian population precisely to "alienate"
their Jewish compatriots.[25] At the very least, Philo must be understood to be arguing here for dual Jewish-Alexandrian "ethnicity"
(and, likewise, Jewish-Roman, Jewish-Asian, Jewish-Syrian, Jewish-
Macedonian, and so on) as over and against a singularly Jewish/Judean
ethnicity, in order for the passages in *Flaccus* and *Embassy* to make sense
in context. There is considerable ancient precedent for understanding
"Alexandrian," "Syrian," "Macedonian," "Antiochene," and the like as
"ethnicities" or ethnic signifiers declaring origin and ancestry.[26] Philo
lays claim to all of these and others as ethnicities rightfully borne by
Jews by birth, descent, kinship, and territorial allegiance/patriotism.

To the extent that Philo here implies that "Jew" is an "ethnicity,"
he indicates that "Jewish ethnicity" is of precisely the same nature

---

Roman Cities, ed. John R. Bartlett (New York: Routledge, 2002), 175–92. On
the Hellenos inscription see, for example, Delia, ibid., 26; Cohen, *Beginnings*, 75.
Scholars are deeply divided on how to interpret the emendation and to what end,
and by whom, it was carried out.

24. See Yehoshua Amir, "Philo's Version of Pilgrimage to Jerusalem," in
Jerusalem in the Second Temple Period, ed. Aharon Oppenheimer et al. (Jerusalem: Yad Izhak Ben-Zvi, 1980); P. Borgen, "Philo of Alexandria," in *Jewish Writings of the Second Temple Period: Apocrypha, Pseudepigrapha, Qumran Sectarian
Writings, Philo, Josephus*, ed. Michael Stone (Philadelphia: Fortress Press, 1984),
269; Aryeh Kasher, "Jerusalem as 'Metropolis' in Philo's National Consciousness," *Cathedra* 11 (1979): 45–56 (Hebrew); *The Jews in Hellenistic and Roman
Egypt: The Struggle for Equal Rights* (Tübingen: Mohr-Siebeck, 1985); and Niehoff, *Philo*. Cf. Sarah Pearce's counter-arguments in "Jerusalem as 'Mother-City'
in the Writings of Philo of Alexandria," in *Negotiating Diaspora: Jewish Strategies
in the Roman Empire*, ed. John M. G. Barclay (New York: T & T Clark, 2004),
19–36.

25. Cf. Josephus, *Ant.* 19.281.

26. Delia, ibid., 23–8.

and quality as "Hellenic ethnicity"—no more particular, no less universalistic. Philo does not assert an ethnic-minority identification in the face of a Hellenistic-majority culture; rather, appropriating the colonial apparatus, he articulates a worldwide Jewish identity in the image of worldwide "Hellenism" and a Jewish map, the boundaries of which match (and exceed) those of either the "Hellenic" or Roman *oikoumenē* ("inhabited world"). According to Philo's paradigm, then, many locales were "colonized" in distant antiquity by both Jews and Hellenes—often concomitantly—such that both are descendents of those locales' "founding fathers" in equal measure and both share the same ancestral and territorial identification with the "colony." Hence, "Jew" and "Alexandrian," for example, could no more be construed as competing allegiances or identities than could "Hellene" and "Alexandrian."

The relationship of ethnicity, class, and gender to diverse and changing notions of "citizenship" in places like Alexandria is, as already noted, an extremely complicated question; but "ethnicity," it must be emphasized, is neither identical to, nor coterminous with, "citizenship" in any Greco-Roman city, much less with "citizenship" in the Roman Empire as a whole. Despite Philo's carefully and cleverly chosen paradigm, a longstanding scholarly tradition persists in reading these *Flaccus* and *Embassy* passages as Philo's demand for a singular Jewish ethnic or national identity at odds with Jews' numerous ancestral, ethnic/national, and particular homelands. It is worth considering that this scholarly tradition holds sway in an era in which the notion of "Jewish ethnoracial particularism" continues to have ideological currency, on the one hand, while, on the other, the creation of a "Jewish national homeland" has played a part in the creation of a far-reaching and encompassing narrative of Jewish national consciousness, history, and allegiance.

Acts of the Apostles

Philo is not the only ancient writer to provide an extensive catalog of Jewish ethnicities and homelands. Another such list is found in a Christian writing of the first century CE: the New Testament Book of Acts:

> It happened that there were staying in Jerusalem Jews, pious men
> from every nation (*ethnos*) under heaven. And when this sound
> was heard, the multitude gathered and were bewildered in mind,
> because each heard them speaking in his own tongue. But they
> were amazed and marveled, saying, "Behold, are not all these that
> are speaking Galileans? And how have we heard each speaking
> his own native dialect *in which he was born*? Parthians and Medes
> and Elamites, and inhabitants of Mesopotamia, Judea, and Cap-
> padocia, Pontus, and Asia, Phrygia and Pamphylia, Egypt and the
> parts of Libya about Cyrene, and visitors from Rome, Jews and
> proselytes, Cretans and Arabians, we have heard them speak-
> ing in our own tongues of the wonderful works of God." (Acts
> 2:5–11, emphasis and translation mine.)

In this fantastical narrative of Christian origins, Luke portrays a Jewish
multitude comprised of "pious men from every *ethnos* under heaven,"
who speak in a dizzying variety of native or "natal" tongues and dia-
lects. Luke's use here of the conceptual categories *ethnos* ("nation/
people") and *genos* ("race/origin/birth") is by no means coincidental
or unconscious. It is, instead, absolutely vital to a universalizing mission that envisions every nation and every people united by the action
of a single Holy Spirit. What is striking, for present purposes, is Luke's
choice of Jews as the template for imagining unity suffusing an otherwise incoherent babble of ethnic distinction and diversity. Luke's
"pious Jews" are united in pilgrimage to Jerusalem for the festival of
Shevuot, even as they are divided by birth and nation—by *genos* and
ethnos until God's Holy Spirit miraculously intervenes. The ethnoracial diversity of the Jews persists and is emphasized in the account; it
is only the nature of their unity that is ingeniously reconceived.

These observations should not be construed as attributing historical accuracy to Luke's catalog of Jewish ethnicities any more than to
his vision of dancing fires and miraculous audition and glossolalia.
Instead, the intent is to highlight Luke's rhetorical deployment of a
Jewish multiethnicity that resonates so strongly with that found in
Philo, despite the radically different aims, eras, locations, and strategies of the two authors. Although modern scholars are, understand-
ably, preoccupied with determining the textual sources, genre, and
ideological underpinnings of Luke's catalog, its author presents it

without qualification or gloss (even the Judean Jews elicit no special note or ranking in the list), suggesting that he anticipated no sense of novelty in his ancient audience's reception of such a description of broad Jewish ethnic diversity.[27]

The same can hardly be said, however, of Luke's modern audience, who, judging by published scholarship on this text, find it virtually impossible to see Jews as comprising the trees of this forest of global ethnic diversity. For example, commentator Bruce M. Metzger finds the first sentence of the passage nothing short of "amazing" and "contradictory": "Most amazing of all is the statement that these Jews were persons from every nation under heaven. Out of all *lands* under heaven could be understood—but since Jews were already an *ethnos*, to say that these were from another *ethnos* is tantamount to a contradiction of terms."[28] As with the audience *in* Luke's account (as opposed to the ancient audience *for* Luke's account), it would seem to require a miracle of divine intervention for the modern reader to make sense of the confusing incoherence attributed to the language of the text. Whence does Metzger's bewildered sense of contradiction derive? I would suggest that it inheres in an uncritical insistence on an ethnoracial particularity of Jews that is neither shared nor borne out by the ancient text itself.

Metzger is hardly alone in his disorientation. C. K. Barrett, noting that "the word [Jews] normally has a racial meaning in the NT," resolves his own discomfort with the "racial" language of the passage by asserting the divisibility of the term "Jews" from the term "pious men" and offering two opposing translations: "If taken with *Jews* the phrase *apo pantos ethnous tōn hupo ton ouranon* must mean, *from* (their

---

27. Notable studies of the catalog in Acts 2:9–11 include J. A. Brinkman, "The Literary Background of the 'Catalogue of the Nations' (Acts 2:9–11)," *CBQ* 25 (1963): 418–27; Bruce Metzger, "Ancient Astrological Geography and Acts 2:9–11," in *Apostolic History and the Gospel*, ed. W. Ward Gasque and Ralph P. Martin (Grand Rapids: Eerdmans, 1970); James Scott, "Acts 2:9–11 as an Anticipation of the Mission to the Nations," in *The Mission of the Early Church to Jews and Gentiles*, ed. J. Adna and H. Kvalbein (Tübingen: Mohr-Siebeck, 2000); and Gary Gilbert, "The List of Nations in Acts 2: Roman Propaganda and the Lukan Response," *JBL* 121, no. 3 (Fall 2002): 497–529.

28. Bruce M. Metzger, *A Textual Commentary on the Greek New Testament* (Reading, England: United Bible Societies, 1971), 290; italics in the original.

residence among) *every nation under heaven*; if taken with *pious men* it could mean, *belonging to every nation under heaven.*"[29] Barrett prefaces his proposals by appeal to "Old Testament" instances in which "nations" is used in contrast to "Israel." Accordingly, Jews of Luke's time *must* be understood to *reside among* every nation under heaven while never, in any coherent sense, being understood to *belong to* any of those nations. "Belonging," it seems, is beyond Jewish capability— or, conversely, Jews "belong" solely to "Jewishness" regardless of where and for how many generations they are in *residence among* those who *truly belong* in and to various *nations* or *ethnē*.

For whom are such distinctions imperative, and in what contexts are they meaningful? Another scholar's ruminations are helpful in deconstructing this imperative and meaning. In an extended footnote on the passage from Acts, Gary Gilbert observes that "the reading of 'Jews' in this verse [Acts 2:5] . . . is problematic." Although the term "Jews" appears in the vast majority of ancient manuscripts, it is omitted in two or three of them. Gilbert suggests:

> If the omission is original and the story referred only to "pious men from every nation under heaven," the text would then present *a more universal perspective than is suggested in the current printed editions. . . .* If, on the other hand, we follow the majority of manuscripts and retain the word "Jews," its deletion by later copyists, presumably intentionally, may indicate a desire to render the narrative audience as *more universal by erasing explicit reference to their Jewish identity.*[30]

Here, the discussion of the "problematic" term comprises theories that attempt to account for either the extremely unlikely possibility of an original omission of "Jews" or else its presumably intentional deletion by one or two later copyists for the identical ideological purpose: in order to transmit a *more universal perspective* than the presence of the term "Jews" could coherently signify. By implication, Luke's decision to use the term "Jews" in this passage must express a

---

29. C. K. Barrett, *A Critical and Exegetical Commentary on The Acts of the Apostles* (Edinburgh: T & T Clark, 1994), 118–19.

30. Gilbert, *List*, 505 n.34; italics added.

desire to present a *less than universal perspective* in his story of Christian origins. Yet it is not at all clear why Luke would desire to do so, nor how this desire would be coherent within the context of his unmistakable *worldwide* mission (or even as an assertion of *universal Jewish guilt*). [31]

All apparent incoherence, contradictions, and problems vanish, however, with the simple recognition that Luke, like Philo and other writers of Greco-Roman antiquity, recognized a world of ethnoracial diversity among the Jews of their era. These writers assumed no definitional conflict or categorical contradiction in imagining Jews as *belonging to* a vast multiplicity of *ethnē* ("nations," "homelands," "peoples") through *genos* ("birth," "race") and ancestral *syngeneia* ("kinship"). If that is the case, then, as noted in my original reading above, Acts 2 presents "pious Jews" gathered in Jerusalem as a template for imagining a kaleidoscopic array of ethnic diversity suffused by a divinely inspired unity. Jews thus provide Luke's *model*—not merely his *foil* or *counterpoint*—for imagining a universal, multiethnic, spirit-filled community. Luke's familiar brands of anti-Judaism and supersessionism conflict not at all with his use of a pious, multiethnic—and subsequently converted—multitude of Jews in this story. What makes perfect sense to Luke leaves his modern interpreters tied up in exegetical knots. Those knots result, in large part, from a rhetoric of Jewish ethnoracial particularism that has long served to constitute (through contrast) and to sustain (through animosity) particular versions of Christian universalism.

A recent generation of scholars of early Christian studies has begun to articulate the ways in which the flourishing "race science" of

---

31. Jack Sanders argues that, "The primary reason, however, for Luke's including representatives of *worldwide Jewry* at Pentecost is not to hint at the universal gospel and not to heighten the miracle of hearing in native languages, but to attest to the universal Jewish guilt in the death of Jesus." *The Jews in Luke-Acts* (Philadelphia: Fortress Press, 1987), 223; italics in original. For a point of view similar to Sanders's, see Lawrence Wills, "The Jews in Acts," in *JBL* 110, no. 4 (1991): 631–51; and Shelly Matthews, "The Stoning of Stephen," in Shelly Matthews and E. Leigh Gibson, ed., *Violence in the New Testament* (New York: T & T Clark, 2005). Whatever the theological intentions attributed to Luke in composing this passage, the point remains that his catalog encompasses broad ethnic diversity among "worldwide Jewry."

the nineteenth and early twentieth centuries shaped and informed the nascent academic field of "ancient Christianity and its Jewish background." "Race" became a handy way to describe the intractable "otherness" of Jews and to account for their continued existence long after the rise of Christianity (and, later, the Enlightenment and "emancipation") should have worked to make them disappear. The "otherness" that resisted all such universalistic human evolutionary projects was seen to be of a *particular* nature. Indeed, it was understood to be in the very nature of Jews as a "race" to remain in an unevolved state of particularity in the face of multiethnic, multinational Christian universalism. Theological blindness or resistance to Christ's universal salvific message was treated as a "genetic trait" of one of religion's evolutionary dead ends. Denise Kimber Buell explains the implicit equation: "If universalism is defined in contrast to racial specificity, and universalism is seen as a distinctive feature of Christianness, then Christianness is defined as not-race particularly over and against Jewishness as race."[32] Within a decade of Europe's failure to exterminate that "defective" race—a race that could *belong* neither to nation-state nor to empire— the term "ethnicity" appeared in the academic vocabulary and slipped more or less seamlessly in to join, if not replace, "race" in the discourse of Jewish particularism versus Christian universalism.[33]

Buell's work has been especially significant in highlighting the stakes of this Christian discourse and in attempting to address the historiographic erasures that enable it. Specifically, her project has been one of bringing to the forefront evidence of early Christian appropriations of the categories "race" and "ethnicity" (*genos, ethnos, laos, phylos*) in formulating that community's own narratives of self-fashioning and group identity.[34] In numerous texts of Christian antiquity, Buell notes, "the multiethnic background of those who became members of

---

32. Buell, "Rethinking", 457.

33. According to the OED, the term "ethnicity" is first used in this sense by David Riesman in 1953 in the journal *American Scholar* XXIII.1.15, where he compares "ethnicity" to "other parochialism[s]." See also Jonathan Hall's comments on "ethnicity" as code for "race." *Ethnic Identity*, 19–20.

34. Buell, "Rethinking", esp. 456; "Race and Universalism in Early Christianity," *Journal of Early Christian Studies* 10, no. 4 (2002): 429–68; *Why This New Race? Ethnic Reasoning in Early Christianity* (New York: Columbia University Press, 2005); and her article in the present volume.

early forms of Christianity did not preclude the depiction of Christians as forming their own *ethnos* or *genos*."[35]

Given the foregoing analysis of images of Jewish multiethnicity, the phenomenon observed by Buell of early Christianity appears to characterize early Judaism as well. To tweak Buell's language just a bit, it appears that the multiethnic background of those identified as Jews in antiquity did not preclude a broad consensus that Jews also formed a distinct *ethnos* or *genos*. In the case of Christianness, as in the case of Jewishness, one could be born into the "race," or one could join it.[36] Legal prohibitions enacted against joining either group, as well as satires demeaning "race traitors" who chose to do so, demonstrate that this perception of multiethnicity and mutability was shared by outside observers of both peoples as well. Perhaps the most significant difference between these two multiethnic "races" is expressed by Clement (who, like his ancestral countryman and literary mentor Philo, was an Alexandrian), when he asserts that Christians are "the one race [*genos*] of saved people," so that one must be of that particular race to be saved.[37]

Given that early writers and epigraphers describe Jews as a people, nation, or race among whom are found members of many *ethnē* and *genē* ("races," "births," "ancestries"), if not always "every nation under heaven," it behooves us to resist blanket assumptions about ancient Jewish ethnic or racial particularity and even to recognize the decidedly "universalistic" elements present in some ancient representations of Jewishness. In a careful and thoroughgoing critique of "the Judaism/Hellenism dichotomy," Dale Martin acknowledges that "both Hellenism and Judaism in the ancient world present important and

---

35. Buell, "Race and Universalism," 467.

36. "A number of early Christian authors find it strategically valuable to speak about Christianness as a racial category, although they formulate it as an inclusive one (as a race that one can join)" (Buell, "Rethinking," 450). Interestingly, and conversely, Origen insists that "The noun *Ioudaios* is the name not of an *ethnos* but of a choice" (commentary on Romans 2:28–29, cited in Cohen, ibid., 134).

37. Clement, *The Stromata* 6.42.2. Buell discusses this and related passages in "Race and Universalism," 429, and "Rethinking," 460. On Clement's debt to Philo, see, for example, David T. Runia, *Philo in Early Christian Literature: A Survey* (Minneapolis: Fortress Press, 1993), ch. 8, "Clement of Alexandria."

irreducible complexities" so deeply interrelated that "to ask whether something is Hellenistic *or* Jewish would seem to be a misleading question."[38] He then goes on, however, to caution against asserting or assuming any kind of "symmetry" between the two:

> Jews were seen as an *ethnos*, like Lydians, Carians, Egyptians, Persians, and Scythians. They might have their own language, ancestral customs, peculiar practices, and religious rites. But already by the time of Jesus, Hellenism was considered by many people—certainly Greeks but other educated persons as well— to have transcended those smaller ethnic boundaries.[39]

Yet, the very "irreducible complexities" of ancient Jewish identities render Martin's summary assertion that Jews were seen as an *ethnos* like other *ethnē* highly problematic. Indeed, the riots in first-century Roman Alexandria, for example, seem to have been precisely about the issue of defining Jewish difference and the lack of any consensus, amid high and shifting legal stakes, on how to do so: Were Jews to be imagined as *like Hellenes* or *like Egyptians*? To what extent and in what respects was one who was "an Alexandrian and a Jew" *like a Hellene* and in what respects *like an Egyptian*? And in the subjective game of claiming ethnicities, which subjects (ancient and modern) get to do the imagining, categorizing, and naming?

Greek colonialism and Roman (and later, Christian) imperialism *are*, in a real sense, the contexts and sources of the category "Jew" (and, likewise, "Hellene") as encountered in the Greco-Roman world. *Ioudaismos* first emerged as a conceptual category exclusively and explicitly in juxtaposition to *Hellenismos* (2 Macc 2:21)—not as a "particular" to a "universal," but as "something like what the Germans would later call *Bildung*," to quote Martin's characterization of "Hellenism."[40] Although there is no apparent "symmetry" between the two with respect to power, it is, nonetheless, precisely the appropriation of Hellenism's conceptual apparatus that underlies most ancient Jewish

---

38. Dale Martin, "Paul and the Judaism/Hellenism Dichotomy: Toward a Social History of the Question," in *Paul Beyond the Judaism/Hellenism Divide*, ed. Troels Engberg-Pedersen; Louisville (Westminster/John Knox, 2001), 30.
39. Ibid.
40. Ibid.

and some non-Jewish expressions of the nature of "Jewish" (and, later, "Christian") identities.[41] That is, those who promoted, accommodated, and resisted Greek colonialism and Roman imperialism first created, then proceeded to answer, the question, "What is Jewishness *like?*" and they did so in far more ways than one.[42]

How might our historiographic and theological narratives change if we were to perceive Jews as a "multiethnic" phenomenon from the earliest emergence of this identity? What might be the effects? Identifying "universalist" or "multiethnic" elements in some early articulations of Jewishness might lead us to recognize the peculiar, imperial "particularism" of some early Christian claims to be the one fully realized human race, to the exclusion of all others. Were this to happen, we might find ourselves on the cusp of a profound paradigm shift. Regardless, acknowledgement of the full spectrum of ancient ethnoracial rhetoric concerning both Jews and Christians might begin, at the very least, to disarm and dismantle some of the rhetorical weapons of mass destruction that our generation has inherited from our own forebears.

---

41. Philo's use of the colonial concept of "mother city" versus "fatherland" to describe Jewish history and identity represents one such appropriation; the letter of 2 Maccabees claiming Jewish kinship with Sparta represents another. The scholarly literature on "Judaism and Hellenism" is vast and accessible and needs no cataloging here.

42. Whereas Cohen ends his final chapter of *Beginnings* with the assertion that, regarding Jewishness in antiquity, "Religion overcame ethnicity" (340), Daniel Boyarin's conclusion is much more in keeping with the evidence: "For the Church, Judaism is a religion, but for the Jews . . . only occasionally, ambivalently, and strategically is it so. . . . Refusing to be different in quite the same ways, not a religion, not quite, Judaism . . . remained something else, neither quite here nor quite there" (*Borderlines: The Partition of Judeo-Christianity* [Philadelphia: University of Pennsylvania Press, 2004], 224-25).

CHAPTER 4

Mimicry and Colonial Differences

Gender, Ethnicity, and Empire in the Interpretation of Pauline Imitation

Joseph A. Marchal

When Paul argues for his audience to imitate him, his argument coincides with what Denise Kimber Buell and Caroline Johnson Hodge have called "ethnic reasoning." The reasoning of ethnicity and racialization are often also gendered in particular ways worth examining if one seeks to engage and assess colonized and colonizing rhetorics of ethnicity. Homi Bhabha's work on mimicry as a strategy in the negotiation of identity in postcolonial contexts could be a resource in recognizing and interrogating these rhetorics; yet his theoretical explication is also incomplete. Hence, we must also reassess the import of Bhabha (and those who might deploy his work) by examining the contributions of scholars such as Rey Chow, Meyda Yeğenoğlu, and Anne McClintock in addressing the intersections among gender, class, ethnicity, and empire. The work of Chow, McClintock, and Yeğenoğlu will highlight how Paul argues in a cross-ethnic, cross-gendered imperial context. We can develop a more complicated picture of colonial and communal dynamics in terms of agency, resistance, and/or cooptation.

Introduction

The category of race developed in a space where rationality, modernity, biology, and imperial expansion intersected in a dizzying array
of formations. As such, though scholars might find analogous ways
of arguing in antiquity, racialization is particularly intertwined with
European empire-building.[1] Furthermore, the academic study of religion in general, and biblical studies in particular, developed in this
particular colonial era.[2] These concurrences suggest that further critical thinking about the role of race, ethnicity, or both in the New, or
Second, Testament should also involve significant attention to imperial and colonial formations. Indeed, given the way race and ethnicity are still used in global, especially neocolonial, contexts, becoming
savvier interpreters of such intersections seems especially pressing to
understand our present and future (and not just the recent and distant
past). Such links between race, ethnicity, and empire are also evident
in a variety of contexts in the ancient Mediterranean world.

These times and topics intersect in compelling ways when one
turns to Paul's letters and the tensive dynamics of imitation in both
ancient and contemporary contexts. Such times, topics, texts, and tensions relate to one major theme of the present volume since, as Denise

---

1. For ancient forms of argumentation similar to racial (stereo)typing, or
what Gay L. Byron calls "ethno-political rhetorics," see her *Symbolic Blackness
and Ethnic Difference in Early Christian Literature* (London: Routledge, 2002).

2. For reflections on the origins of the term "race," as it coincides with the
academic study of religion and the Bible, see Shawn Kelley, *Racializing Jesus:
Race, Ideology, and the Formation of Modern Biblical Scholarship* (London: Routledge, 2002), 1–32; and Denise Kimber Buell, *Why This New Race: Ethnic Reasoning in Early Christianity* (New York: Columbia University Press, 2005), 5–33.
As Buell succinctly puts it, even as one might think the links between religion
and race are separated by academic disciplinary specialization, "religion itself
gets produced as an object of scientific inquiry, *parallel* to race, rather than the
site of production of 'race.'" See Buell, *Why This New Race*, 21, emphasis original. For further reflections on multiple periods of imperial-colonial activity as
relevant to biblical studies' formation and the practice of postcolonial studies,
see Fernando F. Segovia, *Decolonizing Biblical Studies: A View from the Margins*
(Maryknoll: Orbis, 2000), 123–31, 153–55.

Kimber Buell and Caroline Johnson Hodge have argued, Paul engaged in rhetorical practices that could be labeled "ethnic reasoning."[3] The insights of Buell and Johnson Hodge are helpful provocations to study Pauline imitation in a decidedly different fashion, yet their approach also can obscure the key roles of gender and empire as these coincide with the operations of ethnicity and racialization.[4] Contemporary postcolonial theory highlights the fact that calls to imitate aspects of the colonizers' culture recur in imperialism. Homi Bhabha's work on mimicry as a strategy in the negotiation of identity in postcolonial contexts could be a resource in interrogating these rhetorics, particularly as the colonized are often classed as inferior in terms of racial or ethnic difference. Indeed, many biblical scholars have already turned to Bhabha's theoretical apparatus to develop postcolonial readings.[5]

---

3. Denise Kimber Buell and Caroline Johnson Hodge, "The Politics of Interpretation: The Rhetoric of Race and Ethnicity in Paul," *JBL* 123, no. 2 (2004): 235–51. Buell coined the term "ethnic reasoning" "to refer to the set of discursive strategies whereby ancient authors construe collective identity in terms of peoplehood." See Buell, "Rethinking the Relevance of Race for Early Christian Self-Definition," *HTR* 94 (2001): 451; "Race and Universalism in Early Christianity," *JECS* 10 (2002): 432–41. For reflections on the intersections of race, ethnicity, and empire, as they also intersect with a range of other discursive dynamics (like sexuality) in both ancient and contemporary contexts, see Tat-siong Benny Liew, "Margins and (Cutting-)Edges: On the (IL)Legitimacy and Intersections of Race, Ethnicity, and (Post)Colonialism," in *Postcolonial Biblical Criticism: Interdisciplinary Intersections*, ed. Stephen D. Moore and Fernando F. Segovia (London: T & T Clark International, 2005), 114–65. Race differs from (but often also overlaps with) ethnicity as a socially constructed category focused often on ostensibly "biological" grounds, especially "phenotypical peculiarity like skin color, skull size, hair type, and/or nose shape." See Liew, "Margins", 114. See also Kelley, *Racializing Jesus*, 14–32.

4. In their coauthored article on Paul, Buell and Johnson Hodge only briefly note that "Paul's image of Gentile upward mobility is highly gendered." See Buell and Johnson Hodge, "Politics", 246 n.39. Buell's monograph (*Why This New Race*), however, shows increasing attention to the precisely imperial context of early Christianities, while Johnson Hodge's recently published work specifies the prominence of patrilineal descent to constructions of kinship and ethnicity. For the latter, see Johnson Hodge, *If Sons, Then Heirs: A Study of Kinship and Ethnicity in the Letters of Paul* (Oxford: Oxford University Press, 2007), especially 19–42.

5. For a few prominent examples of the use of Bhabha in biblical interpretation, see Tat-siong Benny Liew, "Tyranny, Boundary, and Might: Colonial Mimicry

Still, even as Bhabha can illuminate some of the colonial contours of imitation, his perspective still leaves several gaps, especially in light of the particular ways colonizing and colonized parties argue in terms of both gender and sexuality.

As a result of these recurring gaps in postcolonial studies (both in and outside of Second Testament studies), it is important to revisit the contributions of feminist scholarship to an intentionally intersectional study of gender, race, ethnicity, and empire. For decades now, innumerable feminist scholars, but especially women of color, have shown that race-critical scholarship proves incomplete when it ignores the roles of women, gender, and sexuality.[6] By engaging such predecessors, feminist scholars working in increasingly global, transnational, and neocolonial contexts can develop approaches attuned to race, ethnicity, and empire alongside and within an analysis of women, gender, and sexuality.[7] In order to reconsider the relevance of mimetic

---

in Mark's Gospel," *JSNT* 73 (1999): 7–31; Erin Runions, *Changing Subjects: Gender, Nation, and Future in Micah* (Sheffield: Sheffield Academic, 2002); Stephen D. Moore, "Questions of Biblical Ambivalence and Authority under a Tree Outside Delhi; or, the Postcolonial and the Postmodern," in *Postcolonial Biblical Criticism: Interdisciplinary Intersections*, ed. Stephen D. Moore and Fernando F. Segovia (London: T & T Clark International, 2005), 79–96; and Robert Seesengood, "Hybridity and the Rhetoric of Endurance: Reading Paul's Athletic Metaphors in a Context of Postcolonial Self-Construction," *Bible and Critical Theory* 1, no. 3 (2005) [Now revised and reprinted as the second chapter of Seesengood, *Competing Identities: The Athlete and the Gladiator in Early Christianity* (New York: T & T Clark International, 2006), 20–34].

6. Among the first to make such points were African-American and Latina/Chicana women, including Angela Davis, bell hooks, Audre Lorde, Barbara Smith, Gloria Anzaldúa, and Cherrie Moraga. See, for example, Angela Y. Davis, *Women, Race, & Class* (New York: Random House, 1981); bell hooks, *Ain't I a Woman: Black Women and Feminism* (Boston: South End Press, 1981); Audre Lorde, *Sister Outsider: Essays and Speeches* (Freedom: The Crossing, 1984); Gloria Anzaldúa, *La frontera/Borderlands* (San Francisco: Aunt Lute Books, 1987); and collections such as Cherrie L. Moraga and Gloria Anzaldúa, eds., *This Bridge Called My Back: Writing by Radical Women of Color* (Watertown, Mass.: Persephone, 1981); Gloria T. Hull, Patricia Bell Scott, and Barbara Smith, eds., *All the Women Are White, All the Men Are Black, but Some of Us Are Brave* (New York: Feminist, 1982); and Barbara Smith, ed., *Home Girls: A Black Feminist Anthology* (New York: Kitchen Table, 1983).

7. See, for example, Inderpal Grewal and Caren Kaplan, eds., *Scattered Hegemonies: Postmodernity and Transnational Feminist Practices* (Minneapolis: University of Minnesota Press, 1994); M. Jacqui Alexander and Chandra Talpade

arguments and practices along these lines, the insights of Rey Chow, Meyda Yeğenoğlu, and Anne McClintock will prove useful both for rethinking the import of Bhabha and for resituating the meaning of calls to imitate in a colonized context like Corinth.[8]

Corinthian Imitation and Bhabha's Mimicry

The dynamics of imitation run throughout Paul's argumentation in 1 Corinthians, but they are most explicit in two particular instances. Elizabeth Castelli, in fact, limited her analysis of Pauline imitation to

---

Mohanty, eds., *Feminist Genealogies, Colonial Legacies, Democratic Futures* (New York: Routledge, 1997); Mohanty, *Feminism Without Borders: Decolonizing Theory, Practicing Solidarity* (Durham: Duke University Press, 2003); Reina Lewis and Sara Mills, eds., *Feminist Postcolonial Theory: A Reader* (New York: Routledge, 2003); and M. Jacqui Alexander, *Pedagogies of Crossing: Meditations on Feminism, Sexual Politics, Memory, and the Sacred* (Durham: Duke University Press, 2005). For two volumes that display some of this "bridging" between periods of race-critical and anti-imperial feminist work, see Kum-Kum Bhavani, ed., *Feminism and 'Race'* (Oxford: Oxford University Press, 2001); and Robyn Wiegman, ed., *Women's Studies on Its Own: A Next Wave Reader in Institutional Change* (Durham: Duke University Press, 2002) (especially the entry by Laura E. Donaldson, Anne Donadey, and Jael Silliman, "Subversive Couplings: On Antiracism and Postcolonialism in Graduate Women's Studies," 438–56).

8. Given that my chapter focuses on 1 Corinthians, the following analysis will not make frequent use of many of the aforementioned feminist, race-critical resources. Nevertheless, I cite them to indicate their formative role in the development of the analytic adopted below and to delineate how such intersections have been rarely explored by the pale malestream of biblical scholarship. Furthermore, scholarship would do well to begin to attend to yet other crucial intersections represented by a queer of color critique [Jose Esteban Munoz, *Disidentifications: Queer of Color and the Performance of Politics* (Minneapolis: University of Minnesota Press, 1999); Roderick A. Ferguson, *Aberrations in Black: Toward a Queer of Color Critique* (Minneapolis: University of Minnesota Press, 2004); and E. Patrick Johnson and Mae G. Henderson, eds., *Black Queer Studies: A Critical Anthology* (Durham: Duke University Press, 2005)], postcolonial queer studies [Gayatri Gopinath, *Impossible Desires: Queer Diasporas and South Asian Public Cultures* (Durham: Duke University Press, 2005); and Sara Ahmed, *Queer Phenomenology: Orientations, Objects, Others* (Durham: Duke University Press, 2006)], or even approaches attending to race, gender, sexuality, nation, ethnicity, and empire as forms of a queer, race-critical, postcolonial analysis [Jasbir K. Puar, *Terrorist Assemblages: Homonationalism in Queer Times* (Durham: Duke University Press, 2007)].

these two instances where the Greek term *mimētēs* ("imitator") appears (4:16, 11:1).[9] As Antoinette Clark Wire demonstrates, though, any analysis of Corinthian imitation cannot be limited to these passages, since Paul uses himself as a model in a number of arguments elsewhere (7:6–9; 8:9, 13; 9:23–24; 13:9–11; and 14:18–20).[10] Indeed, in the following reflections, I will have ample reason to include these and expand beyond them in order to think more carefully about the intersections of gender, ethnicity, and empire in 1 Corinthians.

Yet, any study of Pauline imitation must begin with Castelli, as most (malestream) biblical scholarship on Paul avoids the issues of power and authority involved when one argues through imitation.[11] Castelli is particularly helpful since her work stresses how exhortations to imitate are inherently hierarchical.[12] Premised upon the apparent superiority of the model to be imitated, imitation assumes an audience is inferior to the superior model. However, in the process of imitation, imitators can never quite become the original model, indicating both the model's elevated position and the hierarchical dynamic at the heart of such argumentation.

Given scholars' tendency to excuse problematic power dynamics in Paul's letters, recognition of the significance of Castelli's perspective is long overdue. The tension between the call to sameness and the inability of the copy to become (enough) like the model underscores the difference between the potential model (Paul) and the hoped-for copies (the audience). In many cases, the differences between Paul and his audience(s) are underexamined. The rare exceptions to this general rule have been the feminist rhetorical work of scholars like Antoinette Clark Wire, Elisabeth Schüssler Fiorenza, and Cynthia Briggs Kittredge. These scholars recognize that, since the letters address their arguments to particular audiences toward particular

---

9. Elizabeth A. Castelli, *Imitating Paul: A Discourse of Power* (Louisville: Westminster John Knox Press, 1991), 90, 97–115. For further reflections on the utility and the limits of both Castelli's approach and Bhabha's theoretical apparatus, see Joseph A. Marchal, *The Politics of Heaven: Women, Gender, and Empire in the Study of Paul* (Minneapolis: Fortress Press, 2008), 59–90.

10. Antoinette Clark Wire, *The Corinthian Women Prophets: A Reconstruction through Paul's Rhetoric* (Minneapolis: Fortress Press, 1990), 35–36.

11. See Castelli, *Imitating Paul*, 23–33.

12. Ibid., 16, 21–22, 86–87.

ends, one can "read against the grain" of such argumentation to discover the possible views of members of these communities other than Paul's.[13] Thus, the letters themselves begin already from a place of difference. In fact, one of the main reasons that the letters are written is likely that some think, speak, or act differently from how Paul wishes. This provides an opportunity to think about others' agency, most especially in the fraught situation of a colonized context, like that of Corinth under the Roman Empire.

This opportunity to rethink difference and agency in such a context could be bolstered by greater engagement with the work of Homi Bhabha, whose theoretical apparatus involves hybridity, ambivalence, and mimicry.[14] Bhabha recognizes that the colonizers' call for imitation involves a claim to racial or ethnic difference, which is explained in dualistic terms of the colonized's savage, uncivilized, or undeveloped status versus the colonizer's masterful, civilized, and superior place. Thus, "mimicry emerges as one of the most elusive and effective strategies of colonial power and knowledge."[15] Mimicry becomes elusive precisely when it slips such hierarchical dichotomization. Since the colonized's mimicry creates a hybridized version of the apparently superior and pure colonial culture, the colonized do not become like the colonizer, but inhabit a third "in-between" space. This hybrid phenomenon fractures the founding dualism that asserts inherent difference and stable identity for both groups. (Indeed, the colonizer's demand for imitation implies that the inferior race can become like the supposedly superior race.) When colonizing discourse calls for imitation, it contradicts itself, since the superiority of the colonized is based on the premise of inherent ethnic, racial, or cultural status.

---

13. For examples of such interpretive strategies, see Wire, *Corinthian Woman*; Elisabeth Schüssler Fiorenza, *Rhetoric and Ethic: The Politics of Biblical Studies* (Minneapolis: Fortress Press, 1999); Cynthia Briggs Kittredge, "Rethinking Authorship in the Letters of Paul: Elisabeth Schüssler Fiorenza's Model of Pauline Theology," in *Walk in the Ways of Wisdom: Essays in Honor of Elisabeth Schüssler Fiorenza*, ed. Shelly Matthews, Cynthia Briggs Kittredge, and Melanie Johnson-DeBaufre (Harrisburg: Trinity Press International, 2003), 318–33.

14. See Homi Bhabha, *The Location of Culture* (London: Routledge, 1994).

15. Bhabha, "Of Mimicry and Man: The Ambivalence of Colonial Discourse," in ibid., 85–92, 85.

Here, Bhabha highlights something missing from Castelli's analysis of the hierarchical dynamics of the model-copy relationship: the instability of the model's authority. If imitation is meant to demonstrate the model's superiority, then, in a sense, the model's authority is not evident without the copy's imitation. It is an anxious request. The authoritative status of the colonizer-model needs to be repeatedly enacted in order to show its authority. Without imitation, the colonizer-model's authority can be questioned. Here is the "paranoia of power," as Bhabha explains: "The colonialist demand for narrative carries, within it, its threatening reversal: *Tell us why we are here.*"[16]

This suggests a conflicted agency for the colonized: imitation of the colonizer can become a form of resistance or mockery. The *appearance* of obedient imitation is a resemblance, or "sly civility." If read between the lines, such mimicry both resembles and disrupts the colonizer.[17] The inexact replication troubles the idea of the "original," as the imitator is "almost the same, but not quite," that is, "almost the same, but not white."[18] The uncertain identity exposes the uncertainty of the colonizer's control of the colonized. Colonial mimicry highlights the potential for the colonized's agency, creating a productive ambivalence where transgressive resistance becomes possible.

As Castelli has stressed, the rhetorics of imitation in 1 Corinthians operate in evidently hierarchical ways. The gap between Paul and his audience is clear in this arrangement not only because he calls for them to "become imitators of me" (4:16; 11:1), but also because he depicts himself as their father (4:15).[19] Twice the community is described as less advanced than Paul (who is himself no longer an

---

16. See Bhabha, "Sly Civility," in *Location of Culture*, 93–101, 100.

17. On this, Bhabha writes: "The *menace* of mimicry is its *double* vision which in disclosing the ambivalence of colonial discourse also disrupts its authority." See Bhabha, "Of Mimicry and Man," in *Location of Culture*, 88. On the move from mimicry to menace or mockery, see also Bhabha, "Of Mimicry and Man," ibid., 91; and "Articulating the Archaic: Cultural Difference and Colonial Nonsense," ibid., 123–38, 137.

18. See Bhabha, "Of Mimicry and Man," ibid., 86, 89. For the conjoined phrase "not quite/not white," see p. 92.

19. On the nonaffectionate, mostly hierarchical nature of ancient parent-child, especially father-child, relations, see Wire, *Corinthian Women*, 45–47; Castelli, *Imitating Paul*, 99–102.

infant, *nēpios*, in 13:11): they are his *tekna* ("children," 4:14) and *nēpioi* ("infants," 3:1) who are not yet ready for solid food. The second time Paul uses the *mimētēs* phrase in the letter, he inserts the phrase "just as I [am] of Christ" (11:1). By arguing this way, Paul closely affiliates his own authority with Christ's. That this can be read as a hierarchical progression is only strengthened by the immediately following "hierarchy of heads," that delineates women's place beneath men, men's beneath Christ, and Christ's beneath God (11:3).

When it comes to specific communal practices, Paul is often quick to reinforce his own preeminent place in comparison to members of his audience. Even as he tries to limit the practice, Paul boasts that he is more gifted than the rest, able to "speak in tongues more than all of you" (14:18). His abilities extend from the ecstatic to the self-disciplined, as he wishes that all could be "as I myself am" (7:7), single and self-controlled erotically (7:8–9). Yet, Paul's advice in this section presumes the inability of many to live in this *kreissōn* ("better," 7:38) "Pauline" state, conceding a variety of conditions for "having" a woman or man when facing temptation and corruption (7:1–16, 25–40).

Throughout the letter, then, Paul crafts several arguments to shape one path for the Corinthians to follow. The letter accomplishes this not only by explicit reference to Paul as model but also through extended contrasts between positive and negative models. As most scholars note, the opening chapters of this letter address the prominent concern of unity through a series of striking reversals that underscore what path should not be followed (an example of antimodel argumentation).[20] The audience should not pursue the typical, human, worldly, or "wordy" wisdom (1:18–25; 2:1–5, 12–14; 3:18–21), or assume that "you" have already achieved status (4:8–10). Rather, the "you" should aspire to be more like the "us" who work in unity and sameness (1:10). The differences outlined between "us" and others reflect the colonizing tendency to dichotomize between strong and weak, wise and foolish, destruction and safety, human and divine, and

---

20. For the importance of unity to the rhetorical plan of 1 Corinthians (and 1:10 as the "thesis statement" about this unity), see, for example, Margaret M. Mitchell, *Paul and the Rhetoric of Reconciliation: An Exegetical Investigation of the Language and Composition of 1 Corinthians* (Louisville: Westminster John Knox, 1991).

physical and spiritual (among others). This dualistic frame clarifies who and what should not be imitated, including the wise one, the scribe, the debaters, and the rulers of this era (1:20; 2:6).

Even as he argues within such a dualistic framework, though, Paul's claims about his own model seem to open up a different kind of hybrid space. As Robert Seesengood has highlighted, one might understand Paul as "Jewgreek" or "Greekjew" for occasions like the arguments in 9:19–23 or 10:32–33.[21] Certainly, Paul cites a baptismal formula where both *Ioudaioi* and *Hellenoi* can be incorporated into one, in Christ (12:13).[22] But he also shows his own model quality (worthy of imitation) when he adapts and becomes like those he seeks: *Ioudaioi*, those under the law and without the law, and the weak (9:20–22).[23] Similarly, regarding food practices, he advises the community to do as he does, and not offend either *Ioudaioi* or Greeks (10:32–33). In both cases, Paul shows a comprehensive ability to adapt, becoming "all things to all" (9:22) and pleasing "all in all [I do]" (10:33) in order to bring safety or salvation to them (9:22; 10:33).

If the assembly community is to imitate Paul, one might expect their practices or identity to reflect Paul's own in-between, hybrid "thirdness." Indeed, when Paul advises the audience to not offend *Ioudaioi* or Greeks, he also advises against offending the assembly of God (10:32).[24] Such consecutive phrasing draws the interpreter back not only to the baptismal formula of 12:13 ("either *Ioudaioi* or Greeks"),

---

21. See, for example, Seesengood, *Competing Identities*, 23–24, 31, where he also is citing Daniel Boyarin, *A Radical Jew: Paul and the Politics of Identity* (Berkeley: University of California Press, 1994), 79. Interestingly, though Boyarin does not directly refer to Bhabha in the work, Bhabha did provide approving comments on the 1997 back jacket of *A Radical Jew*.

22. Following Johnson Hodge, this study will simply transliterate the Greek term alternately translated Jews or Judeans (*Ioudaioi*) in order to signal the complexity and variety of such ethnic descriptive terms. See Johnson Hodge, *Heirs*, 11–15.

23. On adaptability in Paul, see Clarence E. Glad, *Paul and Philodemus: Adaptability in Epicurean and Early Christian Pedagogy* (New York: Brill, 1995); and Glad, "Paul and Adaptability," in *Paul in the Greco-Roman World: A Handbook*, ed. J. Paul Sampley (Harrisburg: Trinity Press International, 2003), 17–41.

24. For arguments related to multiple identities for those in the assembly (especially Gentiles), see Johnson Hodge, *Heirs*, 126.

but also to the letter's opening dual claims that Christ is "a stumbling block to *Ioudaioi* and foolishness to the *ethnē* ('nations')" (1:23) and that both *Ioudaioi* and Greeks can be called (1:24). The assembly community is itself a third entity, differentiated from *Ioudaioi* and the nations, but also comprising Greeks and *Ioudaioi*.

This hybrid version of communal identity and practice, as modeled by Paul, potentially fractures Paul's preceding arguments for unity. Furthermore, a vision of community that is somehow neither *Ioudaios* nor Greek yet also comprised of *Ioudaioi* and Greeks indicates that some of the boundaries constructed by Paul's dualistic framework can be crossed. Indeed, Paul's own boasting about his ability to be "all things" suggests that he himself is somehow almost the same, but not quite Greek, or almost the same, but not quite *Ioudaios*. Are the resemblances Paul seeks then transgressive? If so, how much do Paul's own arguments about adaptation undercut his more authoritative dichotomization? Such questions open up the interpretive possibility that there are other ways to proceed in the community than the path laid out by Paul's arguments in 1 Corinthians (including where Paul might be dualistic on other factors).

Even within the hierarchical chain presented in several of the arguments for imitation, the role of the intermediate figure is raised. Certainly, letters like 1 Corinthians make frequent references to divine power and authority in order to bolster Paul's point of view. In line with this rhetorical tendency, then, Paul's exhortation to "become imitators of me, just as I [am] of Christ" (11:1) positions Paul as a necessary intermediary between the audience and the model of Christ. This grants Paul a divinely-imbued privilege, yet it also opens up an additional "in-between" space of continuously descending, almost but not quite right imitations (Paul of Christ, the audience of Paul). Thus, both Christic and Pauline authority are, in a sense, fractured.

The tendencies towards hierarchy and its destabilization in Paul's arguments carry over to additional intermediates like Timothy. After all, immediately after the first explicit call to imitate Paul, he connects his model to the reminders that Timothy will provide (4:17; cf. 16:10). That Timothy is, like the community, also cast as Paul's *teknon* ("child") and is sent at Paul's orders underscores the persistently hierarchical tenor of Paul's argument. Yet, if Timothy, the "mimic man," is a suitable replacement for Paul's own presence, what keeps Paul's pre-eminently authoritative position unique?[25] The letter operates under the claim that the Corinthian community specifically needs Paul (for unity and most especially for safety or salvation), yet such supporting figures indicate that Paul and others might not be so different after all. As in Bhabha's scenario for mimicry, this weakens the letter's claim to Paul's superior model status.

Indeed, from Paul's point of view, the problems at Corinth seem to involve claims of relative closeness to his own status and position. In the opening chapters, he meditates on the difference between Apollos and himself as a source of disunity among the Corinthians. He first claims that it is important to follow neither of them, and then extols his own model over and against Apollos (1:10–17; 3:1–5; 4:6–7, 14–21). Thus, one trajectory in the letter distances Paul from Apollos and other community members in a hierarchical chain, while another trajectory urges all to become like Paul.

If being "like Paul" is at all possible, however, his authority could be minimized. Moreover, the way this call to imitate him is so repetitive (in this and other letters) indicates how anxious a request it is. If, as it seems, the Corinthian community is not imitating Paul "correctly," his authoritative status would be relativized. This imitation with a difference makes a difference. For Castelli, the inability to achieve sameness with a model exemplifies the impossibly impregnable authority of a model. But to Bhabha, this same inability indicates the model-colonizer's lack of definitive control over the copy-colonized. This lack of control reminds us of the community's opportunities to follow other models (like Apollos) or to adopt more transgressive forms of imitation.

Paul makes many attempts to convince the community that his exhortations to imitate him are seamless and self-evident. At many turns, Paul's argumentation reflects strategies akin to colonizers' in terms of hierarchy, exclusive authority, and conformity to one side of dichotomizations. Yet, the letter also bears signs of a continuing slippage, an undoing of the authority Paul attempts to install for himself, a slippage that opens the meaning of Pauline mimicry. Bhabha's

---

25. For the "mimic man," see, for example, Bhabha, "Of Mimicry and Man," in *Location of Culture*, 87.

perspective highlights some fruitful possibilities for engaging these arguments as forms of ethnic reasoning, even as one cannot yet assume an inherent subversiveness to such forms of mimicry.

Complicating Colonial Mimicry: Ethnos and Ethos

Colonial powers often show remarkable flexibility in maintaining or reconsolidating their own authority, even through the transgressions and traversals of those moving in resistance to empire, a point that Bhabha's work mostly misses. Rey Chow, for example, cautions against Bhabha's valorization of mimicry, ambivalence, and hybridity. Chow points out that the terms of the resistance Bhabha theorizes begin with and remain rooted in the colonizer's discourse, which "makes it unnecessary to come to terms with the subaltern since she has already 'spoken,' as it were, in the system's gaps."[26] This kind of strategy only reinforces the centrality imperial discourse claims for itself and, thus, operates as a kind of assimilation or reconsolidation rather than resistance.[27] Colonialism is successful because it takes multiple, diffuse,

---

26. See Rey Chow, "Where Have All The Natives Gone?" in *Feminist Postcolonial Theory*, 324–49, 330. Reprinted from *Displacements: Cultural Identities in Question*, ed. Angelika Bammer (Bloomington: Indiana University Press, 1994), 125–51. Here, Chow is engaging Benita Parry who implements Bhabha to critique Gayatri Spivak's essay, "Can the Subaltern Speak?" in *Marxism and the Interpretation of Culture*, ed. Cary Nelson and Lawrence Grossberg (Urbana: University of Illinois Press, 1988), 271–313. See Parry, "Problems in Current Theories of Colonial Discourse," *Oxford Literary Review* 9, no. 1-2 (1987): 27–58.

27. To continue Chow's incisive argument, "What Bhabha's word 'hybridity' revives, in the masquerade of deconstruction, anti-imperialism and 'difficult' theory, is an old functionalist notion of what a dominant culture permits in the interest of maintaining its own equilibrium" (*Natives*, 330). In a similar manner, Liew contrasts his use of "colonial mimicry" to Bhabha's definition: "I am using 'mimicry' to refer to a reinscription or a duplication of colonial ideology by the colonized" (*Tyranny*, 13 n.9). Liew's article also refers to and elaborates upon Chow's earlier work on Diaspora. See Chow, *Writing Diaspora: Tactics of Intervention in Contemporary Cultural Studies* (Bloomington: Indiana University Press, 1993). For an interrelated, if different approach to these issues of ethnicity, empire, gender, and embodiment in 1 Corinthians, see also Liew, "Redressing Bodies in Corinth: Racial/Ethnic Politics and Religious Difference in the Context of Empire," in *What is Asian American Biblical Hermeneutics? Reading the New Testament* (Honolulu: University of Hawaii Press, 2008), 75–97, 175–188.

various, and even contradictory forms in order to secure its authority.[28] The fractures Bhabha finds are more often signs of colonialism's subtle vitality than its undoing.

Still, it remains important to think further about mimicry, as Chow maintains that "mimeticism is, perhaps, the central problematic of cross-ethnic representation in the postcolonial world."[29] For Chow, however, this problematic involves three overlapping and coexistent levels of mimeticism. The first level, which is akin to Castelli's analysis of imitation above, involves the white man's claim to be the original model, founding the imperative for the colonized and racialized other to become like the ruler.[30] This level echoes Trinh T. Minh-ha's observations of the European call to the natives: "'Be like *us*' . . . Don't be us, this self-explanatory motto warns. Just be 'like.'"[31] This first level is qualified by the second kind of mimeticism, which Chow mostly describes in terms similar to Bhabha's ambivalent form of mimicry.[32]

In addition to these forms of imitation, Chow suggests a third kind, which she calls "coercive mimeticism." Coercive mimeticism does not demand the imitation of a "superior," but expects the ethnic to mime or perform what is most recognizable as ethnic.[33] Unlike the analysis of Frantz Fanon (upon which Bhabha elaborates), where, "For the black man there is only one destiny. And it is white,"[34] the

---

28. Indeed, within this multiplicity, the hybridized mimicry can operate as an extension of the drive toward proliferation that is characteristic of a kind of turbo-capitalism that is increasingly evident globally. See, for example, the argument in Chow, "Keeping Them in Their Place: Coercive Mimeticism and Cross-Ethnic Representation," in *The Protestant Ethnic and the Spirit of Capitalism* (New York: Columbia University Press, 2002), 95–127, 106.

29. Ibid., 103.

30. See ibid., 104. Even as the "whiteness" on which these sources reflect is mostly (though not entirely) a more recent racialized formation, these critical insights still might apply to first century contexts where ethnic differentiations are used to enact and reinforce similar (if non-identical) schema of supremacy and subordination.

31. See Trinh T. Minh-ha, *Woman, Native, Other: Writing Postcoloniality and Feminism* (Bloomington: Indiana University Press, 1989), 52. Trinh is considerably less sanguine than Bhabha about the possibilities for resistant imitation.

32. See Chow, "Coercive Mimeticism", 104–6.

33. See Chow, ibid., 107–08.

34. See Frantz Fanon, *Black Skin, White Masks*, trans. Charles Lam Markmann (New York: Grove Press, 1967 [1952]), 10, 228.

only destiny in coercive mimeticism is to be ethnic. Chow argues that ethnic subjects must be recognized as conforming to the stereotype of their ethnicity, developing a kind of self-mimicry, where certain images are affirmed as exemplary embodiments of a communal *ethos* in a process of containment. Such internal policing of group boundaries and characteristic dispositions (*ethos*) becomes a way to shame others for not being properly "authentic," leading to lateral violence within or across ethnic groups rather than resistance.

Chow's conception of the potential for ambivalence *and* coercion in mimicry illuminates Paul's rhetorics of imitation in a different manner. Indeed, the way ethnic identity vacillates between the particular and the universal in Chow's analysis interconnects with Buell and Johnson Hodge's views of ethnic reasoning as moving between fixity and fluidity.[35] As Paul hopes that the members of this new kind of community will imitate him (following Paul's construction of his character, or *ethos*, as a "speaker"), he depicts his elevated status as relatively fixed. Not only is Paul the authoritative model, but he is also a (divinely-endorsed?) apostle with considerable capabilities for control and prophecy (2:6–7, 12–13; 4:14–21; 7:7–9; 14:18–19). In two passages demonstrating his *ethos* as a model, Paul attempts to establish himself as the conduit for collective safety (9:22; 10:33). Yet, in both instances, Paul models his own fluidity, adaptability, or even ethnic instability (9:20–22; 10:32). While Bhabha might lead us to view this ambivalence as the unstable fracturing of Pauline identity and authority, Chow alerts us to the possibility that these might be variously contradictory strategies toward the same end. Such negotiations between fixity and fluidity are examples of the effective dynamism of ethnic reasoning as consistent with colonizing coercion, rather than its transgression, dissolution, or transcendence.

The processes of ethnic identification and differentiation are also prominent in the letter's efforts at creating a particular group identity to be followed by the audience. Mimetic arguments like the one in

---

35. See Buell and Johnson Hodge, "Politics", 236–38. For Chow's elucidation of the simultaneous understanding of ethnicity as universal (something everyone has/is) and particular/local (something only others or foreigners have/are), see Chow, "The Protestant Ethnic and the Spirit of Capitalism," in ibid., 19–49.

10:32–11:1 set the assembly community parallel to the ethnic groups mentioned here and elsewhere in the letter (*Ioudaioi* and Greeks, 1:22–24; 9:20; 10:32; 12:13; cf. 9:21–22). Paul's treatment of circumcision (7:17–20) and "intermarriage" (7:12–16) also suggests that questions about how to be ethnic in the community were live ethical issues at Corinth. Paul proffers forms of ethnic differentiation as the path toward a new kind of ethnic solidarity.[36] Shortly after the first explicit instance where he calls them to imitate him, Paul condemns the community for acting even worse than *ta ethnē* ("the nations," 5:1) in permitting the presence of immorality (5:6–13). If the Corinthian community is to become an *ethnos* unlike the *ethnē* antimodels, it must cast out offenders so that assembly members themselves can be saved (5:3–5, 12–13). The ethics of unity expresses itself through the maintenance of boundaries for the community as a body (6:13–18). "The nations" appear twice elsewhere as negative contrasts for the assembly community to avoid, as those who see Christ as foolishness (1:23) and those who sacrifice to demons rather than to God (10:20).[37] Furthermore, when it comes to speaking in tongues, Paul exhorts the community not to act like barbarians, lest they obstruct the proper kind of assembly building (14:11–12).[38]

In 1 Corinthians, Paul works to found a particular ethnic identity for the assembly community using a series of ethnic differentiations. For the Corinthians, though, this would take concerted efforts, since they used to be "the nations" (12:2) and, according to Paul, acted like they did not belong in the kingdom of God (6:9–11). As such

---

36. See, for example, David G. Horrell, *Solidarity and Difference: A Contemporary Reading of Paul's Ethics* (London: T & T Clark International, 2005), 133–65.

37. In the second instance (10:20), "the nations" may only be implied, as those who sacrifice not to the real God but to idols/demons, though *ta ethnē* does appear in a number of manuscripts for the verse.

38. This passage's argument asking the audience to not act like *barbaroi* might also connect to those places where Paul depicts the community as childish (*nēpioi*, 3:1) with a term that stresses the element of immaturity where one cannot yet speak, or can but without appropriate forethought or reflection. Such intertwined claims about conquered and foreign peoples being immature, childish, or less linguistically advanced echo long-standing imperial and colonial rationales based on ethnic difference.

arguments remind us, by using terms akin to the founding of an *ethnos*, most of the people in the community at Corinth likely were not of the same *ethnos* as Paul (hence, his famous moniker: "apostle to the Gentiles").[39] Thus the letter's calls to imitate Paul (and his vision of community) are acts of "cross-ethnic representation" in a colonized context.

Indeed, on occasion it seems that Paul seeks to incorporate this group as a particular kind of *ethnos* in relation to *Ioudaioi*. In one instance where "the nations" appear as an ethnic antimodel (10:20), Israel is used as a counterexample of appropriate affiliation (10:18). Furthermore, Paul uses both the creation stories (11:7–12; 15:45–50) and the wilderness accounts (10:1–13) in order to explain proper conduct for the community. In the latter case, he even specifies a new ancestry, calling the generation of Moses "our fathers" (10:1), both Paul's and the community's. Yet, even as Paul seeks a communal identification with Israel, he also uses the grumbling and disobedient wilderness generation as an antimodel (10:5–10). Their fate would be destruction (10:9–10) just as Paul has warned on numerous other occasions in the letter (1:18–21; 3:13, 17; 5:5; 6:13; 7:16; 9:22; 10:33; 11:29–34; 15:2, 24–28). The coercive tenor of such mimetic arguments is hard to miss.

Thus, the assembly members are exhorted to be like neither the nations, nor the barbarians, nor the ancestors of the *Ioudaioi* (even as they are now their ancestors, as well). The conceptualization of Paul's "us" is clarified through a range of fixed examples, yet is somehow different from all previous groups. Furthermore, this "us" must be clear enough to deserve safety in the face of destruction, but fluid enough to allow those who are convinced to imitate Paul to become part of the "us." As Chow's work shows, the seeming contradiction of this fluid, yet fixed ethnic-communal identity does not necessarily signify a failure on the part of the argument, but instead its effectively coercive adaptabilities. As Paul's arguments convince, the boundaries

39. For social-historical modeling about the mixed social, ethnic, and communal relations within Corinth and within the assembly community there, see Craig S. de Vos, *Church and Community Conflicts: The Relationships of the Thessalonian, Corinthian, and Philippian Churches with Their Wider Civic Communities* (SBLDS 168; Atlanta: Scholars Press, 1999), 179–232, especially 185–90, 195–203.

created by such rhetorics will be enacted by the community to police itself in accordance with Paul's vision, often phrased in terms of ethnicity. In the imperial context of the Roman *colonia* at Corinth, these arguments for violent exclusion seem to be directed less at the ruling administration than at other people and perspectives in the prospective community.[40] The specter of safety gained and withdrawn recalls instances of lateral violence in colonized contact zones rather than resistance. In this way, Paul's arguments coincide with and reinforce imperial power: the common strategy of divide and conquer. Even if they are somehow aimed against the empire of the time (as some scholars maintain), they are easily misdirected, co-opted, and reassimilated to an imperial-colonial agenda.[41]

If the assembly community followed this model to "shore up" their boundaries, the organization within the new *ethnos* would proceed along hierarchical lines of difference. As is evident by the arguments for imitation in the letter, Paul attempts to claim an almost exclusive place of authority in comparison to others in the assembly. This authority is not so absolutized that it prevents Paul's commendation of other figures, from Timothy and Apollos to the household of Stephanas (16:15–18; cf. 1:14–16), even as each is somehow subordinated to Paul. Elsewhere, Paul admits a variety of gifts present in

---

40. Musa W. Dube's work has analyzed how collaboration leads colonized peoples to fight against each other. While this study focuses on such possibilities within communities that know Paul (or between Paul and them), Dube refers to the internal divisions of various competing interest groups in Roman Palestine. See Dube, *Postcolonial Feminist Interpretation of the Bible* (St. Louis: Chalice Press, 2000), 51–52. Furthermore, Dube argues that Matthew is an example of "a collaborative postcolonial narrative that arises from among the colonized but that deflects the focus from the root cause of oppression, the imperialists, and focuses instead on other victims." Ibid., 135.

41. On the potentially anti-imperial resonance of Paul's arguments in the letter, see, for example, Richard A. Horsley, "Rhetoric and Empire—and 1 Corinthians," in *Paul and Politics: Ekklesia, Israel, Imperium, Interpretation; Essays in Honor of Krister Stendahl*, ed. Horsley (Harrisburg: Trinity Press International, 2000), 72–102. For further reflections on such claims, see Marchal, "Imperial Intersections and Initial Inquiries: Toward a Feminist, Postcolonial Analysis of Philippians," *JFSR* 22, no. 2 (Fall 2006): 5–32. For the possibility that Paul is arguing in terms of a solidarity that can cut across "the nations," see Davina C. Lopez, *Apostle to the Conquered: Reimagining Paul's Mission* (Paul in Critical Contexts; Minneapolis: Fortress Press, 2008).

the Corinthian community, from healing and speaking in tongues to prophecy and teaching (12:4–11; cf. 7:7). Still, he clarifies the proper order of things, with apostleship and prophecy as the first and the second of "the greater gifts" (12:28–31). Paul enjoys pride of place in this arrangement, standing in for "the head" of the community, which is now incorporated into one body (10:32–11:3; 12:12–27).

Such argumentative efforts make clear that this letter is "ethnically complex *and* asymmetrical"[42] in relation to both outsiders and insiders. In developing such cross-ethnic calls for imitation, Paul's multivalent strategies also function coercively, given the mechanics of communal exclusion and the threats of divinely executed destruction articulated in the letter. The ambiguity of these strategies does not need to undo such hierarchical authority or internalized coercion. Still, in response to Bhabha, Chow enjoins us to focus on more than the canonized discourse as the source of interstitial, resistant agency. Paul's view of his authority was far from established for the first-century context of Corinth, reminding us that there are still possibilities for perspectives besides Paul's. The three levels of mimeticism explain how there could be many, simultaneous understandings of Pauline (or scholarly) attempts at cross-ethnic representation, but this study has yet to consider how these imitation arguments are simultaneously gendered.

Engendering Ethnic Resistance to and through Mimicry

Like Chow, both Meyda Yeğenoğlu and Anne McClintock also examine Bhabha's notion of colonial mimicry, but they do so to question how the dynamics of race, ethnicity, and empire all critically intersect with gender. As McClintock quite pointedly observes, this complication seems especially necessary for utilizing Bhabha's conceptual

---

42. See Buell and Johnson Hodge, "Politics", 249. For a different conception of Paul's efforts at "ethnic reconstruction" that also reflects around these dynamics of fixity and fluidity, see Sze-Kar Wan, "Collection for the Saints as Anticolonial Act: Implications of Paul's Ethnic Reconstruction," in *Paul and Politics: Ekklesia, Israel, Imperium, Interpretation; Essays in Honor of Krister Stendahl*, ed. Richard Horsley (Harrisburg: Trinity Press International, 2000), 191–215.

apparatus, since he writes only "Of Mimicry and Man."[43] Indeed, by ignoring women, gender, and sexuality, appending them after the fact, or treating them as peripheral to the "main" task, postcolonial theory risks replicating structures within the colonialism it seeks to upend.

Yeğenoğlu highlights as one prominent example the colonial effort to "unveil" Algerian women, since colonizing forces "must first of all conquer the women."[44] Here is coercive mimeticism, not just in terms of ethnicity, but precisely where ethnicity, colonialism, and gender intersect. In this light, the act of veiling frustrates the demands of colonial power.[45] Colonized women mimic the male colonialist discourses about women, but by doing so, they threaten the colonizer's ability to recognize and, in turn, control the colonial subjects. Indeed, a veiled woman can see without being "seen."[46] Despite the militant agency of such women, Fanon characterizes them as the anticolonial males' "women-arsenal," assuming that they are only involved as widows or wives of the revolutionaries.[47]

Such acts of reincorporation into the male-dominated heterosexual family typify how colonizing and colonized imaginations function "porno-tropically" to sexualize and gender peoples and locations in accordance with the rationales and fantasies of colonialism. By invoking the analogy of family, empires could domesticate and naturalize their claims to authority.[48] Since the familial orders that subordinate

---

43. McClintock writes: "The ironically generic 'Man' in Bhabha's title ("Of Mimicry and Man") both conceals and reveals that Bhabha is really only talking about men. By eliding gender difference, however, Bhabha implicitly ratifies gender power, so that masculinity becomes the invisible norm of postcolonial discourse." See Anne McClintock, *Imperial Leather: Race, Gender, and Sexuality in the Colonial Conquest* (New York: Routledge, 1995), 64–65.

44. See Fanon, *A Dying Colonialism*, trans. Haakon Chevalier (New York: Grove Press, 1965), 37–38. As quoted in Meyda Yeğenoğlu, "Veiled Fantasies: Cultural and Sexual Difference in the Discourse of Orientalism," in *Feminist Postcolonial Theory*, 542–66, 543.

45. See Yeğenoğlu, "Veiled Fantasies", 557–58; Fanon, *Colonialism*, 44; and Malek Alloula, *The Colonial Harem*, trans. Myrna and Wlad Godzich (Minneapolis: University of Minnesota Press, 1986), 7.

46. See Yeğenoğlu, "Veiled Fantasies", 557.

47. See McClintock, *Imperial Leather*, 365–68; Fanon, *Colonialism*, 48–58.

48. See McClintock, ibid., 42–51. On these "porno-tropics," see McClintock, "The Lay of the Land: Genealogies of Imperialism," *Imperial Leather*, 21–24; and

women and children were and often still are seen as natural and self-evident, the empire that mimes "family" can extend its authoritative reach with paternalistic beneficence. Within such an argument, showing how women's sexual roles fulfill certain constrained expectations becomes especially important. McClintock charts how colonized women (particularly in Africa) are classed as degenerate and primitive by virtue of their apparently aberrant bodies and sexuality, while the "good" woman bears the responsibility of properly reproducing racial, ethnic, national, or imperial differences through the physical and social-pedagogical production of equally "good" subjects (children) representative of these kinds of differences.[49]

Thus, McClintock, like Yeğenoğlu, cautions that not all practices of mimicry work subversively. For example, a native with apparently "in-between" characteristics does not necessarily disrupt the categories of savage and civilized as Bhabha's hybrid "mimic man" would, but reinforces an argument for imperial supremacy: linear progress, where "in-between" characteristics mark some point along a map toward perfect civilization. When empires stress their cultural forward progress and their primitive subjects' degeneration, discovering "improved" colonized subjects demonstrates the subjects' historical "lateness" and their place in lower rungs in the "family tree of man."[50] Bhabha also fails to consider the various roles a "white" male can adopt in colonized locales, passing as whatever race or class he prefers, while other lower-class native mimics are seen as unfortunate monsters. As McClintock notes: "Evidently, passing 'down' the cultural hierarchy is permissible; passing 'up' is not."[51] In both their gendered and imperial aspects, males' racial or ethnic transvestism needs to be examined as "the colonial who passes as Other the better to govern."[52]

Laura E. Donaldson, "The Breasts of Columbus: A Political Anatomy of Postcolonialism and Feminist Religious Discourse," in *Postcolonialism, Feminism, and Religious Discourse*, ed. Kwok Pui-lan (New York: Routledge, 2002), 41–61.

49. See McClintock, ibid., 41–42, 353–57. For the particular ways women have been figured in nationalist discourses as reproducers, signifiers, and transmitters of ethnic boundaries or difference, see Nira Yuval-Davis and Floya Anthias, ed., *Woman-Nation-State* (Hampshire: MacMillan, 1989), 7–10.

50. See McClintock, ibid., 66.

51. See McClintock, ibid., 70 (see the longer analysis on pages 66–71).

52. See McClintock, ibid., 70.

For McClintock and Yeğenoğlu, then, only an imitation that departs from such narratives of family and advancement could be effectively resistant, a "purposeful but distorted imitation,"[53] or a "delicious impersonation that belies complete disguise."[54] These dissonances are more easily comprehended when the analysis is fine-tuned to the collaborations and juxtapositions of mimetic practices in and through multiple social categories, such as gender, sexuality, race and ethnicity, class, nation, and empire. McClintock and Yeğenoğlu's reflections on mimicry stress the importance of perceiving multiply intersecting categories of analysis, particularly when arguments like the calls to imitate in 1 Corinthians have multiple interpretive possibilities. This is also emphasized by a number of feminist and postcolonial feminist biblical scholars, including Elisabeth Schüssler Fiorenza, Musa Dube, and Kwok Pui-lan.[55]

Such work should elucidate that Paul's letter is not only "cross-ethnic" (communicating across various ethnic divides), but it is also cross-gendered: Paul directs his imitation rhetorics to a community with both women and men. While the presence of specific arguments about women's roles in the Corinthian assembly makes this clear (for example: 7:1–40; 11:2–16; 14:34–36), the connections between the imitation arguments and women's roles merit further consideration. For example, Paul's calls for women to cover their heads when prophesying (11:5–16) quickly follow an argument to imitate his own

---

53. See Yeğenoğlu, ibid., 559.

54. See McClintock, ibid., 175.

55. Schüssler Fiorenza's neologism "kyriarchy," for example, highlights how multiple and mutually influential structures of domination and subordination function together, evident not only in sexism, but also in racism, classism, ethnocentrism, heterosexism, colonialism, nationalism, and militarism. For an introductory definition to this neologism, see Schüssler Fiorenza, *Wisdom Ways: Introducing Feminist Biblical Interpretation* (Maryknoll: Orbis Books, 2001), 1, 118–19, 211; and idem, *Rhetoric and Ethic*, ix. See also Schüssler Fiorenza, *Bread Not Stone: The Challenge of Feminist Biblical Interpretation* (rev. ed.; Boston: Beacon, 1995), 211 n. 6; and idem, *But She Said: Feminist Practices of Biblical Interpretation* (Boston: Beacon, 1992), 8, 117. For critiques of kyriarchy, as well as further observation on overlapping or intersecting dynamics, see Dube, ibid., 16–21, 28–37, 43, 111–15, 185; Kwok Pui-lan, *Postcolonial Imagination and Feminist Theology* (Louisville: Westminster John Knox, 2005), 16, 21–23, 49–50, 55, 81–82.

actions (10:32–11:1) and a linking sentence that hails the Corinthians for keeping Paul's traditions (11:2). I have already noted the hierarchical tendencies in this section of the letter (10:33–11:1, 3), as well as the ways Paul uses his people's creation stories (11:7–9, 11–12) to assert these claims as part of the letter's ethnic reasoning. These intersections make it even more striking that a patriarchal demand about women's head coverings appears as a marker of gendered and communal difference in an imperial context (strangely akin to a number of more contemporary efforts focusing on women in colonial, postcolonial, and neocolonial contexts).[56]

Nevertheless, Paul's efforts in this letter could indicate that he seeks to "first of all conquer the women" in the Corinthian audience. Indeed, Paul's attitude towards the women also seems to coincide with Fanon's view of a "women-arsenal" when he instructs women to be silent in the assembly and to "ask their men" (14:34–35) when they need to know more. Such argumentation not only attempts to enforce passivity among women, but it also relocates charismatic women within more normative familial (and likely sexual/erotic) arrangements. Yet, as Yeğenoğlu might question Fanon's assumptions, biblical scholars must not simply assume women's monolithically obedient response to such hierarchical arguments for imitation and order. One might still envision a range of transgressive practices in the context of these cross-gendered, cross-ethnic calls to imitate.

In order to establish such possibilities, interpreters also cannot ignore the gendered significance of the ongoing rhetorics of kinship in 1 Corinthians. As scholars have often noted about this letter, Paul particularly stresses familial dynamics in describing the community, calling them *adelphoi* ("brothers" or, more optimistically, "siblings") thirty-nine times in 1 Corinthians. As I have highlighted above, Paul portrays himself as the father of the assembly and presents Timothy, his "child," as an intermediate model (4:14–17). Not only does such an arrangement indicate a patriarchal order, but it also coincides with the colonizing vision

---

56. Though the remaining reflections cannot consider this particular intersection further, it does suggest the need for more cautiously critical engagement around the varying significance of "the veil" in relation to gender, class, race and ethnicity, and empire.

of linear progress where descending levels of authority and identity are correspondingly derived from the superior above. The intermediate place of Timothy or of the household of Stephanas, baptized by Paul (1:16) and deserving of acquiescence (16:15–16), reinforces this scaled concept of a gendered hierarchy in this new "family of man."[57]

Contrary to recent work on the maternal imagery in Paul's letters, the way Paul briefly depicts himself as a nursing mother to the Corinthian assembly (3:1–3) neither qualifies nor undermines these authoritative dynamics of social control in continuity with patriarchy, ethnic privilege, and imperialism.[58] Indeed, this might fit with a larger argumentative strategy evident in Paul's letters: his arguments that one must suffer in order to gain, or descend in order to ascend.[59] Although Paul characterizes himself as an underling and a household manager for the divine (4:1), suffering a series of trials and tribulations (4:9–13), he still gains authority by association with the divine and occupies a preeminent place atop the human chain of command (2:7, 10; 3:9–11; 4:14–16; 5:2–4; 9:1–2, 8; 11:1; 12:28; 14:18–19, 37–38; 15:30–31). This could be one example of where Paul "passes as Other the better to govern." Certainly, such an image puts Paul's repeated claims to adaptability in another light. Paul stresses that he can "pass down," while trying to keep a range of parties, from Apollos to the prophetic women, in their place. He insists that they cannot "pass up" to the status that he maintains for himself.[60]

---

57. These references to the *oikos* of Stephanas (1:16; 16:15) also recall the importance of an ancient *imperator* learning to manage an empire by first managing his household, including especially his women, children, and slaves. Thus, household arrangements are not disconnected from these wider imperial-colonial dynamics, but are often extensions and microcosms of an interrelated order of subjection and domination.

58. For the argument that familial images build up the community and minimize Paul's authority, see Beverly Roberts Gaventa, *Our Mother Saint Paul* (Louisville: Westminster John Knox, 2007), 41–50.

59. For further reflections on this pattern in Paul's argumentation in both 1 Corinthians and Philippians, see Wire, ibid., 58–71; Marchal, *Hierarchy, Unity, and Imitation: A Feminist Rhetorical Analysis of Power Dynamics in Paul's Letter to the Philippians* (Academia Biblica 24; Atlanta: Society of Biblical Literature; Leiden: Brill, 2006), 142–43, 171–73, 185–86, 199–200.

60. Paul's ability to sacrifice or suffer a descent indicates that he has status that he can afford to lose. Such an argument for imitation would likely look very

These dynamics of imitation and communal belonging are further gendered by the way Paul seeks adherence to particular concepts of erotic normativity. As argued above, Paul argues in terms analogous to ethnic or national identity in colonized contexts by holding that communal cohesion in Corinth is threatened by improper sexual practices (5:1–2; 6:9–10, 16–20). The right kinds of eroticism involve imitating Paul's own model of self-control (7:7–9, 38). Of course, not all are as advanced as Paul, so not all will be capable of such virtuous control. In cases where a man in the community cannot behave appropriately, it is assumed that his prospective female partner will forego her opportunity for chaste elevation so that he will not descend into sin (7:36–40).[61] This androcentric plan for "saving" one partner continues an earlier argument for the sanctifying power of a believing partner and parent on an unbeliever and their children (7:12–16).[62] Similar to the conceptual and political work done by casting women as reproducers and transmitters of ethnic, racial, national, or cultural identity and difference, Paul particularly marks the women in the audience as bearers of this differentiated identity with the responsibility to imitate him and his vision of communal unity.

These rhetorics of imitation in 1 Corinthians attempt, then, to enact a form of coercive mimeticism that weaves gender and sexuality into ethnicity and empire. Yet, to accept that these arguments were as normative and authoritative as Paul implies is to reinscribe these differences without considering that the dynamics of the Corinthian community were likely varied. Accepting Paul's point of view ignores the potential import of the conspicuous and even anxious efforts of

---

different to those who have little to no status in the audience, including (at least some) women and slaves. A longer examination of the intersections of gender, sexuality, race and ethnicity, and empire should, of course, consider further the role of slaves in the community and in Paul's arguments about the community, as this also relates to Paul's ethnic reasoning and more contemporary racializations (see especially 6:19–20; 7:17–24).

61. See Wire, *Corinthian Women*, 78–90.

62. This argument violates the previous passages' arguments for keeping separate from outsiders, unbelievers, or the "immoral" inside in order to maintain the communal purity (5:1–13; 6:9–11, 15–20). For some reflections on this contradiction of sorts, see Dale B. Martin, *The Corinthian Body* (New Haven: Yale University Press, 1995), 218–19.

Paul. He attempts to convince the audience to adopt his perspectives on the wide range of issues that he intertwines with this concept of a new *ethnos* for the assembly. These rhetorical developments indicate that Paul is responding to a situation where people in Corinth are thinking and acting differently. Indeed, this might explain the targeted ways in which Paul addresses women at key points in the letter, for example, suggesting that he is more concerned with *their* imitation and obedience than others'.

This stress in the letter's mimicry argumentation might coincide with the imperial-colonial strategy to contend over the ethnically or racially "inferior" women in colonial locales. It might be especially important for Paul to convince women, especially recognizable figures like the prophetic women, to don the "Paulish" clothing of mimicry. If they did so, it would be a clear sign of his authority and an immense aid for convincing others of his legitimacy. The more well-known these women were, the more likely their conformity would encourage wider assimilation to such calls for imitation. Yet, this potential need to convince women to imitate him (or to convince others that nonconformists were a problem for the community) raises the possibility that Paul was responding to models in use in the Corinthian community that differed from his own. Instead of immediately assuming the point of view of Paul's arguments, scholars could posit that other Corinthians initiated or engaged in imitation practices.

By following another model, or following Paul's in ways he did not expect or approve, some in the community likely refused to assimilate. Otherwise, how could Paul recognize it from afar? For the Corinthians' behavior to be bothersome to Paul, writing from some distance, their imitative practice would have needed to be somehow different from Paul's (or, at least, from what Paul expected). If their imitation was, in the words of Yeğenoğlu, "purposeful and distorted," it seems more likely to have drawn Paul's attention and efforts in the ways found in 1 Corinthians. Imitation with some kind of difference cannot be received seamlessly, but registers as a dissonant practice that refuses to erase the imitator's agency. Paul's directed calls to the Corinthian women prophets, or indeed the whole letter of 1 Corinthians, could indicate that Paul has seen such dissonant imitation by these women and other members of the communities.

Once Paul's calls to imitate are considered in light of an analysis that includes gender, ethnicity, and empire, different historical and rhetorical dynamics become possible, indicating the continuing utility of feminist approaches when attending to issues of difference involved in negotiating ethnicity, one's position in relation to empire, and choices regarding erotic practices. This suggests the still vital importance of reconsidering feminist approaches to race-critical, ancient imperial, or postcolonial projects, as well as the importance of a complex feminist analysis. As the Corinthians struggled over whom, what, how, or why to imitate, similar interpretive struggles still lie before us in selecting and refining new models of teaching, thinking, and communal transformation. Such examinations of mimicry can become useful sites for rethinking agency and assimilation, resistance and reinscription, subversion and co-optation in contexts both ancient and contemporary.

CHAPTER 5

"To the Jew First and Also to the Greek"

Reading Romans as Ethnic Construction

Sze-kar Wan

In Romans, Paul attempts a construction of the Jewish *ethnos* by subverting and redefining prevailing ethnic categories used by his Roman audience and, contrary to conventional wisdom since the Reformation, by focusing on what circumcision represents: namely, a deeper commitment to the law (Rom 2:25–29). While the letter addresses Gentile converts, Paul incorporates them through code-switching into this expanded Jewish *ethnos*, changing their ethnic division, "Greeks and barbarians," into his own, "Jews and Greeks." While "Gentile" in Paul's usage retains much of its pejorative connotations, "Greek" connotes commonality and unity with "Jew."

The term *Ioudaioi* in Rom 2:17–29 might well refer to *Gentile* converts rather than to people born Jewish. In Epictetus's derisive comparison of nominal philosophers to make-believe "Jews" who in spite of their "baptism" remain unchanged in their "inner sentiments" (*pathos*), such people are "Jews" (i.e., converts to the Jesus-movement) in name only but not in reality. Paul's description of *Ioudaioi* in Romans bears remarkable similarity to Epictetus's and may reflect a concerted effort to deepen the Gentile converts' commitment to the Law, symbolized by circumcision.

Ironically, while circumcision is often constructed as a boundary separating Jews from non-Jews, it is also the path through which someone from the outside can enter the Jewish *ethnos*.

By focusing on circumcision as the central symbol of Jewishness, Paul defines Judaism in the exclusive terms of the male body. Thus, in deploying the arsenal he acquires under the Empire for his construction of Jewish universalism, he also runs the risk of re-erecting an ideological and *kyriarchal* edifice. On the surface, Paul could claim to have overcome the problem by his thoroughgoing allegorization, but his insistence on using circumcision as a synecdoche for all Jews, when it is practiced only on men, threatens the whole project.

Introduction: Ethnicity versus Ethnic Construction

There is no such thing as ethnicity. There is only ethnic construction. Thus, any appeal to such observable traits as custom, belief, taste, behavior, language, accent, phenotypes, belief system, or putative common ancestry in the pursuit of a stable definition of ethnicity is bound to fail. Ethnicity is a dynamic social phenomenon that changes with time and place and is always negotiated between potential members of an ethnic group. Different people define ethnic groups differently, depending on their status, ideological allegiance, relative position, and their purpose for group identification. The main reason for the current disagreements is that most mistake ethnic construction, which is a deliberate, conscious formulation, for a value-free, universally valid definition. In the effort to find a constant among competing formulations of ethnicity, the only constant is the lack of a constant. Ethnicity is not based on natural law, as if an "invisible hand of God" has guided a people to its formation and ultimate recognition of a "manifest destiny"; that is a national mythology. Ethnicity is the product of a deliberate construct brought into the consciousness of a group by an intentional manipulation of symbols and resources deemed common to potential members of the group.[1]

---

1. This approach to ethnicity as construct is an elaboration of Fredrik Barth's original thesis that ethnicity has more to do with boundary maintenance than cultural essentialism. See Fredrik Barth, *Ethnic Groups and Boundaries: The*

One necessary ingredient to ethnic construction is a self-conscious belonging to an ethnic group. Max Weber first introduced the notion that formation of an ethnic group depends on the subjectivity of the agents: An ethnic group "entertains . . . a *subjective belief* in their common descent . . . in such a way that this belief is important for the continuation of the nonkinship communal relationship."[2] The key phrase here, "subjective belief," places ethnicity in the realm of ideological construction. Though Seth Schwartz broadly accepts Weber's suggestion, he rightly questions its "schematic simplification." Do all agents, he asks, need to be conscious of belonging to a group? Do they need to be self-conscious to the same degree?[3] Without resolving these questions, my approach here shifts the discussion from the subjectivity of members to the intentionality of the framer of any definition of ethnicity. In other words, although it is legitimate to question whether

_____

Social Organization of Culture Difference (Bergen: Universitetsforlag; Boston: Little, Brown & Co., 1969), 9–38; repr. "Ethnic Groups and Boundaries," in *Theories of Ethnicity: A Classical Reader,* ed. W. Sollors (New York: New York University Press, 1996), 294–324. I have previously discussed Barth's theory and applied it to a reading of Romans in "Collection for the Saints as Anti-Colonial Act: Implications of Paul's Ethnic Reconstruction," in *Paul and Politics: Ekklesia, Israel, Imperium, Interpretation; Essays in Honor of Krister Stendahl,* ed. Richard Horsley (Harrisburg: Trinity Press International, 2000), 191–215. Recent attempts to supplement Barth's constructivist definition of ethnicity with "cultural" elements, as exemplified in the works of Shaye Cohen, *The Beginnings of Jewishness: Boundaries, Varieties, Uncertainties* (Berkeley: University of California Press, 1999), 5–8; and Philip Esler, *Conflict and Identity in Romans: The Social Setting of Paul's Letter* (Minneapolis: Fortress Press, 2003), 41–53, represent in my opinion a misunderstanding of Barth's fundamental position. An excellent example of created ethnicity can be found in nineteenth- and twentieth-century Shanghai. Residents of the northern Jiangsu Province, overwhelmingly women, were discriminated against and ethnicized on basis of their geography and class rather than on race. See Emily Honig, *Creating Chinese Ethnicity: Subei People in Shanghai, 1850–1980* (New Haven: Yale University Press, 1992).

2. *Max Weber on Charisma and Institution Building: Selected Papers,* ed. S. N. Eisenstadt (Chicago: University of Chicago Press, 1968), 389; emphasis added. See also his *Economy and Society: An Outline of Interpretive Society* (Berkeley: University of California Press, 1978), 4–5.

3. Seth Schwartz, *Imperialism and Jewish Society, 200 BCE to 640 CE* (Princeton: Princeton University Press, 2001), 5. In this connection, Schwartz suggests that Jewish historians have largely ignored the constructive nature of Jewishness but have simply assumed the Jews' unity and nationhood because of the historians' "Romantic nationalist ideology."

the construction of ethnicity requires all in-group members to be aware of belonging to a particular group, the framer must ultimately explain how an ethnicity is structured, what its most essential characteristics are, and who is in and who is out. The framer must persuade potential members that they will gain the most from subscribing to this particular definition of their ethnic group.[4]

This approach to ethnicity reflects both the history of the term and its current usage. The Greek term *ethnos* could mean "group," "guild," "rural folk" (as opposed to "city folk"), as well as "nation" or "people" in classical and Hellenistic literature.[5] It was an infinitely malleable term, dependent on context. The enduring question of whether to take *ethnē* as the pejorative "Gentiles" or the more neutral "nations," even within the relatively confined New Testament world, illustrates the issue. Historically, the notion of "ethnicity" gained wide currency as a result of colonization, when dominant groups brought peoples of various cultures and nationalities into contact with each other. As a rule, the dominant group does not define itself in ethnic terms, while it collects subordinate groups under different ethnic headings.[6] This is true whether we speak of settler colonization, where a dominant group installs itself as master and defines the natives as ethnic groups;[7] or of involuntary trafficking of peoples from their native lands to the metropolitan center;[8] or of voluntary migration from former colonies to

---

4. One must distinguish the subjects' awareness of the political utility of belonging to an ethnic group, which can be and often is inarticulate and non-existent, from their awareness of being members of an ethnic group, which is conscious and active even when it is not always embraced. Bill Ashcroft, Gareth Griffiths, and Helen Tiffin, *Post-Colonial Studies: The Key Concepts* (1st ed.; London: Routledge, 2000), 83.

5. Anthony Saldarini, *Matthew's Christian-Jewish Community* (Chicago: University of Chicago Press, 1994), 59–60.

6. Ashcroft, Griffiths, and Tiffin, Post-*Colonial Studies*, 83–84, which relies in part on W. W. Isajaw, "Definitions of Ethnicity," *Ethnicity* 2 (1974) 111–74, who emphasizes the experience of immigration for his understanding of ethnicity. Donald Horowitz, *Ethnic Groups in Conflict* (Berkeley: University of California Press, 1985), 149–60, has demonstrated that ethnicity is often manipulated by colonial powers to create interethnic competition, conflict, and tension.

7. Take, for example, the cases of the United States, Canada, New Zealand, Australia, or South Africa.

8. For instance, the forced transport of African slaves to Europe and its diasporized colonies.

colonial centers, where the host nation ghettoizes the new immigrant groups by insisting on identifying them by their lands of origins.

Today, the term "ethnicity" still connotes marginalization, since only the minoritized are marked by their ethnicity. When an ethnic group is identified by its country of origin, ethnicity is constructed as foreignness. Behind the question, "Where are you from?" stands a statement: "You are not one of us." As one might expect, such a construction, imposed by the dominant group, relies chiefly on observable traits such as phenotypes, language, accents, or customs that distinguish "them" from "us." This myth of difference also trades on a myth of sameness. All who are different from us are assumed to be the same as each other. For example, the dominant construction of Asian identity in the United States insists on a common Asianness among the diverse populations and cultures across Asia, even though "Asia" is the result of colonial cartography and even though "Asian" in reality embodies diverse, multiform cultures and religions. It also threatens to mask over gender and class differences—until one subclass or subgroup is elevated to the status of "honorary white."[9]

On the other hand, the marginalized often use ethnicity to inculcate group identity, build cohesion, resist assimilation, and gain political power through collective effort. Such ethnic construction is a means of survival. Initially a construction is forced upon a group by the dominant group's prior choice, but is often embraced by members of the ethnic group because of potential advantages in being so constructed. The emphasis is then placed on similarity between group members as symbolized by common ancestry, shared political aspirations, or politically expedient common experiences. For example,

---

9. The womanist problematization of feminism might illustrate the point: bell hooks writes, "By calling attention to interlocking systems of domination—sex, race, and class—black women and many other groups of women acknowledge the diversity and complexity of female experience, of our relationship to power and domination." bell hooks, "Feminism: A Transformational Politic," in *Feminist Theory: A Reader*, ed. W. K. Kolmar, F. Bartkowski (Boston: McGraw-Hill Higher Education, 2005), 466. See also her *Feminism Is for Everybody: Passionate Politics* (Cambridge, Mass.: South End, 2000); and Rey Chow, "Violence in the Other Country: China as Crisis, Spectacle, and Woman," in *Theorizing Feminism: Parallel Trends in the Humanities and Social Sciences*, ed. A. C. Herrmann and A. J. Stewart (2nd ed.; Boulder, Colo. & Oxford: Westview, 2001), 345–64.

Asians and Pacific Islanders in the United States, despite longstanding hostility at times and differences in national origin, language, and history, embrace the "Asian American" identity, because it helps organize them into a politically powerful bloc in American society.[10]

Romans as Ethnic Construction

What has all this to do with the book of Romans? It is my contention that in Romans, Paul is engaged in ethnic construction. Paul does not create what second-century writers later called a "third race" above and beyond Jews and Gentiles, or subsume Jews and Gentiles under some subgroup within Judaism.[11] Rather, Paul attempts to redefine Jewishness itself. While the affirmation of Jesus as Christ is indispensable in his reconstruction, it in no way obviates the need for other central symbols of first-century Judaism, namely belief in God and the law.[12]

---

10. An important related corollary of ethnicity as construction is multiple or "embedded" ethnic identities. Each ethnic group embodies members of multiple identities, and that allows them to form different, even competing, subgroups within the boundaries of the larger group. Under the name "Asian American," for example, can be grouped Korean American, Chinese American, Japanese American, and so on. Even though on occasions these groups choose to function as a unified movement for political reasons, and even though one could discern broad common features in Asian American "culture" (in Fredrik Barth's sense of being the by-product of group formation), on other occasions, these subgroups might choose to express their identities separately. Two recent studies have explored the possibility of understanding Paul's letters through his multiple identities: Caroline Johnson Hodge, "Apostle to the Gentiles: Constructions of Paul's Identity," *BibInt* 13, no. 3 (2005): 270–88; Jerry Sumney, "Paul and Christ-Believing Jews Whom He Opposes," in *Jewish Christianity Reconsidered: Rethinking Ancient Groups and Texts*, ed. Jackson-McCabe (Minneapolis: Fortress Press, 2007), 57–80.

11. This is basically the position of the so-called "New Perspective" school. The contours of their arguments are well known and need not be rehearsed here. See summary and critique in Pamela Eisenbaum, "Paul, Polemics, and the Problem of Essentialism," *BibInt* 13, no.3 (2005): 222–38, especially 227–32; Neil Elliott, "An American 'Myth of Innocence' and Contemporary Pauline Studies," *BibInt* 13, no.3 (2005): 239–49, especially 242–45. The recent statement, "[Paul] subsumes both Jews and Gentiles under the category of Christ-believers," by Sumney, "Paul", 64, would seem to be arguing for a similar position.

12. See Schwartz, *Imperialism*, 49–99, where he discusses the various ways of appropriating the three central pillars of Second Temple Judaism: "The one God, the one Torah, and the one Temple" (49). It should be noted that these three

In fact, contrary to ancient and modern views that Paul advocates abrogating the law, his discussion of circumcision upholds the inner spirit of the law. What complicates matters is the influx of Gentile converts who normally would undergo the rite of circumcision to signify their conversion. Paul tacitly acknowledges the centrality of circumcision by arguing that it is the means not only of keeping Gentiles out but also of providing a path for conversion to Judaism.[13] But moving beyond the physical act itself, Paul focuses on what it signifies, namely, a deeper commitment to the law. Thus, Gentiles, or as Paul prefers in Romans, "Greeks," can be included as full members of the Jewish *ethnos*.

The question must be raised, however: when Paul zeroes in on circumcision as the identity marker, has he committed himself to interpreting Jewishness as maleness? Even if my thesis is correct, that he is more concerned with reinterpreting circumcision and shifting the discussion from the signifier to the signified, one still cannot escape the implications of the central rite itself, which is applicable to only male members of this ethnic group. Can Paul's reinterpretation of circumcision overcome the limitations imposed by the maleness of the metaphor? Or does he end up perpetuating a myth of sameness that homogenizes Jewish identity by denying the reality of women? Before we can examine in detail his discussion of circumcision in 2:25–29, it is necessary to set it in the context of Paul's overall program of ethnic reconstruction.

"Jew" or "Judean"?

In translating *Ioudaios* as "Jew," I am going against the recent trend of rendering the Greek term as "Judean."[14] Historically, tying the Jewish

---

pillars are not always present at the same time in all Jewish ethnic constructions or to the same extent. That is why the absence of the Temple in Paul's formulation should not automatically rule its Jewishness out of court, just as the relative neglect of the Temple in Philo's Middle-Platonic allegorical system should not make us doubt its general Jewishness.

13. The importance of this double function of circumcision will become clear towards the end of this essay.

14. Most recently, Esler, *Conflict*, 63–74; Johnson Hodge, "Apostle", 272–73; Neil Elliott, *Arrogance of Nations: Reading Romans in the Shadow of Empire* (Minneapolis: Fortress Press, 2008), 16.

way of life to the homeland of Judea was part of a state construction of the Jewish ethnicity. According to Tacitus:[15]

> [The Jewish] rites [i.e., frequent fasts, the Sabbath, unleavened bread], whatever their origin, can be defended by their antiquity; their other customs are sinister and abominable, and owe their persistence to their depravity; for the worst rascals among other peoples, renouncing their ancestral religions, always kept sending tribute and contributing to Jerusalem, thereby increasing the wealth of the Jews. Further, the Jews are extremely loyal toward one another, and always ready to show compassion, but toward every other people they feel only hate and enmity. They sit apart at meals and they sleep apart, and although as a nation they are prone to lust, they abstain from intercourse with foreign women; yet among themselves nothing is unlawful. They instituted circumcision of the genitalia so that they could be recognized by their difference. Those who are converted to their ways follow the same practice, and the earliest lesson they receive is to despise the gods, to disown their country, and to regard their parents, children, and brothers as of little account. (*Histories* 5.5.1–2)

This passage deals with two coordinated concerns of the Romans: the containment of the Jews as a separable ethnic group and converts to Judaism. The former is evidenced by the broad stereotyping of the Jewish way of life, an act of essentializing a subject people. The latter is indicated by references to "[those] renouncing their ancestral religions" and "those who are converted to their ways." But Romans do not regard these converts in the same way as they do devotees of the Isis or Cybele cults: they construct them as disloyal to "their ancestral religions," "despising the gods," disregarding "their parents, children, brothers." Worst of all, these converts send "tribute and [contribute] to Jerusalem, thereby increasing the wealth of the Jews." The Romans thus deliberately set the Jewish converts' religious affiliation in a geopolitical binary of Rome *versus* Jerusalem (that is, Judea), thus equating their entrance into Judaism with disloyalty to the empire.

---

15. Quoted in Cohen, *Beginnings*, 43.

In this context, translating *Ioudaioi* as "Judeans" perpetuates Rome's propaganda of constructing Jews as foreigners and enemies of Rome.

Would converts themselves accept this construction? According to Suetonius:[16]

> Besides other (taxes), the Jewish tax was levied with the utmost vigor; (both) those who lived a Jewish life without registering (themselves as Jews), as well as those who concealed their origin and did not pay the tribute levied on their nation, were prosecuted as subject to the tax. (*Domitian* 12.2)

According to Shaye Cohen, "those who lived a Jewish life" but did not register themselves as Jews were converts or "Judaizers," whereas "those who concealed their origin" were Jews by birth.[17] But that would strongly indicate that converts and the state assessed Judaism differently. It seems quite possible that converts saw themselves as devoting to a Jewish cult, just as they would any of the numerous cults available in the empire, which is to say, without renouncing their allegiance to the empire or attaching themselves to the land of Judea. That is one plausible reason for refusing to pay the Jewish tax. The state, on the other hand, constructed Judaism as a political allegiance rather than a cult, thus legitimating the prevailing convention of naming residents by their countries of origin.[18] Thus, converts to Judaism are automatically constructed as "Judeans," while converts would most likely consider themselves "Jews," that is, adherents to a cult or a philosophy. How one translates *Ioudaioi*, therefore, depends entirely on whose construct one wishes to validate.

In other words, ethnic identity was a site of contestation between the converts and the state. The state conceived of conversion to Judaism as abandoning the affairs of the empire and joining another people, whose origins were traceable to Judea, but it is possible that converts did not register as *Ioudaioi* because they did not regard their adherence to Judaism as a political act in conflict with their original citizenship.

---

16. Cited in ibid., 42.

17. Ibid.

18. Amy-Jill Levine, *The Misunderstood Jew: The Church and the Scandal of the Jewish Jesus* (San Francisco: HarperSanFrancisco, 2006), 161.

Even if they realized the consequences of their conversion, and even if, occasionally, it might be advantageous to declare themselves Jews,[19] equating "Jew" (a religious or cultural adherent to the Jewish way of life) with "Judean" (a resident of the foreign land of Judea) was a legal myth imposed by the state. If this was the case, "Judean" was part of a state ideology constructed for the purpose of othering certain residents of their cities identifiable by their way of life.[20]

Identifying a group by its supposed connection to a foreign sovereign power is a standard ploy in colonialism, as well as in modern states with multiethnic groups. It designates the group as "other," "foreign," and possibly "hostile." It was a quantum leap in social construction in the United States, for example, to go from the pre-civil rights ethnic names of "negro," "black," or "African," to "African *American*," as it was a conscientized moment of self-realization for Asians living in the United States to adopt the self-identifier "Asian *American*." To support her elimination of "Jew" in favor of "Judean" for *Ioudaios*, Johnson Hodge reasons that a "double nomenclature permits an artificial separation between our understandings of *Ioudaioi* in antiquity and connection to homeland including the local temple and cult."[21] In spite of her good intentions, such a proposal holds a hidden danger. In a multiethnic state, a double nomenclature is often the only way to maintain two identities simultaneously, identities that the dominant group would prefer to conflate: "Either you are one of us or one of them." In straining at creating "Asian American" as an acceptable intellectual category, Asians living in the United States have succeeded in constructing—so far, only for themselves—a hybrid space between "us" and "them," a space that has yet to gain official recognition. To

---

19. Cohen, *Beginnings*, 68.

20. Levine raises another objection to the translation of *Ioudaioi* as "Judeans": "The argument that Jesus is not a Jew but a Galilean and then the severing of the Jews today from any connection to the people of Israel in the late Second Temple period lead to the inevitable conclusion that Jews have no connection—historically, ethically, spiritually—to the land of Israel." *Misunderstood*, 165. Levine's point is made with regard to substituting "Jew" with "Galilean," but her point still applies.

21. Johnson Hodge, "Apostle", 273. Johnson Hodge cites for support Esler, *Conflict*, 66, who makes the same point.

this day, only "Asian" appears in the United States census, not "Asian American."[22]

"Greeks and Barbarians"

In examining Paul's ethnic terminology, I start with the premise that the same ethnocentricity governs Paul as would govern anyone in his position.[23] In Romans 1:13, Paul addresses the Romans as *ethnē:* "I often intended to come to you . . . in order to have some fruit among you just as among the remaining nations (*en tois loipois ethnesin*)."[24] The phrase "the remaining nations" stands in parallel to "among you," indicating that Paul includes his Roman hearers among the *ethnē*. As to whether *ethnē* should be understood as "nations" or "Gentiles," the clue lies with the next verse (1:14), where *hellēsin te kai barbarois* ("to both the Greeks and the barbarians") functions grammatically as the dative of *opheiletēs eimi* ("I am a debtor"), but stands rhetorically in apposition to *tois loipois ethnesin* ("to the remaining nations") of the previous sentence. Greeks and Romans used the standard formula "Greeks and barbarians" to construct the peoples and nations of the world, that is, "us" versus the rest of humanity.[25] Paul uses it here in

---

22. Similarly, instead of "Turkish Germans," "Chinese Malaysians," and "Korean Japanese," the dominant elites recognize only "Turks," "Chinese," and "Koreans," all ideological classifications designed to construct these groups as foreign and therefore potentially disloyal. It is remarkable to me that, so far as I know, few if any Jewish scholars have come out in support of translating *Ioudaios* strictly as "Judean," whereas two (Cohen and Levine) have openly voiced their dissent. See footnotes 16–18 above.

23. I use "ethnocentricity" here in the neutral sense of favoring insiders over outsiders in constructing group identity. I take ethnocentricity to be an ineluctable human condition and therefore a fundamental method in analyzing any group formation and ethnic construction. So Cohen, who starts with the premise that "like numerous other groups, both ancient and modern, Jews see the world in bipolar terms: Jews versus Gentiles, 'us' versus 'them'," *Beginnings*, 1.

24. I am responsible for all translations of biblical texts except where otherwise noted.

25. This is how Josephus (*Ant.*, 16.177) uses the phrase: "It is most profitable for all people, *Greeks and barbarians* alike, to practice justice, about which our laws are most concerned and, if we sincerely abide by them, they make us well disposed and friendly to all people" (adapted from Josephus, *Jewish Antiquities*, trans. H. St. J. Thackeray (LCL; Cambridge, Mass.: Harvard University Press, 1963), 8.279); italics added.

the sense of *his readers'* ethnic categories. In that case, *ethnē* should be translated not as "Gentiles," but as "nations" or "peoples."[26]

Such a purview of the whole of humanity fits the universal scope of the book of Romans. This is already adumbrated in the thanksgiving prayer, "Your faith is announced to *the whole world*" (1:8).[27] In 15:19, Paul constructs a map that begins from Jerusalem, goes through Illyricum, and ends in Spain.[28] This move imitates Roman imperial cartography,[29] which Gayatri Spivak calls "worlding of the world on uninscribed earth."[30] This was Rome's favorite colonial strategy: inscribing an imperial discourse on the colonized space.[31] As part

---

26. So Elliott, *Arrogance*, 44–46. Translating *ethnē* as "nations" or "peoples" would resolve a longstanding problem of why Paul would want "to bear some fruit" among "Gentiles" in Rome, when the congregations had already been established by someone else and after he had vowed not to tread on grounds ploughed by someone else (2 Cor 10:13–15). For discussion of problem, see Robert Jewett, *Romans* (Minneapolis: Fortress Press, 2006), 925. If my reading is right, that Paul's scope is universal, he is using his Roman hearers' terminology to convey his evangelistic obligation to the whole inhabited world.

27. By contrast, a comparable formulation in 1 Thessalonians 1:7–8 goes no farther than Macedonia and Achaia: "You have become a model to believers in *Macedonia and Achaia*, for from you the word of the Lord has reverberated not only in *Macedonia and in Achaia*, but your trust in God has gone out in every place."

28. John L. White, *Apostle of God: Paul and the Promise of Abraham* (Peabody, Mass.: Hendrickson, 1999), 132. On the previous page, White suggests that Paul uses the phrase "Greeks and barbarians" to refer to only Gentiles. His own qualifier, that Paul does not devote much space to or detail the region he considers non-Greek (that is, the barbarians), should give us a hint that Paul intends with the phrase to refer to the inhabited *oikoumen*, which in this case he describes using his Roman hearers' preferred terminology.

29. White writes, "the physical specificity of his obligation as Christ's ambassador was probably inspired by the boundaries of the Roman Empire (to the extent he was conversant with these)." Ibid., 132.

30. Gayatri Spivak, "The Rani of Simur," in *Europe and Its Others: Proceedings of the Essex Conference on the Sociology of Literature*, vol. 1, ed. Francis Barker, Peter Hulme, Margaret Iversen, and Diana Loxley (Colchester: University of Essex Press, 1985), 128, 135. More below.

31. See the charge given to Aeneas by his father Anchises in Book 6 of the *Aeneid*, but especially 6.851–53: "Roman, remember by your strength to rule earth's peoples—for your arts are to be these: to pacify, to impose the rule of law, to spare the conquered, battle down the proud." Vergil, *The Aeneid*, trans. Robert Fitzgerald (New York: Vintage Books, 1984), 190.

of the same strategy to unify the Empire, they placed Rome in the center of the Peutinger Map, while labeling the "barbarians" on the periphery as "other."[32]

Paul alludes to, adopts, adapts—and subverts these strategies. In place of a Rome-centered map, he proposes a new metropolitan center, Jerusalem, from which the new world extends through Illyricum and ends in Spain, the ends of the earth. In this regard, Paul's friend Luke gets it right: the new gospel will propagate from Jerusalem to Judea to Samaria, "until the end of the earth" (Acts 1:8). Luke mistakes "the end" for Rome, however, when Paul really means Spain. If the world revolves around Jerusalem, eschatological events are naturally centered there as well. So, in his climactic discussion of the salvation of Israel (in reality, all humanity), Paul changes *heneken Siōn* ("on behalf of Zion," LXX Isa 59:20) to *ek Siōn* ("out of Zion," Rom 11:26b). The change is not just a matter of wanting to avoid offending his Gentile hearers,[33] but a declaration that Jerusalem shall be the Messiah-king's new seat of power. Jerusalem is not the redeemer's final destination, but his starting point, the center of his authority, indeed his capital.

I would argue that one of Paul's goals in Romans, if not the goal, is to establish Jerusalem as a new capital of an alternate empire, which is intended to replace Rome. Paul does not want to make Rome his own domain, not because he wants to avoid building on someone else's foundation or to be diplomatic,[34] but because to him, its centrality has already been displaced. Paul learns the empire-building impulse from his imperial masters but constructs a new script of sweeping cosmic scope.[35] While Paul in no way advocates any political or military revolution, he actually constructs an anti-imperial discourse in which the God of the Jews, through an apocalyptic upheaval, will triumph over

---

32. See Jewett, *Romans*, 912, for an ingenious discussion of the Peutinger Map.

33. So ibid., 703.

34. Ernst Käsemann senses Paul's insecurity and awkwardness in proposing to visit Rome in 1:11–12, which is not clarified until 15:22–29; *Romans*, trans. G. W. Bromiley (Grand Rapids: Eerdmans, 1982), 18–19; 397; see also Jewett, *Romans*, 924.

35. So also White, *Apostle*, 130–32, who argues that Paul's presentation of Christ was greatly influenced by popular imperial images prevalent around the Empire.

all earthly authorities. With Christ's death and resurrection, the end time is already breaking into the imperial arena hitherto thought to be inhabited only by the Roman colonizers. The Jewish cosmic vision is about to be realized, in which the underclasses of the rmpire will be elevated from their lowliness and the overlords of the worldly regime will be humbled in an eschatological reversal.[36]

Such a theory of Romans would go a long way towards explaining why Paul would subject his Gentile hearers to a series of discussions on Jewish topics, especially in chapters 1–11. Here, I agree with many recent scholars that Paul's primary audience is Gentiles, specifically Gentile converts.[37] To Dieter Georgi, Paul is simply "disguising his political program," since "debate with Judaism was the code for a more far-ranging conflict that brought Paul into mortal danger."[38] I would say, rather, Paul co-opts the Gentile converts into his apocalyptic framework, thus making these "Jewish" topics into their topics and installing Jerusalem as their new metropolis. Paul treats them as *Ioudaioi*.[39]

---

36. This argument is laid out in my "Collection" (see note 1, above), which depends in part on the works of Johannes Munck, *Paul and the Salvation of Mankind*, trans. Frank Clarke (Richmond: John Knox, 1959); and Dieter Georgi, *Remembering the Poor: The History of Paul's Collection for Jerusalem* (Nashville: Abingdon, 1992). An irony of this reversal is, of course, Paul's own essentialism and his definition of Judaism as male allow him no room to speak of reversal in gender terms. As for Rom 13:1–8, a passage that appears to counsel submission to the state, it can be read "from the bottom up" as a hidden, subversive script; see Sze-kar Wan, "Coded Resistance: A Proposed Rereading of Romans 13:1–7," in *The Bible in the Public Square*, ed. C. B. Kittredge, E. B. Aitkin, and J. A. Drapper (Minneapolis: Augsburg/Fortress Press, 2008), 173–84.

37. To name just a few representatives of this position: Stanley Stowers, *A Rereading of Romans: Justice, Jews, and Gentiles* (New Haven: Yale University Press, 1994), 21–33; and Elliott, *Arrogance*, 20, 44–50. But note the dissenting voice of Esler, *Conflict*, 54–63, whose reading of Romans as Paul's attempt to resolve conflicts between two ethnic groups requires him to postulate the presence of both Jews and Greeks ("Gentiles") in the Roman congregations.

38. Dieter Georgi, *Theocracy in Paul's Praxis and Theology* (Minneapolis: Fortress Press, 1991), 81.

39. Several scholars have suggested that Paul's Gentile audience might have been God-fearers who were already familiar with biblical themes: Peter Lampe, "The Roman Christians of Romans 16," in *The Romans Debate*, rev. & exp. ed., ed. K. P. Donfried (Peabody, Mass.: Hendrickson, 1991), 225; idem, *From Paul to Valentinus: Christians at Rome in the First Two Centuries* (Minneapolis: Fortress

"To the Jew First and also to the Greek"

Paul follows his announcement of indebtedness to "Greeks and barbarians" with a statement on his apostolate in 1:16–17. These two verses have frequently been viewed as the theme of the whole letter, but recently Neil Elliott has persuasively argued that they are a continuation of the thanksgiving prayer.[40] *Gar* links v. 16 with the foregoing, explaining Paul's attitude toward the *euangelion* ("I am not ashamed") and, more importantly for our purpose, the intended object of his apostolate: "Everyone who believes, to the Jew first and also to the Greek." The phrase is equivalent to "Greeks and barbarians," since both vv. 14 and 16 detail the scope of Paul's obligation to preach the *euangelion*, but Paul "code-switches" by turning a Greco-Roman universalism into his own *Jewish* universalism: As soon as he establishes the universal context with a phrase familiar to his hearers, he turns it into his own—by dividing humanity into "Jews" and non-Jews.[41]

An example of such code-switching can be found in Josephus, who in the preamble of the *Jewish War* gives the reason for writing the book:

> In these circumstances, I . . . propose to provide the subjects of the Roman Empire with a narrative of the facts, by translating into Greek the account which I previously composed in my vernacular tongue and sent to the *barbarians in the interior* [*hoi anō barbaroi*, lit., "the upcountry barbarians"]. (*J.W.* 1.3)[42]

Josephus in 1.6 clarifies that by *barbaroi* he refers to his own "kinsfolk":

> I thought it monstrous, therefore, to allow the truth in affairs of such moment to go astray, and that, while Parthians and

---

Press, 2003), 69–70; John Dominic Crossan and Jonathan Reed, *In Search of Paul: How Jesus's Apostle Opposed Rome's Empire with God's Kingdom* (New York: HarperSanFrancisco, 2004), 38–40.

40. Elliott, *Arrogance*, 17.

41. For code-switching, see Anthony Thiselton, *First Corinthians* (Grand Rapids: Eerdmans, 2000), 930.

42. Josephus, *The Jewish War*, vol. 2, trans. Henry St. John Thackeray (LCL; Cambridge: Harvard University Press, 1997), 3–5; italics added.

Babylonians and the most remote tribes of Arabia with our *kinsfolk* beyond the Euphrates and the inhabitants of Adiabene were, through my assiduity, accurately acquainted with the origin of the war . . . the *Greeks* and such *Romans* as were not engaged in the contest should remain in ignorance of these matters, with flattering or fictitious narratives as their only guide.[43]

To ingratiate himself with his Greek and Roman readers, Josephus follows Roman usage, using the derogatory "barbarian" for his fellow Jews. He even reinforces the Roman perception by mentioning the Jews in relation to the Parthians, Babylonians, and Arabs. Once he establishes this context, though, he turns the table and criticizes the Greeks and the Romans for being ignorant of the truth, which the barbarians ironically already know.

In this connection, the term "Greeks" represents all non-Jews who are as ignorant as the Romans against whom the Jews fought the war. In the *Jewish Antiquities*, Josephus uses "Greeks" in the same way (*Ant.* 16.160–61). Regarding the mistreatment against the Jews in Libyan cities in spite of the equal rights previous kings have granted them, Josephus blames the "Greeks." But it is clear from the context that to Josephus, the conflict was not just between one minority group and another, as if only the Greek residents of these cities fought against the Jews. Instead, Josephus must have intended to implicate the general citizenry of these cities, since the Jews had to appeal to Caesar for a blanket reaffirmation of the rights they had under previous regimes. Josephus's accuracy is not the question, but how he labels all non-Jews "Greeks" in order to set up an ethnic binary, "Jews" and "Greeks." Paul's subdividing of humanity is no less or more ethnocentric than Josephus's. Both make an in-group discourse universal, and both try to objectify an in-group language. "Greek" is less derogatory than "Gentile," but it is no less ethnocentric.

In using the ubiquitous phrase "Jew and Greek," Paul appeals to two ethnic myths simultaneously. All "Jews" stand together in a self-diasporizing unity in an ethnic myth of sameness, set apart from the

---

43. Ibid., 5; italics added.

"Greeks," who are all Gentiles.[44] All non-Jews are thus flattened into a sameness, regardless of their self-constructed ethnicity, for no other reason than that they are different from insiders, the "Jews." Here, Paul adopts the language of insiders—that is, *insiders* as defined by the old genealogical boundaries. Only a Jew would find it acceptable to divide humanity into "Jews and Greeks." Only a Greek or a Roman would divide the world into "Greeks and barbarians." Only a Chinese would bifurcate the world into "Chinese and barbarians." All these statements are self-evidently ethnocentric in that they privilege one ethnic group by using in-group language as the standard to evaluate others.[45] Thus, in a monstrous inversion, Paul turns the imperial ideology on its head and constructs a counter-ideology. If the Roman discourse can be termed, following Spivak, "a colonial worlding," Paul's construction is an anticolonial worlding, a counter-hegemony that ironizes and interrogates the hegemonic insistence of the imperial discourse.

Paul's adoption of the master's language to his own ends is precisely what Mikhail Bakhtin describes as the doubling or hybridity of the language.[46] It is important to note that this doubleness is not the result of juxtaposing one speaker with another, but syntactically and semantically involves the same writer, the same speaker whose use of one's voice is immediately ironized, interrogated, subverted by another, often the audience's. Linguistic hybridity is the very matrix within which two voices are held in dialogue with each other. This is

---

44. Christopher Stanley, "'Neither Jew nor Greek': Ethnic Conflict in Graeco-Roman Society," *JSNT* 64 (1996) 101–24, argues that since no one in the ancient world would call himself or herself a "Gentile" but "Greek," "Persian," and so on, Paul does not use "Greek" here to mean all Gentiles. This suggestion has proved popular in recent years: see Sumney, "Paul", 59; Elliott, *Arrogance*, 46. What must be remembered, though, is that Paul is not engaged in a sociological exercise, but in an ideological construct of ethnicity.

45. To construct outsiders as "other" by insiders' standards is of course a longstanding practice in colonial discourse. The old apartheid distinction between the neutral "white" and "colored," or "black," was similarly based on a fixed, essentialist definition of white ethnicity.

46. Basing his observation primarily on novelistic conventions and the use of "double voice" in the construction of every discourse, Bakhtin asserts that every utterance is in fact double-voiced and double-accented. Mikhail Bakhtin, *Dialogic Imagination: Four Essays* (Austin: University of Texas Press, 1981), 259–366.

exactly what Paul does here in his inversion of the Greek–barbarian distinction to his advantage.

Paul's construct is also an example of what Elisabeth Schüssler Fiorenza has termed *kyriarchy*, a comprehensive system of "domination by the emperor, lord, master, father, husband, elite propertied male."[47] Schüssler Fiorenza developed her terminology in part in conversation with Michael Halliday's concept of "anti-language":

> Anti-language . . . is a replication and subversion of the grammar and vocabulary of the dominant speech community. Anti-language is used by outsiders for constructing a reality that is an alternative reality to that of the dominant society. Even though anti-language uses words of the dominant group in a different way . . . , anti-language still reinscribes language patterns of the dominant speech community. Although language and anti-language stand in opposition to each other, both the dominant society and the subgroup share the same overarching system of meaning, since they are both part of the same imperial order.[48]

In other words, it is not merely a matter of using the master's tools for the noble purpose of resistance. In using language and categories enabled by the imperial order, Paul's construction risks falling prey to the world created by the very imperial pretension responsible for the tools, with their "message of emancipation subtly [mutating] into oppression."[49]

---

47. Elisabeth Schüssler Fiorenza, *The Power of the Word: Scripture and the Rhetoric of Empire* (Minneapolis: Fortress Press, 2007), 14.

48. Ibid., 5; Michael Halliday, *Language as Social Semiotic: The Social Interpretation of Language and Meaning* (Baltimore: University Park Press, 1978).

49. Stephen Moore, *Empire and Apocalypse: Postcolonialism and the New Testament* (The Bible in the Modern World 12; Sheffield: Sheffield Phoenix, 2006), 31; see also R. S. Sugirtharajah, *The Bible and the Third World: Precolonial, Colonial, and Postcolonial Encounters* (Cambridge: Cambridge University Press, 2001), 259–62, according to whom the questioning of internal integrity of the biblical constructs is one of the important insights of postcolonial biblical scholarship. Biblical writers themselves are complicit, even when they actively resist the colonizing forces of the empire.

Paul's Use of the Term "Greek"

Most commentators equate Paul's use of "Greek" with "Gentile."[50] But "Greek" is more neutral and less pejorative,[51] and Paul chose it over "Gentile" for a reason. "Greek" is used six times in Romans. Other than the first appearance of "Greek" in 1:14, all subsequent uses appear in the formula "Jew and Greek" (1:16; 2:9, 10; 3:9; 10:12). After Paul establishes his ethnic division in 1:16, he uses the same expression, "to the Jew first and also to the Greek," in a couplet: "There will be anguish and distress for everyone who does evil, to the Jew first and also to the Greek, but glory and honor and peace for everyone who does good, to the Jew first and also to the Greek. For God shows no partiality" (2:9–11 NRSV). The last line, "For God shows no partiality," is obviously meant to indicate symmetry between "Jew" and "Greek." The addition of "first" complicates things a bit, for it might well indicate an effort at prioritizing the Jews over Gentiles. But it does not detract from the central notion that Jews and Greeks will be judged by the same standard. Paul's point in 2:1–11 is that those who do the very things for which they criticize others (especially 2:3) deserve their just punishment, whereas those who do good will be rewarded. God does not favor one group over the other. The only criterion is the performance of good deeds.

If "Jews" and "Greeks" are placed on the same scale, then Paul can conclude that they are equally culpable. They are both, in fact, "under sin": "We charged beforehand that Jews and Greeks—all—are under sin" (3:9). The only common criterion by which both groups are accepted, therefore, is faith: "For scripture says, 'No one who believes in him will be put to shame' [Isa 28:16]. For there is no distinction between Jew and Greek; the same Lord is above all and is generous to all who call on him" (10:11–12 adapted from NRSV). In all these cases, the phrase "Jew and Greek" stresses commonality and unity between these two groups.

If "Greek" is used as a largely positive image of non-Jews, "Gentile" might well be used pejoratively, standing in distinction from Jews. The Gentiles are given the possibility of fulfilling the law, even

---

50. Most recently, Martin Goodman, *Rome and Jerusalem: The Clash of Ancient Civilizations* (New York: Alfred Knopf, 2007), 114. Goodman cites in support Josephus, *Ant.* 18.183; 20.173–78; *J.W.* 2.266–68; 3.409.

51. So Jewett, *Romans*, 140.

though "by nature" they do not possess the law: "For when Gentiles, who by nature do not have the law, do what is in the law, they without the law are a law to themselves" (2:14). Here, *physei* ("by nature") should be taken with the previous phrase rather than with the following, especially since Paul repeats the Gentiles' lack of the law. The qualifier "by nature" therefore describes the identity of the Gentiles, rather than their action.[52] In spite of the endless debate on whether or not these Gentiles are converts, Paul's point, established already in 2:1–11 and maintained through 2:12–16, is that *all*—Jews and Greeks (2:9–10)—are judged by the same criterion, namely, whether they obey the law. In this context, *nomos* ("law") refers to the Torah, the lack of which separates the Gentiles from Jews. Non-Jews are called "Gentiles" in this passage rather than "Greeks."

The citation of Isa 52:5 in Rom 2:24 also distinguishes between "Jews" and "Gentiles": "For the name of God on account of you is blasphemed among the Gentiles." "You" harks back to one who calls oneself *Ioudaios* (2:17), in particular, the one who boasts in the law but dishonors God by transgressing the law (2:23). This indictment makes sense only if it is assumed that the "Jew" is distinguished from, indeed superior to, the "Gentile" (not "Greek") because the former has the law.

Constructing "Jewishness"

If there is a difference between "Greek" and "Gentile," we should also expect different connotations of "Jew," depending on whether it is constructed as the opposite of "Greek" or of "Gentile." Using "Jew" in conjunction with "Greek" (1:16; 2:9, 10; 3:9) emphasizes the symmetry between Jews and non-Jews. Paul does not deny the priority enjoyed by the "Jew," though he does not spell it out fully. Whether one understands *prōton* of 1:16 and 2:9–10 either in the chronological or logical sense, its disappearance in 3:9, where both "Jew" and "Greek" are "under sin," should perhaps caution against attaching too much significance to it. Using "Jew" with "Gentile," either explicitly or implicitly, emphasizes the differences between Jews and non-Jews. In that case, "Jew" in 2:17 should be understood in light of "Gentiles" of 2:24 (Isa

---

52. So, among others, Jewett, ibid., 214.

52:5), since the Gentiles' taking the Lord's name in vain is construed as the direct result of the "Jews" having violated the very commandments they espouse (2:17–23). Because the insider ("Jew") has given lie to the very law of God in which they boast, the name of God has also become a byword for hypocrisy to outsiders ("Gentiles"). In this connection, Paul does not criticize mere boastfulness,[53] but the contradiction between the high-sounding moralist's words and his deeds.

If this indictment reminds us of the opening critique in 2:1–11, it is not accidental. Paul says that those who pass judgment on others ought to examine themselves, for they do the very things they condemn others for doing:

> In passing judgment on another you condemn yourself, because you, the judge, are doing the very same things. You say, "We know that God's judgment on those who do such things is in accordance with truth." Do you imagine, whoever you are, that when you judge those who do such things and yet do them yourself, you will escape the judgment of God? (2:1–3)

On the strength of this premise, Paul develops the general principle that rewards and punishments to both "Jews" and "Greeks" are based on the common criterion of obeying the law. If so, in 2:17–31, he must be criticizing those who exhibit the same penchant to commit the exact same sin of doing the opposite of what they preach.

The trouble is, in 2:1–11, Paul has the Gentiles in mind, as Stowers has convincingly shown,[54] while 2:17 addresses the "Jew" rather explicitly. At least, that is what appears on the surface. In this context, it may be wise to remember that the definition of Jewishness in the first century was decidedly fluid. It was difficult to tell a Jew from a Gentile,[55]

---

53. Stowers, *Rereading*, 143–53.

54. Ibid., 110–109; Stowers is followed and amplified by Jewett, *Romans*, 196–98; Elliott, *Arrogance*, 83–85.

55. So concludes Cohen: "How, then, did you know a Jew in antiquity when you saw one? The answer is that you did not"; *Beginnings*, 67. To respond to the charge that he neglects social distinctiveness of Jewish institutions, Cohen further explains, "On an individual-by-individual basis, the establishment of Jewishness is not clear at all. I am arguing that our modern scholarly difficulty in distinguishing Jews from non-Jews in antiquity faithfully mirrors the thinness of the boundary between Jews and Gentiles in antiquity." Ibid., 67 n. 175.

but it was nearly impossible to distinguish between members of the Jewish *ethnos* who followed the Jesus movement and those who did not. Paul's converts most likely regarded themselves as "Jews," so much so that Paul himself could facilely make that assumption, describing their conversion as turning to a "living God" (1 Thess 1:9–10). Even so erudite a philosopher as Epictetus could not distinguish between Jesus-followers and non-Jesus-followers within Judaism. Discussing the marks of a true philosopher, he compares a nominal philosopher who does not practice what he preaches to someone play-acting the part of a "Jew":

> Why then do you call yourself a Stoic? Why do you mislead the common folk? Why do you act like [*hypokrinesthai*] a Jew even though you are Greek? Don't you know how each is called a Jew, a Syrian, an Egyptian? Whenever we see someone equivocating, we are wont to say, "He is not a Jew but is only acting [*hypokrinesthai*]." But when he adopts the inner sentiments [*pathos*] of one who has been baptized [*baptizesthai*] and made his choice, then he both is in fact and is called a Jew. Likewise we are also falsely baptized [*parabaptistai*], in name Jews but in reality something else, [if we are] unsympathetic [*asympathēs*] to our own reason, far from practicing what we say, haughty as if we knew them. (Arrian, *Epictetus Diss.* 2.9.19–21)[56]

Judging from the references to baptism and to someone "hypo-critizing" as a "Jew," Epictetus must have mistaken Gentile conversion to the Jesus movement for conversion to Judaism. These converts, because they are unsympathetic to Jewish *philosophia*, are little more than play-acting "Jews." In other words, as late as the end of the first century, the dividing line between Jesus-followers and non-Jesus-followers was nonexistent to outsiders. Thus, Martin Goodman concludes: "No one in the Christian community before 70 seems to have seen any problem in a Jew who had joined the assembly of the faithful

---

56. The reference was first made known to me in Jewett, *Romans*, 221–22. Epictetus relies on a series of repetitions and word plays to make his point: *hypokrinesthai* used twice, and the contrast between *pathos* and *asympathēs* and between *baptizesthai* and *parabaptistais*.

continuing to think of himself or herself as Jewish as well as a follower of the new movement."[57]

All this raises the possibility that by *Ioudaios*, Paul might also be referring to Gentile converts who are consciously joining a movement within Judaism that honors Jesus as Messiah. In fact, several clues in the ensuing passage detailing the supposed hypocrisy of the "Jew" point in that direction. The use of *eponomazesthai* ("to call oneself") in connection with *Ioudaios* in 2:17 echoes Epictetus's mocking derision that someone calls himself (*legein heauton*) a Stoic. The strength of Epictetus's remark is derived from a distinction between being a Jew "in reality" (*tō onti*) and being "called" (*kaleitai*) one, a distinction he makes explicit in the next line using the more conventional contrast between *logō* and *ergō*. Just as Epictetus uses the notion to describe (false) converts, Paul might well use it for the same purpose. The use of *katēchousthai* ("to be instructed") to describe the self-designated Jew's instruction in the law reminds one of the use of the same word in Galatians 6:6, where the instruction of converts is in view.[58] Likewise, what Jewett calls the philosophical notion of "proof" used to demonstrate hypocrisy in 2:18 also suggests that the "Jew" might be more at home in the Hellenistic philosophical tradition than in traditional Judaism.[59]

The Ambivalence of Circumcision

The most prominent part of Paul's argument in 2:17–29, of course, elaborates on circumcision (2:25–29), an issue that thrusts to the forefront the question of insider-outsider boundaries. But this discussion is perhaps the strongest argument that Paul includes Gentile converts

57. Goodman, *Rome and Judaism*, 525. See also Denise Kimber Buell and Caroline Johnson Hodge, "The Politics of Interpretation: The Rhetoric of Race and Ethnicity in Paul," *JBL* 123, no.2 (2004): 235–51; Sumney, "Paul", 76–77. Acts 11:26 and 1 Peter 4:16 are evidence that by the end of the first century or start of the second, Jesus-followers began to adopt the self-referential term *christianoi*. This raises the question of how Nero was able to distinguish Christians from Jews in the mid-sixties or, perhaps more relevantly, if he ever was.

58. Jewett, *Romans*, 224.
59. Ibid., 223–24.

as "Jews." While circumcision during the Second Temple period had become the defining characteristic of Judaism,[60] it received the most intense attention when confronted by the non-Jews' abhorrent revulsion.[61] After all, circumcision became problematic only for those who did not grow up with a cultivated disposition towards it. Circumcision was singled out as an ethnic marker when Gentiles used it to construct the otherness of Judaism and when Jews relied on it to distinguish themselves from outsiders. Both sides used it to separate one from another. Thus, circumcision became a central symbol of Judaism if and only if there was opposition to it. It is a classic case of an ethnic identity constructed by outsiders, imposed on but also embraced by insiders.[62]

But if circumcision separates Jews from non-Jews, it also marks a path for inclusion into the Jewish community.[63] It is therefore no accident that Paul seizes on the topic to teach his Gentile converts the true meaning of being Jewish. Paul does so by distinguishing circumcision from doing the law. The theme of obeying the law runs through 1:18–2:29, thereby establishing it as *the* criterion for judgment. As Jouette Bassler has shown, 1:18–32 and 2:1–11 are linked by a repetition of *prassein* ("to practice," 1:32 [2x]; 2:1–3), *poiein* ("to do," 1:28, 32; 2:3), and cognates of *krinein* ("to judge," 2:1–3).[64] In fact, the linkage goes even deeper, as the act of circumcision gives way to doing the law: *nomon prassein* ("to practice the law," 2:25); *ta dikaiōmata tou nomou phylassein* ("to keep the righteous requirements of the law," 2:26); *krinein* ("to judge," 2:27). The true Jew is one who

---

60. Survey of material can be found in Jewett, ibid., 231–33.

61. All the texts surveyed by Jewett, *Beginnings*, 231–32, have to do with distinguishing Jews from Gentiles.

62. According to Cohen, ibid., 109–39, especially 135–39, circumcision became a prominent ethnic marker for Jews in mid-second century BCE, coinciding with the time Jewishness was constructed as separation from Gentiles. By the end of the second century, Greek writers began emphasizing the Jewish refusal to intermingle with them. What had been a survival strategy on the part of diaspora Jews had become a prominent issue among Jews living in Judea as well by the second half of the second century BCE.

63. So Paula Fredriksen, *From Jesus to Christ: New Testament Images of Jesus of Nazareth* (New Haven: Yale University Press, 2000), 142–53; and Cohen, *Beginnings*, 136.

64. Jouette Bassler, *Divine Impartiality and a Theological Axiom* (Chico, Calif.: Scholars Press, 1982), 131–33.

moves beyond the physicality of circumcision and does what circum-cision signifies.

Paul's contemporaries, including Josephus and Philo, had been reluctant to abandon the rite of circumcision. Even Philo, while extol-ling what circumcision stands for allegorically, namely, the excision of fleshly passion, excoriates the extreme allegorists who conclude that the rite of circumcision is thus no longer needed (*De migratione Abrahami* [On the Migration of Abraham] 89–93).[65] Paul, by con-trast, abandons circumcision altogether as an ethnic marker by driv-ing a wedge between the rite and what it points to, namely, the law. Whereas before, circumcision took on the essentialist characteristic of Jewishness, Paul replaces circumcision with praxis by refocusing on the inner requirements of the law. The replacement of circumci-sion by the law is so thorough that circumcision can, allegorically speaking, be reversed: "If you are a transgressor of the law, your cir-cumcision has become uncircumcision" (2:25), and "he who keeps the requirements of the law can turn his uncircumcision into cir-cumcision" (2:26). The roles of the judge and the judged are reversed accordingly, for "the natural uncircumcision, by completing the law, will judge [him] who is, through the letter and circumcision, a trans-gressor of the law" (2:27). Doing what is required by the law has replaced circumcision as the ultimate condition for Jewishness. Thus constructed, Jewishness depends on fulfilling the law, and uncircum-cised Gentile converts can be accepted as genuine Jews, provided they do what the law says.[66]

---

65. See David M. Hay, "Philo's References to Other Allegorists," *SPhilo* 6 (1979–80): 41–75; Richard D. Hecht, "The Exegetical Contexts of Philo's Inter-pretation of Circumcision," in *Nourished with Peace: Studies in Hellenistic Juda-ism in Memory of Samuel Sandmel*, ed. Frederick E. Greenspahn, Earle Hilgert, and Burton L. Mack (Chico, Calif.: Scholars Press, 1984), 51–79; John M. G. Barclay, "Paul and Philo on Circumcision: Romans 2:25–29 in Social and Cul-tural Context," *NTS* 44, no.4 (1998): 536–66.

66. Whether or not *Ioudaios* of 2:17 is intended to include converts or refer to them exclusively does not ultimately invalidate my point here, which is that Paul has redrawn the ethnic boundaries that distinguish true Jews from outsiders. In so doing, Paul has not created what later Christians called the "third race," since, lest we forget, the central criterion is fulfillment of the *Jewish* Torah, which, along with God and the Temple, remained one of the three major symbols of Judaism during the Second Temple period, as Schwartz has shown (*Imperialism*,

Conclusion

Recently, Mark Nanos has called for a new model of interpreting Paul's letters in the context of an inter/intra-Jewish discourse instead of an inter/intra-Christian discourse.[67] This essay is a contribution in that direction. In particular, I suggest it may be more profitable to evaluate Paul as a framer of ethnic construction driven by his own theological and anti-imperial ideology. He is as much concerned with including Gentile converts in his Jewish construct as he is with elaborating an alternative empire that centers in Jerusalem.

But in deploying the arsenal he acquires under the empire, he also runs the risk of re-erecting its ideological and *kyriarchal* edifice. The insistence on using circumcision as a synecdoche for all Jews, when it is practiced on men, threatens the whole project. On the surface, Paul could claim to have overcome the problem by his thoroughgoing allegorization, which enables him to distance Jewishness from the physical rite itself. But his final formulation of genuine faith cannot escape his male limitations. As Joel Marcus has argued, *akrobystia* means literally "foreskin."[68] In so, the contrast between *peritomē* ("circumcision") and *akrobystia* in 2:25–29 is between two types of Jewish identity, both centered around the male gender. Thus, 4:10–12 literally reads:

> How then is righteousness reckoned [to him]? While he was in circumcision or in his foreskin? Not in circumcision but in his foreskin. And he received the sign of circumcision as a seal of the righteousness of his in-the-foreskin faith, in order that he be the father of all who believe through the foreskin (in order that righteousness be reckoned to them), as well as the father

---

49–99; see note 12 above). There might be an infinite number of permutations of these elements, but all constructions of Jewishness appeal to at least one of these elements in some form. If that is the case, Paul is not creating a new race but is redefining an old one. Naturally uncircumcised outsiders can be considered *Jewish*, provided they follow the law.

67. Mark Nanos, "How Inter-Christian Approaches to Paul's Rhetoric Can Perpetuate Negative Valuations of Jewishness—Although Proposing to Avoid That Outcome," *BibInt* 13 (2005): 255–69, especially 267.

68. Joel Marcus, "The Circumcision and the Uncircumcision in Rome," *NTS* 35, no.1 (1989): 67–81.

of circumcision—not only to those of circumcision but also to those who walk in the footstep of the foreskin faith of our father Abraham.

The contrast here is not between circumcision and uncircumcision, but between two types of faith, one while the foreskin is still on, the other when it is removed. Paul at the end cannot escape the trap he laid for himself.

PART II

Race, Gender, and Ethnicity

Shaping the Discipline of Early Christian Studies

CHAPTER 6

God's Own People
Specters of Race, Ethnicity, and Gender in Early Christian Studies

Denise Kimber Buell

The figures of "haunting" and "inheritance" can contribute to ethically engaged forms of New Testament and Early Christian studies. Haunting enables us to think about how ancient texts have variously helped produce, resist, and transform contingent, modern forms of human classification. Haunting also helps us to speak about how our visions for the future are unpredictably yet ethically bound up with our relationship to what has come before us.

Ancient texts inside and outside the New Testament presume that humans can be classified in terms of kinds of difference, including differences in *genos, ethnos,* and *laos,* as well as gender, status, forms of religious worship, age, wealth, and other factors. Some texts define those who are "in Christ," who obey Christ (or obey God as Jesus did), and/ or who avow Jesus' messianic or saving status as forming a people (a *laos, ethnos,* or *genos*). These are the people of the God whose belonging may be charted through patrilineal descent (for example, God, Abraham, Christ) or from a mother with the correct status (for example, from Sarah, not Hagar). Claims of peoplehood in texts *re-membered* as Christian are resources from which hegemonic religious, ethnic, national, and racial belonging have subsequently been constructed. But they also have been used to challenge and transform dominant meanings of race and ethnicity. Some racialized practices in specific modern contexts constitute an inheritance from different early Christian traditions. Unless we adequately acknowledge that inheritance, we are at risk of passing on those practices to future generations.

⑤⑤⑤⑤⑤⑤⑤⑤⑤⑤⑤⑤⑤

Introduction

> I will call them my people (*laos*), who were not my people (*laos*);
> and her beloved, who was not beloved.
>
> ROMANS 9:25

For many white, liberal Christians in the United States, speaking in terms of being the people of God may have no racial or ethnic connotations.[1] But consider two strikingly different contemporary appeals to New Testament texts regarding peoplehood that are made precisely in the context of contemporary race issues. As Vincent Wimbush notes, Romans 9:25 (see epigraph above) serves as the epigraph to Toni Morrison's novel *Beloved*.[2] In this context, the Pauline text, itself a reworking of earlier prophetic claims in Hosea, seems to counter a denial of peoplehood (and belovedness) to those who share the legacy of enslavement. In addition, this Romans passage foregrounds change: a shift from non-people to a people.[3] The choice of a biblical text for the novel's epigraph is unlikely to be coincidental, but Morrison does not use it to say that peoplehood entails membership in a Christian community.

---

1. This essay is revised from a paper delivered at the "Race, Gender, and Ethnicity in Early Christian Studies" conference, Harvard Divinity School, Cambridge, Mass., March 2007. I am especially grateful to Melanie Johnson-DeBaufre, Christina Fanciullo, Laura Nasrallah, and Elisabeth Schüssler Fiorenza for critical feedback in the revision process. My thanks also to Wallace Best for his response to the conference version of the paper.
2. Vincent Wimbush, "'We Will Make Our Own Future Text': An Alternate Orientation to Interpretation," in *True to Our Native Land: An African American New Testament Commentary*, ed. Brian K. Blount (Minneapolis: Fortress Press, 2007), 49–51.
3. See also 1 Peter 2:9–10, cited above. Thanks to Melanie Johnson-DeBaufre for this point (conversation).

In sharp contrast to Morrison's use of Romans, the white suprem-acist Christian preacher Jarah Crawford interprets a different Pauline passage from Galatians to justify his sense of the racialized limits of Christian belonging.[4] While Crawford does not deny the possibility that Jews and those racialized as other than "white" can convert to Christianity, he insists that they become Christians "not as heirs in the family of God but as servants" because "they are not from the seed of Abraham. They will not share the inheritance of Israel."[5] Craw-ford clearly has in mind Galatians 3:28–29. ("There is neither Jew nor Greek, there is neither slave nor free, there is no male and female; for you are all one in Christ Jesus. And if you are Christ's, then you are Abraham's offspring (*sperma*), heirs (*klēronomoi*) according to the promise.") He seems both to presume a notion of race as "fixed" and that Christian belonging preserves hierarchies of differences, includ-ing racial differences, among humans.

Crawford racializes Christian belonging by naturalizing "white-ness" as a fixed characteristic, linked putatively to genealogy ("seed"), signifying superior access to salvation. At the same time, he seems to suggest that religious identity is fluid. Morrison more radically under-mines the idea that race is fixed by highlighting transformation from nonpeople to people, yet her novel does not depict Christian conver-sion as the solution for racism.

Both Crawford and Morrison show that ideas re-membered and transmitted as Christian have been inherited and claimed in very dif-ferent contexts towards very different ends, including differing under-standings of race. In his invocation of heirs and distinction between "family" and "servants," Crawford makes chillingly clear that our present contexts inform the kind of "inheritance" we craft from bibli-cal sources, and that contests over inheritance are a matter of power

---

4. See Denise Kimber Buell, "Early Christian Universalism and Modern Forms of Racism," in *The Origins of Racism*, ed. Benjamin Isaac, Miriam Eliav-Feldon, and Joseph Ziegler (Cambridge: Cambridge University Press, forthcom-ing 2009); see also analysis of Crawford's sermons and writings in James A. Aho, *The Politics of Righteousness: Idaho Christian Patriotism* (Seattle: University of Washington Press, 1990).

5. Jarah Crawford, *Last Battle Cry* (Middlebury, Vt.: Jan, 1984), 67; cited and analyzed in Aho, *Politics*, 99.

struggles that often define some as incapable of being heirs. Morrison poses a challenge to Crawford's claim to embody the authentic and authorized heir to Christian testament texts, but her novel ends by suggesting that there are inheritances passed down over time that future generations might not want to inherit.[6]

Inside and outside the New Testament, texts remain that presume that humans can be classified in terms of kinds of difference, including differences in *genos, ethnos,* and *laos,* as well as differences in gender,[7] status, forms of religious worship, age, wealth, and other factors. Some texts define those who are "in Christ," obey Christ (or obey God as Jesus did), and who avow Jesus' messianic or saving status as forming a people (a *laos, ethnos,* or *genos*)—the people of the God who made a covenant with Abraham and Israel, a people with unique access to salvation, a people whose belonging may be charted through patrilineal descent (for example, God, Abraham, Christ), or a people from a mother with the correct status (for example, from Sarah, not Hagar). Claims of peoplehood in texts *re-membered* as Christian are resources from which hegemonic religious, ethnic, national, and racial belonging have been constructed.[8] But they also have been used to challenge and transform dominant meanings of race and ethnicity.[9] When belonging

---

6. See especially the final, unpaginated pages of *Beloved*, which include:

> Everybody knew what she was called, but nobody anywhere remembered her name. Disremembered and unaccounted for, she cannot be lost because no one is looking for her. . . . It was not a story to pass on. They forgot her like a bad dream. . . . Remembering seemed unwise. . . . It was not a story to pass on. . . . This is not a story to pass on. Down by the stream in back of 124, her footprints come and go, come and go. They are so familiar. Should a child, an adult place his feet in them, they will fit. Take them out and they disappear again as though nobody ever walked there. By and by all trace is gone, and what is forgotten is not only the footprints but the water too and what is down there (Morrison, *Beloved* [New York: Penguin, 1987], epilogue).

7. In some contexts, *genos* can denote gender difference.

8. One might also add "nation" to the list here. Anthony D. Smith makes an extended argument for the centrality of biblical notions of peoplehood, interpreted through various Christian vectors, for the production of the "nation." *Chosen Peoples: Sacred Sources of National Identity* (Oxford: Oxford University

to a *genos, ethnos,* or *laos* is articulated using genealogical or procreative rhetoric or is regulated through norms and practices that classify humans into different sexes, such belonging is also gendered. Scholars of the New Testament and early Christian history must wrestle with how to make sense of ancient rhetoric and practices about peoplehood.[10] We should expose and assess their ambivalent legacies inside and outside of Christian contexts.[11]

In discussing Morrison and Crawford, I may appear to advocate that New Testament and early Christian studies address "reception history" and ignore ancient contexts and rhetoric. But this is not the case. As my recent study of second- and early-third-century sources that construe "Christian" belonging as membership in a *genos, ethnos,* or *laos* demonstrates, I also value close readings of ancient texts.[12] But

---

Press, 2003). Benjamin Isaac has argued that classical sources, rather than Christian or Jewish ones, anticipate and serve as a source for the modern constructions of racism. *The Invention of Racism in Classical Antiquity* (Princeton: Princeton University Press, 2004).

9. See, for example, "the cross of Christ has created a new nation of men [sic] . . . This new nation, this sturdy race is unique in the history of mankind [sic]. It is a race created not by blood, but by grace." John LaFarge, Catholic leader in Jamaica, from his book, *The Catholic Viewpoint on Race Relations* (Garden City, N.Y.: Hanover House, 1956), 111; cited in Franklin H. Littell, "Religion and Race: The Historical Perspective," in *Race: The Challenge to Religion: Original Essays and an Appeal to the Conscience from the National Conference on Religion and Race,* ed. Mathew Ahmann (Chicago: Henry Regnery Co., 1963), 44; see also the rethinking of "people of God" in Rena Karefa-Smart with Gordon E. Truitt, "A Call to Move Beyond the Heritage of Christian Racism," in *Ending Racism in the Church,* ed. Susan E. Davies and Sister Paul Teresa Henesee (Cleveland: Pilgrim, 1998), esp. 114–19.

10. See now Lawrence M. Wills, *Not God's People: Insiders and Outsiders in the Biblical World* (Lanham, Md.: Rowman & Littlefied, 2008), 1–14 and 101–215. Although her focus is not on New Testament or early Christian texts, see the important study by Regina Schwartz, *The Curse of Cain: The Violent Legacy of Monotheism* (Chicago: University of Chicago Press, 1997).

11. Regardless of a scholar's own theological commitments—or lack thereof—we all can articulate what kinds of claims about peoplehood and difference will help or hinder the kind of world we want to inhabit and be accountable to how our views are partial and located. For an excellent recent example, see Sylvester A. Johnson, *The Myth of Ham in Nineteenth Century American Christianity: Race, Heathens, and the People of God* (New York: Palgrave, 2004), 112–31.

12. Denise Kimber Buell, *Why This New Race: Ethnic Reasoning in Early Christianity* (New York: Columbia University Press, 2005).

I presume that my readings are contingent and situated, informed by locations and commitments. These interpretations are informed by my concerns to trace how self-definition as a people in these texts rhetorically structures inclusions and exclusions in ways that anticipate or contrast with later racist, ethnocentric, or anti-Jewish rhetoric. In that book, I also show that some modern encounters, especially liberal "secular" and Christian encounters, with these early texts have too often produced interpretations of early Christian history that efface, ignore, or deem "heterodox" early Christian rhetoric of peoplehood. This tendency may arise from a laudable goal—to define and produce Christianity as a nonracist formation—but one that has paradoxically reinforced white, Eurocentric privilege and anti-Judaism.[13]

Not surprisingly, some readers are uncomfortable with my use of "race" for ancient texts and my deliberately provocative interchangeable use of "ethnicity" and "race" in *Why This New Race*. There, I used "race" deliberately to trouble the sense that we automatically shut off contemporary presuppositions when considering temporally and culturally distant discussions of human difference and to sharpen the possibility that texts produced in different languages and contexts might nonetheless be resources for the production of modern materializations of "race" and "ethnicity." Without arguing that ethnicity and race are always the same, I also wanted to trouble the easy assumption that any difference between them is stable; too often, "ethnicity" is now used to speak about ancient ways of marking collective difference, when "race" was used in the nineteenth and early-twentieth centuries.

I have also realized that my analysis in *Why This New Race* performs its own kind of occlusion by (too implicitly) focusing on modern interpretive practices emblematic of those with socially or theologically privileged locations. That is, I spend less time articulating my project's relationship to interpretive countertraditions than I do in producing my own readings of ancient texts. In seeking to address these two disparate issues, I have come to view *haunting* and *inheritance* as valuable, interlocking figures. This essay considers how these

---

13. See Buell, ibid., especially 10–21, 166–69.

terms can contribute to ethically engaged forms of New Testament and Early Christian Studies.

I argue that haunting offers New Testament and early Christian studies a useful way to negotiate the insistence on situational particularity (for example, the widespread view that "race" is a "modern" construct, but also that "race," "ethnicity," and "gender" have only context-specific meanings) while also allowing us to consider the evidence for the "afterlives" of ancient texts and ideas, including Christian Testament ones. Haunting enables us to think about how ancient texts have variously helped produce, resist, and transform contingent, modern forms of human classification.[14] Haunting also helps us to speak about how our visions for the future are unpredictably yet ethically bound up with our relationship to what has come before us. That we are dealing with legacies materialized in specific contexts makes the concept of inheritance also important to foreground.[15]

After expanding these points in the next section, I focus on the category of "race" with attention to how race articulates with ethnicity and gender. Both the mobile and variable instantiations of race and Christian articulations of collective belonging as membership in a people unsettle assertions of race as a category distinguished from ethnicity, national, civic, or religious identities by attributions of both "fixity" and modernity. I then suggest three of many possible

14. My motivation in using the imagery of haunting, specters, and ghosts arises in part because, since the early 1990s, an astonishing number of works in literary theory, sociology, history, and political philosophy have appeared in which foreground haunting is a conceptual rubric. Often feminist, queer, poststructuralist, or otherwise committed to cultural critique and ethical transformations, these works show little evidence of recognizing their theological resonances and implications. Some of the many examples include: José B. Monléon, *A Specter is Haunting Europe: A Sociohistorical Approach to the Fantastic* (Princeton: Princeton University Press, 1990); Jacques Derrida, *Specters of Marx: The State of the Debt, the Work of Mourning, and the New International*, English trans. by Peggy Kamuf (French original, 1993; New York: Routledge, 1994); Avery Gordon, *Ghostly Matters: Haunting and the Sociological Imagination* (Minneapolis: University of Minnesota Press, 1997); Wendy Brown, *Politics Out of History* (Princeton: Princeton University Press, 2001); Helen Sword, *Ghostwriting Modernism* (Ithaca: Cornell University Press, 2002); and Carla Freccero, *Queer/Early/Modern* (Durham: Duke University Press, 2006).

15. See Derrida, *Specters*, especially 16.

inheritances from New Testament and early Christian texts and traditions with which scholars and activists have reckoned or might reckon further. Finally, the conclusion situates my remarks more specifically in terms of disciplinary training and approaches.

Haunting and Inheritance

> In the world and between us as analysts and the worlds we encounter to translate into world-making words are hauntings, ghosts, and gaps, seething absences, and muted presences.
>
> AVERY GORDON, *GHOSTLY MATTERS*[16]

> One never inherits without coming to terms with some specter.
>
> JACQUES DERRIDA, *SPECTERS OF MARX*[17]

For the last decade, I have offered a course on haunting.[18] Haunting offers a powerful way to speak about forces that affect us profoundly

---

16. Gordon, *Ghostly*, 21.

17. Derrida, *Specters*, 21.

18. The most recent version of this course is REL 305T—Haunted: Ghosts in the Study of Religion (Williams College). The course description on my syllabus includes:

> Haunting offers a powerful way to speak about forces that affect us profoundly while remaining invisible or elusive. "What is it that holds sway over us like an unconditional prescription? . . . The distance between us and that which commands our moves—or their opposite, our immobility—approaches us: it is a distance that closes in on you at times, it announces a proximity closer than any intimacy or familiarity you have ever known" (Avital Ronell, *Dictations: On Haunted Writing* [1986] xvi–xvii). The figure of the ghost has been developed by those grappling with the ongoing effects of modern slavery, colonialism, state-sponsored terrorism, the holocaust, and personal trauma and loss. This course takes memory, history, and "identity" as three central concepts through which haunting has been explicitly elaborated, or from which it can be extrapolated (for example, where vision and visibility are salient to cultural analysis). The relationship of haunting/ghosts to social arrangements of power will be especially important, as we explore how ghosts disrupt, critique, or expose prevailing arrangements of power. Also central for discussion will be

while remaining invisible or elusive. More than simply the stuff of campfire stories or teen horror flicks, the figure of the ghost has been developed by those grappling with the ongoing personal and collective effects of rape, gender and sexual identity, modern slavery, colonialism, state-sponsored terrorism, and genocide.

I am using haunting not simply as "shorthand . . . for just about any kind of troubled or troubling relationship," but rather as a call to transformative ethics.[19] In this sense, I draw especially on Avery Gordon's and Jacques Derrida's suggestions that justice ought to be the motivation for speaking in terms of hauntings and ghosts.[20] As Gordon puts it, "if the *dead* start to take the *living* back to the past, *it is connected to the labor aimed at creating in the present a place (a past or future), a something that must be done.*"[21] But as Derrida stresses, haunting is not simply the force exerted by the past on the present, the dead on the living; the specter is *untimely*, bringing future possibilities both dreaded and utopian, as in the opening line of Marx's *Manifesto of the Communist Party*: "A specter is haunting Europe—the specter of communism."[22]

To speak in terms of haunting is to question assumptions about continuities and discontinuities between the past, present, and future, even as it centers the present (one is haunted in the present). To speak

---

the usefulness of the ghostly in complicating how we imagine the relationship between the individual and the social. Building on the insights about memory, history, and identity that haunting has been used to address, this course will challenge you to explore the study of religion by way of its "seething absences." We shall ask how the study of religion has endeavored to address loss, trauma, and its persistent effects, what "holds sway" over various approaches to the study of religion, as well as how "religion" constitutes its own ghostly presence, haunting other domains.

19. Helen Sword has wryly and accurately noted that "ghosts" and the verb "to haunt" as these appear especially in literary criticism and new historicism have an "extraordinary flexibility" that can offer "a kind of interpretive cloud cover" to those seeking "to escape semantic precision." Sword, *Ghostwriting*, 165.

20. Derrida, *Specters*, xix–xx; Gordon, *Ghostly*, for example, 63–64.

21. Gordon, *Ghostly*, 182–83, italics in the original. Gordon is here revising a statement by Michel de Certeau in his *The Writing of History*, trans. Tom Conley (New York: Columbia University Press, 1988), 101.

22. Derrida, *Specters*, 4.

in terms of haunting helps us to reject the equally problematic notions of causal determinism or sameness between ancient and modern contexts. For the topics of race, ethnicity, and gender in early Christian studies, haunting offers one way to avoid the trap of anachronism or the implication that concepts we might wish to transform or undo are timeless, static, or inevitable.

Instead, a haunting expresses a relationship or possibility not yet fully realized or one that has become shadowy in the present. Always double-edged, a "haunting always harbors the violence . . . that made it, and the . . . utopian," the potential for alternatives to present social structures and ethical relations.[23] To attend to ghostly presences is to write "stories that repair representational mistakes, but also strive to understand the conditions under which a memory was produced in the first place, toward a countermemory, for the future."[24] For those committed to social and ethical transformation but who do not fit comfortably within a religious community, haunting offers a rubric comparable to the language of theological re-visioning.[25]

That is, what I am proposing shares important features with (indeed, is inspired by) both liberation theologians and scholars concerned with the legacies and implications of New Testament and early Christian materials, regardless of religious affiliation (or lack thereof). All of us center inquiry about the past in the present, with a view to the future. The primary historical narrative generated and employed by such scholars and activists is one of struggle and multiplicity: there was no original essence of Christianity; instead, we should imagine struggles of earnest, if often contentious, individuals and groups framing and enacting their differing visions of God's *basileia*.[26]

---

23. Gordon, *Ghostly*, 207.

24. Ibid., 22.

25. I see haunting as one mode of memory transmission, one that preserves the ethical accountability of the living without denying agency to nonhuman, nonliving phenomena. I am currently writing a book that elaborates these questions of agency, haunting, and memory further.

26. See especially the works of Elisabeth Schüssler Fiorenza, including *In Memory of Her: A Feminist Theological Reconstruction of Christian Origins* (New York: Crossroads, 1983), esp. 92; *Sharing Her Word: Feminist Biblical Interpretation*

When this narrative is conjoined with contemporary struggles
to create the structures and conditions for ethical relations and to
repair existing material injustices (including poverty, racism, heterosexism, and sexism), visions for the future may be linked with
re-visions of suppressed, marginalized perspectives based on our readings of ancient sources.[27] These submerged perspectives are made visible precisely because of contemporary reflections and future visions.
But the interpreter may also understand these traces, these "seething
absences" as, in a crucial sense, evidence for paths-not-taken which
may bear an imperfect, wavering resemblance to those being charted
for the future. The element of the labor that modulates between envi-
sioning a more just future and the re-visioning needed to see these
traces can be imagined as a willingness to acknowledge and engage
haunting presences.

Haunting suggests that invisible forces have a sort of agency; they
have desires and designs upon the living. Interpreters such as Avery

in Context (Boston: Beacon, 1998), especially 113–14; and Jesus and the Politics
of Interpretation (New York: Continuum, 2000), 28, 48–51, 168–74; see also
Sheila Briggs, "'Buried with Christ': The Politics of Identity and the Poverty of
Interpretation," in The Book and the Text, ed. Regina Schwartz (Oxford: Basil
Blackwell, 1990), 276–303; Elizabeth A. Castelli and Hal Taussig, "Drawing
Large and Startling Pictures: Reimagining Christian Origins by Painting Like
Picasso" in Reimagining Christian Origins: A Colloquium for Burton L. Mack, ed.
Castelli and Taussig (Valley Forge, Pa.: Trinity Press International, 1996), 3–20;
Karen L. King, The Gospel of Mary of Magdala: Jesus and the First Woman Apostle
(Santa Rosa, Calif.: Polebridge, 2003), 155–90; Elizabeth A. Castelli, Martyr-
dom and Memory: Early Christian Culture Making (Gender, Theory, and Religion;
New York: Columbia University Press, 2004); Melanie Johnson-DeBaufre, Jesus
among Her Children: Q, Eschatology, and the Construction of Christian Origins
(Harvard Theological Studies 55; Cambridge: Harvard University Press, 2005).
    27. I think here, for example, of the work of the Feminist Sexual Ethics
Project, directed by Bernadette Brooten at Brandeis University, with its work on
the legacies of slavery in the lives of girls and women in Christianity, Judaism,
and Islam (see http://www.brandeis.edu/projects/fse/). See also Clarice Mar-
tin, "The Haustafeln (household codes) in African American Biblical Interpreta-
tion: 'Free Slaves' and 'Subordinate Women,'" in Stony the Road We Trod: African
American Biblical Interpretation, ed. Cain Hope Felder (Minneapolis: Fortress
Press, 1991), 206–31; Curtiss Paul DeYoung, Michael O. Emerson, George
Yancey, and Karen Chai Kim, United by Faith: The Multiracial Congregation as an
Answer to the Problem of Race (Oxford: Oxford University Press, 2003).

Gordon interpret hauntings in terms of the often unnoticed but real effects of "worldly power" and the "shared structure of feeling, a shared possession, a specific type of sociality" that subtly connect individuals materially, emotionally, and conceptually in specific contexts.[28] I would add that haunting also leaves room for agencies that exceed human dimensions. Thus, haunting creates a space for religious and theological discourses to be examined, engaged, and critiqued without requiring that these be reductively "translated" or "demythologized" into humanist terms.[29]

I am not, however, proposing that the living lack accountability or agency: it is the living, situated and embodied, who must reckon with hauntings. Derrida uses the concept of inheritance to speak about this process of reckoning.

The term "inheritance" evokes questions about identity and agential relations among the one who wills, the content of the inheritance, and the heirs.[30] Inheritance may connote something controlled by the one who wills. But in relationship to haunting, the inheritance may not be consciously willed but rather passed on despite the best efforts not to transmit habits, patterns, traumas; and the living may have to reckon with that which is literally unspeakable and not of their own experience.[31] As Derrida insists, an inheritance is the "*injunction to reaffirm by choosing . . . one must* filter, sift, criticize; one must sort out the several different possibles that inhabit the same injunction."[32]

---

28. Gordon, *Ghostly*, esp. 193–208.

29. Mary Keller's work on possession informs my thinking here; see her *The Hammer and the Flute: Women, Power, and Spirit Possession* (Baltimore: The Johns Hopkins University Press, 2002).

30. The question of who inherits not only threads through biblical texts, but preoccupies its interpreters; see Galatians, but also Philo, *Who Is the Heir*.

31. Toni Morrison's term "rememory" captures this beautifully (*Beloved*, 35–36); see discussion by Gordon, *Ghostly Matters*, 164–69. See also Esther Rashkin, *Unspeakable Secrets and the Psychoanalysis of Culture* (Albany: SUNY Press, 2008).

32. Derrida, *Specters*, 16. I do not mean to suggest that Derrida is the first to articulate this point; this is a central insight and basis for authorizing virtually all feminist, womanist, postcolonial, queer, and other liberationist as well as deconstructive engagements with biblical texts.

Those who undertake this process are situated and partial. To take an obvious example, a collection such as the New Testament was produced as a seemingly fixed and unified inheritance for Christians long after the composition of its constituent texts;[33] its fixity and unity has been repeatedly questioned both in terms of what counts as Scripture and canon and in terms of interpretation and use. The New Testament "speaks at the same time several times—and in several voices."[34] What constitutes the broader inheritance for Christians is contested by different heirs, as indicated by both the categories of "heresy" and "orthodoxy" and the plural forms of Christianity.

Less metaphorically, "inheritance" is a term that has a troubled history itself in relationship to gender, status, and race. To put it bluntly, not all humans have been able to be heirs (at least not in publicly or legally recognized ways); and in some contexts (such as slavery and colonialism), status and race have been defined so as to classify certain kinds of humans *as* inheritance. Furthermore, the idea that one "inherits" characteristics from one's "blood" or environment[35] has been an insidiously powerful and flexible one, used to naturalize binary, heterosexist notions of gender as well as race, ethnicity, national identity, class, and religious identity.[36]

As the next section shows, haunting highlights the instability of "race" conceptually and temporally and allows us to reconsider the racialized material and discursive formations that have dominated New Testament and early Christian studies so that we can craft a better inheritance for the future.

---

33. Of course, not even the content of these texts was fixed, as the subfield of textual criticism has demonstrated. See, for example, Bruce Metzger and Bart Ehrman, *The Text of the New Testament: Its Transmission, Corruption, and Restoration*, 4th ed. (New York: Oxford University Press, 2005).

34. Ibid.

35. Of course it is important to note how different these two ideas about inheritance are: "blood" can be invoked to define inheritance as fixed, whereas "environment" may be used to define inheritance as mutable.

36. See Anne McClintock, *Imperial Leather: Race, Gender and Sexuality in the Colonial Contest* (New York: Routledge, 1995).

"Race" as a Haunted Concept

Racial discourse emerged as a species of theological evaluation.

JAMES PERKINSON, *WHITE THEOLOGY:*
OUTING SUPREMACY IN MODERNITY[37]

Despite the extraordinary multicultural, multiethnic, multireligious populations in the United States, with quite varied traditions of signifying time and community, U.S. scientific culture is replete with figures and stories that can only be called Christian.

DONNA HARAWAY, *MODEST _ WITNESS@SECOND _ MILLENIUM*[38]

We "know" that "race" is modern. We "know" there was a time before Christianity.[39] Most of us also have a healthy suspicion of origin stories. The majority of scholars agree that race was manufactured in the context of European "contact" and colonization of the "New World" in the early-sixteenth century or at least as "a constitutive feature of modern power."[40] A number of scholars have also persuasively linked binary, heterosexist gender norms and the naturalization of class difference to the articulation and materialization of race.[41] Perkinson's

---

37. James Perkinson, *White Theology: Outing Supremacy in Modernity* (New York: Palgrave, 2004), 53.

38. Donna J. Haraway, *Modest_Witness@Second_Millenium.FemaleMan©_Meets_OncoMouse™: Feminism and Technoscience* (New York and Routledge, 1997), 10.

39. Of course, early Christian authors such as Justin Martyr and Eusebius construct elaborate narratives that harness biblical and Greek universal histories to push back the origins of Christianity.

40. Michel Foucault is a notable exception to this consensus, preferring to locate race's origins in the nineteenth century (see Ann Laura Stoler's analysis in her book *Race and the Education of Desire: Foucault's History of Sexuality and the Colonial Order of Things* [Durham: Duke University Press, 1995]). Stoler has also offered an incisive and persuasive critique of the historiography of the origins of race in "Racial Histories and Their Regimes of Truth," *Political Power and Social Theory* 11 (1997): 183–206.

41. For example, Angela Y. Davis, *Women, Race, and Class* (New York: Random House, 1981); Audre Lorde, *Sister Outsider: Essays and Speeches* (Trumansburg, N.Y.: Crossing, 1984); Dorothy Allison, *Skin: Talking about Sex, Class, and Literature* (Ithaca, N.Y.: Firebrand Books, 1994); Ann Laura Stoler, *Carnal Knowledge and Imperial Power: Race and the Intimate in Colonial Rule* (Berkeley: University of California Press, 2002); McClintock, *Imperial Leather.*

provocative statement about racial origins is itself loaded, of course, but invites us to ask how racialized practices of specific modern contexts were constituted as an inheritance from "several different possibles" in early Christian traditions in ways that we have failed to adequately acknowledge and thus are at risk of continuing to pass on to future generations.

In recent years, medievalists in particular have taken on the dominant narrative about the origins of race.[42] Geraldine Heng's study of the first crusade, for example, elaborates a specific context for mobilizing the notion of Christian peoplehood: "Over and over, the crusaders describe themselves as a special transnational people defined by their religion and blazoned on the cross they bore: *gens Christiana*, a race/nation/community of Christian subjects constituting the privileged army of God (*excercitus Dei*)."[43] David Nirenberg has written about Spain, beginning in the 1430s, as an infamous setting for defining Christian belonging in terms of reproductive lineages in the contexts of debates about the conversion of Jews and Muslims, debates that "explained and legitimated the creation and perpetuation of certain hierarchies and discrimination through the language of reproduction."[44]

These scholars have argued that medieval European Christian theological renderings of human difference undergird those expressions of race identified as distinctly modern. As Lisa Lampert points out, "using nineteenth- and twentieth-century biological models as the standard for determining whether one can make connections between ideological formations . . . hinders investigations into how medieval concepts, particularly theological ones, may have shaped

---

42. In addition to references below, see also the special issue of the *Journal of Medieval and Early Modern Studies* 31 (2001), which is devoted to this topic.

43. Geraldine Heng, *Empire of Magic: Medieval Romance and the Politics of Cultural Fantasy* (New York: Columbia University Press, 2003), 26.

44. David Nirenberg, "Race and the Middle Ages: The Case of Spain and Its Jews," in *Rereading the Black Legend: The Discourses of Religion and Racial Difference in the Renaissance Empires*, ed. Margaret R. Greer, Walter D. Mignolo, and Maureen Quilligan (Chicago: University of Chicago Press, 2007), 80–83 (quote from 83). Irene Silverblatt explores how these formations interact with New World colonial projects: *Modern Inquisitions: Peru and the Colonial Origins of the Civilized World* (Durham: Duke University Press, 2004).

later ones in ways about which we are still unaware."[45] So, too, earlier Christian materials and their legacies may have informed later practices of racism and corresponding definitions of race in unexpected ways; we must attend carefully to this issue when interpreting these texts.

We need not insist on any stable, transhistorical, universal essence to race (or other categories), but instead can attend to how our contingent circumstances, commitments, and blind spots inform *without strictly predetermining* our reconstructions and evaluations of the contingent constructions and ethical, material consequences of discourses of peoplehood made in another contingent location. This means that we need to tackle, minimally, the widespread presumption that "race" is built primarily on assertions of fixed characteristics shared by all members of a putative racial group.

Fixity and Fluidity

> The confounding problem of race is that few people seem
> to know what race is.
>
> IAN F. HANEY LÓPEZ, "THE SOCIAL CONSTRUCTION OF RACE"[46]

One of the ways in which "race" has been cordoned off from both "religion" and "ethnicity" has been to distinguish race as immutable— at least putatively—while defining other forms of collective identity as voluntary or mutable.[47] Understanding race and racism as primarily

---

45. Lisa Lampert, "Race, Periodicity, and the (Neo-)Middle Ages," *Modern Language Quarterly* 65, no. 3 (2004): 396.

46. Ian F. Haney López, "The Social Construction of Race," in *Critical Race Theory: The Cutting Edge*, ed. Richard Delgado (Philadelphia: Temple University Press, 1995), 193.

47. This cordon has been seen also as a temporal one, insofar as medieval texts are seen to differ from some modern notions of racial essence because they "point to the possibility of change, although this change requires conversion and is based on a fixed belief in Christianity as the only true religion." Lampert, "Race", 409. Some critical race theorists have also challenged sharp distinctions between race and ethnicity; see for example, Naomi Zack, *Thinking about Race*, 2nd edition (1998; Belmont, Calif.: Wadsworth, 2006). But others have made a strong case for distinguishing between race and ethnicity either to: (a) emphasize that racial and ethnic identities need to be distinguished in the United States

about attributions of fixity is insufficient. Not only am I convinced, as Paul Gilroy puts it, that "race" is the "complex, unstable byproduct" of racism,[48] but also that, as Ann Stoler has helped me to see: "The porousness we assign to the contemporary concept of race may be a fluidity fundamental to the concept itself and not a hallmark of our postmodern moment."[49]

I want to emphasize this double-sided character of racial discourse, in part to indicate its resonances with theological and ethnic discourses that similarly modulate between an insistence on essences while accommodating change.[50] While one reviewer of *Why This New Race* despaired that I offer a rubric so broad that it can apply also to honey,[51] this is actually the point. The stickiness of racial discourse is its ability to ooze and transform; it may even appear sweet in contexts where it can serve as a basis to claim a collective identity or as sustenance for claiming civil rights.

After all, as Stoler notes, "race has not always been what we might assume, a discourse forged by those in power, but on the contrary, a counternarrative, embraced by those contesting sovereign notions of power and right, by those unmasking the fiction of natural and legitimate rule."[52] This is part of the double-edged legacy I see in interpretations of ancient claims of peoplehood preserved in the New

---

to understand whiteness (see David Roediger, *Towards the Abolition of Whiteness: Essays on Race, Politics, and Working Class History* [London: Verso, 1994]); or (b) to produce nonessentialist forms of strategic ethnic identities (see Avtar Brah, "Difference, Diversity, Differentiation: Processes of Racialisation and Gender," in *Theories of Race and Racism: A Reader*, ed. Les Back and John Solomos [New York and London: Routledge, 2000], 431–46).

48. Paul Gilroy, *Postcolonial Melancholia* (New York: Columbia University Press, 2005), 14.

49. Stoler, "Racial Histories and Their Regimes of Truth," 198. See also the work of David Theo Goldberg, who also emphasizes the fluidity of race: *Racist Culture: Philosophy and the Politics of Meaning* (Oxford: Blackwell, 1993).

50. For further discussion, see Buell, *Why This New Race*, 5–34; see also Sneja Gunew's discussion of the relationship between race, ethnicity, and national belonging in *Haunted Nations: The Colonial Dimensions of Multiculturalisms* (Transformations: Thinking Through Feminism; New York: Routledge, 2004), 15–29.

51. Peter Oakes, "Christianity and Ethnicity (review of Buell, *Why This New Race*)," *Classical Review* 56, no. 2 (2006): 501.

52. Ann Laura Stoler, *Race and the Education of Desire*, 69.

Testament and developed in some early Christian writings. To claim to be a people can be an assertion of the right to exist despite proscriptions or denials; when voiced by those socially and structurally disenfranchised, it may be a powerful statement indeed. But to claim that all must join one's people in order to count as fully human or to be saved is ethically suspect, even when those making the claims are socially marginalized or subjugated.[53]

We need to bear in mind that "ethnicity" and "religion" have been formulated and deployed as putatively fixed assignments as well. Colonial projects may classify the colonized into distinctive ethnic groups, for example; suspicions may be voiced about whether or not one can truly convert from one religious group to another.[54]

Moreover, race, ethnicity, gender, and religion interact in complex ways in different situations. As Sneja Gunew has noted with respect to the Bosnian War, gender, ethnicity, and religion converged in ways that "matched the absolutism associated with race in an earlier age."[55] In this context, the "ethnic groups" of Bosnian Serbs and Bosnian Muslims were configured in terms of religion, not "the expected racist model of the racially pure family (in the sense of bloodlines)."[56] She suggests that the systematic rape of Bosnian Muslim girls and women as a form of ethnic cleansing "was constructed in this case . . . not as genealogical contamination but as blasphemy. . . . Thus the bodies of Muslim Serbian women were figured as the reliquary of the 'ethnically homogenous' family and coherent with this figurative logic, as the sanctuary of the Muslim faith."[57] This violence—gendered, religious, and ethnic—simultaneously denied the possibility of consent to the raped girls and women (and their wit-

---

53. See especially Sylvester A. Johnson's problematization of the Christian notion of the "people of God" for African Americans, in Johnson, ibid., 112–31. See also Buell, "Early Christian Universalism and Modern Forms of Racism."

54. See, for example, on the former: *The Politics of Ethnic Consciousness*, ed. Cora Grovers and Hans Vermeulen (New York: St. Martin's Press, 1997); on the latter, Gauri Viswanathan, *Outside the Fold: Conversion, Modernity, and Belief* (Princeton: Princeton University Press, 1998).

55. Gunew, *Haunted*, 25.

56. Ibid.

57. Ibid.

nesses) and reintroduced a genealogical dimension to the production of the nation.[58]

Here is where speaking in terms of haunting and inheritance seems particularly apt. Familiar modern racial discourses and religious discourses about salvation and belonging intersect to the extent that they can be spoken about in terms of inheritance, claims that collective identity is assured through the transmission of tradition, culture, or genetic material. To insist on race's modernity or to insist that any discourse that "points to the possibility of change" has nothing to do with race or racism prevents us from asking questions that might otherwise allow us to critically engage the multiple inheritances conveyed by premodern ghosts.

That There Be Ghosts: Three Inheritances

There is always a time-lag and an overlap.

E. R. DODDS, *PAGANS AND CHRISTIANS*
IN AN AGE OF ANXIETY[59]

In writing, what is no longer of its time can endure and speak.
It becomes a place of refuge to which the repressed and
inopportune can retreat, and a background from which what
is forgotten can reemerge, a place of latency.

JAN ASSMAN, *RELIGION AND CULTURAL MEMORY*[60]

In this section, I sketch three kinds of arguments that appear in New Testament and/or early Christian texts, those that (1) articulate "roots" of collective belonging, especially in terms of genealogies and kinship; (2) articulate universal access and aspirations of Christian belonging in terms of membership in a people; and (3) read the surfaces of the body to classify individuals into varying types/groups. All of these

---

58. Ibid., 25–26.

59. E. R. Dodds, *Pagans and Christians in an Age of Anxiety: Some Aspects of Religious Experience from Marcus Aurelius to Constantine* (Cambridge: Cambridge University Press, 1965), 3.

60. Jan Assmann, *Religion and Cultural Memory* (Cultural Memory in the Present; Stanford: Stanford University Press, 2006), 99.

arguments haunt contemporary scholarship because their influence occurs largely in the context of disavowal among the mainstream forms of scholarship and theology. Those who have called attention to the way that these arguments are racially, ethnically, or gender inflected are almost all scholars using feminist, womanist, postcolonial, or other approaches grounded in attention to the interpreter's own social location and a concern for the ongoing ethical implications of historical interpretation.[61]

Roots

Modern presumptions that race is immutable have tended to lead scholars to interpret early Christian collective identity as nonracial because it has been depicted as an identity one acquires. Even when race and ethnicity are held to be distinct, one also finds similar claims that early Christians did not constitute an ethnic group.[62] But if we approach these ancient writings instead from the perspective that our embodied existence and structural locations gain their sense of fixity and fluidity only through our relation to others and systems of power, we might understand differently ancient writings that frame belonging to a *genos, ethnos,* or *laos* in terms of shared ancestry, kinship, and intergenerational transmission of teachings that one can or must acquire in order to count as a member.

I'm proposing, for example, that we interrogate as rhetorical, racializing strategies the second-century writings by Aristides, Justin, and Clement that make Jesus the founder of a new descent group. Aristides notes that Christians trace their *genos* back to Christ, even though Jesus was a Hebrew (*Apology* 2.4; 15.2). As Aristides hints, early Christian texts also often locate Christian belonging in a temporal framework,

---

61. See also the new work that proposes a new subfield of minority biblical criticism, *They Were All Together in One Place? Toward Minority Biblical Criticism*, ed. Randall C. Bailey, Tat-Siong Benny Liew, and Fernando F. Segovia (Atlanta: SBL, 2009).

62. For a number of examples of this disavowal, see Buell, ibid., 1. See also Ben Witherington III, *Acts of the Apostles: A Socio-Rhetorical Commentary* (Grand Rapids, Mich.: Eerdmans, 1998), 371; cited approvingly in DeYoung, Emerson, Yancey, and Kim, *United*, 29.

positioning Christianness as the *ethnos* or *genos* formed out of all types of humans, as well as the one *genos* that brings humanity into a universal and superior state. Christ's life—and often also death—has begun a new race, open to all, as Justin and Clement also assert.[63]

To understand how peoplehood haunts New Testament and early Christian studies, we must always consider the violence entailed in installing a rupture between "Christian" and "Jew."[64] Astute critical scholarship has examined the contexts that inflect nineteenth- and twentieth-century scholarship and theology for how "race" matters. Susannah Heschel and Shawn Kelley's studies, for example, demonstrate clearly how modern interests in defining and distinguishing Jew (and other "others") from Christian inform historical interpretations of Jesus and Christian history in racialized and racist ways.[65] Scholar-theologians such as Jacqueline Grant, Musa Dube, and Kwok Pui-lan emphasize both historical contexts of racialized and racist historical interpretations and outline legacies and strategies of resistance.[66] The racialized readings exposed by these scholars are, to be sure, the product of specific, contextualized encounters with ancient texts.[67]

---

63. See Buell, ibid., 35–36, 46.

64. Of course, in addition, there is no singular moment when such a rupture occurred. This is an area that has received considerable scholarly attention, both in terms of the history of the disciplines and reconstructive narratives of the first through seventh centuries.

65. Susannah Heschel, *Abraham Geiger and the Jewish Jesus* (Chicago: The University of Chicago Press, 1998); and *When Jesus Was an Aryan: Christians, Nazis, and the Bible* (Princeton: Princeton University Press, forthcoming); Shawn Kelley, *Racializing Jesus: Race, Ideology, and the Formation of Modern Biblical Scholarship* (New York: Routledge, 2002).

66. Jacqueline Grant, *White Women's Christ and Black Women's Jesus* (Atlanta: Scholars, 1989); Musa Dube, *Postcolonial Feminist Interpretation of the Bible* (St. Louis: Chalice, 2000); and Kwok Pui-lan, "Jesus/the Native: Biblical Studies from a Postcolonial Perspective," in *Teaching the Bible: The Discourses and Politics of Biblical Pedagogy*, ed. Fernando F. Segovia and Mary Ann Tolbert (Maryknoll, N.Y.: Orbis Books, 1998), 69–85.

67. See also recent studies that tend not to be in direct conversation with womanist and other liberation theological scholarship; for example, William E. Arnal, *The Symbolic Jesus: Historical Scholarship, Judaism, and the Construction of Contemporary Identity* (Oakville, Conn.: Equinox, 2005); *Apocalypticism, Anti-Semitism, and the Historical Jesus: Subtext in Criticism*, ed. John Kloppenborg and John W. Marshall (London: T & T Clark, 2005).

Nonetheless, it is instructive to consider also the spectral resonances among the works of nineteenth-, twentieth-, and twenty-first-century interpretations about the historical Jesus or reconstructions of early Christian history and *ancient* works that struggle with situating Jesus in relation to collective identity.

I am calling for more studies that triangulate close attention to contexts of modern scholarship, including how this encounter echoes, refracts, suppresses, and distills possibilities from earlier moments and from the interpreter's own location.[68] Insisting on race's modernity allows scholars to avoid haunting questions: how do *ancient* writings, both canonical and noncanonical, "racialize" Jesus and those "in Christ" in ways that "heirs of the Enlightenment" recuperate and transform? One example of scholarship well suited to address such questions is that which focuses on the Roman imperial period and also aims to reconstruct a "parting of the ways" between Jews and Christians, or a lack thereof, and to assess who should be held accountable for any such parting and on what grounds.[69] Yet those who *complicate* narratives of the parting of the ways between "Christians" and "Jews"—a proclivity

---

68. In addition to the scholarship by Grant, Dube, and Kwok cited above, which emphasizes the interpreter's location and the political and ethical effects of theological reception and creation of understandings of Jesus, I think here of work by scholars such as Elisabeth Schüssler Fiorenza (*Jesus and the Politics of Interpretation* [New York: Continuum, 2000]) and Melanie Johnson-DeBaufre, *Jesus*.

69. For example, *The Ways that Never Parted: Jews and Christians in Late Antiquity and the Early Middle Ages*, ed. Adam H. Becker and Annette Yoshiko Reed (2003; Minneapolis: Fortress Press, 2007); James G. D. Dunn, *The Partings of the Ways between Christianity and Judaism and Their Significance for the Character of Christianity* (Philadelphia: Trinity Press International, 1991); Rosemary Radford Reuther, *Faith and Fratricide: The Theological Roots of Anti-Semitism* (New York: Seabury, 1974); John G. Gager, *The Origins of Anti-Semitism* (New York: Oxford University Press, 1983); *Reinventing Paul* (Oxford: Oxford University Press, 2000); Jeffrey S. Siker, *Disinheriting the Jews: Abraham in Early Christian Controversy* (Louisville, Ky.: Westminster/John Knox, 1991); David M. Olster, *Roman Defeat, Christian Response, and the Literary Construction of the Jew* (Philadelphia: University of Pennsylvania Press, 1994); Daniel Boyarin, *A Radical Jew: Paul and the Politics of Identity* (Berkeley: University of California Press, 1994); *Dying for God: Martyrdom and the Making of Christianity and Judaism* (Stanford: Stanford University Press, 1999); *Border Lines: The Partition of Judaeo-Christianity* (Philadelphia: University of Pennsylvania Press, 2004).

that I share—have not fully reckoned with the significance of language of peoplehood for the production of "Christian" belonging.[70] Nor has this scholarship always attended to how questions about differences between Jews and Christians in antiquity not only displace modern concerns about the differences between Jews and Christians but also modern concerns about racial and ethnic difference more broadly.[71]

Any consideration of writings now canonical for Christians must grapple with the fact that, in the mid-late first century C.E., "Christianity" is only a spectral possibility that subsequent generations of readers either materialize in competing ways or refuse to materialize. I am thinking especially of texts that never adopt the term "Christian" as a term of self-identification, but this needs to be considered also for texts such as 1 Peter in which the term *christianos* ("Christian") does appear. 1 Peter addresses readers by positioning their affirmation of an obedient, suffering, resurrected, and returning Jesus as God's Christ using scriptural imagery and paraphrasing that situates readers inside the history of Israel. By alluding to proclamations in texts such as Isaiah and Hosea, 1 Peter presents itself and its listeners as the authentic heirs of these proclamations, the God about whom they speak, and the people to whom these prophecies and promises have been addressed. "You are a chosen *genos*, a royal priesthood, a holy *ethnos*, God's own *laos*, in order that you may declare the wonderful deeds

---

70. Judith M. Lieu's work constitutes an important exception. See *Christian Identity in the Jewish and Graeco-Roman World* (Oxford: Oxford University Press, 2004). See also Tessa Rajak, "Talking at Trypho: Christian Apologetic as Anti-Judaism in Justin's *Dialogue with Trypho the Jew*," in *Apologetics in the Roman Empire*, ed. Edwards, Goodman, and Price (Oxford: Oxford University Press, 1999), 59–80.

71. Paul, as a figure, and writings attributed to Paul, have served as one major locus for debates about when and how Christianity "breaks" from other forms of Judaism. The plurality of legacies of Paul, in antiquity and beyond, makes Pauline materials ripe for an investigation of their haunting effects and possible inheritances. Paul has recently become a favored "ancestor" from whom continental philosophers hope to inherit a vision for progressive ethics, a move that I view with considerable ambivalence; see, for example, Giorgio Agamben, *The Time That Remains: A Commentary on the Letter to Romans*, trans. Patricia Daley (Stanford: Stanford University Press, 2005); Alain Badiou, *Saint Paul: The Foundation of Universalism*, trans. Ray Brassier (Cultural Memory in the Present; Stanford: Stanford University Press, 2003).

of the one who called you out of darkness into marvelous light. Once you were no people (*ou laos*) but now you are God's people (*laos*)" (1 Peter 2:9–10). To follow the textual rhetoric, being a member of God's people also means being eligible for "an inheritance which is imperishable, undefiled, and unfading, kept in heaven for you . . . a salvation ready to be revealed in the last time" (1 Peter 1:4–5).[72] As Elisabeth Schüssler Fiorenza succinctly notes: "Israel is not yet seen as the 'other' of the community but as its constitutive identity."[73]

The text presupposes that members of God's people consist of free (or freed) women and men, some of whom are married, and enslaved women and men. The (free) married women are specifically instructed to imagine themselves as "children" (*tekna*) of Sarah (1 Peter 3:6), whom the text invokes to exhort wives to be submissive to their husbands. While female readers, free and slave, may have resisted such an exhortation, the text's rhetoric raises the question of what kind of ancestry an enslaved or free unmarried woman might have claimed, if any. It should also make us think again about the gendered- and status-linked functions of appeals to ancestors, appeals that may simultaneously aim to produce or index membership in a people.

While the term *christianos* appears as a charge for which a reader might suffer (1 Peter 4:16), there is no indication that it is either the term readers used for themselves or that this term marked collective belonging apart from Judaism.[74] For subsequent readers, the term

---

72. Paul, in the letter to the Galatians, also explains the consequences of being in Christ in terms of descent and inheritance: "If you belong to Christ, then you are Abraham's offspring, heirs according to the promise" (Gal 3:29). That is, becoming a son (*huios*) of God through Christ makes Abraham one's ancestor, making one eligible to inherit the promises God made to Abraham. For extensive analysis, see Caroline Johnson Hodge, *If Sons, Then Heirs: A Study of Kinship and Ethnicity in the Letters of Paul* (Oxford: Oxford University Press, 2007); Denise Kimber Buell and Caroline Johnson Hodge, "The Politics of Interpretation: The Rhetoric of Race and Ethnicity in Paul," *JLB* 123 (2004): 235–52; Sze-kar Wan, "Does Diaspora Identity Imply Some Sort of Universality? An Asian-American Reading of Galatians," in *Interpreting Beyond Borders*, ed. Fernando F. Segovia (The Bible and Postcolonialism 3; Sheffield: Sheffield Academic, 2000), 107–31.

73. Elisabeth Schüssler Fiorenza, *The Power of the Word: Scripture and the Rhetoric of Empire* (Minneapolis: Fortress Press, 2007), 169.

74. See ibid., 168.

offers a lens through which to read the entire text, even as it remains equally possible to read the text as one whose readers understand themselves in complete continuity with the history of Israel and the will and actions of Israel's God.

The text charts no tensions or divisions among Jews; the addressees seem to include former Gentiles who have been reborn and await salvation by virtue of becoming members of God's people, even as this membership is marked by their love for and faith in Jesus, a faith that the text defines especially in terms of obedience and submission.[75] Nevertheless, we know that 1 Peter was preserved and transmitted as a text whose contents would help to index both a distinctive form of belonging separate from Judaism (as "Christian" comes to be understood) and the authoritative form of that distinctive Christian belonging (as a canonical text).

While "Christianity" may be a specter in 1 Peter that has been materialized by most subsequent readers, it is not the only one. The possibility that Christianity might never have arisen, or that *christianos* might never have become distinct from "Judaism," haunts the reader's encounter with this text and most other New Testament writings. Is the kind of peoplehood imagined in 1 Peter radically different from that imagined in other forms of Judaism? The claim that members of a nonpeople have become members of God's people might be made by Christians and Jews alike seeking to assert, explain, and preserve differences. The idea that those who have not counted as a people, or at least as God's people, can become members of a people characterized by divine favor and promises of salvation is one activated by mid-second-century writers who self-consciously use the term "Christian" for insiders, portraying this membership in terms of descent and kinship as well as transformation.[76]

---

75. See especially 1 Peter 1:1–9.

76. From a different vantage point, to claim that those who were not God's people (free "Gentiles" but also enslaved women and men whose status legally precluded membership in a *genos* or *ethnos*) now could be members of God's people is the kind of inheritance that Morrison activates (by way of Romans) in *Beloved*.

Universalism

Early Christian texts regularly depict membership as ideally universal in scope. Yet such claims are not only presented in terms of peoplehood, but can also be expressed as the disenfranchising of other groups: "join us to count as human" or "we are you, really" (especially others who also claim to be Israel or Abraham's descendants).

Even if 1 Peter communicates access to God's people for those who were previously excluded and do not imagine a distinctive "Christian" collective identity as the result, authors from the second half of the second century begin to make such claims. Justin and Clement assert that this new Christian *genos* has as its ancestors Abraham and Jacob, meaning that Justin can depict Christians as the true Israel, the descendants and heirs of God's promises to Abraham and Jacob.[77] To what extent do these early Christian claims anticipate racist logic as it emerges in the European imagination and material practices of radically disinheriting non-Christians, especially Jews but also later Muslims, from claims to be the heirs of God's promises?[78]

Indeed, Justin—as well as others, such as Clement of Alexandria—makes Christians not simply the rightful heirs to biblical traditions but also the heirs to Greek and Roman philosophical patrimony.[79] This move, perhaps already anticipated in the speech attributed to Paul in Acts 17, raises questions about how Christian universalizing claims presuppose multiple human groups even as they deny the possibility that any group but a Christian one fully embodies the truth.[80]

---

77. See Buell, *Why This New Race*, 94–115.

78. See Kathleen Biddick, *The Typological Imaginary: Circumcision, Technology, History* (Philadelphia: University of Pennsylvania Press, 2003), and Lampert, "Race".

79. Justin uses the idea that all humans have the *Logos* implanted in them, but that few were able to access it before the arrival of the incarnated *Logos* in the world. This universal framing allows Justin to argue that Greek and Jewish texts and traditions contain truth, but that Christians uniquely embody correct access to this truth (see Buell, *Why This New Race*, 79–81).

80. I discuss Acts 17 at some length in Buell, "Early Christian Universalism and Modern Forms of Racism," forthcoming.

Emma Dench has provocatively suggested that "we might think of Christianity from around the later second-century AD [sic], as a new, comparatively large-scale, and suggestively exclusive way of character-izing identity, framed in opposition to Roman identity."[81] It would be valuable to examine further the double-edgedness of Christian uni-versalizing aspirations, aspirations that simultaneously produce "oth-ers" as those left behind—Jews, idolaters, heretics, heathens—and by implication, inferior humans or less than fully human.[82] Such work could draw, as Dench herself does, on analyses of religious and ethnic responses to globalization: "It is becoming increasingly clear in the modern world that, just as the creation of the modern nation-state fostered smaller ethnic or religious identities,[83] so 'globalization' has frequently led to the reformulation and bolstering of national, ethnic, or religious identities, ranging from the self-consciously new to the studiedly traditional."[84] Particular kinds of Christian affiliation may serve as the index for ethnically-, racially-, or nationally-linked iden-tity claims (think of the Bosnian example above); nonetheless, when Christianity serves transnational, "globalizing" claims, we must be careful to examine how such claims resist, incorporate, or otherwise negotiate notions of distinctive peoplehood.

Physiognomy

Awareness of how race has been adduced by means of visible percep-tion has inspired considerable attention to how ancient sources antici-pate or differ from this preoccupation. How do early Christian (and

81. Emma Dench, *Romulus' Asylum: Roman Identities from the Age of Alex-ander to the Age of Hadrian* (Oxford: Oxford University Press, 2005), 218. I like this example in part because Dench offers it specifically on the heels of an observation about the present, indicating how her point about early Christian-ity arises both from her analysis of Roman identities and from her views about current ethnically- and religiously-framed responses to globalization. See also James B. Rives, "The Decree of Decius and the Religion of the Empire," *JRS* 89 (1999): 135–54.
82. For further discussion of "compulsory mutability," see Buell, "Early Christian Universalism", forthcoming.
83. For example, being Breton, Catalan, or Catholic in Northern Ireland.
84. Dench, *Romulus' Asylum*, 218.

other ancient) discourses about reading surfaces of the body constitute an inheritance for later European and North American preoccupations with skin color (but also gender, sexuality, and class) and reading the surfaces of the body for moral traits? Shelley Haley, Robert Hood, Vincent Wimbush, Gay Byron, and Emma Dench have all explored the ruptures and resonances between modern and Roman periods.[85]

The relationship between the visible and invisible was certainly a concern for many early Christians, and many did cultivate distinctively Christian ways of reading the surfaces of the body to discern underlying moral truths and characteristics.[86] Ancient texts provide here an inheritance of the instability between surface and exterior, which echoes in literature about "passing" and transformation. We could also do more to inquire about how Christian discourses of holiness are transformed and resituated in European discourses that yoke whiteness and Christianness together as indexes of national and ethnic identities, such as Englishness.[87]

I have only touched briefly on three areas worth further exploration, but I hope it will stimulate further consideration of how we can come to grapple with disavowed inheritances, ones both that we need to exorcise and ones that we might wish to conjure for future transformations.

---

85. Vincent Wimbush, "Ascetic Behavior and Color-ful Language: Stories about Ethiopian Moses," *Semeia* 58 (1992): 81–92; Shelley Haley, "Black Feminist Thought and Classics: Re-membering, Re-claiming, Re-empowering," in *Feminist Theory and the Classics*, ed. Nancy Sorkin Rabinowitz and Amy Richlin (New York: Routledge, 1993), 23–43, and contribution in this volume, 27–49; Robert Hood, *Begrimed and Black: Christian Traditions on Blacks and Blackness* (Minneapolis: Fortress Press, 1994); David Brakke, "Ethiopian Demons: Male Sexuality, The Black-Skinned Other, and the Monastic Self," *Journal of the History of Sexuality* 10, no. 3/4 (2001): 501–535; Gay Byron, *Symbolic Blackness and Ethnic Difference in Early Christian Literature* (New York: Routledge, 2002); Dench, *Romulus' Asylum*.

86. See especially Georgia Frank, *The Memory of the Eyes: Pilgrims to the Living in Christian Late Antiquity* (The Transformation of Classical Heritage; Berkeley: University of California Press, 2000).

87. See Heng, *Empire of Magic*.

Conclusion

> Disavowed, [a] haunting will undo the present as
> it works according to its own logic;
> yet when avowed, it does not make perfectly clear
> what its meaning and effects are.
>
> WENDY BROWN, *POLITICS OUT OF HISTORY*[88]

> We can agree, I think, that invisible things are not
> necessarily 'not-there'.
>
> TONI MORRISON, "UNSPEAKABLE THINGS UNSPOKEN"[89]

Haunting and inheritance bear directly on how we engage race, ethnicity, and gender in New Testament and early Christian studies because they highlight and trouble assumptions about continuities and discontinuities between the past and the present. E. R. Dodds hints at this: "Strictly speaking, there are no periods in history, only in historians. . . . And when hindsight enables us to cut it through at a critical point, there is always a time-lag and an overlap."[90] Dodds speaks here especially to the difference between the messiness on the ground and the clarity that a historian imposes. But his remarks also suggest a more complicated notion of temporality. Not only does the past inform the present—as a kind of cultural inertia (time-lag)—but unseen forces also operate on the present from the future. As Dodds puts it: "C[arl] G. Jung remarks somewhere that 'long before 1933

---

88. Brown, *Politics Out of History*, 153.

89. Toni Morrison, "Unspeakable Things Unspoken: The Afro-American Presence in American Literature," *Michigan Quarterly Review* 28 (1989): 11.

90. Dodds, *Pagans and Christians*, 3. By time-lag and overlap, Dodds in part means that there is no neat distinction possible between retrospectively designated time periods: "When Marcus Aurelius came to the throne no bell rang to warn the world that the *pax Romana* was about to end. . . . For a long time the majority of individuals must have continued to think and feel as they had always thought" (3–4). Dodds was a long-time member of the British Society for Psychical Research, serving as its president from 1961–63. The British SPR was founded in the early twentieth century to pursue scientific evidence for spiritual entities, including the life after death (See Hugh Lloyd-Jones, *Blood for the Ghosts: Classical Influences in the Nineteenth and Twentieth Centuries* [London: Duckworth, 1982], 287–94).

there was already a faint smell of burning in the air.' "[91] Whether it is fascism, existential anxiety, lynchings, universal suffrage, regime change, radical democracy, or God's *basileia*, this "in-the-air-ness" is the sign of a haunting; it signals the alternative inheritances possible in the present.[92]

Dodds challenges historical-critical interpretive approaches. Historical criticism calls for stories with clear, linear narratives and also posits a sharp break between the present of the narrator-scholar and the past. Historical critical frameworks do not accommodate the possibility of ghosts—that there might be something that could disrupt the assertion of linear temporalities and of neat distinctions between temporalities. This emphasis on historical discontinuity asserts a lack of inheritance between the present and the past, or disparages claims of inheritance as problematic. That is, it asserts that what a religious community claims as having inherited from the tradition really is a corruption or later addition.[93] This approach also requires the interpreter to mask or deny her contingency in the interpretive process.

Along with many other scholars (including those in this volume), I favor critical approaches to biblical studies and early Christian texts that challenge the historical-critical ideal that one can lay bare the original meaning of a text by peeling back its promiscuous reception history; such approaches refuse historical criticism's

---

91. Dodds, *Pagans and Christians*, 4.

92. In a context very different from Dodds, Jacques Derrida makes a similar point about ghosts and their hauntings. He notes that, in the mid-nineteenth century, Marx and Engels wrote of a specter of communism haunting Europe before communism was "nameable . . . but still to come"; Derrida contrasts this haunting from the future with reflections on communism after the dissolution of the Soviet Union and reunification of Germany, asking: "What exactly is the difference from one century to the next? Is it the difference between a past world—for which the specter represented a coming threat—and a present world, today, where the specter would represent a threat that some would like to believe is past and whose return it would be necessary again, once again in the future, to conjure away?" (Derrida, *Specters*, 38–39).

93. This position can, paradoxically, serve to authorize religious reform in the name of recuperating the lost original. But this strategy problematically envisions a singular essence to original Christianity—even if it denies that no one can access that original.

denial that we play a role in making the meaning of the text.[94] Ethically engaged interpretive frameworks are unruly heirs to historical-critical approaches. But to the extent that other scholars and I have been trained in historical-critical frameworks, we have been disciplined to deny the existence of ghosts in two ways. First, we are taught not to see or name what haunts the discipline—at least not without significant professional risk. We would do well to remember that spiritualist proclivities and fascination with psychical research was a major component of the context in which the late nineteenth- and early-twentieth-century scholars pursued their work, work which shaped major questions and lines of research for the fields of Ancient History, Classics, and Biblical Studies.[95] Second, especially if we

---

94. Although I speak throughout this essay as if scholars in New Testament and Early Christian Studies belong together, we tend to do our work more apart than together. We could use more communication across the subfields of New Testament Studies and Early Christian Studies. On the one hand, those working with texts and sites from the mid-second century on can serve as vital resources for the early inheritances of texts that became part of the New Testament anthology (for example, *Early Patristic Readings of Romans*, ed. Kathy Gaca and L. L. Wedborn [Romans Through History and Culture Series; London: T & T Clark, 2005]). On the other hand, those working in New Testament tend to be more practiced in articulating the contemporary stakes of textual interpretation and the significance of the interpreter's location (for example, Elisabeth Schüssler Fiorenza, *In Memory of Her: A Feminist Theological Reconstruction of Christian Origins* [New York: Crossroads, 1983]; Schüssler Fiorenza, *Rhetoric and Ethic: The Politics of Biblical Studies* [Minneapolis: Fortress, 1999]; *Stony the Road We Trod: African American Biblical Interpretation*, ed. Cain Hope Felder [Minneapolis: Fortress, 1991]; *Reading from this Place*, Volume 1: *Social Location and Biblical Interpretation in the United States* and *Reading from This Place*, Volume 2: *Social Location and Biblical Interpretation in Global Perspective*, both volumes ed. Fernando F. Segovia and Mary Ann Tolbert [Minneapolis: Fortress Press, 1995]; Fernando Segovia, *Decolonizing Biblical Studies: A View from the Margins* [Maryknoll: Orbis, 2000]; *African Americans and the Bible: Sacred Texts and Social Textures*, ed. Vincent L. Wimbush with the assistance of Rosamond C. Rodman [New York: Continuum, 2000]; as well as ongoing work of the Institute for Signifying Scriptures, directed by Vincent Wimbush at the Claremont Graduate School; *Feminist New Testament Studies: Global and Future Perspectives*, ed. Kathleen O'Brien Wicker, Althea Spencer Miller, and Musa Dube [New York: Palgrave, 2005]; *Her Master's Tools? Feminist and Postcolonial Engagements of Historical-Critical Discourse*, ed. Caroline Vander Stichele and Todd Penner [Atlanta: SBL, 2005]; and *They Were All Together in One Place? Toward Minority Biblical Criticism*).

95. I am currently working on these issues further.

have appointments in research universities or liberal arts colleges, we learn to distance ourselves from those who believe in divine powers, spirits, and ancestors (regardless of the interpreter's own religiosity). For women and men marked "other" by race, class, educational background, sexuality, language, culture, as well as religion, this has been in effect a requirement to become ghostly.[96] We need to be attentive to how such training may haunt us by being as explicit as possible about what kinds of heirs we choose to be.

There is no singular essence to Christianness, now or in the past—no single or unified inheritance. But there are ancient textual strategies for producing Christianness that continue to be claimed as resources for authorizing and creating present Christianness. These include narratives, inside and outside the canon, that define Christians as a people, God's people. These texts, in their own contexts, in the history of their reception, and in our various uses of them, trouble an easy distinction between race, ethnicity, and religion and vex any assertions that our modern formations of racism and race have nothing to do with ancient articulations of human difference, human salvation, and the inheritance of God's promises.

---

96. I acknowledge, however, the strategic and theological uses of historical criticism to intervene in the present—to authorize reform of present thinking in the name of the past.

CHAPTER 7

Race, Aesthetics, and Gospel Scholarship

Embracing and Subverting the Aesthetic Ideology

Shawn Kelley

᠋᠋᠋᠋᠋᠋᠋᠋᠋᠋᠋᠋᠋

Racialized thinking entered New Testament scholarship by a variety of routes, the most successful being those couched in the dignified language of the intellectual. Perhaps the most cunning of these covert forms of racialized discourse is the aesthetic ideology that permeates post-Romantic modernity. It is through this aesthetic ideology that the morally destructive, and highly gendered, categories of nation and race have become hopelessly intertwined with the elevated and inspiring categories of art and beauty. Aesthetics led to the racialization of much formative historical-critical New Testament scholarship and renders problematic any attempt to escape from the discipline's racialized ideology.

This aesthetic ideology can be felt most acutely in parable scholarship, which became the gateway through which racialized aesthetics entered historical-critical biblical scholarship. Parable scholarship was the single aspect of historical criticism that maintained its appeal to those scholars who otherwise rejected historical criticism on methodological grounds. As a result, it was through parable scholarship that racialized aesthetics spread far beyond more traditional forms of scholarship.

The methodological innovations of the past two decades simultaneously reinscribe aspects of racialized discourse in new scholarly terrain (by embracing a parabolic aesthetic) and provide critical space for challenging racialized discourse within the discipline (by developing alternative reading strategies and interpretive goals).

⑤⑤⑤⑤⑤⑤⑤⑤⑤⑤⑤⑤.

Introduction

Throughout the modern era, European and American thought was preoccupied with racial issues. Most of this thought tended towards the brutal: analyzing the mental and spiritual deficiencies of the non-white races, defending slavery and legalized segregation, outlawing miscegenation, supporting eugenics, and constructing elaborate laws and practices in support of racial hierarchies. This harsh racial discourse was supported by the crassest of stereotypes, by shocking, state-sanctioned violence, and by the long arm of the law. All of this added up to a world where racism and brutality were intimately connected and where racial violence was socially and intellectually sanctioned.

While it is important to draw attention to the persistence of systematized racial violence, it would be a mistake to assume that racial thinking can be limited to instances and practices of overt cruelty. There are times when racial thought shuns the vile rhetoric of the demagogue in favor of the dignified discourse of the poet and the intellectual. There are times when racialized thinking is grounded in the realm of the aesthetic rather than in the realm of the lynch mob. This form of racial thinking appears in discourse that is decidedly gentle and in rhetoric that can tend towards the inspirational, which renders it particularly difficult to identify and to confront.

In this chapter, I wish to analyze the lingering effect of aestheticized racial thinking in the discipline of biblical scholarship. The goal of the chapter will be to help identify this particular discourse within the discipline and to begin the process of extricating the discipline from its snares.

Let me start by sharpening the question a bit. In *Racializing Jesus*, I argued that much formative, historical-critical New Testament scholarship was thoroughly racialized.[1] This formative New Testament criticism has faced a withering methodological and ideological critique.[2] I wish to explore the following question: in parting ways with historical criticism, has recent criticism also managed to free itself from the sort of racialization that I have identified in formative biblical scholarship? Or might some forms of recent criticism have reinscribed historical-criticism's racialization in new and ever more complicated ways?

Race and Modernity

I shall begin by articulating some of the argument I put forth in *Racializing Jesus*, which explores the role of race in modernity in general and in modern New Testament scholarship in particular. Throughout the course of my work, I argue that race is a social construct that functions within the discourse of modernity.[3] I also argue that modern racial thinking is as conceptually empty as it is pervasive, and that it gains its intellectual potency by penetrating other intellectual discourses. As an empty category, race tends to be both protean and parasitic, infusing itself into the fabric and economy of the foundational aspects of modernity. Instead of existing alongside, say, literature or anthropology, racial thinking wove itself into these modern discourses. This process by which race permeates particular modern discourses can be defined as "racialization."

In many ways, the modern process of racialization is entwined with modern views of gender.[4] Much racial thinking is explicitly or implicitly sexualized, with the colonizing race often conceiving of itself in stereotypically male terms (that is, active, dominant, aggressive,

---

1. Shawn Kelley, *Racializing Jesus: Race, Ideology and the Formation of Modern Biblical Scholarship* (London: Routledge, 2002).

2. See, for example, Elisabeth Schüssler Fiorenza, *Rhetoric and Ethic: The Politics of Biblical Studies* (Minneapolis: Fortress Press, 1999), 44–46; Fernando Segovia, *Decolonizing Biblical Studies: A View from the Margins* (Maryknoll, N.Y.: Orbis Books, 2000), 18–22, 26–29.

3. Kelley, *Racializing Jesus*, 17, 26–31.

4. For a discussion of gender and modernity, see Elisabeth Schüssler Fiorenza, *Jesus and the Politics of Interpretation* (New York: Continuum, 2001), 9–11; Stephen Moore, *God's Beauty Parlor and Other Queer Spaces in and around the Bible* (Stanford: Stanford University Press, 2001), 135–69.

in control) and conceiving of the colonized races in stereotypically female terms (that is, passive, invaded).[5] Notions of racial superiority are often metaphorically sexualized. On a less metaphoric level, much racial anxiety is explicitly sexual in nature. Most racial economies are founded on the fear of miscegenation and ensuing interracial procreation, creating enormous anxiety about the sexual violation of white women at the hands of nonwhite men.[6] The obsession with biological, racial, and reproductive purity provided fundamental support for many aspects of modern racial brutality, from Jim Crow segregation, to widespread laws against interracial marriage, to anti-immigration hysteria, to the eugenics movement.[7]

It is my contention that this widespread, modern obsession with sexual and reproductive purity is often translated into the world of culture, which results in the widespread, modern obsession with cultural purity. Blood and soil racism can often be extended to cultural and artistic racism, with an equally obsessive fear of cultural miscegenation. In this way, modern aesthetic ideologies and modern debates about culture and its debasement can allegorically reflect modern anxieties about racial and sexual purity and about the modern desire to expel that which potentially taints the pure.

The Aesthetic Ideology

It is tempting to assume that the pursuit of beauty is inherently less dangerous than the pursuit of a racially pure gene pool and the maintenance of racial hierarchy. For are not the humane values of art and

---

5. See Sander Gilman, *The Jew's Body* (London: Routledge, 1991), 136–37, 187–91, 219; *Freud, Race, and Gender* (Princeton: Princeton University Press, 1993), 36–48.

6. For further discussion, see Robert J. C. Young, *Colonial Desire: Hybridity in Theory, Culture, and Race* (London: Routledge, 1995), 126–27, 131–33, 141–42, 144–48, 150–58.

7. See Henry Friedlander, *The Origins of the Nazi Genocide: From Euthanasia to the Final Solution* (Chapel Hill: University of North Carolina Press, 1995); Stefan Kühl, *The Nazi Connection: Eugenics, American Racism, and German National Socialism* (New York: Oxford University Press, 1994); Joel Williamson, *A Rage for Order: Black-White Relations in the American South Since Emancipation* (Oxford: Oxford University Press, 1986), 117–91.

literature antithetical to the mind-numbing violence of racial oppression? This section of the chapter will challenge this assumption by exploring the intertwining of racial values and modern views of art, literature, and beauty.

This intertwining of race, nationalism, and art and culture emerged in the early modern period and hardened into an aesthetic ideology that helped to structure much of European and American nationalism.[8] This aesthetic ideology works by a series of elisions. The quest for higher consciousness is silently transformed into a quest for corporative or collective authenticity which itself becomes synonymous with racialized consciousness.

This ideology is structured around a fundamental illusion, which posits the existence of homogenous national cultures, racially pure peoples, and authentically unified nations. The illusion is also fundamentally aesthetic. Racial thinking posits a unified national culture that reflects the essence of the people. Furthermore, the people's national health is nurtured by its embrace of the primordial, and therefore racialized, works of culture and art.[9] This assumption leads to the simultaneous aestheticizing of race and the racializing of aesthetics, with the aesthetic ideology providing the crucial link between art and literature, on the one hand, and race and nation, on the other.[10] The general problem concerns the intertwining of art and aesthetics, on the one hand, and race, ethnicity, and nation, on the other. Nation/race/ethnicity/people become defined in aesthetic terms, and art/literature/culture become defined in nationalistic and racial terms.[11]

---

8. See Kelley, *Racializing Jesus*, 44–47.

9. For a discussion of primordiality and its roots in Romanticism, see Kelley, ibid., 37–39. See also Hans Sluga, *Heidegger's Crisis: Philosophy and Politics in Nazi Germany* (Harvard: Harvard University Press, 1993), 37, 102, 106, 115–19.

10. See Kwame Anthony Appiah, *In My Father's House: African in the Philosophy of Culture* (New York: Oxford University Press, 1992), 48.

11. This particular ideology was identified and deconstructed by the literary critic Paul de Man. Paul de Man, "Sign and Symbol in Hegel's *Aesthetics*," *Critical Inquiry* 8, no. 4 (1982): 761–75; "Hegel on the Sublime," in *Displacement: Derrida and After*, ed. M. Krupnick (Bloomington: Indiana University Press, 1983), 139–53; "Phenomenality and Materiality in Kant," in *Hermeneutics: Questions and Prospects*, ed. G. Shapiro and A. Sica (Amherst: University of Massachusetts Press, 1984), 121–44.

In *Racializing Jesus*, I explore in some detail the origins of such an ideology and its role in New Testament scholarship, and I do not wish to repeat that analysis here.[12] Instead, I shall briefly summarize my conclusions. The aesthetic ideology is constructed around two fundamental gestures: the nurturing of the positive and the simultaneous expulsion of the negative. The expulsion of pollutants makes it possible to nurture the primordially healthy. The positive values and the negative values are both conceived of in explicitly aesthetic terms, with the positive (that is, immediacy, dynamism, authenticity, primordiality, organicity) made possible by the purging of the negative (that is, what is mediated, inauthentic, static, inorganic). When read as political allegories, the ominous nature of strategies of expulsion and purgation come to the fore. It is a thin line from expelling polluting art to expelling polluting people; this is a line that was continually crossed in so many of the modern genocides.[13] In short, the aestheticized dichotomy (between pure and impure, between nurturing and polluting, between engaging and expelling) is promptly and repeatedly politicized and racialized, as purity of culture elides into purity of nation and race.[14]

This ideology can be found throughout modernity. It has particular political appeal to the eugenics movement[15] and to various sorts of fascism.[16] While it is less influential on the particulars of American racism, one can see its presence in the thought of post-Reconstruction

---

12. See Kelley, *Racializing Jesus*, 59–61, 70–80, 116–21, 145–54.
13. For a discussion of the role purity played in a variety of modern genocides, see Ben Kiernan, *Blood and Soil: A World History of Genocide and Extermination from Sparta to Darfur* (New Haven: Yale University Press, 2007), 27–29, 193, 316–18, 378, 401, 461–63, 472–75, 477, 551, 564–66.
14. For further discussion, see Young, *Colonial Desire*, 37, 39, 46–50, 62–89, 102, 104–6, 140.
15. See Friedlander, *Nazi Genocide*, 1–22; Kühl, *Nazi Connection*, 13–26; Robert Jay Lifton, *The Nazi Doctors: Medical Killing and the Psychology of Genocide* (New York: Basic Books, 1986), 22–44.
16. See David Carroll, *French Literary Fascism: Nationalism, Anti-Semitism, and the Ideology of Culture* (Princeton: Princeton University Press, 1995), 18–48; Philipe Lacoue-Labarthe, *Heidegger, Art and Politics*, trans. C. Turner (Cambridge, Mass.: Blackwell, 1990), 61–104; Philipe Lacoue-Labarthe and Jean-Luc Nancy, "The Nazi Myth," trans. Brian Holmes, *Critical Inquiry* 16, no.2 (1990): 291–312.

Southern radicals.[17] It also has particular resonance for intellectuals of a variety of different stripes, especially, but not limited to, those with fascist tendencies: Heidegger and a youthful Paul de Man, to name only two examples.[18]

The Aesthetic Ideology and Formative Biblical Scholarship

The aesthetic ideology works by racializing aesthetics—that is, by thinking about human collectivity in both racial terms (that is, as ethnicities or "peoples," grouped together by common racial attributes) and in aesthetic terms (that is, by ascribing particular aesthetic values to these peoples and by associating these particular aesthetic values with specific peoples). This ideology encourages a variety of different thinkers, poets and philosophers to slide freely from artistic categories to racial ones and back again, and it ensures that certain aesthetic categories are structurally racialized, despite (or, perhaps, because of) their invocation of humane values.[19] Within New Testament scholarship, the effect of the aesthetic ideology can be felt whenever scholars interpret early Christian texts with a range of appealing yet ideologically loaded aesthetic values and terms, especially *immediacy, authenticity, primordiality, organicity,* and *metaphoricity.* Nowhere have these aesthetic terms presented themselves more fully than in the field of parable scholarship.

I have argued elsewhere that, within post-Bultmannian New Testament scholarship, the aesthetic ideology is most visible in the parable scholarship of Wilder, Dodd, Funk, and Crossan.[20] These aesthetic

---

17. See Williamson, *A Rage for Order,* 17–29, 99–116.

18. *Racializing Jesus* has extensive bibliography on Heidegger's Nazism (see Kelley, chapter 4). For a recent study, see Charles Bambach, *Heidegger's Roots: Nietzsche, National Socialism, and the Greeks* (Ithaca: Cornell University Press, 2003). On de Man, see Werner Hamacher, Neil Hertz, and Thomas Keenan, eds., *Response: On Paul de Man's Wartime Journalism* (Lincoln: University of Nebraska Press, 1989); Christopher Norris, *Paul De Man: Deconstruction and the Critique of the Aesthetic Ideology* (London: Routledge, 1988), 177–98.

19. The postcolonial concept of hybridity functions to disrupt these elisions and to provide an aesthetic alternative to purity. See Homi Bhabha, *Location of Culture* (London: Routledge, 1994), 2–3, 7, 54–55.

20. See Kelley, *Racializing Jesus,* chapter 6.

values are employed to delineate the nature of parabolic language, to discern how parabolic language functions, and to help shape the very definition of parable itself.[21] Parable scholarship is fundamentally dependent upon the ideology's central gesture of expulsion of the inorganic (that is, allegory) to better nurture the originary and primordial text (that is, the properly reconstructed parable). Such analysis is consistently and thoroughly aestheticized, with both parable and allegory defined in terminology culled from the ideology.[22]

This type of analysis is consistently racialized, as the negative terms are identified with either Eastern Judaism or decadent Romanic early-Catholicism while the positive terms are identified with the Hellenistic West.[23] As a result, the teachings of Jesus, which have been constructed around fundamentally racialized categories, become the ground for Western identity.[24]

The analysis is consistently politicized as well, with Jesus representing the freedom that comes with higher consciousness and the allegories representing the servility that comes with stunted consciousness. The categories are also implicitly gendered, with their reliance upon the opposition between purity and miscegenation and with their repeated claim that authentic parables are misunderstood by being domesticated. This oft-repeated term nicely reveals together racial and gendered anxieties, since the fear of racial contamination elides into the fear that association with the realm of the female (that is, the domestic) will defuse Jesus' teachings of their power.

---

21. See ibid, 172–90 (on the nature of parabolic language) and 190–99 (on the function of parabolic language).

22. See ibid., 173, 178, 190.

23. In much of the philosophical tradition appropriated by New Testament scholarship, Greece was seen as the primordial birthplace of the West, where freedom first triumphed over Eastern despotism. In this schema, Rome was seen as the place where Western-Hellenistic freedom is compromised, resulting in a return to Eastern, spiritually tyranny. One can see this schema in Hegel (see ibid., 42–62, 65–66), in Heidegger (ibid., 100–121), as well as in their heirs within New Testament scholarship (ibid., 70–79, 82–87, 139–54).

24. This occurs by creating a number of aesthetic categories that are associated with either the West (i.e., primordial, authentic, etc.) or with the East (i.e., inorganic, mediated, etc.) and then by attributing the Western categories to Jesus and the Eastern categories to his opponents or to his misguided followers. For examples, see Kelley, ibid., 70–72, 78–79, 177–82, 200–203.

Finally, the ideology embraces the notion of historicized primordiality, where a primal originary text is buried under millennia of stultified misreading and misinterpretation. Authentic freedom is to be found by reconnecting with the powerful, primordial, originary voice of Jesus, although that reconnection can only occur after the tainted text has been successfully purged.

The Prison House of Parables: The Aesthetic Ideology and Recent Methodologies

Let us turn to the era of methodologically motivated alternatives to historical criticism, an era that, as Segovia observes, began in the mid-1970s and continues to this day.[25] This revolt was in part methodological, as narrative and structuralist critics challenged historical-critical approaches to reading early Christian texts. The revolt was equally ideological, spurred on by feminist, African-American, and Jewish-friendly critics who challenged historical-criticism's claims to objectivity and socio-political neutrality. Historical criticism was coming under increasing assault on methodological as well as ethical grounds.

There seems to be, then, an entirely understandable and laudatory desire for a clean break with historical criticism. Would such a *methodological* clean break from form criticism and historical Jesus research also mean an *ideological* clean break from the racialized discourse of the aesthetic ideology? This is the question that I wish to take up for the remainder of my analysis. The desire to break free from the hegemony of historical criticism does not necessarily guarantee that scholarship will free itself from the aesthetic ideology that structures so much historical criticism. My thesis is that the aesthetic ideology, outlined above, is attractive enough to appeal to a diverse range of scholars and is fluid enough to inform readings from a variety of different methodological perspectives

Let us begin by reiterating the fundamental gesture of the aesthetic ideology: the expulsion of the pollutant so as to make possible

---

25. Segovia, *Decolonizing*, 3.

the nurturing of the primordial. The primordial is fundamentally originary, meaning that it is not only historically prior, but that it also provides fundamental ground for identity. Encounter with the pure and primordial will produce authenticity and higher consciousness for the individual and for the group. Ultimately, it is this encounter that grounds Western, ethnic, and racial identity. This primordial ground is not immediately accessible because it is buried deep in the past, at the misty moment of Christian origins. Traces of this originary ground can be glimpsed beneath layers of inauthentic, derivative, domestic, and hopelessly impure texts. It is the scholar's job to purge the authentic moment of these (racial, ethnic, female) impurities to open up the possibility of authentic encounter and to make possible an authentic grounding for Western identity.

I hope to show that this gesture occurs in a variety of different scholarly discourses. Ironically enough, the aesthetic ideology is one of the few aspects of modern scholarship that is capable of transcending the methodological divide.

Displacing the Historical Jesus

The fundamental gesture of the aesthetic ideology involves the recovery and nurturing of early Christianity's primordial, formative moment. This primordial moment is most often associated with the teachings of the historical Jesus. For parable scholarship, the parables of Jesus formed the primordial moment that makes it possible to glimpse fleeting experiences of authenticity. Some historical reconstructions of emerging Christianity do not build their analysis around the figure of the historical Jesus. In so doing, these studies open up critical space for challenging the aesthetic ideology and the ensuing scholarly racialization. At the same time, their choice of aesthetic categories has led to the ideology's ever-widening dissemination. Given the space constraints here, I propose looking at one particular example: Burton Mack's research on Q.[26] In this case, a historical reconstruction is

---

26. Q is the name scholars have given to the reconstructed source that is posited to be independent of the Gospel of Mark and shared by the Gospels of Matthew and Luke. The reconstructed Q consists primarily of sayings of Jesus.

caught between the desire to decenter the historical Jesus (and thus to move away from the aesthetic ideology) and the embrace of problematic aesthetic categories (which leads to the reinscribing of the aesthetic ideology). It is this reinscribing of the aesthetic ideology that ensures that these forms of historical reconstruction will continue to construct a primitive Christianity that grounds Western identity and that does so in strikingly masculine terms.

Burton Mack has proposed an ambitious reconfiguration of Christian origins that simultaneously puts forth a blistering moral indictment of Christianity.[27] His project is complex and multifaceted, complete with intricate historical reconstructions, forceful yet controversial textual analysis, theological critique, and ultimately an ideological assault on Christianity itself and on Western-Christian imperialism. For Mack, the teachings of the early Jesus movement are buried in the earliest layers of Q (that is, Q1). It is these teachings and the movement that they reflect that provide the hermeneutical key to the emergence of formative Christianity.

Mack is particularly interested in the earliest Jesus movement, rather than the person of Jesus. By directing scholarly attention away from Jesus, he implicitly directs it away from the aestheticized quest for primordiality that so often follows the quest for the historical Jesus. At the same time, crucial moments in Mack's historical reconstruction of emerging Christianity are heavily dependent upon the gestures and values of the aesthetic ideology. Thus, for Mack, there is an early originary moment that is constructed with the help of the aesthetic ideology's positive axis. This primordial moment is the early Jesus movement as reflected in the earliest phase of the Q movement. According to Mack, we learn from Q1 that Jesus and his followers formed a countercultural movement that criticized conventional values and advocated an authentic approach to life. The Jesus of Q1 created this world by means of his witty aphorisms, which heightened awareness and challenged the hollowness of customary

---

While Q was initially proposed as a solution to the knotty problem of the textual relationship between the Synoptic Gospels, some recent scholars (including Mack) have come to see Q as an autonomous Gospel with its own point of view.

27. Burton Mack, *A Myth of Innocence: Mark and Christian Origins* (Philadelphia: Fortress Press, 1988), 368–76.

pretensions.[28] The taming and domesticating of the authentic teachings occur almost right away, in Q2 and in Q3.[29] "The teasing invita-
tion to reconsider things has been transformed into *hardened* polemic
in the course of the *domestication* of the chreia."[30] The process of
domestication culminates when the moribund aphorisms are buried
in the Gospel of Mark. "The most devastating mode of *domestication* of the parables occurred already in the earliest gospel."[31] Rather
than decentering or deconstructing the dominant aesthetic ideology,
his embrace of these aesthetic categories ensures that the ideology is
displaced onto new scholarly terrain.

For Mack, virtually the entire early Christian movement must be
purged if we are to rediscover the early, aesthetically authentic aphorisms of the Jesus movement. Under Mack's guidance, the ideology
(its aesthetic values, its logic of expulsion, its historical narrative) is
transposed from the parables of the historical Jesus to the aphorisms
of the earliest Jesus movement of Q1. The original (Western) voice,
standing behind the (female, foreign) domestication of that voice, is
found in the aphorisms of the earliest Jesus movement. Once the pollutants have been purged, this voice can be rediscovered and can provide proper grounding for an undomesticated Western identity.

Literary Criticism

As historical critics set out to reinvent historical-critical methodology,
many literary critics (and their allies or rivals in semiotics and struc-
turalism) seek to displace the historical-critical method in its entirety.
These methods reject the historical-critical goal of reconstructing the
teachings of Jesus or his earliest followers and the historical-critical
method of carving up the Gospels into disparate sources. Rather than
looking through the text, literary critics opt to stand before the text to
engage each Gospel on its own terms. These new methods represent
fundamental challenges to historical criticism, seeking, in the words

---

28. Burton Mack, *The Lost Gospel: The Book of Q and Christian Origins* (San
Francisco: Harper San Francisco, 1993), 111.
29. See Mack, ibid., 131–37.
30. Mack, *Innocence*, 187–88; italics added; see also pp. 192, 169–70.
31. Mack, ibid., 171; italics added.

of Robert Fowler, "to hasten the metamorphosis of my critical guild."[32] The discipline is, indeed, being transformed in any number of ways, and literary criticism has played a role in that transformation. It is less clear, however, that literary criticism has brought about an ideological transformation of the discipline. Once again, I wish to stress that this is not the place for a thorough airing of methodological debates among literary critics. Instead, I wish to maintain the same narrow focus as above and to ask if literary criticism has challenged the aesthetic ideology, with its racialized logic of nurturing and expulsion.

A significant portion of narrative critics structure their analysis around the quest for a singular, primordial, parabolic moment, although they argue that this moment need not be traced back to the nebulous world of pre-Gospel history. It is the earliest of Gospels, the Gospel of Mark, which is constructed as the primordial text destined to be domesticated by its aesthetically inferior heirs. For the influential historical critic turned literary critic Norman Perrin, the unique literary stance of Mark's Gospel is expressed in the same sort of primordial, universal themes that Perrin found in the parables of Jesus.[33] Perrin's suggestions were expanded by several of his students, notably John Donahue and Werner Kelber. In an early, influential reading of Mark's Gospel, John Donahue argued that "Mark's Gospel can be presented as a narrative parable of the meaning of the life and death of Jesus."[34] Kelber in turn reads Mark in light of a confrontation between orality and textuality. Arguing that the process of textualizing the oral voice is inherently stultifying, Kelber draws terms from the ideologically loaded aesthetic values of parable criticism.[35] He then pivots

---

32. Robert Fowler, *Let the Reader Understand: Reader-Response Criticism and the Gospel of Mark* (Minneapolis: Fortress Press, 1991), 1.

33. Norman Perrin, *The Resurrection according to Matthew, Mark and Luke* (Philadelphia: Fortress Press, 1977), 35, 83; *Jesus and the Language of the Kingdom: Symbol and Metaphor in New Testament Interpretation* (Philadelphia: Fortress Press, 1976).

34. John Donahue, "Jesus as the Parable of God in the Gospel of Mark," in *Interpreting the Gospels*, ed. James Luther Mays (Philadelphia: Fortress Press, 1981), 149, see also 156–66.

35. Werner Kelber, *The Oral and the Written Gospel: The Hermeneutics of Speaking and Writing in the Synoptic Tradition, Mark, Paul, and Q* (Philadelphia: Fortress Press, 1983), 62, 91–94.

and argues that Mark's textualization also has a parabolic logic all of its own and that Mark is a "rigorous . . . parabolic thinker" who articulates "the parabolic nature of Jesus' story."[36] For Kelber, "Jesus' life and death, as narrated by Mark, transpires according to the hermeneutical process of parable."[37]

For the literary critic Robert Fowler, it is Mark's Gospel that actually originated parabolic discourse; in this way, Fowler once again displaces the aesthetic ideology and reinscribes it into new scholarly terrain. It is only Mark's narrative skill that has allowed critics mistakenly to give parabolic credit to the historical Jesus. "Readers have been accustomed to giving all of the credit for parabolic speech to the protagonist (the historical Jesus), which would probably please a master of indirection such as Mark."[38] Fowler's reader-response analysis of the second gospel is an attempt to demonstrate its thoroughly parabolic nature.

The logic of the aesthetic ideology, especially as it has been shaped within New Testament scholarship, necessarily produces the aesthetic opposite to Mark's originary Gospel. There must be a textual turning point; something that is both ossified and stultifying, something that impedes the reception of Mark's primordial Gospel and that misshapes Christian history. As Fowler explains, "only in recent decades have we made significant progress in freeing the parables of the historical Jesus from the smothering embrace of Matthew and Luke. A similar mission for Mark's parabolic discourse must also be conducted."[39] It is the later Synoptic Gospels that crush the originary spirit of Mark's Gospel. Matthew's Gospel "represents perhaps the first such revision and the first great step toward the *domestication*, literalization, and historicization of the parabolic discourse of the Gospel of Mark."[40] For Fowler, Matthew blocks access to what is genuinely liberatory and antiauthoritarian in Mark's Gospel.

Under the guidance of some influential forms of literary criticism, the aesthetic ideology (its aesthetic values, its logic of expulsion, its

---

36. Ibid., 125, 124.
37. Ibid., 124.
38. Fowler, *Let the Reader Understand*, 183, see also 146–47.
39. Ibid., 256.
40. Ibid., 255–56; italics added.

historical narrative) is transposed from the parables of the historical
Jesus to the Gospel of Mark. It is there that one can find the original
(Western) voice, standing behind the (female, foreign) domestication
of that voice. Once the pollutants have been purged, this voice can be
rediscovered and can provide proper grounding for an undomesticated
Western identity.

Postmodernism

Historical criticism and many newer methodologies tend to work
within a largely positivistic framework where meaning is singular and
recoverable. For postmodern and ideological critics, this assumption is
theoretically problematic. For these critics, the newer methodologies
do not go far enough in separating themselves from the objectivist
stance assumed by historical criticism. In particular, postmodern-
ists object to the assumption that texts are unified, harmonious, and
monological.[41] Part of the challenge faced by postmodernism is to
develop reading strategies that highlight the divided, contradictory,
and dialogical nature of these texts.

Postmodernism would seem to provide the theoretical grounding and reading strategies that would be ideal for resisting the power
of the aesthetic ideology. The aesthetic ideology is a system which
helps shape the meaning of its central terms, it functions by a series
of elisions that cover up theoretical and textual aporias, and its logic
works by forceful, racialized, and gendered exclusions. Derridean
deconstruction has provided Paul de Man and Homi Bhabha with the
critical tools for identifying and challenging the ideology and its fundamental exclusions. While deconstruction's central reading strategy
(that is, identifying textual aporias to highlight and deconstruct systems of meaning) seems particularly promising, it is worth asking if
it is sufficient, in and of itself, to resist an ideology that has become
deeply ingrained in the disciplinary consciousness.

41. For a discussion, see "The Bible and Culture Collective" (George Aichele,
et al.), *The Postmodern Bible* (New Haven: Yale University Press, 1995), 9–11,
42–45, 128–35. See also the work of Stephen Moore, which is discussed below.

Some of the earliest New Testament forays into postmodernism came out of parable scholarship, which suggests a link between the parabolic aesthetic ideology and particular constructions of postmodernism. John Dominic Crossan, in particular, attempted to ground his reading of the parables in the postmodernist theories of Jacques Derrida, Michel Foucault, and Roland Barthes. Despite the substantial shifts in theory and terminology, the later Crossan's parables do more or less the same thing that they had done throughout his earlier *In Parables:* they elevate consciousness that has been degraded by the forces of domestication. As the central teachings of the historical Jesus, parables "shatter the deep structure of our accepted world"[42] and open the path to higher consciousness. The question was not what parables did (that is, they shattered the world of fallen conventionality), but how they did it. Increasingly unhappy with the Romantic assumptions in his earlier analysis of metaphor,[43] Crossan turned to the category of polyvalence. Crossan determined that parables work by means of polyvalence rather than metaphoricity.

This is not the place to take up the scholarly debates about Crossan's postmodern view of parables. I do, however, wish to highlight that, despite the theoretical promise of polyvalence, the initial application of the term did not lead towards a confrontation with the aesthetic ideology. Instead, the ideology's fundamental gestures once again have been reinscribed in new scholarly terrain. For Crossan, paradox, polyvalency, and mystery produce a higher consciousness, liberating the hearer from authoritarianism and despotism. It is the polyvalent parable that smashes the idols of the totalitarian imagination, and frees the hearer from the world of the aesthetically ossified, alien, domesticated consciousness. It is paradox that humbles the stultifying forces of domestication and ensures that Jesus will remain robustly Western. The parables are polyvalent, multiple, and therefore inexhaustible, while allegories are monological and univocal.[44]

---

42. John Dominic Crossan, *The Dark Interval: Towards a Theology of Story* (Sonoma, Calif.: Polebridge, 1988), 122.

43. See John Dominic Crossan, *Raid on the Articulate: Cosmic Eschatology in Jesus and Borges* (New York: Harper & Row, 1976), 115–30; *Cliffs of Fall: Paradox and Polyvalence in the Parables of Jesus* (New York: Seabury, 1980), 5–13.

44. Crossan, *Cliffs,* 10; see also Kelley, *Racializing Jesus,* 235 n. 11.

Crossan's second crucial interpretive move is to conceive of his parabolic theory in political terms. Alienation and its ensuing spiritual slavery now stem from belief in a single, authoritative interpretation of a text. Freedom is found in multiple interpretations, in texts that demand more than one reading (that is, the parables), and in theories that are open to more than one reading. *Cliffs of Fall* argues that a literal or univocal reading produces alienated consciousness and all that follows. In *Raid on the Articulate*, Crossan contrasts "the magic of multiplicity" with "the tyranny of univocity,"[45] as multiplicity comes to represent freedom, while univocality stands in for totalitarianism.[46]

One could argue that Crossan's steps towards postmodernism remain within the orbit of more conventional parable scholarship. One cannot say the same thing about Stephen Moore, who has consistently pushed mainstream scholarship to take up the full array of challenges posed by the turn to postmodernism. Yet, even here, one can find traces of the aesthetic ideology as mediated through parable scholarship. One can see these traces in Moore's initial critique of the emerging literary criticism of the late 1980s, where Moore contrasts the aesthetic shock of historical criticism[47] with the tedium of more conventional forms of literary criticism. He objects to literary readings which remain too "comforting", too "conventional", and unable to "startle" those who consume them.[48] This is the language and logic of the parable translated to the debates over theory, with poststructuralism taking the role of parable, and narrative criticism assuming the role of allegory. One can also see traces of this ideology in Moore's first consistently poststructural reading of the Gospels. With the help of Derridean deconstruction, Moore proposes a reading of the Gospel of Mark where the interpretation is every bit as parabolic as the Markan

---

45. Crossan, *Raids*, 125.

46. See Crossan, *Cliffs*, 56; for similar claims about Mark, see Fowler, *Let the Reader Understand*, 251–62.

47. See Stephen Moore, *Literary Criticism and the Gospels: The Theoretical Challenge* (New Haven: Yale University Press, 1989), 128; *Poststructuralism and the New Testament: Derrida and Foucault at the Foot of the Cross* (Minneapolis: Fortress Press, 1994), 117.

48. See Moore, *Literary Criticism*, 54–55.

text.[49] His critique, in other words, is that recent Markan scholarship is not parabolic enough. The aesthetic ideology is more than capable of prospering in the rarefied air of postmodern criticism.

Conclusion

I am not recommending that we turn our backs on the methodological innovations of the past two decades. While both historical criticism and the newer methodologies are implicated in modern racialization, neither are so ideologically contaminated as to be hopelessly racialized. Furthermore, there is no new method that could somehow magically free itself from the ideological constraints of a racist and sexist modernity. Any new method we develop could well open itself up to the same aestheticizing and racializing tendencies. While some forms of postmodernism, particularly those in dialogue with postcolonial criticism, are especially well-suited to confront the racialization that permeates modernity, there is every reason to fear that they too could become ideologically ensnared, and there is every reason to assume that more conventional forms of criticism are equally capable of ideological disentanglement.

What I am suggesting is a revisiting of the methodological debates of the past two decades, but with aesthetically defined ideological questions coming to the fore. The challenge, I would suggest, is to identify the precise moments that various movements open themselves up to racialization, and, having identified those moments, to begin the slow and arduous process of shifting the analysis in another direction. It is through this process that the discipline can begin the process of developing alternative aesthetic categories, assumptions, and reading strategies.

I have repeatedly drawn attention to the fact that much recent criticism has desired to produce a decolonized Gospel. Yet these noble ideals are unrealizable, I would suggest, as long as they are propped up by an ideology built around purity, expulsion, and fear of

---

49. See especially Stephen Moore, *Mark and Luke in Poststructuralist Perspectives: Jesus Begins to Write* (New Haven: Yale University Press, 1992), xviii, 74.

domestication. What I wish to highlight is the gap between the ideals of a methodology and the aesthetic assumptions that simultaneously pull the analysis in the opposite direction.

I would like to conclude by holding out hope for optimism. Perhaps, with the aesthetic ideology unmasked, the discipline will take one step closer towards the decolonized and liberatory hermeneutic that seems to be honestly desired by so many scholars working out of so many diverse methodologies.

CHAPTER 8

Race as Incarnational Theology

Affinities between German Protestantism and Racial Theory[1]

Susannah Heschel

During the Third Reich, German Protestant theologians, motivated by racism and tapping into traditional Christian anti-Semitism, redefined Jesus as an Aryan and Christianity as a religion at war with Judaism. In 1939, these theologians established the Institute for the Study and Eradication of Jewish Influence on German Religious Life. The surprisingly large number of distinguished professors, younger scholars, and students who became involved in the effort to synthesize Nazism and Christianity should be seen not simply as a response to political developments, nor simply as an outgrowth of struggles within the field of Christian theology, but as suggesting underlying affinities between racism and Christian theology, affinities they recognized and promoted. In tracing the work of the Institute, its funding, publications, and membership activities, the emergence of a Nazi Christianity comes to light.

Introduction

The question I want to pose is why Christian theology is drawn to racism. Specifically, I am examining German Protestant New Testament scholarship in the early-twentieth century, prior to and during the Nazi era. The surprisingly large number of distinguished professors, younger scholars, and students who became involved in the effort to synthesize Nazism and Christianity should be seen, I want to argue, not simply as a response to political developments, nor simply as an outgrowth of struggles within the field of Christian theology, but as suggesting underlying affinities between racism and Christian theology, affinities they recognized and promoted. What did these German theologians feel they could achieve by synthesizing Protestant theology and racism?

Already in 1971, the late historian Uriel Tal challenged the entrenched view that racist anti-Semitism is a new phenomenon that repudiates Christianity by arguing that such anti-Semitism was actually utterly dependent on Christian anti-Judaism for its success:

> It was not the economic crises that brought about this new political, racial, and anti-religious anti-Semitism, but completely the reverse, it was precisely the anti-Christian and anti-religious ideology of racial anti-Semitism which hampered the first anti-Semitic parties in their efforts to utilize the economic crisis for their political development . . . [because] what still attracted the masses was the classical, traditional Christian anti-Judaism, however adapted it may have become to the new economic conditions.[2]

---

1. This article is based on a paper I delivered at the superb seminar on New Testament and race, organized by Professors Elisabeth Schüssler Fiorenza and Laura Nasrallah, at Harvard Divinity School. I appreciate very much the insightful comments by the seminar participants, and, in particular, the formal response to the paper by Jennifer Knust.

My mother, Sylvia Heschel, died the day after the seminar concluded in March of 2007 and this article is dedicated to her memory.

2. Uriel Tal, "Religious and Anti-Religious Roots of Modern Antisemitism," Leo Baeck Memorial Lecture, No. 14 (New York: Leo Baeck Institute, 1971); reprinted in Uriel Tal, ed., *Religion, Politics, and Ideology in the Third Reich: Selected Essays* (London and New York: Routledge, 2004), 177.

Tal demonstrated that Germany's anti-Semitic, *völkisch* ("racial")
movements that arose in the nineteenth century had to abandon their
initial anti-Christian stances in order to win supporters for whom
Christian anti-Jewish arguments were of profound political appeal.[3]

Even within the so-called "church struggle" for control of the
Protestant church between members of the pro-Nazi German Christian movement and the Confessing Church, anti-Semitism became
the glue that united the otherwise warring factions.[4] Similarly, however much Hitler made use of images of messianism, redemption,
and other Christian motifs, the most useful and consistent aspect of
Christianity for the Nazi movement was its anti-Judaism, just as the
single most consistent and persistent feature of Nazism was its anti-
Semitism.

While seeking to undermine the political power and moral authority of the churches, Nazism simultaneously appropriated key elements of Christian theology into its own ideology both for purposes
of winning adherents accustomed to Christian arguments and to give

---

3. "In reality Nazism accomplished but few of its goals. But in one area, that
of the Jewish question, political myth achieved its purpose to the full. Here the
regime met the least opposition from those who in other matters were hardly
in accord with Nazism—be it intellectuals, the churches, or public opinion in
the Reich or abroad. The Jew served as the focal point round which Nazism
turned and on which the structural process of value-transformation and reversal
of meanings took place. Among the values and meanings that were transformed,
the symbol itself was turned into substance; consequently, the negation of Judaism had to be transformed into the annihilation of the Jew, this time not spiritually but rather physically, not symbolically but in substance." Tal, ibid., 111.

4. The German Christian movement began as a coalition of Protestant clergy
and laity with strong nationalist and racist convictions who sought to alter Christianity in accord with those convictions. Formed in 1932, its ideology was shaped
by ideas that emerged in the nineteenth and early twentieth century. Strongly
supportive of the Nazi Party, German Christian leaders wanted to create a Reich
church, led by a pro-Nazi bishop, which would implement Nazi racial policies
and create a manly, antidoctrinal, anti-Semitic Germanic Christianity. The Confessing Church, which emerged in 1934 from the Pastors' Emergency League
that was formed in response to a German Christian rally in Berlin in November,
1933, opposed alterations of Christian Scripture and doctrine and insisted that
the sacrament of baptism could not be overridden by Nazi racial laws. It thus
offered support to baptized Jews, but most of its members did not offer support
to Jews who had not been baptized.

its own message a coherence and resonance with the age-old Christian teachings that had shaped European culture. The German Christians reversed the process, appropriating Nazi rhetoric and symbols into the church to give its Christianity a contemporary resonance. Both the Nazis and the German Christians identified Hitler as Christ's second coming. They spoke, for example, of the "Führer Jesus" and described Hitler as "God's agent [Beauftragter] in our day."[5] That gave Hitler the status of a supernatural being and gave Christ renewed glory as a contemporary figure of enormous political significance.

Meanwhile, Jews were not simply despised, but came to be presented as a danger to be eradicated. In this, as in so many other issues, theologians anticipated and suggested anti-Jewish policy before it was formulated by the Nazi regime. On February 24–25, 1936, a few months after the proclamation of the Nuremberg Laws,[6] a group of theologians[7] met in Dresden to discuss merging the German Christian factions of the state churches of Thuringia and Saxony. During the course of the meeting, Siegfried Leffler, a German Christian leader, official in the Thuringian Ministry of Education, and, by 1939, official head of the Institute, stated:

> In a Christian life, the heart always has to be disposed toward the Jew, and that's how it has to be. As a Christian, I can, I must, and I ought always to have or to find a bridge to the Jew in my heart. But as a Christian, I also have to follow the laws of my nation [Volk], which are often presented in a very cruel way, so that again I am brought into the harshest of conflicts with the Jew. Even if I know "thou shalt not kill" is a commandment of God or "thou shalt love the Jew" because he too is a child of the eternal Father, I am able to know as well that I have to kill him,

---

5. From "Bericht über die Arbeitstagung der 'Deutschen Christen' Gruppe Rheinland," 144–46, cited by Heiner Faulenbach, *Ein Weg durch die Kirche: Heinrich Josef Oberheid* (Cologne: Rheinland Verlag, 1992), 161.

6. This was still long before Jews were being deported and murdered.

7. Some of these theologians subsequently became leaders of the German Christian–sponsored Institute for the Study and Eradication of Jewish Influence on German Church Life, founded in 1939.

I have to shoot him, and I can only do that if I am permitted to say: Christ.[8]

That meeting took place just a few months after the Nuremberg Laws of September 1935, which were viewed as an encouragement by the German Christians to take even more radical positions. Legal cases in German courts, brought in the wake of the Nuremberg Laws' criminalization of sexual relations and marriage between Jews and Aryans, and widely reported in the German press, implicated Jews as sexual predators of Aryans. That further encouraged Christian theologians to insist on protecting Christian purity by eradicating Jewishness with even more radical measures.[9] The penetration of Christian bodies by Jewish sex reiterated a typical motif of racist rhetoric—the dangers of miscegenation—and reinforced fears that Aryanism was not immutable, but subject to destruction by Jews.[10] It is commonly and incorrectly assumed that modern racism promotes a notion of race as an immutable essence; biological immutability, it is argued, differentiates modern racism from earlier forms of prejudice.[11] Whereas the church historically advocated the conversion of the Jews

---

8. *Akte Thüringisches Volksbildungsministerium* Signatur A 1400, Blatt 293; my translation. The meeting was held February 24–25, 1936. Present: Paul Althaus, Martin Doerne, Erich Fascher, Meyer Erlach, Dedo Müller, pastors, church superintendents; Leffler, Leutheuser, Hugo Hahn, a church superintendent in Saxony who led the Confessing Church movement there, and Grundmann. It is striking that Anja Rinnen, in her biography of Siegfried Leffler, does not cite this document, and that Hahn does not describe the meeting in his detailed memoir of the period nor mention Leffler's comments. See Anja Rinnen, *Kirchenmann und Nationalsozialist: Siegfried Lefflers ideelle Verschmelzung von Kirche und drittem Reich, Forum zur Pädagogik und Didaktik der Religion;* 9 (Weinheim: Deutscher Studien Verlag, 1995). Hugo Hahn and Georg Prater, *Kämpfer Wider Willen. Erinnerungen aus d. Kirchenkampf 1933–1945* (Metzingen: Brunnquell-Verl., 1969).

9. Patricia Szobar, "Telling Sexual Stories in the Nazi Courts of Law: Race Defilement in Germany, 1933 to 1945," *History of Sexuality* 11, no. 1–2 (2002): 131–63.

10. On the centrality of fear of miscegenation in the racist discourse of colonialism, see Ann Stoler, "Racial Histories and Their Regimes of Truth," *Political Power and Social Theory* 11 (1997): 183–206.

11. For a recent expression of this assumption, see Aaron Rodrigue, "Totems, Taboos, and Jews: Salomon Reinach and the Politics of Scholarship in Fin-de-Siecle France," *Jewish Social Studies* 10, no.2 (2004): 1–19.

to Christianity, so this line of reasoning goes, modern racists reject the possibility that Jews can become Christians because Jewishness is biological and cannot be erased. Yet this assumption overlooks the complexity of racial thinking.

Wherever racist ideas have held sway, it has always been assumed that racial status could be altered by, for example, marriage, making miscegenation a central concern of European racism. In the Third Reich, Jews were racially elevated by marriage to an Aryan, while Aryans married to Jews were corrupting their race. The defilement of pure Aryan descent was presumed to be all too easy and to occur through pollution of the body. Racial theory is thus concerned not only to promote the superiority of the Aryans, but also their vulnerability to the pollutions of lesser races and the degeneracy that has supposedly resulted from it.[12]

Indeed, the Aryan fear of compromised racial purity, expressed through strict laws prohibiting sex with non-Aryans, indicates that the mutability was believed to occur via sexual relations, even without conception and reproduction, as expressed in Artur Dinter's bestselling novel, *Die Sünde wider das Blut* ("Sins against the Blood"), in which the children of an Aryan couple are tainted as a result of their mother's sexual relationship with a Jew many years earlier that left her blood permanently polluted.[13] Fantasies of losing one's racial spiritual purity via the body abounded among modern racial theorists and their literary popularizers. Such vulnerability of Aryan blood to corruption by Jewish semen mirrors the vulnerability of holiness to profanation in religious systems and illustrates that the instability of race, not its immutability, lies at the heart of its invention. As Ann Stoler has concluded from her studies of race and colonialism, "the

---

12. The work of Comte Joseph-Arthur de Gobineau (1816–82), which influenced Houston Stewart Chamberlain, Alfred Rosenberg, and Hitler, is a good example of the argument that mixing with other races had caused a degeneracy of the European Aryans. See his *Essai sur l'inegalite des races humaines*, 4 vols. (Paris: Didot, 1853–55).

13. Artur Dinter, *Die Sünde wider das Blut. Ein Zeitroman*, 11th ed. (Leipzig: Matthes and Thost, 1920). Dinter was active in *völkisch* and Nazi politics in Thuringia during the 1920s. He held Nazi party membership number 5 and served as Gauleiter of the party in Thuringia, but was expelled from the Nazi party in 1928.

force of racial discourse is precisely in the double-vision it allows, in the fact that it combines notions of fixity and fluidity in ways that are basic to its dynamic."[14]

No Aryan was immune from potential judaization, not even the most passionate Nazis. Indeed, charges of Jewish thinking (sometimes called "Pharisaic") abounded as "holier than thou" Nazi sympathizers traded accusations.[15] Anti-Semites had long insisted that German Aryan women were vulnerable to Jewish predation, and Jesus, whose gentleness and suffering was viewed as effeminate by German Christians, was depicted in one Nazi caricature as an Aryan woman on a cross with a lecherous Jewish man in the foreground: the crucifixion as the Jewish rape of Germany.[16]

The use of laws and court procedures to control sexual relations within Germany and thereby create the Aryan racial nation was not in contradiction to Christian teachings; after all, as Jennifer Knust points out, the apostle Paul, Justin Martyr, and other early Christian writers asserted that those who reject Christ are by definition sexually repulsive, licentious, and "unnatural" in their sexual behavior.[17] Among the postapostolic writers, the physical, and especially sexual, purity of Christians was the safeguard of moral and religious purity. Thus, the Nuremberg Laws easily could be read as upholding classical Christian values and calling forth the sort of theological action that Leffler proposed just months after they were announced. The affinities theologians sought with racism were challenged by the image of Christianity as a "Jewish" religion. While some pastors, already during

---

14. Ann Stoler, "Racial Histories and Their Regimes of Truth," *Political Power and Social Theory* 11 (1997): 198.

15. For example, in a privately printed pamphlet, Hans von Soden, professor of NT at the University of Marburg and an opponent of the German Christians, termed Grundmann's book, *Jesus der Galiläer*, a piece of "Pharisaic" scholarship for trying to construct Jesus as an Aryan. Grundmann, in turn, accused anti-Christian Nazi ideologues of having been "judaized" by the eighteenth-century Jewish philosopher, Moses Mendelssohn, for their claim that Jesus was a Jew.

16. Kurt Plischke, *Der Jude als Rassenschänder: Eine Anklage gegen Juda und eine Mahnung an die deutschen Frauen und Mädchen* ["The Jew as Race Defiler: An Accusation against Judah and a Warning to German Women and Girls"] (Berlin-Schöneberg: NS.-Druck und Verlag, 1934).

17. Jennifer Wright Knust, *Abandoned to Lust: Sexual Slander and Ancient Christianity* (New York: Columbia University Press, 2006).

World War I, called for the rejection of Jewish elements from Christianity, adherents of the anti-Christian, neopagan movements, as well as some Nazi theorists, such as Alfred Rosenberg, mocked those efforts, on the grounds that once the "Jewish" was removed from Christianity, nothing would remain.[18] Within the theological community, debates were more specific: how was the "Jewish" to be defined? Was the Old Testament Jewish? What about Jesus, Paul, and the gospel authors? To arrive at those decisions and carry out the necessary consequences of purging Christianity of Judaism, in 1939, a group of theologians established a "dejudaization institute" (*Entjudungsinstitut*). A wide range of Protestant church leaders offered public sanction to the Godesberg Declaration of March 1939, which asserted that Christian churches could not be international; that National Socialism is an extension of Martin Luther's efforts; and that Christianity repudiates Judaism.[19] The centerpiece of the declaration was its question and answer: "Is Christianity derived from Judaism and is it its continuation and completion, or does Christianity stand in opposition to Judaism? We answer this question: Christianity is the unbridgeable religious opposition to Judaism."[20]

Outline of the Institute

At noon on Saturday, May 6, 1939, a group of Protestant theologians, pastors, and churchgoers gathered at the historic Wartburg Castle, resonant with Lutheran and nationalist significance, to celebrate the

---

18. Alfred Rosenberg, *der Mythus Des 20. Jahrhunderts: Eine Wertung der Seelisch-Geistigen Gestaltenkämpfe unserer Zeit* (Munich: Hoheneichen, 1930). On Rosenberg, see Ernst Piper, *Alfred Rosenberg: Hitlers Chefideologe* (Munich: Blessing, 2005).

19. Signatories were the German Christian leaders of eleven regional churches: APU, Saxony, Nassau-Hessen, Schleswig-Holstein, Thuringia, Mecklenburg, Pfalz (Palatinate), Anhalt, Oldenburg, Lübeck, and Ostmark (Austria), all of which were dominated by the German Christian movement. The Confessing Church denounced the declaration, as did the Reformed Confederation for Germany, and the World Council of Churches issued a statement opposing it.

20. My translation. Documents related to the formulation and signing of the Godesberg Declaration, which was published by the church in its official Gesetzblatt, can be found in the Zentralarchiv der Kirche, Berlin, Bestand 7/4166.

official opening of the "Institute for the Study and Eradication of Jewish Influence on German Church Life" (*Institut zur Erforschung und Beseitigung des jüdischen Einflusses auf das deutsche kirchliche Leben*). The Institute's goals were both political and theological. Seeking to create a dejudaized Church for a Germany that was in the process of ridding Europe of all Jews, it developed new biblical interpretations and liturgical materials. In the six years of its existence, as the Nazi regime carried out its genocide of the Jews, the Institute redefined Christianity as a Germanic religion whose founder, the Aryan Jesus, had fought valiantly to destroy Judaism, falling victim to that struggle. Germans were now called upon to be the victors in Jesus' own struggle against the Jews.[21]

On the theological level, the Institute achieved remarkable success, winning support for its radical agenda from a host of church officials and theology professors who welcomed the removal of Jewish elements from Christian Scripture and liturgy and the redefinition of Christianity as an Aryan religion. These included both senior and junior scholars in the field of theology, ranging from Martin Redeker, professor of systematic theology at the University of Kiel and an expert on the work of Friedrich Schleiermacher, to Georg Bertram, professor of New Testament at the University of Giessen and an expert on the Septuagint. Members of the Institute worked devotedly, as did so many others in the Reich, "towards the Führer," in Ian Kershaw's phrase, to win the fight against the Jews.[22] Their devotion took them to greater and greater extremes, abandoning traditional Christian doctrine in exchange for coalitions with neo-pagan leaders, and producing vituperative propaganda on behalf of the Reich's measures against the Jews.

---

21. On the history, funding, and activities of the Institute, see Susannah Heschel, *The Aryan Jesus: Christians and the Bible in Nazi Germany* (Princeton: Princeton University Press, 2008).

22. Kershaw took the phrase "working towards the Führer" from a speech delivered by Werner Willikens, State Secretary in the Prussian Agriculture Ministry, at a meeting of representatives from state agriculture ministries held in Berlin on February 21, 1934. Ian Kershaw, *Hitler 1889–1936: Hubris* (New York: W. W. Norton, 1998), 529.

Aryan, in turn, meant not simply a physical or biological body type, but much more an inner spirit that was simultaneously of great power and also profoundly vulnerable to the degeneration threatened by non-Aryans, particularly Jews. In Nazi Germany, "racial hygiene" became the field to teach how to protect the body housing the Aryan spirit; the Institute's theology attended to caring for that spirit. In its idiosyncratic gender politics, the spirit was to protect the body from racial impurity and for that protective task the spirit required a masculinization that these theologians contended would be achieved by abandoning the old, "judaized" Christianity for a new, Nazified, dejudaized Christianity.

Most members of the Institute, particularly its academic director, Walter Grundmann, a professor of New Testament at the University of Jena, saw themselves in the theological avant-garde. They believed that they addressed and resolved a problem that had long plagued Christian theology: how to establish clear and distinct boundaries between earliest Christianity and Judaism and to eliminate all traces of Jewish influence within Christian theology and religious practice. As a mostly younger generation of scholars, trained by Germany's leading scholars of early Christianity—many members of the Institute were students of the distinguished Tübingen professor, Gerhard Kittel—they considered themselves able to recover the historically genuine, non-Jewish Jesus and a Christian message compatible with contemporary German identity. Theirs was a goal of purification, authenticity, and theological revolution, all in the name of historical-critical methods and commitment to Germanness, to be achieved by eradicating the Jewish from the Christian. A Christian message tainted by Jewishness could not serve Germans, nor could a Jewish message be the accurate teaching of Jesus.

The Institute's goals were stated forthrightly at its opening by Grundmann, who delivered the keynote lecture on "The Dejudaization of the Religious Life as the Task of German Theology and Church." The present era, he declared, was similar to the Reformation: Protestants had to overcome Judaism just as Luther had overcome Catholicism. "The elimination of Jewish influence on German life is the urgent and fundamental question of the present German religious situation."[23] Yes, Grundmann noted, people in Luther's day could not imagine Christianity without the pope, just as in his day, they could not imagine salvation without the Old Testament, but the goal could be realized. Modern New Testament scholarship had made apparent the "deformation of New Testament ideas into Old Testament preconceptions, so that now angry recognition of the Jewishness in the Old Testament and in parts of the New Testament has arisen, obstructing access to the Bible for innumerable German people."[24]

The Bible would have to be purified, Grundmann continued, restored to its pristine condition, proclaiming the truth about Jesus: that he was an Aryan who sought the destruction of Judaism. Grundmann outlined the scholarly tasks that the Institute would undertake. This included clarifying the role of Judaism in early Christianity and its influence on modern philosophy. Any opposition to National Socialism from within the church, claimed Grundmann, arose from nefarious Jewish influence, such as the arguments of Jewish scholars that Jesus was a Jew. The Jews had destroyed Germans' *völkisch* thinking, Grundmann continued, and, with help from Bolshevism, they were now striving for world conquest, the *Weltherrschaft des Judentums* ("world domination of Jewry"). The Jewish threat to Germany was grave: "For these reasons," Grundmann stated, echoing Nazi propaganda, "the struggle against the Jews has been irrevocably turned over to the German *Volk*."[25] The war against the Jews was not simply a military battle, but a spiritual battle: "Jewish influence on all areas of German life, including on religious-church life, must be exposed and broken,"[26] a phrase Grundmann repeatedly used in defining the Institute's purpose.

From 1939 to 1945, the Institute functioned as a broad tent, under which both scholars and pastors could articulate a range of anti-Jewish theological positions, most of which had already been proposed long before 1933 by various theologians and pastors, though without entering mainstream discussion within the church. Some,

23. Walter Grundmann, *Die Entjudung des religiösen Lebens als Aufgabe deutscher Theologie und Kirche* (Weimar: Verlag Deutsche Christen, 1939), 9. My translation.
24. Ibid., 9–10. My translation.
25. Ibid., 9. My translation.
26. Ibid., 17. My translation.

like Grundmann, called for the removal of the Old Testament from the Christian Bible on the grounds that the Old Testament was a Jewish book, while others, such as Johannes Hempel, professor of Old Testament at the University of Berlin, tried to retain the Old Testament for Christians, on the grounds that its core was a message about the *Volk* ("nation" or "race") Israel (not the Jews) that was important for the German *Volk* to hear. Active members of the Institute included internationally renowned scholars of Jewish texts, such as Hugo Odeberg, but also theology students and demagogues, such as Hans-Joachim Thilo and Wolf Meyer-Erlach. By 1942, the year most European Jews were murdered, the Institute broadened its membership and its themes, inviting *völkisch* writers to lecture on Germany's Teutonic heritage and its compatibility with Christianity.

What united Institute members was a commitment to eradicating Jewishness as a means of purifying both Christianity and Germany. Known popularly as a dejudaization institute, it was the Protestant church's instrument of anti-Semitic propaganda. Theological conclusions regarding Jesus' teachings and his interactions with the Jews of his day were shaped into a rhetoric that endorsed Nazi ideology, making Nazism appear to actuate in the political sphere what Christians taught in the religious sphere. Institute conferences and publications were notable not for scholarly originality, but for developing biblical exegesis and religious history using racial methods. With members who were leading scholars of theology, professors or instructors at universities throughout the Reich, the Institute provided a scholarly and religious mantle for a politicized anti-Semitism that mirrored the Propaganda Ministry's rhetoric, which described the war as a defense against an alleged Jewish war on Germany. Grundmann wrote in 1941: "Our *Volk*, which stands above all else in a struggle against the satanic powers of world Jewry for the order and life of this world, dismisses Jesus, because it cannot struggle against the Jews and open its heart to the king of the Jews."[27] In proving that Jesus was not a Jew

---

27. Walter Grundmann, "Das Messiasproblem," in *Germanentum, Christentum und Judentum: Studien zur Erforschung ihres gegenseitigen Verhältnisses. Bd. 2. Sitzungsberichte der zweiten Arbeitstagung des Instituts zur Erforschung des jüdischen Einflusses auf das deutsche kirchliche Leben vom 3. bis 5. März 1941 in Eisenach*, ed. Walter Grundmann (Leipzig: Georg Wigand, 1943). My translation.

but an opponent of the Jews, Grundmann allied the Institute's work with the Nazi war effort.

The extent of the Institute's appeal was remarkable: university professors, instructors, and students of Protestant theology in the Reich became Institute members; they represented a cross-section of disciplines, geographic locations, ages, and levels of scholarly accomplishment. Let me mention a few. Walter Grundmann was professor of New Testament at the University of Jena, where two other Institute members taught, Heinz Eisenhuth, systematic theology, and Wolf Meyer-Erlach, practical theology. Johannes Hempel was an active member from the outset and close to Grundmann, who solicited his assistance in winning Institute support from church officials in Berlin. Hempel was professor of Old Testament at the University of Berlin and editor of the *Zeitschrift für alttestamentliche Wissenschaft* ("Journal for Old Testament Studies") until 1959. Georg Beer, New Testament professor at the University of Heidelberg, was one of the Institute's most senior members, and himself an expert on rabbinic Judaism. Systematic theology was represented by Martin Redeker, the Schleiermacher scholar, from the University of Kiel, and Theodor Odenwald, University of Heidelberg; New Testament was represented by Johannes Leipoldt, from the University of Leipzig, Herbert Preisker, from the University of Breslau, and Hugo Odeberg, from the University of Lund. Younger members included Georg Bertram, Gerhard Delling, and Karl Euler, all trained as theologians.

Some were Nazi party members of long standing, while others never joined. The Institute offered precisely what academics seek: support for publications, conferences to present ideas, gatherings to meet colleagues, and a sense of self-importance. For members who were pastors, teachers of religion, or students of theology, the chance to gather with well-known professors from all over the Reich and Scandinavia was certainly of great appeal, especially since all expenses were paid. Opportunities to publish in Institute-sponsored books were also valuable, because paper and funding were scarce during the war years.

Members were divided into working groups and, within a year, produced a dejudaized version of the New Testament, *Die Botschaft Gottes* ("The Message of God"); a dejudaized hymnal, *Grosser Gott Wir loben Dich* ("Mighty God We Praise You"); a Nazified catechism,

Deutsche mit Gott: Ein deutsches Glaubensbuch ("Germans with God: A German Catechism"); as well as numerous books and pamphlets for lay and scholarly audiences, in which the Institute's theological arguments were presented. The Institute held numerous conferences and established a branch in Romania to serve "ethnic Germans." Though closed in 1945 by the Thuringian church due to lack of funds, members of the Institute were never censured by their postwar churches for their anti-Semitic work. Hempel, for example, who had transformed the prestigious Institutum Judaicum in Berlin, which he directed from 1937–45, into a center for racially based scholarship,[28] retained his editorship of the distinguished journal *Zeitschrift für alttestamentliche Wissenschaft.*

Racial Theory and Theology

My larger question is why racial theory was so appealing to Protestant theologians in Germany during the first half of the twentieth century, and why it was so easy to racialize Christianity. The racism that emerged in Europe during the second half of the nineteenth century appealed to German Protestants at first as a component of nationalism, but by the twentieth century, racism, particularly anti-Semitism, became a vehicle to modernize Christianity and to legitimate its tenets. Jesus was first presented in opposition to Judaism, then as its enemy, finally as an Aryan.

Numerous historians have traced the origins of racist thought to the period of the Enlightenment and blamed its emergence on the decline of religious belief. The historian Colin Kidd, however, recently has argued not that race emerges as a consequence of the undermining of religion, but that race is implicated as a major factor in bringing about the "unraveling of Christian certainties."[29] Starting in the

---

28. For a history of the Institutum Judaicum, see Ralf Golling, Peter von der Osten-Sacken, eds., *Hermann L. Strack und das Institutum Judaicum in Berlin: mit einem Anhang über das Institut Kirche und Judentum* (Berlin: Institut Kirche und Judentum, 1996).

29. Wolfgang Fenske, *Wie Jesus zum "Arier" wurde. Auswirkungen der entjudaisierung Christi im 19. und zu Beginn des 20. Jahrhunderts* (Darmstadt: Wissenschaftliche Buchgesellschaft, 2005). Colin Kidd, *The Forging of Races: Race and*

eighteenth century, race, according to Kidd, helped to undermine the foundations of Christian belief: the universalism of its message, the uniqueness and historicity of its teachings, and the reliability and coherence of its Scriptures. Race argued for a differentiated classification of human beings, whereas the Bible claimed that God created all humans equally. Science trumped religion, and race, Kidd argues, undermined theologically-rooted belief in monogenesis, and made religion seem regressive and undermined faith. By the Nazi era, however, the very same racial claims played the opposite function: in its specific iteration as anti-Semitism, race was used by some theologians as a restorative force of coherence for Christian theology and for interpretations of the New Testament. Monogenesis was no longer the central concern; instead, biblical passages were uncovered to demonstrate support for racial hierarchy, and anti-Semitic passages in the New Testament were highlighted to demonstrate Christian conformity with racist suppositions. Racism was viewed by many theologians not only as a political tool, but as an avant-garde method for understanding society and human nature.

By making use of racial arguments in their presentations of Christianity, members of the Institute thought they could bolster the appeal of Christianity to its Nazi despisers. Racism's argument that distinct and immutable orders exist in society lent support to a "theology of creation." Biblical hierarchies were also invoked to support racism. One Institute member, Wilhelm Stapel, attempted to demonstrate that racism supported Christian claims to divine creation: just as God had created societal orders—marriage, family, hierarchy, property, and so forth—God had given each *Volk* a task and place on earth.[30]

Scripture in the Protestant Atlantic World, 1600–2000 (Cambridge: Cambridge University Press, 2006), 122.

30. Stapel, who lectured at Institute conferences, was widely read and was one of the more sophisticated exponents of *völkisch* theology. Some of his publications include *Die Kirche Christi und der Staat Hitlers* (Hamburg: Hanseatische Verlagsanstalt, 1933); *Antisemitismus und Antigermanismus. Über das seelische Problem der Symbiose des deutschen und des jüdischen Volkes* (Hamburg: Hanseatische Verlagsanstalt, 1928); *Der christliche Staatsmann. Eine Theologie des Nationalismus* (Hamburg: Hanseatische Verlagsanstalt, 1932); *Volk. Untersuchungen über Volkheit und Volkstum*, 4th ed. (Hamburg: Hanseatische Verlagsanstalt, 1942).

Believers in racial hierarchy could see it as an extension of the biblical account of God's creation of hierarchical orders within nature and society. Christians were told that racial hierarchies were an extension of the divine order. In both cases, the subservience of women to men and the dominance of animals by humans eased the acceptance of racism.

Within the field of Christian Protestant theology, racism was thought to restore the uniqueness, historicity, and significance of Jesus and his teachings that had been undermined by historicism. Even if Jesus' teachings did not seem different from those of other Jews of his day, he was distinct in his race, as an Aryan and not a Jew. His racial identity was then used to read his teachings not as reflections of Judaism, but as repudiations of it. The goal of the Institute was to use racial theory to eradicate all traces of Jewishness and to restore the original, authentic teachings of Christianity. That goal was simultaneously political; Institute publications argued that the Jews were violent people who sought the destruction of Jesus and continued to strive for world domination and the subjugation of all Gentiles. The Institute presented the war as a defensive life and death struggle against the Jews, and also as a Christian war in the name of the authentic non-Jewish Jesus, the Christianity he sought to bring into being, and the battle to destroy Judaism that he failed to win. Like the German military, the Institute presented its cause as a total eradication of the enemy, Judaism, and not simply its segregation or expulsion from the Reich.

The dejudaization effort of the Institute must be examined both in terms of Third Reich politics and as a Christian theological dilemma that engaged a vast number of pastors, bishops, and academic theologians. That theological dilemma was to explain the origins of Christianity within Judaism. Christianity came into being by resting on the theological foundations of Judaism, and the relationship of Judaism to Christianity has often been described as a "mother-daughter" relationship. Nearly every central theological concept of Christianity rests on a Jewish foundation, from messiah to divine election. Affirming what is central to Christian teaching usually entails an affirmation of a Jewish idea or a text from the Old Testament, so that attempting to eradicate the Jewish was a kind of "theological bulimia."[31] Yet modern historical scholarship, by contextualizing the message of Jesus within Judaism, demonstrated that his teachings were not new or original, but similar to those of other Jews of his day. Historicism led to the problem of defining the distinctiveness of Christianity, and raised the shameful specter that Jesus did not offer a new religious message, or else that Christianity was simply a version of ancient Judaism; this also carried a valence of shame, given Jews' inferior status in Christian Europe. The rise of modern anti-Semitism intensified the theological dilemma: how could Christianity be extricated from Judaism? Theologians turned to racial theory in order to solve a theological dilemma, and the project of the Institute—eradicating Christianity of Jewish influence—was racism at the theological level.

Racial theory was not simply a tool for theological research. The appeal of racism, and particularly anti-Semitism, to German Protestant theologians went deeper. Theologians found affinities with racial rhetoric because, I would like to argue, they perceived that racism is ultimately concerned not with biology but rather with the human spirit. That was recognized by the racists themselves, who were concerned to define the spiritual natures of those they studied. Walter Wüst, professor of linguistics at the University of Munich and rector of that university from 1941–1945 and head of the Ahnenerbe, a research center established by SS chief Heinrich Himmler to study Indo-Germanic origins, made the link between race and religion clear: "Today we know that religion is basically a spiritual-physical human activity and that it is thereby also racial."[32] Indeed, in the context of the SS, religion could survive only by being redefined as a racial phenomenon.

---

31. I would like to thank Richard M. Gottlieb for stimulating conversations about the metaphor of theological bulimia. I have developed that theme more extensively elsewhere; see Susannah Heschel, "Theology as a Vision for Colonialism: From Supercessionism to Dejudaization in German Protestantism," in *Germany's Colonial Pasts: An Anthology in Memory of Susanne Zantop*, ed. Eric Ames, Marcia Klotz, and Lora Wildenthal (Lincoln: University of Nebraska Press, 2005); "Theological Bulimia: Christianity and Its Dejudaization," in *After the Passion Is Gone: American Religious Consequences*, ed. Michael Berenbaum and Shawn Landres (Walnut Creek, Calif.: AltaMira, 2004).

32. Walter Wüst, *Indogermanisches Bekenntnis* (Berlin: Ahnenerbe-Stiftung Verlag, 1942), 68; cited by Stefan Arvidsson, *Aryan Idols: Indo-European*

Even before the Nazis came to power, the concern of racists was not so much the inferiority of certain peoples' bodies—the shape of the cranium or the color of the skin—as the degeneracy of their morality and spirituality and the alleged threat posed by such degeneracy to superior races. The body was presented as the physical representation of moral and spiritual qualities. Physiognomy was interpreted by philologists as signifying linguistic ability, language differences were taken as indicators of cultural levels, and "culture" was often interchangeable with "race."

Indeed, scientific measurements of the body were rejected by leading race theorists, such as Houston Stewart Chamberlain, as irrelevant to Aryans, for whom knowledge was intuitive. Grundmann revived this argument in his claim that Jesus knew God's wishes intuitively, through his heart, in contrast to Jews who know God through reason.[33] Developing the proper hermeneutics became key to racialist thinking: knowing how to "read" the body to learn what sort of moral and spiritual qualities are incarnate in it. The goal of anti-Semitic texts was to train readers in the proper hermeneutics for interpreting the Jewish body and knowing its inherent danger.

Thus, if physiognomy was described at length as signaling racial difference, it never stood alone. Rather, modern race theorists saw the body as a carrier of the soul, of moral and spiritual potencies, making race theory a kind of theology. As Richard Dyer writes in his study of whiteness, "For all the emphasis on the body in Christianity, the point is the spirit that is 'in' the body. What has made Christianity compelling and fascinating is precisely the mystery that it posits, that somehow there is in the body something that is not of the body that may be

---

Mythology as Ideology and Science, trans. Sonia Wichmann (Chicago: University of Chicago Press, 2006), 187. Examples of collaboration between theologians and Nazi race theorists deserve further exploration; see, for example, Eugen Fischer and Gerhard Kittel, *Das Antike Weltjudentum: Tatsachen, Texte, Bilder* (Hamburg: Hanseatische Verlagsanstalt, 1943).

33. Houston Stewart Chamberlain, *The Foundations of the Nineteenth Century*, trans. John Lees, 2 vols. (New York: John Lane Co., 1910); Walter Grundmann, *Die Gotteskindschaft in der Geschichte Jesu und ihre religionsgeschichtlichen Vorausetzungen, Studien zu deutscher Theologie und Frömmigkeit 1* (Weimar: Verlag Deutsche Christen, 1938).

variously termed spirit, mind, soul, or God."[34] Racists worried about the moral and spiritual threat of lesser races, such as Jews; the inferior bodies of those races were carriers of their corrupt spirits, not causes of the corruption. Within the Aryan body, the womb was central as the location for breeding pure Aryans and, at the same time, the place vulnerable to contamination by non-Aryan racial seed. Aryan women were thus encouraged by a conflicted Nazi ideology both to breed and to remain chaste.

The tired argument that racism is about biology fails to recognize that racism emphasizes the dangers posed by the body to the spirit. Flesh is crucial to racialist thinking because the body is not simply a symbol of the degenerate spirit; rather, moral degeneracy is incarnate within the body and the two cannot be separated. The Jewish nose, for instance, is not dangerous in itself, but incarnates a moral decadence. The fundamental relationship between body and soul characterizing modern racist discourse is a mirror of the body-soul dilemma at the heart of Christian metaphysics, and is precisely the stamp that Christianity has placed on Western philosophy.[35] Race additionally reinscribes the classical Christian distinction between the carnality of Judaism and the spirituality of Christianity, itself heir to older Western traditions, rooted in Aristotelian philosophy, distinguishing between the "female" body and the "male" soul. Indeed, as Elizabeth Spelman has argued, the soul is to the body as men are to women, and Christians are to Jews.[36]

Furthermore, both racism and theology present themselves as discourses of morality, with particular attention to sexual morals. Therefore, it is not surprising that National Socialism professed support of Christianity in its early years, with Hitler portraying himself as a religious man defending Christian faith against the enemies of the church—Leftists and Jews. Claus Ekkehard Bärsch has demonstrated the extensive presence of Christian motifs in the work of key

---

34. Richard Dyer, *White: Essays on Race and Culture* (London and New York: Routledge, 1997), 16.

35. John L. Hodge, "Domination and the Will in Western Thought and Culture," in *Cultural Bases of Racism and Group Oppression,* ed. Donald K. Struckmann, John L. Hodge, and Lynn Dorland Trost (Berkeley: Two Riders, 1975).

36. Elizabeth V. Spelman, *Inessential Woman: Problems of Exclusion in Feminist Thought* (Boston: Beacon, 1988).

Nazi theorists.[37] Hitler's use of Christianity was encouraged by the emergence of racial theology; for some Nazi propagandists, Christianity was a wonderful wellspring of anti-Semitism in creating what Richard Steigmann-Gall has called the Nazis' "Holy Reich."[38] Yet my analysis is not simply that the Nazi state made use of Christian symbols, but that Nazism sought a supersessionist position in relation to Christianity, incorporating very specific key teachings into its own, more elevated political ideology, exploiting the language and ideational framework of Christianity, rather than trying to imitate or destroy it. Reciprocally, the Institute's theology treated Christianity as the body and National Socialism as the spirit, making the church the bodily carrier of a Nazi soul, thus attempting to make Nazism incarnate in Christianity.

Racism as Incarnational Theology

The question of blood, which unites both Christian theology and racist discourse, extends the link between theology and race further. It is through blood that race is carried and transmitted, according to most of the racial discourse of the Nazi era, and it is blood, too, that supposedly carries and transmits gender. At the symbolic heart is the blood of Jesus, redemptive and sacramental, both in his shedding of it and in the believer's swallowing of it at the Eucharist. The centrality of blood to both the Christian and Nazi narratives permitted a congeniality between the two systems of thought, but also gave rise to competition and conflict. For National Socialism, blood was fixed and determinative, allowing no possibility for change or conversion. The Lutheran understanding of the Eucharist was less rigid: the wine was not actual blood, though the real presence of Christ was in the wine and wafer. One might expect the Eucharist to have been redefined with the advent of Nazism to give it a more fixed and less symbolic meaning, rigidifying its definition of blood to bring it in accord with

---

37. Claus Ekkehard Bärsch, *Die politische Religion des Nationalsozialismus* (Munich: Fink-Verlag, 1997).

38. Richard Steigmann-Gall, *The Holy Reich: Nazi Conceptions of Christianity, 1919–1945* (Cambridge: Cambridge University Press, 2003).

racial ideology, yet theological reinterpretations of the Eucharist did not take place.[39] The antidoctrinal stance of the German Christian movement focused attention away from refinements of traditional dogma, and Eucharistic celebrations continued at their conventional monthly pace in Protestant churches during the Third Reich, including those led by German Christians.

As a religion of incarnation, Christianity rests on a fragile boundary between the human and divine, the carnal and spiritual, the Jewish and Christian. Its instability was brought to light both by the rise of theological historicism and by the question pursued by Jewish theologians of the nineteenth century: Where, in fact, does Christianity begin and Judaism end? The very figure of Jesus is the lynchpin: he is at once a Jew and the founder of Christianity. Jesus begins his life as a Jew, but ends his life as a Christian. Christianity itself is achieved, as the narrative of Jesus' life implies, through a process of emergence, a religious purification that attempts to rid the Jewish from the Christian. That Jewishness, neither wholly carnal nor spiritual, is an undefined, vague threat that can purge either body or soul, and enter the one through the other—polluting the body through a corruption of the mind. Purity of the self can be achieved through a Christianization of the self, a removal of the Jewish, just as purification from the Jewish marks the creation of the Christian. Thus, the emergence of a racialized Protestant theology in the early decades of the twentieth century should be viewed not only as a response to political developments in Germany, but as a recognition of the aporia of Jesus the Jew, who was also the first Christian.

Theological historicism has been fascinated with the possibility of determining the point of Christian origins. Yet, as James Donald writes, "there is no possibility of defining clear-cut boundaries between reality and imagination."[40] So, too, reconstructions of early Christianity are always imaginative, always, in Michel de Certeau's words, haunted: "Haunted places are the only ones people can live

---

39. Doris Bergen, *Twisted Cross: The German Christian Movement in the Third Reich* (Chapel Hill, N.C.: University of North Carolina Press, 1996), 45.

40. James Donald, *Imagining the Modern City* (Minneapolis: University of Minnesota Press, 1999), 17.

232 🗐 Prejudice and Christian Beginnings

in."[41] The theological roots of the Institute's dejudaization venture are deeply imaginative and can be traced to questions about Jesus' identity that began to be raised at the earliest moments of Christian theological self-formation. Yet, the question of his identity became much more vital and tense with the onset of the historical investigation of Christian origins in the nineteenth century and the repudiation of dogmatics and the supernatural. Theology was to be based on the historical figure of Jesus—his actions and teachings. While many political, social, and economic factors contributed to the rise of anti-Semitism in modern Germany, the Aryan Jesus also emerged as the result of theological processes internal to Christianity and was brought to the fore as a consequence of the historical-critical methods of modern, liberal German Protestantism.

Conclusion

Eradicating the Jewish from the Christian was thus no simple task. Alfred Rosenberg, among other Nazis, recognized the difficulty of that task and mocked the efforts of Christian theologians to carry it out. Remove the Jewish from Christianity and there will be nothing left, he insisted. Even the Institute members were not able to agree on an answer to the central question: What was the Jewish that required eradication? The Old Testament from the Bible, the Jewishness from Jesus, Paul from the New Testament, Hebrew from the hymnal—the task was enormous. With each effort, a new task appeared: In November 1933, the Berlin German Christian leader Reinhold Krause's call for rejecting the Old Testament was shocking; in 1939, declaring Jesus an Aryan was less troubling; by 1942, with the murder of the Jews underway, purging the Jewish was no longer the central concern and was replaced by efforts to synthesize the Teutonic with what remained of the dejudaized "Christian."

While the racial origins of Jesus' blood were sufficiently unstable that they could be declared Aryan, the identity of Paul left no such

---

41. Michel de Certeau, *The Practice of Everyday Life*, trans. Steven Rendell (Berkeley: University of California Press, 1984), 108; cited by Donald, *Imagining*, 17.

indeterminacy. Identifying himself as a Jew and as a Pharisee in his own writings, a conversion of Paul to Christianity was unacceptable in the Nazi racist schema that declared it impossible to divest a Jew of Jewishness. Yet, rejecting Paul would undermine Christian theology and, in particular, the work of Martin Luther, whose affinity to Paul formed one of the bases of the Reformation. Sharp adherence to the historical-critical methods that were central to the German Christian movement were helpful in unmasking the Jewish Jesus to see the genuine Aryan, but the same methods forced the recognition that Paul was unalterably a Jew. Moreover, the methods of the History of Religions School that had been adopted by the German Christians had shifted away from theological interests in Pauline doctrine to Paul as a religious individual, which further called attention to his spiritual training with the Pharisees, historical environment, educational background, and cultural setting.

A complete dejudaization of Christianity was ultimately a hopeless goal; Judaism was too deeply incarnated within Christian Scriptures, doctrine, and theology. The effort was also intangible: Judaism could not be reduced to a particular text or concept, but came to be seen as a spiritual quality that could not be defined and delimited so easily. Its influence on Christianity was inchoate, leaving the theologians who were Institute members in an endless debate over defining Jewish-Christian boundaries. Ultimately, Christianity remained in the uncomfortable position of being the physical transporter of Jewishness as it spread its message throughout the course of history, working as the body of what the Nazi theologians considered the degenerate soul of Judaism.

Asserting that Jesus was an Aryan was a polysemic message, affirming German identity and repudiating the Jews, and thus participating in a long Christian theological tradition of defining Christianity in contrast to Judaism. The Institute picked up that theological tradition, fertilized it with the anti-Semitism of the 1930s, and repackaged it as Christian theology for both the Nazi regime and the church. As anti-Semitic theology, it could survive the Third Reich and enter postwar Germany (minus the word "Aryan," which was dropped after 1945) as if it were legitimate Christian thought, but in fact the Institute's teachings became the vehicle for Nazi anti-Semitic ideas to be

234 ⑤ Prejudice and Christian Beginnings

preserved and transported into postwar Germany. The fiction that the church had been in the opposition to Nazism, and that the Nazis had been anti-Christian, allowed theology to evade the kind of scrutiny that other German cultural traditions and institutions had to undergo after the war.

CHAPTER 9

Religion, Ethnicity, and Ethnoreligion

Trajectories of a Discourse in German-Speaking Historical Jesus Scholarship[1]

Gabriella Gelardini

German-speaking Protestant theology was caught in a real dilemma through its inquiry into the historical Jesus, since from its very beginnings with Reimarus it had to grapple with the fact that Jesus was a Jew in more than a casual sense. This suited neither orthodox dogma nor modern Protestant theology's arrangement with historical criticism. In order to maintain theological control, scholars described a tension between Jesus' "religion" and his "ethnicity" (or "nationality"). Jesus was construed as a figure whose religion conflicted with or transcended his (Jewish) ethnicity or nationality, which were understood as merely external or formal facts. Further, when, in the late nineteenth and early twentieth centuries, the non-dissoluble cohesion of Jesus' ancient

---

1. I am sincerely grateful to Elisabeth Schüssler Fiorenza and Laura S. Nasrallah for inviting me to contribute to this volume; I also extend my warm thanks to Mark Kyburz for proofreading this paper. All translations of citations from German articles and books are my own.

ethnoreligious Jewish identity had to be acknowledged, the pattern shifted to (Christian) transethnic religion versus (Jewish) ethnoreligion (including the historical Jesus). In the quest for the historical Jesus, the modern concept of "religion" was conceived as a separate sphere; a modern conception of individualism allowed scholars to construe a historical Jesus along lines in which the nature of his "religion" could be distinguished or even separated from his "ethnicity." Examples include the "de-nationalizing" of Jesus' religion in the First Quest (Herder, Baur) and his "de-Christianizing" in the so-called No Quest (Wellhausen, Bultmann), which paved the way for the return of the Life-of-Jesus-theology in the New or Second Quest (Käsemann). Although the Third Quest locates the Jesus movement clearly within Judaism, a number of scholars have recently questioned whether Jesus' Judaism is really acknowledged everywhere.

Introduction

As recently as 1974, a well-known German New Testament scholar declared that "Jesus as a Jew was not ready to live a Jewish life in the sense of a Jewish self-conception . . . of whatever shading," since he was engaged in "a conflict" of "principal importance" with contemporary Jews, which "affected the foundations of Jewish faith."[2] Almost exactly two centuries earlier, Gotthold Ephraim Lessing had established this very contradiction in his edition of "Fragments of an Anonymous Writer." According to Albert Schweitzer, Lessing's deliberations ushered in the First Quest for the historical Jesus.[3] Lessing's unnamed author—later identified as Hermann Samuel Reimarus, a Deist and a professor in Hamburg—argued that Jesus "was born a

---

2. Ferdinand Hahn, "Methodologische Überlegungen zur Rückfrage nach Jesus," in *Rückfrage nach Jesus: Zur Methodik und Bedeutung der Frage nach dem historischen Jesus*, ed. Karl Kertelge (Quaestiones disputatae 63; Freiburg i.B.: Herder, 1974), 11–77, esp. 42–43.
3. Following its first publication in 1906 as *Von Reimarus zu Wrede: Eine Geschichte der Leben-Jesu-Forschung*, an edited and expanded edition appeared under the now customary title in 1913. The current and readily available German edition is *Geschichte der Leben-Jesu-Forschung*, 9th ed. (Uni-Taschenbücher 1302; Tübingen: Mohr Siebeck, 1984).

Jew and wanted to remain a Jew."[4] He also asserted that "Jesus did not want to abolish the Jewish religion, in no article, in order to introduce a new one instead."[5] Apparently alluding to Martin Luther's famous treatise "That Jesus was born a Jew," Reimarus challenged both the orthodox christological doctrine of *anhypostasis* (according to which the human nature of the "son of God" has no state of *persona*) and the rapprochement of modern theology with historical hermeneutics. If Jesus' human nature—and of course, for Reimarus, no divine nature of Jesus Christ existed as postulated by Christian dogma—was actually Jewish by birth, nation, and religion, the attack on the Christian view of Jesus as the "originator" (*Urheber*) or "founder" (*Stifter*) of Christianity could not have been more radical.

German-speaking Protestant theology faced a dilemma due to its inquiry into the historical Jesus, since from its very beginnings with Reimarus, it had to grapple with the fact that Jesus was a Jew in more than a casual sense. This, of course, suited neither orthodox dogma nor Protestant theology, which had already adopted historical criticism of the Bible. If the historical Jesus was a Jew and nothing but a Jew, the Protestant conception of Jesus as a heroic and ingenious teacher, as well as a free and, of course, male individual, was seriously called into question.[6] Given the heavily distorted image of the Jews, their social disparagement, and their lack of equal civil rights until the mid-nineteenth century in Germany, one can readily imagine what

4. Gotthold Ephraim Lessing, *Theologiekritische Schriften I und II*, Vol. 7 of *Werke*, ed. Herbert G. Göpfert (Munich: Hanser, 1976), 502.

5. Ibid., 522.

6. Dieter Georgi, "Leben-Jesu-Theologie/Leben-Jesu-Forschung," *TRE* 20 (1990): 566–75, esp. 566–67; "The Interest in Life of Jesus Theology as a Paradigm for the Social History of Biblical Criticism," *HTR* 85, no. 1 (1992): 51–83; Elisabeth Schüssler Fiorenza, *Jesus and the Politics of Interpretation* (New York: Continuum, 2000); further, Ekkehard W. Stegemann, "Jesus von Nazareth," *DNP* 5 (1998): 910–22, esp. 910–11; Gerd Theißen and Annette Merz, *Der historische Jesus: Ein Lehrbuch*, rev. and enl. 3rd ed. (Göttingen: Vandenhoeck and Ruprecht, 2001), 21–26; N. T. Wright, "Quest for the Historical Jesus," in *The Anchor Bible Dictionary*, ed. D. Freedman (New York: Doubleday, 1992), 3:796–802, esp. 796–98; for a more recent study of Liberal Theology, see Werner Zager's *Liberale Exegese des Neuen Testaments: David Friedrich Strauß, William Wrede, Albert Schweitzer, Rudolf Bultmann* (Neukirchen-Vluyn: Neukirchener, 2004).

offense it caused by declaring Jesus a Jew and denying that he was the founder of Christianity. It should also be mentioned that an anti-Judaic construction of gender was encoded in the prevalent image of the Jews, according to which Jewish males were deemed effeminate and unable to conduct a heroic life;[7] the reverse principle, by implication, applied to Jewish females. Jews themselves struggled for emancipation and integration into civil society, and non-Jews like Lessing supported their claim for equal civil rights. In one of his plays, Lessing even depicted a Jew as able to live "up to the standard of enlightened humanity," notably "in striking contrast" to Christian characters.[8]

As Hans Liebeschütz has shown in a brilliant study, Judaism of antiquity assumed outstanding importance in German historical research beginning in the eighteenth century, not least because historical criticism of the Bible had to deal with the undeniable "connections with the Jewish world"[9] from which Christian religion had emerged. Before Lessing's innominate author shattered its foundation, the consensual response to the obvious cohesion of Jesus (and his disciples) with Judaism of antiquity was to marginalize the connection. Jesus only accommodated his teaching to his contemporary Jewish audience. Judaism was not the essence or nature of his religion but only the nutshell, as Johann Salomo Semler (1725–1791) and others argued.[10]

---

7. Matthew Biberman, *Masculinity, Anti-Semitism, and Early Modern English Literature: From the Satanic to the Effeminate Jew* (Burlington: Ashgate, 2004); Roy S. Wolper, "The Lustful Jew in the Eighteenth Century: A Sympathetic Stereotype?" in *Proceedings of the Sixth World Congress of Jewish Studies*, Held at the Hebrew University of Jerusalem, 13–19 August, 1973, Under the Auspices of the Israel Academy of Sciences and Humanities, 4 vols., ed. Avigdor Shinan (Jerusalem: World Union of Jewish Studies, 1977–1980), 3:147–57; Daniel Boyarin, *Unheroic Conduct: The Rise of Heterosexuality and the Invention of the Jewish Man* (Berkeley: University of California Press, 1997). Boyarin seems to argue that this stereotype originated in rabbinical concepts, rather than in anti-Jewish fantasies.

8. Jacob Katz, *Out of the Ghetto: The Social Background of Jewish Emancipation 1770–1870* (New York: Schocken Books, 1978; repr. Cambridge: Harvard University Press, 1973), 69.

9. Hans Liebeschütz, *Das Judentum im deutschen Geschichtsbild von Hegel bis Max Weber* (Schriftenreihe wissenschaftlicher Abhandlungen des Leo Baeck Instituts 17; Tübingen: Mohr Siebeck, 1967), 15.

10. Stefan Alkier, *Urchristentum: Zur Geschichte und Theologie einer exegetischen Disziplin* (Tübingen: Mohr Siebeck, 1993), 21–44.

Hence, a tension had already been established between the historical Jesus and Judaism before Reimarus. In order to exercise theological control over historical hermeneutics, scholars resolved this tension by putting Jesus' "religion" (or "culture") totally or partly against his "ethnicity" (or "nationality"), albeit in two characteristic and distinct manners. First, the historical Jesus was primarily construed as a figure whose religion clashed with or transcended his (Jewish) ethnicity or nationality, rendering negligible the latter aspect of his identity as a merely external fact. Second, however, when late nineteenth and early twentieth religious-historical research more or less had to concede the Jewishness of Jesus' religion, the underlying pattern shifted from (Christian) religion versus the (Jewish) ethnicity of Jesus to a pattern of (Christian) (transethnic) religion versus (Jewish) ethnoreligion (including that of the historical Jesus).

In this article, I'll start by mentioning present discussions concerning the terminology and the disputed application of the categories "religion" and "ethnicity" to ancient history. I comment briefly on the collective identity discourse of ancient *Ioudaioi* in the work of several scholars, including Shaye J. D. Cohen, Steve Mason, and David Goodblatt. In subsequent sections, I will deal with some characteristic examples to substantiate my principal claim. First, I consider Reimarus, according to whom the historical Jesus was religiously and nationally a Jew. Then, I examine two examples of responses to this challenge that follow the pattern "religion versus ethnicity," namely Johann Gottfried Herder and Ferdinand Christian Baur. Section four deals tersely with Julius Wellhausen and Rudolph Bultmann; considering the historical Jesus more or less reluctantly a Jew both religiously and, of course, ethnically, they separated him from the Christian religion, the "gospel" (Wellhausen), and the "kerygma" (Bultmann). Here, one can also speak of an overshadowing of the quest for the historical Jesus by the controversy between theological self-conception over against the challenges of modern *Historismus*. This is apparently the background of the so-called New or Second Quest, which started among Bultmann's disciples. I argue that particularly Ernst Käsemann's position in this dispute is controlled by the heritage of Liberal Theology and anti-Judaic resentment. The final section considers the Third Quest.

"Religion," "Ethnicity," and "Ethnoreligion"—Some Remarks on Terminology

Like the English word "Judaism," the German *Judentum* means the Jewish religion in modern usage. But the German word also comprises the actual and historical performance of Jewish culture or religion ("Jewishness") and the collectivity of the Jews (*Judenheit* or *Judenschaft*: "Jewry"). Thus, the German term can signify both the religious and cultural expressions of Jews, and their constitution as a collective, people, or nation. Potentially, however, German usage also encodes the distinction between belonging to the Jews, the Jewish people or nation or an ethnic collective, and belonging to Judaism as a cultural identity, which is mostly understood as a specific religious system. It is thus possible to speak of Jesus as a Jew, as a figure whose ancestry is Jewish or who belongs by birth to the Jewish people or nation, while denying that he wanted to follow the Jewish way of life, Judaism, or Jewishness. Hence, one could speak of Jesus as a Jew without automatically implying that he shared the self-conception of contemporary Judaism in whichever variety. This is a completely modern concept. I indicate the potential already inscribed in language by using the terms "religion," "ethnicity," and "ethnoreligion." But I employ them as etic categories in order to explain what distinct matters are meant by distinct or non-distinct words.

The problem of applying habitual language use to ancient history is well-known. Since words like "nation," "nationality," "nationalism," and particularly "race" seem to carry narrow and sometimes ideologically loaded modern concepts into ancient sources, "ethnicity" enjoys a good reputation among scholars today. David Goodblatt's illuminating study and its theoretical analysis of the terminology used in historiographical research on Greek, Roman, and Jewish antiquity provide much insight into this debate.[11] While he aims to reestablish the use of "nationality" and "nationalism" as adequate terms, Goodblatt finds it "difficult and not helpful to distinguish ethnicity from nationality,"[12]

---

11. David Goodblatt, *Elements of Ancient Jewish Nationalism* (Cambridge: Cambridge University Press, 2006), 1–27.
12. Ibid., 26.

although he does not argue against "ethnicity" as an appropriate etic category.[13]

The use of "religion" for ancient history is a different matter. Concerning the Greek terms *Ioudaios* and *Ioudaïsmos*, Steve Mason's recent and rich investigation attempts to demonstrate that it is not only anachronistic to use the term "religion" as an etic category, but it is even problematic.[14] Mason's linguistic analysis is indeed persuasive inasmuch as it underlines the enduring relationship of the mentioned Greek terms to the discourse of ethnicity with regard to the Jews as a people or nation in antiquity. For the Mediterranean Diaspora, John M. G. Barclay had previously already argued that the "evidence indicates that it was ethnicity—precisely the *combination* of ancestry and custom— which was the core of Jewish identity in the Diaspora."[15] Likewise, Shaye J.D. Cohen, with whom Mason engages in a fruitful debate, is certain that the "Jews (Judeans) of antiquity constituted an *ethnos*, an ethnic group."[16] He argues, however, that a cultural or religious accentuation had occurred since the time of the Hasmoneans. Therefore, he characterizes Jewish identity at the end of the Second Temple as "ethnoreligious": "For most *Ioudaioi* in antiquity, the ethnic definition was supplemented, not replaced, by the religious definition."[17] Cohen

---

13. Over the past three decades, various scholars applying social methods, and most recently Denise Kimber Buell (*Why This New Race: Ethnic Reasoning in Early Christianity* [New York: Columbia University Press, 2005]), have suggested that early Christianity, particularly in late antiquity, quite naturally invoked ethnic categories to assert its collective self-definition. The rediscovery of ethnicity in the course of secularization and nationalism was thus important, and its anti-Semitic instrumentalization, of course, proved to be problematic.

14. Steve Mason, "Jews, Judaeans, Judaizing, Judaism: Problems of Categorization in Ancient History," *JSJ* 38 (2007): 457–512.

15. John M. G. Barclay, *Jews in the Mediterranean Diaspora: From Alexander to Trajan (323 BCE–117 CE)* (Berkeley: University of California Press, 1996), 404; cf. idem, "Constructing Judean Identity after 70 CE: A Study of Josephus's Against Apion," in *Identity & Interaction in the Ancient Mediterranean: Jews, Christians and Others: Essays in Honour of Stephen G. Wilson*, ed. by Zeba A. Crook and Philipp A. Harland (Sheffield: Phoenix Press, 2007), 99–112.

16. Shaye J. D. Cohen, *The Beginnings of Jewishness: Boundaries, Varieties, Uncertainties* (Berkeley: University of California Press, 1999), 7.

17. Ibid., 137: Cohen refers for the concept and term to John A. Armstrong, *Nations before Nationalism* (Chapel Hill: University of North Carolina Press, 1982), 201–203.

242 ⌘ Prejudice and Christian Beginnings

sees the distinct difference in the identity-concept of the *ethnos* of the *Ioudaioi* juxtaposed with other *ethnē* in the characteristic manner, "in which they worshiped their God, what we today would call their *religion*."[18] Mason argues that it is all about discourses of *ethnicity* in which the distinctions were made by certain specific ethnic-identity boundary-markers, such as customs, laws, traditions, and ritual interactions with divine worlds; Cohen argues that although the ethnic connection is never invalidated or even abrogated, one has to recognize a progress "from *ethnos* to ethnoreligion."[19]

Cohen is indebted to modern sociological and ethnological theories of "imagined communities" (Benedict Anderson), according to which national or ethnic groups construe their identities; as particularly Fredrik Barth has argued, groups do so by drawing boundaries on the basis of "continuing dichotomization between members and outsiders."[20] The contents of this delineation are occasionally disputed and have therefore sparked controversy. For Cohen, "the sum total of these distinctive characteristics was designated by the Greek word *Ioudaïsmos*," which "means more than just religion" or "Judaism," but instead, means, "Jewishness."[21] Mason convincingly argues,[22] however, that *Ioudaïsmos*, which indeed does not denote Judaism or the Jewish religion (at least not before the third century CE), was a watchword referring to the identity of *Ioudaioi* as members of their specific *ethnos*. The contenders of *Ioudaïsmos* preferred their ancestral customs over against an alleged alteration, for instance *Hellenismos*, which would make or change *Ioudaioi* to *Hellenes*. *Ioudaïsmos* thus signifies the activities in which members of the *ethnos* of the *Ioudaioi* engage to lead a life according to what are considered required standards, customs, and laws, or the activities of those forcing others into compliance ("Judaizing").

We can leave open for discussion whether or not to accept Goodblatt's characterization of a "belief in a common descent and a shared

---

18. Cohen, *Beginnings*, 7.
19. Ibid., 109.
20. Fredrik Barth, ed., *Ethnic Groups and Boundaries: The Social Organization of Cultural Difference* (Bergen: Universitets Forlaget, 1969), 14 (as cited in Cohen, *Beginnings*, 5).
21. Cohen, *Beginnings*, 7–8.
22. Mason, "Jews", 460–76.

culture available for mass political mobilization" as a "national identity."[23] Nor do we need to decide here whether we follow Cohen in linking the cultural aspect of ethnic identity to the category of "religion." It is clear, however, that "religion," as applied by Cohen to the ancient history of the Jews, does not correspond to its modern sense, since he combines it with an indissoluble embeddedness in ethnic identity. Religion as a sphere apart, that is, separated from other cultural, social, and ethnic discourses, is not conceivable in antiquity. It is perhaps worth indicating two working assumptions at this juncture: first, when applying "religion," "ethnicity," and "ethnoreligion" as etic categories, I presuppose them to be modern terms; second, I assume that "religion" as a term that has been part of historical Jesus research since the eighteenth century makes evident that it (according to the modern concept) emerged simultaneously as a discrete and independent sphere.[24] The paradox that Jesus' ethnic identity as a Jew, that is, his status as a member of the Jewish people or nation, holds true at one and the same time with his separation from Judaism needs to be seen in the same larger context of the emerging modern concept of religion. This coincides with an inherent tendency therein to understand religion as something clear and exclusive without fuzzy borders. Finally, the seventeenth- and eighteenth-century concept of religion is linked to an area of conflict between the concept of a "natural" or "reasonable" religion on the one hand, and a "revealed" or "positive" religion on the other. This conflict also affects the controversy over the religion of Jesus.

Jesus: A Jew Who Wanted to Remain a Jew (Reimarus)

Hermann Samuel Reimarus (1694–1768) was convinced that the historical Jesus shared at the very least the *Deistic* view of religion that Reimarus himself favored: "The pure doctrine of Christ, which flowed from his own mouth, in as much as it does not belong particularly

---

23. Goodblatt, *Elements*, 26–27.
24. Wilfred C. Smith, *The Meaning and End of Religion: A New Approach to the Religious Traditions of Mankind* (New York: MacMillan, 1962).

to Judaism, but can become universal, contains nothing more than a reasonable practical religion."[25] Therefore, a kind of reason-religion was a force in Jesus' "reformation of the Jewish superstition,"[26] which Reimarus took for granted. To that extent, Jesus should be considered both a "reformer of Judaism" and a teacher of humankind. Reimarus represents a tradition that had already started with Baruch Spinoza.[27] For Reimarus, however, Jesus' teachings were directed only towards the Jews and concerned only their religion and nation. For Jesus not only taught "moral law" (*Sittengesetz*) but also "ceremonial laws," that is, the specific customs of the Jews. Jesus did not want to abolish or alter the ordained laws and customs (Reimarus refers explicitly to Matthew 5:17), although he widely preferred an "internal conversion of the heart," over against "ceremonial laws and outward bearings."[28] Thus, Jesus did not want to reach beyond the Jewish nation. Although his gospel refers to a coming of the kingdom of heaven, this relates to a "theocracy," to a Jewish nation reestablished by Jesus. As a "worldly Messiah," he wanted to erect only a "temporal realm."[29] Spinoza and John Toland obviously come to mind here.[30] Jesus wanted the Jews to regard him as the promised national Messiah. Although his main aim (*Hauptzweck*) "was not that he wanted to suffer and die, but to erect a worldly realm and deliver the Jews from their captivity," instead, "therein God had forsaken him, therein his hope had failed."[31] Only after his death did the apostles invent, for rather base motives, a "new religion," that is, the Christian belief system. They erected an "edifice of doctrine" (*Lehrgebäude*), in which Jesus now appeared as "a religious (*geistlicher*) redeemer of the human race."[32] They also borrowed

25. Lessing, Schriften, 314.

26. Hermann Samuel Reimarus, *Apologie: Oder Schutzschrift für die vernünftigen Verehrer Gottes*, vol. 2, ed. Gerhard Alexander (Frankfurt: Insel-Verlag, 1972), 39: Lessing's fragments avoided most of Reimarus's contemptuous assertions concerning Jews and Judaism.

27. Peter Eicher, *Bürgerliche Religion: Eine theologische Kritik* (München: Kösel, 1983), 145.

28. Lessing, *Schriften*, 521.

29. Ibid., 523, 539, 552.

30. Liebeschütz, *Judentum*, 2–5.

31. Lessing, *Schriften*, 555.

32. Ibid., 577.

from Jewish traditions to achieve this end. For example, Reimarus refers to the "son of man" concept of Jewish apocalyptic. But "the new religion" rests on "fabled (*erdichteten*) facts."[33] What should therefore become universal after Jesus' death was not his "reasonable and practical religion," but a new "positive" one, the Christian religion. Albeit a "fraud," it was universalized beyond the borders of the Jewish nation by missionary activities. Not Jesus but instead his disciples were the originators and founders of Christianity.

Reimarus compiled his radical denial of the Christian nature of Jesus' teachings by using and developing contemporary historical hermeneutics.[34] Crucially, he designed a historical Jesus from the texts of the Gospels; Reimarus considered Jesus to be a Jew both religiously and nationally, a Jew and nothing else, even if he wanted to reform Judaism in the direction of a "reasonable religion." If theological control should somehow be recovered from the historical Jesus as the "founder" of the Christian religion, Jesus had to be distinguished from the Jewish religion, if not even separated from it. Phrased differently, Jesus' religion had to be stripped of its cohesion with his Jewish ethnicity or nationality. Reimarus regarded the historical Jesus as a representative of the national religion, that is, the "ethnoreligion" of the Jews. A supranational or transethnic Christian religion stems only from Jesus' followers. It is therefore no coincidence that subsequent challenges to the Jewishness of Jesus' "ethnoreligion" had to refer to the two principles through which Reimarus defined the national identity of the Jewish religion of Jesus, namely the law (as a unity of moral *and* ceremonial laws or customs) and the national concept of God's realm and/or the Messiah as Jesus' Jewish "worldly" eschatology. Of course, one could easily adopt Reimarus's view on Jesus as a reformer. But there remained the problem of a historical Jesus as a figure who obeyed and observed the "ceremonial laws" and thus expressed his adherence to the Jewish "ethnoreligion." And the same is true of Jesus' messianic idea. One could hardly deny attributing a messianic concept

---

33. Ibid.
34. Peter Stemmer, *Weissagung und Kritik: Eine Studie zur Hermeneutik bei Hermann Samuel Reimarus* (Veröffentlichung der Joachim Jungius-Gesellschaft der Wissenschaften Hamburg 48; Göttingen: Vandenhoeck and Ruprecht, 1983).

to Jesus, but an exclusively "worldly realm," and even more, a "national" Jewish kingdom and Messiah, were inconceivable, since the historical Jesus had to have something to do with the Christian Messiah.

Therefore, the alleged national Jewish ambitions of Jesus' teachings and expectations played a prominent and lasting role in the quest for the historical Jesus far beyond the short and fierce "fragments-controversy," and without explicitly relating to Lessing's innominate author. I refer to this trend in the First Quest as the "de-nationalizing" of Jesus' ethnoreligion. In a certain sense, it also denotes a "de-Judaizing," and often is connected to various anti-Judaic resentments. But that is another matter.

"Denationalizing" Jesus' Ethnoreligion (Herder and Baur)

Two examples must suffice here. The first comes from the influential *Ideas upon Philosophy and the History of Mankind* (1784–1791) by the poet, philosopher, and theologian Johann Gottfried Herder (1744–1803). Although he was opposed to the moral criticism of the Hebrew Bible by Semler, Immanuel Kant, and others, for Herder, the historical Jesus essentially put an end to all "musings" of a national, messianic Jewish "theocracy."[35] "What now was this realm of heaven?" Herder asks. "Not a worldly highness," he replies, as Jesus' "speeches and deeds" show. For Jesus wanted to be "a spiritual rescuer of his race". And he adds:

> A man from the people appeared, whose spirit was elevated above wool-gathering of terrestrial highness, combined all hopes, desires and divinations of the prophets to the system of an ideal realm, which should not be less than a Jewish heaven. Even the close revolution of its nation he would foresee in this high plan and presaged its magnificent temple, its whole to superstition turned service a fast sad end. Among all nations the realm of

---

35. Johann Gottfried Herder, "Ursprung des Christentums samt den Grundsätzen, die in ihm lagen (IV 17,1)," in *Ideen zur Philosophie der Geschichte der Menschheit*, Vol, 6 of *Werke*, ed. Martin Bollacher (Frankfurt a.M.: Deutscher Klassiker, 1989), 711.

God should come, and the people, who believed to possess such one peculiar for it, was regarded by him as a deceased body.[36]

Opposed to all "national religions" and accused of committing a "crime against the offended nation" and of an "unpatriotic" destruction of his nation's hopes, Jesus represented a kind of "Ex-Judaism" and a "popular belief" (*Volksglaube*), "which turned all peoples to one people."[37] Herder considered this to be in stark if not paradoxical contrast to the origins of this belief in "an obdurate nation, which regarded itself otherwise as the first and unique among all nations."[38] Thus Jesus' "revolution arose from the contempted Judea." But this nation was doomed and, by the time of its demise after the destruction of the Second Temple, had given way to the "most genuine humaneness," [39] which Jesus, represented.

Herder's concept of Jesus was part of his theory of decline, not only of the Jewish nation and Judaism, but also of Rome and other nations of antiquity, and the decline even included Christianity. Where rise occurs, so does decline. In Herder's pattern, the historical Jesus represents the pure and genuine rise of Christianity, while Judaism before and Christianity after him represented decline. Therefore, if Jesus taught "the most genuine humaneness,"[40] his teachings—articulated in the simple message: God is your father and all of you are brothers— transcended not only ceremonial Jewish laws, but also later Christian ceremonial worshipping.

Quite characteristically, Ferdinand Christian Baur (1792–1860), the most influential German New Testament scholar in the nineteenth

---

36. Herder, ibid.: "Es erschien ein Mann aus dem Volk, dessen Geist, über Hirngespinste irdischer Hoheit erhaben, alle Hoffnungen, Wünsche und Weissagungen der Propheten zur Anlage eines idealischen Reichs vereinigte, das nichts weniger als ein jüdisches Himmelreich sein sollte. Selbst den nahen Umsturz seiner Nation sähe er in diesem hohem Plan voraus und weissagte ihrem prächtigen Tempel, ihrem ganzen zum Aberglauben gewordnen Gottesdienst ein schnelles trauriges Ende. Unter alle Völker sollte das Reich Gottes kommen, und das Volk, das solches eigentümlich zu besitzen glaubte, wurde von ihm als ein verlebter Leichnam betrachtet' ".
37. Ibid.
38. Ibid.
39. Ibid.
40. Ibid.

century and beyond, hailed Jesus' "purer idea of the Messiah" and Paul's "sublimation of the messianic idea."[41] Unlike Herder and his idea of a sudden, nearly unprepared appearance of a new ingenious originator of the religion of humaneness, Baur is convinced that everything is interconnected and a product of permanent development generated by antagonistic parties and their clashing principles. Although Baur considered Jesus' history as the primordial and prototypical period of Christianity, since Jesus was the first to express the idea of the Christian religion, even Jesus had to develop a "messianic consciousness," which finally corresponded to his role as the founder of the Christian religion and the moral reformer of the Jewish law. He thus had a "purer idea of the Messiah,"[42] but only a "purer" one and only an "idea," since he did not separate it from the form of the national messianic idea. This "purification" occurred through Paul's universalization of the idea, but only after the first disciples had developed it in a particular Jewish (*judaistische*) form, and by means of antithesis. So Jesus had the "idea," but he dissociated neither it nor himself from the national and religious Jewish form or concrete shape.[43]

The same pattern is applied to Jesus' and Paul's doctrine of the law. For Baur, Jesus undoubtedly emphasized moral law and even the "cleanliness and pureness of ethos"[44] in the Sermon on the Mount over against a merely outward and literal observance of the commandments. But did he oppose moral law to the Mosaic law, which included the "ritual laws"? Baur immersed himself particularly in exegetical deliberations on Matthew 5:17, which, as noted, buttressed Reimarus's main argument, as well. But Baur's conclusion was ambivalent. On the one hand, Matthew 5:17 could reflect Jesus' teaching and also include the demand to observe the ceremonial laws. On the other hand, this verse could represent a later "Judaistic version"[45] of Jesus' sayings, given its context in the Gospel of Matthew and its "Judaistic" theological tendency, which Baur assumed. Thus, there was already in Jesus himself a consciousness of the moral spirit of Christianity as opposed

---

41. Baur, 131.
42. Ibid., 94.
43. Cf. Alkier, *Urchristentum*, 242.
44. Baur, *Vorlesungen*, 48.
45. Ibid., 55.

to Judaism, but again it was not until Paul that this antithesis was for-mally and explicitly articulated as the abolition of the characteristic "ceremonies" of the Jewish religion, its "customs for festive days and dietary laws,"[46] and so on. Thus, Paul became the "second founder" of Christianity, and Baur thereby initiated a shift within the research undertaken by the *Religionsgeschichtlichen Schule* and its heirs.

Baur's concept included the notion that the history of Christian-ity had never included anything that could be identified as its absolute initiation, not even the historical Jesus. Unlike Reimarus, Baur did not argue that Jesus was a Jew and wanted to remain a Jew. But unlike his disciple David Friedrich Strauss, who—as Dieter Georgi has put it—"nearly succeeded in derailing the Life-of-Jesus-Theology,"[47] Baur did not disconnect the historical Jesus from his role in the history of the "dogma," which started with his disciples. This was reserved for the Life-of-Jesus-Theology and above all for Adolf von Harnack (1851–1930), the German theologian and prominent church historian who considered the Gospel of Jesus to be a religion of its own, indeed religion itself.[48] Unlike Christian theologians, the few nineteenth-century Jewish Jesus scholars, most prominently Abraham Geiger, who conducted historical Jesus research, welcomed Jesus' attribution to Jewish religion. Susannah Heschel has shown[49] that Geiger's *Das Judenthum und seine Geschichte: In 12 Vorlesungen*,[50] first published in 1864, can be read as a "counter discourse," that is, as an attempt to "reverse the theological gaze,"[51] much like the impact it made on the contemporary representatives of "Christian" Jesus research. Geiger's

---

46. Ibid., 171.

47. Georgi, "Leben-Jesu-Theologie," 570.

48. Wolfgang Stegemann, "Die historische Jesusfrage—auch ein *religious turn*: Bemerkungen zu einem christologischen Konzept der Moderne," in *Reli-gious Turns—Turning Religions: Veränderte kulturelle Diskurse—Neue religiöse Wissensformen*, ed. Andreas Nehring and Joachim Valentin (ReligionsKulturen 1; Stuttgart: Kohlhammer, 2008), 179–206.

49. Susannah Heschel, *Abraham Geiger and the Jewish Jesus* (CSJH; Chi-cago: University of Chicago Press, 1998, esp. 1–22. See also her article in this volume, 211–234.

50. Abraham Geiger, *Das Judenthum und seine Geschichte: In 12 Vorlesungen* (Breslau: Schletter, 1864).

51. Heschel, *Abraham Geiger.*

placement of Jesus within the Pharisaic Judaism of his time must have offended Christian scholars even more, since Geiger attributed the historical Jesus precisely to that group within Judaism that Christian theologians identified as the epitome and acme of alleged "decadence" and "lawfulness."

"De-Christianizing" the Historical Jesus (Wellhausen, Bultmann)

In the view of the famous scholar of Old Testament and historian of religion, Julius Wellhausen (1844–1918), Harnack and Life-of-Jesus-theology had "elevated the historical Jesus . . . to a religious principle and played him off against Christianity," although the idea itself that Jesus was "the religious ideal" originated from Christianity and not from the historical Jesus: "Without the Gospel and without Paul, Judaism sticks to Jesus, to which he adhered, although he outgrew it."[52] Wellhausen's text reveals its vicinity to Reimarus's theses throughout. Above all, the shift from the "Jewish" to the "Christian," that is, the "heavenly" Messiah after the crucifixion and on the basis of an "ecstatic vision," constituted a sudden and "tremendous leap from the proper Messiah to another one who had only the name in common and was indeed no one (*sc.* Messiah)": "The Messiah at the gallows, a paradoxical *contradictio in adjecto*, has become the shibboleth of an enthusiastic faith and the foundation of the Christian Gospel."[53] The historical Jesus did not share the later "enthusiasm" of his disciples and had not been an enthusiast. Like Reimarus's Jesus, Wellhausen's Jesus' messianic concept was "political."[54] Unlike Reimarus's Jesus, Wellhausen's Jesus planned neither "an insurgence against the Romans" nor "to liberate his people from foreign rule," but instead to set it free "from the yoke of the hierocracy and nomocracy,"[55] that is, from "theocracy" as a rule of priests and laws. Wellhausen thus

---

52. Julius Wellhausen, *Einleitung in die drei ersten Evangelien*, 2nd ed. (Berlin: Reimer, 1911), 104.
53. Ibid., 81, 149.
54. See ibid., 151, where he rejects Albert Schweitzer's concept of "consequent eschatology."
55. Ibid., 83.

avoids mention of a "national" Messiah. His Jesus claimed a "messianic authority to rule inwards,"[56] that is, within the Jewish nation. This, however, included use of violence, leading Wellhausen to assert that, "Reimarus could be correct to a certain degree."[57] Alluding to Reimarus's famous and aforementioned characterization of the historical Jesus' death as a failure of his national hope and messianic expectation, Wellhausen concluded: "Without his death he would not have become historic. The impression of his career rested upon the fact that it had not been completed, but abruptly intermitted. His defeat became his victory."[58] Even when they took up traditions of a realm of God provided by Jewish apocalypticism, the disciples did not include its "nationalism, politics, and hostility against the Gentiles."[59]

Thus, Wellhausen formulated his famous and often cited sentence: "Jesus was not a Christian, but a Jew."[60] He added, and by no means accidentally, that "one can reckon the non-Jewish(ness) in him, the humaneness, more characteristically than the Jewishness."[61] Here, he also echoes Reimarus and displays his own averseness to trends in the Judaism of the Second Temple period (and beyond). Wellhausen could understand that Jesus' compatriots conceived of him as a figure who aimed "to destroy the foundations of their religion."[62] But this was not Jesus' intent at all: "He was only sent to the Jews and wanted to remain within Judaism (*Judentum*)."[63] This assertion seems to be puzzling and even contradictory. As Liebeschütz has pointed out, it was nonetheless coherent for Wellhausen, since he distinguished encompassing historical processes in religion, such as the economy, law, and so forth, from individual freedom and opportunity,[64] or, to phrase it in the Lutheran tradition of Wellhausen's family background, the individual and his or her God. Even more than the prophets of old in Israel, Jesus represented this proud individualism (in both senses

56. Ibid.
57. Ibid.
58. Ibid., 104.
59. Ibid., 93.
60. Ibid., 102.
61. Ibid., 103.
62. Ibid.
63. Ibid.
64. Liebeschütz, *Judentum*, 263.

of the word) for Wellhausen, while Jesus' disciples' gospel came to terms with a social community: not the Jewish nation, of course, but the church. This is the background of Wellhausen's curious remark on "humaneness" versus "Jewishness."

In distinguishing historical facts, including those of the "earthly" Jesus, from the proclaimed or kerygmatic Christ, Rudolf Bultmann's (1884–1976) approach also returned to a Reimarian concept.[65] Adopting a historical perspective, Bultmann argued that Jesus could not be separated in religious or ethnic-racial terms from contemporary Judaism, nor could one argue that Jesus exceeded it. Like his earlier study of Jesus (1926),[66] Bultmann's monumental *Theology of the New Testament*, originally published as *Theologie des Neuen Testaments* (1958),[67] dispenses with the criterion of dissimilarity and accepts Jesus as a Jew. For Bultmann, Jesus' historical message did not, therefore, form part of New Testament theology, but served instead as one of its "presuppositions."[68] Bultmann, who, because of the break with Liberal Theology together with contemporary events, turned into a historical skeptic, had already doubted that the historical method and New Testament sources upon which he had conducted form-historical research could help reconstruct the life of Jesus.[69] Through Schweitzer's work, Bultmann had realized that any history of Jesus necessarily involves construal. Crucially, Bultmann's radical questioning

---

65. Walter Schmithals, "Bultmann, Rudolf (1884–1976)," *TRE* 7:387–96, esp. 387–90; Andreas Lindemann, "Bultmann, Rudolf," *RGG*₄ 1:1859–60; Martin Evang, "Bultmann, Rudolf (Karl)," *Deutsche Biographische Enzyklopädie der Theologie und der Kirchen* 1:205–206.

66. Rudolf Bultmann, *Jesus* (Uni-Taschenbücher 1272; Tübingen: Mohr, 1988); see also Ekkehard W. Stegemann, "Ein Jesus ohne Jesus: Theologische Bibliothek III, Rudolf Bultmann, Jesus (1926)," *Reformatio* 38, no. 3 (1989): 174–78; and Ulrich H. J. Körtner, *Jesus im 21. Jahrhundert: Bultmanns Jesusbuch und die heutige Jesusforschung* (Neukirchen-Vluyn: Neukirchener, 2001).

67. Rudolf Bultmann, *Theologie des Neuen Testaments*, 9th ed., ed. Otto Merk (Uni-Taschenbücher 630; Tübingen: Mohr Siebeck, 1984); see also Ekkehard W. Stegemann's outstanding "Zwischen religionsgeschichtlicher Rekonstruktion und theologischer Interpretation: Rudolf Bultmanns 'Theologie des Neuen Testaments' in ihrem forschungsgeschichtlichen Kontext," *Theologische Zeitschrift* 55, no. 2–3 (1999): 137–55.

68. Bultmann, *Theologie*, 1–2.

69. Bultmann, *Jesus*, 7–15.

of historical reconstruction along the lines of Dialectical Theology situated the historical Jesus within Judaism—although Bultmann did subject Jesus to the usual stereotypes—because he deemed Jesus' historicity and cultural boundedness *irrelevant* for Christianity.[70] Bultmann asserted two crucial claims: on the one hand, that the faith of the followers of Jesus as the "kerygmatic Christ" represented neither the continuation of Jesus' faith nor his proclamation, since this made the historical Jesus the object of faith and proclamation, as history proved. He therefore concluded, on the other hand, that Christian faith could not simply be a continuation or variation of either Jewish faith or religion. Only the mythical and hypostatized interpretation of Jesus as a (historical) person enabled the innovation of Christian faith and kerygma, and consequently, the emergence of Christianity as a new universal religion.

Bultmann's "radical solution for the historical quest for Jesus" strove, as Martin Laube has recently argued, "to dismiss this quest as such," since in the context of justifying Christian theological claims for normative validity, Bultmann shared "the anti-historicist line of attack of early Dialectical Theology" and its attempt "to elude the relativity of historicity"[71] of all things. This is plausible in one sense, but not in another. Although Bultmann evidently knew that it was impossible in historical hermeneutics to adopt a position beyond history

---

70. Even though a structural anti-Judaism demonstrably pervades Bultmann's writings (see, for instance, Bultmann, *Die Theologie des Neuen Testaments*, 10–21, or Bultmann, *Jesus*, 16–18), he was evidently not an anti-Semite. While based in Marburg, Bultmann attracted various acclaimed Jewish scholars, among others Hannah Arendt and Hans Jonas (see also Hans Jonas, *Erinnerungen*, ed. Christian Wiese [Frankfurt a.M.: Insel, 2003], esp. 111). As a member of the Confessing Church, and in his first lecture of the 1933 Marburg summer semester, Bultmann also criticized Nazi Jewish policies, particularly the introduction of the Aryan Paragraph into the church constitution. His brother even died in a concentration camp (Leonore Siegele-Wenschkewitz, *Neutestamentliche Wissenschaft vor der Judenfrage: Gerhard Kittels theologische Arbeit im Wandel deutscher Geschichte* [München: Kaiser, 1980], 20–21; Ulrich Neuenschwander, *Denker des Glaubens: Martin Buber, Albert Schweitzer, Karl Barth, Rudolf Bultmann, Dietrich Bonhoeffer*, 2nd ed. [Gütersloh: Gütersloher and Mohn, 1975], 99–128, esp. 99–100).

71. Martin Laube, "Theologische Selbsterklärung im Angesicht des Historismus: Überlegungen zur theologischen Funktion der Frage nach dem historischen Jesus," *Kerygma und Dogma* 54, no. 2 (2008): 114–37, esp. 118–19.

and therefore left this open to an existential "moment of decision" (*Entweltlichung* in Heidegger's terminology), he thought that such a moment presupposed a historical framework. For Bultmann, this was established by the Christian myth of Jesus Christ (*Kerygma*), whose followers believed he linked eternity to history and heaven to earth. Moreover, Bultmann argued that only a combination of "demytholo-gizing" and "existential interpretation" of the New Testament could decipher the sense of this myth for the present time.

But without the myth of exceeding time and eternity or heaven and earth, typified by the cultic adoration of Jesus Christ as the Lord in heaven that began with the Hellenistic community and Paul, Bult-mann did not consider Christianity a historical possibility. Therefore, the historical Jesus, however radically he may have challenged his Jewish coreligionists, was and remained a Jew. He was a subject, a teacher, a prophet, or a rabbi who taught his fellow Jews, rather than an object of the *kerygma* preached by his future disciples to Jews and Gentiles alike. Bultmann thus introduced to the quest of the histori-cal Jesus not only historical skepticism but a conviction that "authen-ticity" (*Eigentlichkeit*), ensuing from a "moment of decision," could not be achieved in Judaism but only in Christianity. Therefore, even Jesus had to be eliminated from the theological establishment of the normative validity of Christianity. He is one of its "presuppositions," nothing less and nothing more. So even if Bultmann was certain, like Wellhausen, that Jesus challenged Jewish "legalism," he had no good reason to separate Jesus from his "ethnoreligion."

In 1953, Ernst Käsemann (1906–1998)[72] asserted programmati-cally that the christological kerygma necessitated a "New Quest for the Historical Jesus" through its invocation of an earthly figure and its narrative account of that figure in the Gospels.[73] What began as a dispute between teacher and student, or what is commonly referred

---

72. Otfried Hofius, "Käsemann, Ernst," *RGG*$_4$ 4:838.

73. Ernst Käsemann, "Das Problem des historischen Jesus," in *Exegetische Versuche und Besinnungen: Erster und zweiter Band*, 6th ed. (Göttingen: Vanden-hoeck and Ruprecht, 1970), 1:187–214; see also Barry W. Henaut, "Is the 'His-torical Jesus' a Christological Construct?" in *Whose Historical Jesus?* ed. William E. Arnal and Michel Desjardins (SCJud 7; Waterloo: Wilfrid Laurier University Press, 1997), 241–68, esp. 247–54.

to as the Bultmann-Käsemann debate, soon became the New or Second Quest for the historical Jesus.[74] One decisive theme shaping the debate was a confidence reaching beyond historical relativity that criticism could furnish minimal evidence for a "genuine" Jesus tradition through discarding everything deducible from Judaism and early Christianity. Methodologically speaking, a religious- and tradition-historical comparison by means of the *criterion of double dissimilarity* now replaced the previous literary critical construction of the oldest sources as practiced by the First Quest.

The radical break with the life-of-Jesus theology had enormous repercussions among many of Bultmann's disciples. They smelled treason. When the historical Jesus did not have "a lasting, normative, absolute importance . . . for the entire historical appearance of Christianity par excellence,"[75] Gerhard Ebeling thought that Christianity would fall. Käsemann strongly objected to Bultmann's position, too, since for him, it was inconceivable that Christianity was beholden to a mythical, kerygmatic version of Jesus Christ. In contrast, he argued that it owed its existence to Jesus acting as its historical founder to surmount Jewish religion. Bultmann's position that the historical Jesus was a Jewish teacher subject to Judaism and thus Jewish law— the Torah—struck Käsemann as outrageous.[76] In his essay, "Die neue Jesus-Frage" (1975), Käsemann summarized their disagreement thus: "This became evident to me in a dramatic discussion, in which Bultmann told his former students that he considered the earthly Jesus

74. James M. Robinson, *Kerygma und historischer Jesus*, rev. and enl. 2nd ed. (Zürich: Zwingli, 1967).

75. Gerhard Ebeling, "Die Bedeutung der historisch-kritischen Methode für die protestantische Theologie und Kirche," in *Wort und Glaube*, 2nd ed. (Tübingen: Mohr, 1960–1975), 1:14.

76. Theißen and Merz, *Der historische Jesus*, 25–27; Bultmann replied to Käsemann's essay with a piece entitled, "Das Verhältnis der urchristlichen Christusbotschaft zum historischen Jesus: Vorgelegt am 25. Juli 1959," in *Sitzungsberichte der Heidelberger Akademie der Wissenschaften: Philosophisch-historische Klasse* (Heidelberg: Winter, 1960); Käsemann responded in turn with, "Sackgassen im Streit um den historischen Jesus," in *Exegetische Versuche und Besinnungen*, vol. 2 (Gottingen: Vandenhoeck & Ruprecht, 1965), 31–68, esp. 33, 47–49, 60–61; finally, Bultmann published another response entitled, "Antwort an Ernst Käsemann," in *Glauben und Verstehen: Gesammelte Aufsätze*, vol. 4, 2nd ed. (Tübingen: Mohr Siebeck, 1967), 190–98.

to be the bearer of the law, corresponding to his radical emphasis on the call for an existential decision. A gulf opened when I said that this meant that it was the duty of the risen Lord to redeem us from the earthly."[77] Thus, the so-called New or Second Quest owed its existence not only to the challenge of modern historicism, but also to the challenge of historical research that had conceded that it was not possible to separate Jesus from Judaism. "Certainly he was a Jew and made the assumptions of Jewish piety, but at the same time he shatters this framework with his claim."[78] When Käsemann stated that Christian faith in Jesus Christ required substantive criteria resurrected from the historical Jesus, he did not really mean it. For if historical criticism could not approve of Käsemann's conviction that the historical Jesus "broke through the boundaries of Jewish religion decisively" and "actually overcame Judaism,"[79] but considered it rather more probable that Jesus was a Jew and wanted to remain a Jew, Käsemann did not care at all about his criteria. What should be affirmed by historical research was only that the historical Jesus was not concordant with Judaism. Therefore, Käsemann preferred the adjective "earthly" to "Jewish,"[80] as if Jesus were a figure transcending his national and ethnic identity.

And the Third Quest?

Gerd Theißen is certain that after "more than two hundred years" of research, the Third Quest for the historical Jesus has finally realized that "Jesus belongs to Judaism."[81] William E. Arnal shares this

---

77. Käsemann, *Jésus aux origines de la christologie*, ed. Jacques Dupont (Bibliotheca Ephemeridum Theologicarum Lovaniensium 40; Gembloux: Duculot and Leuven: Leuven University Press, 1975), 47–57, esp. 52.

78. Käsemann, "Das Problem des historischen Jesus," 1:206.

79. Käsemann, "Sackgassen im Streit um den historischen Jesus," 2:31–68, esp. 47–48.

80. Käsemann, paradoxically enough, considered historical criticism to be a means against "Docetism," and accused Bultmann and others of that heresy; A. K. M. Adam, *Faithful Interpretation: Reading the Bible in a Postmodern World* (Minneapolis: Fortress Press, 2006), 37–55.

81. Gerd Theißen, *Jesus als historische Gestalt: Beiträge zur Jesusforschung: Zum 60. Geburtstag von Gerd Theißen*, ed. Annette Merz (FRLANT 202; Göttingen: Vandenhoeck and Ruprecht, 2003), 35.

assessment, but refers to recent controversies, particularly among American scholars. In his discussion of the so-called Jesus Seminar, he adds that what is at stake is "what it means that Jesus was a Jew" and "what kind of Jew he was."[82] He thus distances himself from a spate of critics, including Birger A. Pearson and John P. Meier. Pearson accused the Jesus Seminar of "robbing Jesus of his Jewishness" and, by further implication, "the Jesus Seminar has finally robbed him of his religion."[83] According to Meier, "some of the Seminar's opponents have accused them of engaging in a new de-Judification of Jesus."[84] One could add a longer list of critics here, including Elisabeth Schüssler Fiorenza, who speaks of a return of the First Quest.[85] Although the Third Quest's declared purpose was "to free history and exegesis from the control of theology,"[86] there is obviously discomfort with its historical and exegetical construals of Jesus. It is indeed true that the historical Jesus is ubiquitously regarded as a Jew. However, that is not really an achievement of the Third Quest, but of its predecessors, except for the racist Nazi theologians and their precursors.

The Third Quest largely locates Jesus *within* Judaism, but in very different ways. In the First and Second Quests, there were heated debates about what it meant that Jesus was a Jew and whether or how such identification coincided with claims that Jesus was at the same time a radical critic of Judaism, if not the very figure who aimed to pierce the boundaries of Jewish ethnoreligion. Thus, it seems necessary to acknowledge the difference between the first two quests and the Third Quest. Notwithstanding this, however, we should survey the Third Quest according to criteria that observe the above discourses about applying the categories of "ethnicity," "nationality," "ethnoreligion," and "religion" to ancient Jewish history. If Jesus was not the

---

82. William E. Arnal, *The Symbolic Jesus: Historical Scholarship, Judaism and the Construction of Contemporary Identity* (London: Equinox, 2005), 29.

83. Birger A. Pearson, *The Gospel according to the Jesus Seminar* (Occasional Papers of the Institute for Antiquity and Christianity 35; Claremont: Institute for Antiquity and Christianity, 1996), 43.

84. John P. Meier, "The Present State of the 'Third Quest' for the Historical Jesus: Loss and Gain," *Biblica* 80 (1999): 459–87, esp. 484.

85. Schüssler Fiorenza, *Jesus*, 42–55.

86. E. P. Sanders, *Jesus and Judaism*, 3rd ed. (Philadelphia: Fortress Press, 1987), 333.

great individual genius, one wonders whether such a composite identity like John D. Crossan's "Jewish Cynic"[87] is really a plausible historical possibility; one also wonders if any convincing evidence exists to
demonstrate the possibility of a comparable Jewish movement within
Galilee and Judea at the end of the Second Temple. Construing a
Mediterranean culture is certainly justified if such an undertaking
involves etic categories of cultural anthropology. But this would seem
to be somewhat abstract.

What a historical investigation has to prove is the very concrete
shape of the culture of a Jewish movement like that of Jesus and what
its interaction with Judaism of that time looked like. Could one plau-
sibly argue that Jesus distinguishes himself from "Mediterranean culture"? Who is able to deliver a judgement concerning what is in and
what is out? And is it really possible to speak abstractly of "inclusive"
and "exclusive" types of Judaism?[88] Schüssler Fiorenza rightly stated
more than two decades ago that "to speak about the Jesus movement
is to speak about a Jewish movement that is part of Jewish history in
the first century CE."[89] Therefore, it has to be discussed whether the
various images of Jesus construed by the Third Quest really represent
a possible "part of Jewish history in the first century CE.," and how
they make sense in the discourse on identity and "ethnicity" among
Jews of that time and territory.

87. John D. Crossan, *The Historical Jesus: The Life of a Mediterranean Jewish Peasant* (San Francisco: Harper, 1991), 421.
88. Ibid., 418.
89. Elisabeth Schüssler Fiorenza, *In Memory of Her: A Feminist Theological Reconstruction of Christian Origins* (New York: Crossroad, 1983), 105.

CHAPTER 10

"No Modern Joshua"
Nationalization, Scriptures, and Race

Vincent L. Wimbush

There is *no modern Joshua* who can command this resplendent orb of popular discussion to stand still. As in the past, so in the future, it will go on. It may be arrested and imprisoned for a while, but no power can permanently restrain it.

—Frederick Douglass, "The United States Cannot Remain Half-Slave and Half-Free," Washington, D.C. April 16, 1883

With the United States as primary context and point of reference, this essay aims to show how inextricably the modern world phenomena of nationalization, scriptures, and race have been inextricably woven together in the United States. The rhetorics and ideological and political orientation of Frederick Douglass offer an analytical wedge. A speech Douglass delivered in Washington, D.C., in 1883 was part of the celebration of the twentieth year of the signing of the Emancipation Proclamation, an event seen as an appropriate and meaning-charged occasion to take stock of the plight of black peoples in the country. His assessment that in the aftermath of the Civil War, black peoples, especially in the South, faced even more challenges with the establishment of new forms and styles of social, economic, and political slavery led Douglass to rail against the nation's conspiracy of "silence" around the "race" question.

Douglass called on the country to accept Lincoln's challenge to decide whether it would tolerate a society half slave and half free. Douglass imaged the United States after the Civil War as a nation needing to be re-founded and re-defined; he likened it to the Jews wandering in the wilderness—and without Moses, that is, without a supreme charismatic leader. This frustrating and challenging situation represented an opportunity to re-make the nation, but on the basis of racial integration and equality. So, Douglass argued, the nation can and should be rebuilt, but only through serious and honest grappling with the poison of slavery and the racialism that is associated with it, and only if it is recognized that there is "no modern Joshua" to take the onus from the people of interpreting, deciding, and acting for themselves.

Douglass's ideology of nationalization highlights the challenge that a mode of discussion located in the public square and focused on the Bible may pose. It is in relationship to the Bible that the most sensitive, even haunting, public policy issues can be addressed.

Introduction

About four years ago, as I walked on one of the campuses of the Claremont Colleges, a white middle-aged woman—I assume she was a visitor, but cannot be sure about this—accompanied by a younger white female, approached me from the opposite direction. Just as we passed each other, the older woman turned my way and commented, "You look just like Frederick Douglass!" I was taken aback, approaching befuddlement if not shock, but without slowing down, I turned back in her direction and responded with something approaching, "Oh, yes, seen him around lately?"

I am not Douglass. My beardedness notwithstanding, I do not look like Douglass. Douglass does not walk among us today. I never knew Douglass. Douglass was not a playmate of mine in the days of my youth. All of this I know with firm conviction. Yet, there is something about this encounter that I must address. I cannot help thinking about it-not so much about what was going on with the woman who addressed me (how could I really ever know what was going on there?), but about *my* reaction, *my* quickness, *my* sharpness. Did I think that the woman was somehow oddly touching upon some strange truth about me, or about Douglass, that I could not grasp? And why Douglass? Was this experience a type of haunting—by Douglass and other "ancestors"? And what might their haunting of me be about?

I wonder—and wander—in this essay about the matters that come from that disturbing experience. I suspect that my having been then, and finding myself even now, on a college campus and a member of (a particular little corner of) the academy has something to do with the sense of a haunting. The discursive houses in which I find myself in the academy, including but going far beyond religious/biblical/Christian Scripture studies, constantly reverberate with questions and issues about the ongoing meanings of "the past," about centers and canons and authorities and their continuing power. And, of course, my being a dark man with a voice in those discursive houses in the early part of the twenty-first century adds more sound and fury to the reverberations. How could I not be persistently haunted by the invented and invoked pasts—"antiquity," "early Christianity," "the West," "America," and so forth—that define the discursive houses in which I find myself in relationship? How could I escape being haunted by (the invocation of) a dark man of a dark past?

It is likely that Douglass is a representative—a powerful one, indeed—of the "ancestors" who accompany me so much these days, some familial in the narrow sense, others in the broad sense. They help me not to forget some things, and to remember some other things. Almost all of these things are disturbing. For me, as for many others, no one has done this more pointedly than Douglass.

Douglass's 1883 Speech in Washington, D.C.

Without putting my head to the ground, I can . . . hear the anxious inquiry as to when [the] discussion [regarding] the Negro will cease. When will he cease to be a bone of contention? . . . it is idle, utterly idle . . . to dream of peace anywhere in this world, while any part of the human family are the victims of marked injustice and oppression.[1]

---

1. "The United States Cannot Remain Half-Slave and Half-Free: Speech on the Occasion of the Twenty-First Anniversary of Emancipation in the District of Columbia, April, 1883," in *The Life and Writings of Frederick Douglass, IV: Reconstruction and After*, ed. Philip S. Foner (New York: International Publishers, 1955), 359. All subsequent citations of Douglass's speech are taken from this source-text and will be indicated by page number(s) in parentheses in the body of the essay.

These words are part of an address entitled, "The Unites States Cannot Remain Half-Slave and Half-Free," which Douglass delivered in the Congregational Church, Washington, D.C., on April 16, 1883, on the occasion of the twenty-first anniversary of Emancipation in the District of Columbia. The year 1883 was an important commemoration year, but not only in the District of Columbia: throughout the nation, it was an emotional marker of the signing of the Emancipation Proclamation. Black folks were determined—through marches, parades, special forums, special public speaking events—to mark the year so that the nation would not forget what had taken place. It was a difficult chore: the South had begun a poisonous turn toward the reactionary violence of Jim Crowism; the North had turned its back on blacks and its attentions elsewhere.

Douglass's riveting and fiery words quoted above reflect this situation, and they reflect his characteristic intensity and lifelong work in challenging the regime of slavery, racialism, and racial apartheid that had defined and corrupted the United States. These words also register a particular rhetorical and political strategy on Douglass's part that has some implications for social historians and religion critics. Like so many public figures of his time, Douglass used the Bible to think about the shape of the larger world and of the United States in particular. This tendency of speaking the biblical worlds into the contemporary situation was so common in the United States of that time that it was hardly noticed and rarely questioned as a strategy, even by parties diametrically opposed to each other.[2] It is instructive that Douglass, a man who in his mature years tended to keep himself at a critical distance from organized religion, nevertheless continued to the end of his public-speaking life to use biblical rhetorics rather creatively.[3]

The words from the Washington, D.C., speech quoted above open a sort of window onto Douglass's views about the use of one of the

---

2. See Nathan O. Hatch and Mark A. Noll, eds., *The Bible in America: Essays in Cultural History* (New York: Oxford University Press, 1982).

3. The reader should note what is written about the religious sentiments of another black intellectual, W. E. B. Du Bois, in Edward J. Blum, *Du Bois: American Prophet* (Philadelphia: University of Pennsylvania Press, 2007); and Phil Zuckerman, ed., *Du Bois on Religion* (New York: Altamira, 2000).

most popular biblical stories in the American culture of his times—
the Exodus story. Used even before the founding of the republic to
help make the case for the idea of the chosenness of those who had
left Europe and who had—to put the matter most euphemistically—
"by God's grace" "discovered" and "settled" the land that they would
come to call the United States, the Exodus story was made the story
by which, with few exceptions, each new theocratic commonwealth,
colony, and state, then the new nation as a whole, was first defined and
made meaningful and "legitimate." For all the differences between
the various colonies (and, later, the states), as reflected in national
origins and ethnic-tribal-denominational associations, geography,
climate, and local and regional economies, these paled and blurred
into insignificance in relationship to the ideological-discursive framework within which almost all the dominant European settlers and
their heirs belonged. Within such a framework, the white settlers/
colonizers made common assumptions, the most important of which
was that their experiences and actions were inscribed in the texts they
called sacred. They understood that they had been commissioned by
the Divine to take and settle upon the land and build a new world as
"God's new Israel." In some places, these ideas even intensified during
the decades following the founding of the first Republic into the second founding of the Republic in connection with the Civil War.[4]

The Exodus Story in United States Public Discourse

As an astute public figure and student of United States and world history, Douglass was keenly aware of the history of the uses of the biblical story of Exodus in United States public and political discourse.
He understood well the dominant group's use of the story as a moral
about the country's chosenness and the divine approval of its actions.
He knew well how American deeds were read into the biblical story

---

4. See Conrad Cherry, ed., *God's New Israel: Religious Interpretations of
American Destiny* (rev. updated ed.; Chapel Hill: University of North Carolina
Press, 1998), for the history of developments in the United States; and William
R. Hutchinson and Hartmut Lehmann, ed., *Many Are Chosen: Divine Election
and Western Nationalism* (Harvard Theological Studies 38; Minneapolis: For-
tress Press, 1994), for discussions regarding the west in general.

as antitype in relationship to type—how, for example, the country was understood as a privileged people, a new Israel, having escaped the Egypt that was Europe; how such people were ordained to settle new lands, subdue the people on them, and enjoy liberty and prosperity; how George Washington, especially, but also some other white, landed male figures of the Revolutionary War era were considered "founding fathers," especially commissioned to lead the people in the tradition of Moses; and how divine providence continued to guide and approve the new Israel in its settlement and expansionist projects and most importantly, in preserving its unity, especially following the trauma of the Civil War.[5]

This sort of biblical hermeneutics functioned as part of a civil hermeneutics heard throughout Douglass's lifetime in public forums on the lips of politicians and public figures, and printed in books and newspapers. It represented an ideologizing of the nation as a biblical nation by sacrificing, erasing, or rendering invisible nonwhite settlers, first native peoples, then black peoples. The latter were not considered part of the story the nation told about itself. The text that was one of the most important sources for nationalization, the Bible, was (indeed, had to be) made into the white Bible. The epic stories in it were understood to be about the elevation and progress of white peoples. Others—nonwhites, especially black peoples—were either ignored or assumed to play minor or marginal and dependent roles in the epic story as spun by the popular hermeneutic.[6]

In light of the continuing racial apartheid, social, political, and economic inequality and violence directed against blacks in the United States, the aged but stalwart Douglass decried this civil-nationalist biblical hermeneutics. He unsparingly denounced the hypocrisy of Bible-believing, Bible-toting American Christians who actively participated in the enslavement and the continuing repression of black people. And the silence on the part of the non-slave-holding others was considered even worse.

---

5. See Francois Furstenberg, *In the Name of the Father: Washington's Legacy, Slavery, and the Making of a Nation* (New York: Penguin, 2006), 53, 57, 87, 88, 176.

6. Ibid., 51, 63, especially regarding discussion of the Bible as "model" for reading civic texts.

In response to this situation, Douglass's rhetorical strategy involved spinning around the nationalist hermeneutical spin. He took white Americans' use of the Exodus story—likening the Jews' oppression by the Egyptians with their own struggles against British oppression—and went a step further than the typical strict inversion found in the popular black interpretation of the story, according to which the United States was viewed as the oppressive Egypt in relationship to black folks.[7]

The 1883 address was given at a time when Douglass had hoped that his faith in the war effort and in the political process would pay off and usher in a new era in race relations and in advancements for black folks. But he had to face the reality that, in the 1880s, little had changed, and in many respects life was as harsh, if not harsher, for most black folks. His address expressed the exasperation he felt in the face of the persistence of problems, challenges, and virulent opposition. Yet, it was also an expression of hope that the persistence of the widespread—worldwide—discussions about, even clamor over, the situation of black peoples in the United States would lead to the radical changes for which he and so many others had long hoped. This led Douglass to a different sort of play—signifying play—with the biblical story of Exodus: it was not enough to invert directly the dominant American identification of the brutal Egyptians and the long-suffering people of Israel. Douglass signified on this interpretation, not by switching the roles of those featured in the biblical story, but by transforming the story from one about liberation through progress, to be realized through the offices of an anointed charismatic leader, Joshua, to another type of story altogether.

---

7. See Michael Walzer, *Exodus and Revolution* (New York: Basic Books, 1985); Eddie S. Glaude, Jr., *Exodus!: Religion, Race, and Nation in Early Nineteenth-Century Black America* (Chicago: University of Chicago Press, 2000); and William Jeremiah Moses, *Golden Age of Black Nationalism, 1850–1925* (New York: Oxford University Press, 1978); and *Afrotopia: The Roots of African American Popular History* (New York: Cambridge University Press, 1998), for discussion regarding larger historical backdrops and engagements of the story.

Douglass's Rereading of the Exodus Story

The new story Douglass presumed is one in which the United States was enthralled in and transfixed by discussion and debate about the presence of black peoples. What to do with them? How to think about them? How to talk about them? How to address or engage them? Given the subjugation, humiliation, and violence that such people had endured and yet survived, there was no wonder, Douglass argued, that they had made themselves "the most prominent and interesting figures . . . of the world" and had inspired a "resplendent orb of popular discussion." They represented a haunting:

> Men of all lands and languages make [black people] a subject of profound thought and study . . . an object of intense curiosity .
> . . Of the books, pamphlets, and speeches concerning [them], there is literally no end . . . [They are] the one inexhaustible topic of conversation at our firesides and in our public halls. (356)

Of course, given the fact that Douglass traveled in some pretty heady company all over the country and throughout Europe, his characterization of the widespread nature of the situation very likely reflected a status-inflected reality.

Douglass understood the widespread and intense preoccupation with black peoples as a mixed blessing; it was exhausting, annoying, sometimes humiliating: "It is a sad lot to live in a land where all presumptions are arrayed against [the black person], unless we except the presumption of inferiority and worthlessness" (357). Yet, he understood that it was ultimately better to be the subject of ongoing discussion than not to be discussed at all:

> One ground of hope is found in the fact [that] the discussion concerning the Negro still goes on. . . . Without putting my head to the ground, I can even now hear the anxious inquiry as to when this discussion concerning the Negro will cease. When will he cease to be a bone of contention. . . ? Speaking for myself I can honestly say that I wish it to cease. I long to see the Negro utterly out of the whirlpool of angry political debate. (358–59)

Then Douglass makes the main point in the speech by registering the strongest possible adversative: "But it is idle, utterly idle to dream of peace anywhere in this world, while any part [*sic*] of the human family are the victims of marked injustice and oppression" (359). This strong statement, in turn, rhetorically sets the stage for the rereading and restructuring of the Exodus story:

> In America, no less than elsewhere, purity must go before tranquility. Nations, no more than individuals, can reverse this fundamental and eternal order of human relations. There is *no modern Joshua* who can command this resplendent orb of popular discussion to stand still. As in the past, so in the future, it will go on. It may be arrested and imprisoned for a while, but no power can permanently restrain it. (359; italics added)

There are several issues in this statement that beg consideration and comment. First, Douglass assumes that the United States is to be identified with the stories of the Bible. This reflects Douglass's acknowledgment of his sociocultural location and his participation in its discursive-rhetorical framework. The United States and the colonies and states that predated the founding of the United States were for the most part biblical formations.[8] Second, it is assumed that identification with the story in the Bible about ancient-world wandering bands of people in the wilderness is an appropriate and compelling reading of the nation that is the modern-world United States. This also reflects Douglass's acknowledgment of his location and the dominant sociocultural psychology. Michael Walzer has captured what I think Douglass noted:

> Since late medieval or early modern times, there has existed in the West a characteristic way of thinking about political change, a pattern that we commonly impose upon events, a story that we repeat to one another. The story has roughly this form: oppression, liberation, social contract, political struggle, new society. . . . We call this process revolutionary. . . . This isn't a story told

---

8. As already indicated above in note 4, see Cherry, *God's New Israel*, 11.

everywhere . . . it belongs to the West, more particularly to Jews and Christians in the West . . . its source, its original version, is the Exodus of Israel from Egypt. . . .

We still believe what the Exodus first taught, or what it has commonly been taken to teach, about the meaning and possibility of politics and about its proper form:

—first, that wherever you live, it is probably Egypt;

—second, that there is a better place, a world more attractive, a promised land;

—and third, that "the way to the land is through the wilderness."[9]

Third, it is assumed by Douglass that the Exodus-reading of the United States as a wilderness-wandering people must be recast, redefined. Nothing short of a second founding of the nation is required. That Exodus-reading nation is now in Douglass's time promiscuous in social—that is, racial and ethnic—composition. Here, Douglass seems to depart most radically from traditional readings, black and white.[10] His view was shared at certain dramatic moments by only thin segments of the populations on both sides of the North Atlantic.[11] He obviously thought the nation should be radically, that is, racially, pluralistic.

Fourth, it is assumed that the situation in which the United States actually finds itself is not so much in forward progress toward any sort of "promised land," but instead "in motion" about issues having to do with racial inequality and oppression and thus a "resplendent orb of popular discussion." According to this interpretive framework—a

---

9. Walzer, *Exodus*, 133, 149.

10. Glaude, *Exodus!*, especially part two regarding Exodus Politics; Moses, *Golden Age*; and Cherry, *God's New Israel*.

11. For more information and perspective see Christopher Hill, *The World Turned Upside Down: Radical Ideas during the English Revolution* (London: Penguin Books, 1975); Gerald Newman, *The Rise of English Nationalism: A Cultural History 1740–1830* (New York: St. Martin's, 1987); Adam Hochschild, *Bury the Chains: Prophets and Rebels in the Fight to Free an Empire's Slaves* (Boston and New York: Houghton and Mifflin, 2005); and David A. Bell, *The Cult of Nation in France: Inventing Nationalism, 1680–1800* (Cambridge, Mass.: Harvard University Press, [2001] 2003).

signifying on reigning interpretive traditions with a vengeance—
Egypt, then, is *not* the imperial British. King George is *not* Pharaoh.
And those wandering in the wilderness are *not* simply or exclusively
black or white; they are the mixed rabble that had always constituted
the nation and that, in Douglass's view, should properly so constitute
and define the nation. They are now recognized for what they are.

Fifth, it is assumed that in such a situation, with Lincoln having
been assassinated, and the North and the United States Congress having betrayed black peoples, there is no "Moses" to lead the people forward. Perhaps Douglass mused about Lincoln having approached the
status of Moses, or thought that had Lincoln not been assassinated,
he would have developed into a "Moses." The reality was that there
was at the time no one who could be thought of in such terms. And
there was no prospect—certainly not in the White House!—of the
appearance and offices of a "modern Joshua," a successor to Moses to
lead the rabble onward and upward in the exercise of dominance and
possession.

Douglass imagines the entire mixed-rabble nation—not only black
peoples—to be situated in a type of wilderness, that is, in the aftermath of the long, ugly, and brutal experience of slavery, the entire
nation was thrown into utter confusion and so lacked direction and
moral purpose, somewhat traumatized. Most interestingly and paradoxically, Douglass assumes the wilderness to be both problem and
salvation. The rabble is depicted as being in the wilderness of incessant debate, chatter, and shouting about black peoples, presumably
without coming to any conclusion or resolution about what to do next.
Such debate, chatter, and shouting easily could be understood as pre-
venting the people from forward movement out of the wilderness. But
the "wilderness" of conversation and debate is for Douglass the only
way forward: there can be no going forward, no progress, until the race
question is addressed. Not merely talked about, but addressed—with
the necessary sociopolitical, structural, and cultural transformation
of a mixed rabble into an ideologically monogenetic or racially unified
nation. So although the "popular discussion" about race that rages all
around can be exasperating, it is the only way out. For Douglass, the
nation's fate—whether the way of destruction in or liberation from
the wilderness—depends upon staying in motion, that is, continuing

the "popular discussion" around and resolution of the problems and challenges having to do with black enslavement, oppression, and the achievement of racial justice.

This is the reason a "modern Joshua" is not needed: Douglass understood such a figure to represent an effort to lead the people out of the "wilderness"—that is, away from focus upon the race question. But only in that place, with earnest and honest focus upon the race issues, can the mixed-race nation of justice and equality for all begin to emerge. A "modern Joshua" is really a threat, a problem: such a figure would make an attempt to get the people ironically and poignantly to "stand still," to go silent, regarding racial conflict. This may mean being oriented so as to forget, to ignore, to erase, to render black folks and the race issues invisible. It may mean a return to framing the nationalization project in nonracial but nonetheless decidedly racist terms, only to make the majority dominant white race into the default unspoken sociopolitical template or baseline. This would mean a "fall" back into the confounding and dishonest language of universals—ironically, through such terms as "man," "men," "mankind," "people"—while meaning only (or sometimes mostly) white men and (perhaps, some of) the women associated with them. It may entail a going forward out of the wilderness with deadly silence—the type of silence that represents denial of the problem, a glossing over the roughness of the pain and deep humiliation of the enslaved and the corrosiveness of the enslaver with obfuscating exegetical practices. The latter may sometimes represent bold efforts to provide divine legitimacy for the brutal order; at other times, they offer the cover of silence about everything having to do with such an order.

But Douglass did not accept "standing still" on the part of the people of the nation. The ramifications were too negative. He remained hopeful that the "resplendent orb of popular discussion" would lead ultimately to nationalization of a different type.

> The voice of popular complaint, whether it is heard in this country or in other countries, does not and cannot rest upon dreams, visions, or illusions. . . . The Negro is now, and of right ought to be, an American citizen in the fullest sense of the word. . . . The amendments to the Constitution of the United States mean this. . . . What Abraham Lincoln said in respect of the United States

is as true of the colored people as of the relations of those States. They cannot remain half slave and half free. You must give them all or take from them all. Until this half-and-half condition is ended, there will be just ground of complaint. You will have an aggrieved class, and this discussion will go on. (360)

What Douglass thought to be important was that there be no lull, no quiet, no peace in the meantime, that is, while racial justice remains elusive. The clatter, the talk, the debates must rage on; the speeches, the sermons, the writing of essays and books must continue as a type of "movement" of the people. It should be plain to all that this represented an exegetical tour de force regarding the Exodus story, essentially rewriting and recasting it for the sake of the welfare of the people with whom he was in solidarity, and for the sake of making Jewish-Christian scriptural traditions compelling.

Over a period of many decades, Douglass was himself one of the most widely known and regular participants in the national debates about the "racial problem." He remained open to engaging almost anyone and any issue in connection with the matter. He tended to respond to any critic raising any sort of question about the ultimate goal or hope. And he also tended to draw upon many different sources and perspectives in order to facilitate and make compelling his stand on the issues. For example, although he obviously entered into partnerships and campaigns with religious people—lay and clergy—in his mature years, he grew wary of and came to distance himself a bit from organized religion. Yet, as his interpretive spin on the Exodus story makes clear, he drew heavily upon the religious language and symbolism that marked the "Christian" nation in which he lived in order to make his case about issues of the day, most especially the issues having to do with racial injustice.

Douglass's Reading Practices and Racial Justice

What can be seen in Douglass's treatment of the Exodus story in the 1883 Washington, D.C., speech is a type of reading practice in which he interpreted the nation in light of Scriptures (as he created and used them) and Scriptures in light of the nation (as he envisioned and structured it). This reading practice was obviously informed by Douglass's own experience as a slave and—even when he was not fully apprised of the facts on the ground about others' experiences—his continuing solidarity with those who remained enslaved and who continued to suffer from brutal racist policies. Douglass's reading practice foregrounded the plight of black folks and forced the nexus of the religious and the political in a particular way. He read the religious as a registration of the political and the political as a registration of the religious. There was no attempt to separate the two. Such reading practice was understood to be important as part of the campaign to effect racial justice. Two examples are in order:

First, Douglass seemed fascinated by a book written by a British cleric turned American missionary named Morgan Godwyn. In 1680, Godwyn had published a little book with one of those typically labored but, in this case, most arresting titles—*The Negro's and Indian's Advocate, Suing for their Admission into Church: Or a Persuasive to the Instructing and Baptizing of the Negros and Indians in our Plantations. Shewing That as the Compliance therewith can prejudice no Man's just Interest; So the willful Neglecting and opposing of it, is no less than a manifest Apostasy from the Christian Faith.* Douglass saw the publication as a provocative and important example of the use of Scriptures:

> This [publication] was . . . the starting point, the foundation of all the grand concessions yet made to the claims, the character, the manhood and dignity of the Negro . . . a book to prove the Negro's right to baptism seems ridiculous, but so it did not seem two hundred years ago. Baptism was then a vital and commanding question, one with which the moral and intellectual giants were required to grapple.
>
> . . . Slaveholders of that day were sharp-eyed and keen-scented, and snuffed danger from afar. They saw in this argument . . . the thin edge of the wedge which would sooner or later rend asunder the bonds of slavery. . . . They contended that [baptism] could only be properly administered to free and responsible agents . . . who in all matters of moral conduct, could exercise the sacred right of choice. . . . Plainly enough, the Negro did not answer that description . . . [he was] no more fitted to be admitted to the fellowship of the saints than horses, sheep, or swine. . . . But deeper

down . . . there was a more controlling motive for opposing baptism. Baptism had a legal as well as a religious significance. By the common law at that time, baptism was made a sufficient basis for a legal claim for emancipation. . . . I should have been baptized if I could have gotten anybody to perform the ceremony.

For in that day of Christian simplicity, honest rules of Biblical interpretation were applied. The Bible was thought to mean just what it said. When a heathen ceased to be a heathen and became a Christian, he could no longer be held as a slave. Within the meaning of the accepted word of God it was the heathen, not the Christian, who was to be bought and sold, and held as a bondman forever. (363–65)

What Douglass does with Godwyn's biblically inflected argument—"a literary curiosity and an ethical wonder" (363)—is important: he argues that for Godwyn and for himself, biblical interpretation is or should be transparently and consistently used to support the cause of the oppressed, the outsider, the marginalized. Godwyn reminded Douglass that the Bible could be used to scramble traditional lines of identity, positionality, status, and association. Drawing directly from Godwyn, and indirectly if not directly from the Christian Scriptures[12]—possibly Galatians and Philemon; perhaps also the book of Acts—in support of racial justice, Douglass plainly made the point that Christian baptism nullified slavery and racial oppression. It was a leveling force. He makes an astounding argument that ensued as part of the exegetical exercises within a particular "reading formation":[13]

---

12. Many black rhetors and white abolitionists of the time in Europe and the United States did so.

13. For the concept of "reading formation," see Tony Bennett, "Texts, Readers, Reading Formations," *MMLA* 16, no.1 (1983): 1–17; and "Texts in History: The Determinations of Readings and Their Texts," *MMLA* 18, no.1 (1985): 1–16. For discussions regarding ideologies of race and literacy, see Dana Nelson Salvino, "The Word in Black and White: Ideologies of Race and Literacy in Antebellum America," in *Reading in America: Literature and Social History*, ed. Cathy N. Davidson (Baltimore: The Johns Hopkins University Press, 1989), 140–56; Srinivas Aravamudan, *Tropicopolitans: Colonialism and Agency, 1688–1804* (Durham: Duke University Press, 1999), 326–31; and Grey Gundaker, *Signs of Diaspora, Diaspora of Signs: Literacies, Creolization, and Vernacular Practice in African America* (New York: Oxford University Press, 1998), esp. 3–13.

When a heathen . . . became a Christian . . . he could no longer be held as a slave. . . . Within the meaning of the accepted word of God it was the heathen, not the Christian, who was to be bought and sold. (365)

Such radicalism found among religious dissenters and others in the eighteenth and nineteenth centuries in the North Atlantic worlds, especially Britain, had great influence upon Douglass. Indeed, he should be understood as having been one of the leading voices in such company, at least in the informal terms of membership in the discursive circle. It is sad that such a coalition was not sustained.[14]

Another example: In the same speech given in the Congregational Church in 1883, Douglass dismissed the rantings of an insecure writer, a "Professor Gilliam," who reportedly argued with paranoid intensity that eventually black peoples would rise up, seek vengeance, and assume a position of "sovereignty" over white peoples. At this point in his speech, Douglass, in a poignant segue, referenced William Miller, widely known even at that time as the prophet of the imminent end of the world.

When the world did not come to its end as Miller had expected, and after he made adjustments in his prediction and tried to reassure people that the end was indeed imminent, cynics and skeptics weighed in—"What if it does not come?" According to Douglass, Miller's response was, "Then we shall wait till it does come." Miller's exhortation to "wait" riveted Douglass. The latter rightly took the term to be a biblical—specifically, a New Testament or primitive Christian eschatological injunction. But Douglass contradicted the longstanding Western world understanding and usage of the injunction and translated it into Bible-inflected political rhetoric that pointed directly to the plight of black peoples in his own time:

---

14. See Hochschild, *Bury the Chains*, and Peter Linebaugh and Marcus Rediker, *The Many-Headed Hydra: Sailors, Slaves, Commoners, and the Hidden History of the Revolutionary Atlantic* (Boston: Beacon, 2000), for discussions regarding histories of radical progressive coalition-building efforts in the early modern period. Some would argue that such efforts were revived in modern civil rights movements. Alas, today they all seem much like far distant echoes.

The colored people of the United States imitate the wisdom [regarding the expectation of the near end of the world] of . . . [William] Miller and wait. But we should work while we wait. For after all, our destiny is largely in our own hands. If we find, we shall have to seek. If we succeed in the race of life, it must be by our own energies, and our own exertions . . . we must go forward, or be left behind in the race of life. (366)

Here, we have another example of the interpretation of Scriptures as the political, the political in terms of the scriptural. Douglass uses Miller's concept of waiting for the end of the world in reference to the end of slavery and the subjugation of black peoples and the realization of racial justice and socioeconomic and sociopolitical progress—in the world as known and experienced by Douglass. Might Douglass have also thought—most interestingly, after the Civil War!—about a social conflagration as the shape of the end time in the absence of the realization of racial justice?[15] This matter is not so clear. But what is clear is that for Douglass, black folks' expectation of real justice in the United States was understood in terms larger than normal life; it was thought about in terms greatly influenced, if not absolutely determined, by the eschatological and apocalyptic rhetorics of the Bible.

It is also important to note that Douglass drew upon the parenetic traditions that sometimes accompanied biblical eschatological-apocalyptic visions and rhetorics. Wait, yes, Douglass exhorted. But not in passive terms—"We should work while we wait." The immediate source or rhetorical background of this exhortation may have been any number of evangelical preachers, pamphlets, or books. But the ultimate and direct source or background here seems to have been Paul's arguments in 1 Thessalonians regarding waiting and working.[16] The elaboration upon the working–waiting motif in the finding-and-seeking theme seems to have its ultimate origins in the Gospels (Matthew 7). The further elaboration in the race of life theme echoes Paul once again (cf. 1 Corinthians 9).

---

15. Regarding messianic ideology, David Walker (*An Appeal in Four Articles* [1830]) should be considered and compared to Douglass.

16. See 1 Thessalonians 4:13–5:11. Also: Matthew 25:13; Mark 13:34–37.

The point of any of these references for Douglass seems to have been to challenge a particular stance in or response to the world among black peoples in late nineteenth century America. He articulates this challenge by demonstrating a particular type of reading or use of the Bible as center-text for the formation of the nation. Douglass engaged the struggle for racial justice as part of the struggle to realize justice for the nation.

> There is but one destiny . . . left for us, and that is to make our-selves and be made by others a part of the American people in every sense of the word. Assimilation and not isolation is our true policy and our natural destiny. Unification for us is life; separation is death. . . . Our own interests will be subserved by generous care for the interests of the Nation at large. (370)

Apparently keeping the theme of expectation—of the end of the world—in mind, Douglass drew at the end of his speech upon Robert Burns's famous end-of-an-era political song "For a' that" (1795)[17] in order to signal most strongly that the struggle for justice for black peoples is related to justice for the oppressed all over the world:

> It's comin' yet for a' that,
> That man to man the world o'er
> Shall brothers be for a' that. (370–71)

It seemed important for Douglass to make the point that the United States-inflected Christian tradition and its Scriptures were political, that reading practices in connection with Scriptures were and should be fundamentally political, that Scriptures always belong to a nation or a people, and that the reading of Scriptures should always be used to advance a particular liberationist/integrationist/monogenetic agenda of nationalization. This means that for Douglass, a reading of scriptures must be honestly acknowledged to have a public or civic function, and it must have as its primary consideration the position of black folks within the nation. The reading of the Bible is *supposed* to

---

17. See Robert Crawford, ed., *Robert Burns and Cultural Authority* (Iowa City: University of Iowa Press, 1997), for background information on this poem.

be race-sensitive in the way that Douglass read. Although he did not argue the point in explicit terms, Douglass implied that a reading of Scriptures is virulently and violently racist in antiblack terms when it is not a public-nationalization reading that is based upon, or determined by, the position of dark peoples. That is the meaning of his insistence that there be "no modern Joshua" to make us "stand still" in relationship to the clamor about the black presence. Silence in this sense is deadly.[18]

No, I am no Frederick Douglass. But as this essay suggests, I am haunted by him—haunted, in particular, by his challenge regarding the silence. I am, I fear, too much a part of an order—sociopolitical, academic-intellectual—that is eerily silent and too easily misled by what Douglass tagged as "modern Joshuas," or at least the idea of such as a panacea. Being in solidarity with Douglass's effort and argument requires, it seems to me, not only a different reading of the Exodus and wilderness situation and other stories of the Bible. It means not merely providing the "black perspective" on, or the "black" figure in, the white text, but now reading all things dark-ly, reading the complexity, the luminescence, of the darkness of existence, thereby making of black selves—or other race-d selves—a "text."[19] Here might be the beginnings of a radical (re)signifying (on) scriptures that at the same time reflects a (re)signifying of the nation, and beyond it, a reconfigured world community. At the very least, it means understanding that the discourse of religious and theological studies, including biblical

18. But Houston Baker's concept of "silence" and of the need for a "criticism of silence" in the study of black folks should be considered in relationship to Douglass's challenge. See his *Afro-American Poetics: Revisions of Harlem and the Black Aesthetics* (Madison: University of Wisconsin Press, 1988), esp. chapter 3, pp. 106–8 ("Lowground and Inaudible Valleys: Reflections on Afro-American Spirit Work").

19. See Ishmael Reed's fascinating work *Mumbo Jumbo* (New York: Scribner Paperback Fiction, 1996 [1972]). And see my essay, which I think is consonant with Reed's argument insofar as it is an attempt to undermine the agenda of the larger project (commentary!) in which it is found, "'We Will Make Our Own Future Text': An Alternate Orientation to Interpretation," in *True to Our Native Land: An African American New Testament Commentary*, ed. Brian Blount, Cain Hope Felder, Clarice Martin, and Emerson Powery (Minneapolis: Fortress Press, 2007), 43–53.

studies, cannot be silent about the stains and pollutions of racial-ism[20] and racism and other such ideologies and projects, the purpose and effects of which are to humiliate and subjugate peoples. Douglass's challenge to us was to engage—seriously, deeply, and with patience, persistence, and honesty.

Translated into our early-twenty-first century situation, and more specifically, the very discursive arrangements and project to which this chapter belongs, Douglass's challenge may appropriately be understood to go to the very heart of the matter about how we sustain the discussion about race, ethnicity, gender, and class. Are these issues, for example, to frame and define the academic-intellectual discussion and project, or are they to be taken up as additive approaches to traditional paradigms and projects? More pointedly, should "race," as Douglass understood the matter—that is, as a conscious-raising problematic and analytical wedge—inform and (re)orient the discourse of Biblical Studies? Such change would mean that Biblical Studies would turn not around the exegesis of ancient world texts but the fathoming of modern or contemporary world sentiments, politics, power dynamics, and practices in relationship to ancient texts.

Through these issues Douglass continues to haunt me. He should haunt all of us.

---

20. The term *racial-ism* refers to the penchant for dividing people, using race as marker, as in race-baiting, usually with dark peoples greatly disadvantaged. Douglass stood against this penchant as well as virulent and violent forms of racism.

CHAPTER 11

Poetics of Minority Biblical Criticism
Identification and Theorization

Fernando F. Segovia

The poetics of minority biblical criticism may be described from two different perspectives. First, *minority* biblical criticism constitutes one variation among many within the conjunction of two fields of study, biblical studies and Racial-Ethnic Studies, both of which possess long-standing foundations in the academy, going back well into the nineteenth century, and which reveal wide-ranging trajectories of scholarship. Second, as a *poetics*, or rhetorical dynamics, of minority biblical criticism, it focuses on the formal features of critical emplacement and argumentation and therefore constitutes but one critical pursuit among many.

Given the wealth of options regarding variations not only in racial-ethnic criticism but also within minority criticism, it is imperative first to ask where minority criticism fits within racial-ethnic criticism in general and to gain a sense of what such interdisciplinary confluence involves. Second, we must ask how the focus on poetics fits within minority criticism as such.

Interdisciplinary Conjunction: Overview

The proposed interdisciplinary conjunction signified by racial-ethnic biblical criticism brings together two well-established fields of study, whose expansive discursive frameworks and extensive disciplinary parameters prove enormously challenging in their own right, let alone taken in unison. On the one hand, critical accounts of the scholarly tradition reveal both fields as highly complex, constantly shifting, and sharply conflicted. On the other hand, critical discussions of scholarly scope show both fields as comprehending a broad variety of areas of interest. Indeed, in any one such area of study, the literature in question emerges as convoluted, changing, and controverted. Any attempt, therefore, at bringing both fields together represents a very tall order indeed. Yet, if confluence is the goal, there is no option but to forge ahead; otherwise, the discussion on race-ethnicity would remain at a thoroughly undertheorized and impressionistic level.

Several options for such interchange readily come to mind. In a more traditional vein, one might proceed by acquiring mastery in both fields before so doing. This is a noble goal, certainly, but one that seems both impractical and unsound. Nowadays, expertise of this sort in any one field lies beyond the realm of possibility. Besides, the concept of "mastery" in the academic world today, where the highlighting of knowledge-construction trumps the accumulation of knowledge-data, is not a given but a problematic. In more recent fashion, one might proceed by rubbing both fields against one another in localized and transitory ways. This is a fruitful exercise, to be sure, but one that comes across as unsatisfactory and unbalanced. Such juxtaposition conveys a certain degree of arbitrariness, insofar as it reveals less than sufficient theoretical grounding and critical engagement. In addition, such rubbing invariably favors one field over the other, as a critical position is lifted from one discursive context and inserted into the other indiscriminately. In more guarded fashion, consequently, one might proceed by attaining a well-informed sense of the layout of each discipline and offering a well-defined vision of any proposed inter-disciplinary focalization. On the one hand, therefore, one develops a mapping of the constitutive components of a field and the relations among them; on the other hand, one develops a blueprint identifying the components from both field(s) to be related and furnishing a sense of the why and the how for so doing. It is this option that I favor, which calls for a manageable sense of working expertise in both fields as well as for a clear sense of the mutual engagement sought.

I begin with a general sense of layout in each field of study. For Biblical Studies, I rely on my own account of disciplinary history, which I have drawn in terms of umbrella models of interpretation, and reach, and which I have approached by way of appropriate realms of study and actual reading traditions of the Bible.[1] For Racial-Ethnic Studies, I have recourse to recent historical overviews regarding the analysis of race and ethnicity, which surface a number of closely related topics within the discussion of this problematic and which record a gradual transition over time from essentialism to constructivism in the understanding and formulation of these concepts.[2]

Contemporary Biblical Studies, as I see it from the inside, addresses the problematic of scriptural interpretation, which revolves around the study of biblical texts and contexts (cultural and social), both in terms of production and in terms of reception, writ broadly. Such criticism covers enormous terrain. To begin with, it involves not only the traditional approach of historical contextualization regarding the biblical texts but also the more recent approaches that accentuate the literary, sociocultural, and ideological dimensions of such texts. Further, it involves not only the received focus on ancient texts and contexts but also a much-expanded focus on modern and postmodern interpretations and interpreters of such texts and contexts, along with their respective contexts (cultural and social). Its object of study thus comprehends, to put it differently, the realm of antiquity as well as the representation of antiquity in modernity and postmodernity. Lastly, it involves attention not only to the academic-scholarly tradition of reading but also to other major traditions of reading, whether in the religious realm (for example, theological-dogmatic; ecclesial-liturgical; popular-devotional) or at large (for example, social-institutional;

---

1. Fernando F. Segovia, *Decolonizing Biblical Studies* (Maryknoll: Orbis Books, 2000).
2. Steve Fenton, *Ethnicity*, Key Concepts (Cambridge: Polity, 2003); Robert Miles and Malcolm Brown, *Racism*, 2nd ed., Key Ideas (London and New York: Routledge, 2003).

cultural-artistic; political-statist). All such components, moreover, stand as interrelated, in one way or another.

Contemporary Racial-Ethnic Studies, as I read it from the outside, has to do with the problematic of race-ethnicity, which revolves around the study of representations of Self and Other (somatic and cultural) that arise as a result of migration and the encounter of population groups. Such study covers immense territory as well. The list of related topics is long: the phenomenon of migration itself (causes, processes, results); the actual representations of Self and Other that emerge in processes of racialization and ethnicization (images, beliefs, evaluations); the signification of race and ethnos as categories of identity (origins, trajectories, debates); the concept of nation or state (boundaries and borderlands, exile and diaspora, assimilation and resistance); and the emplacement of dominant and minority groups (group formations and perspectives; vertical relations between such categories; horizontal relations among minority groups). All such components stand, again, as interrelated, in some fashion or another.

I turn, then, to a specific consideration of vision regarding interdisciplinary focalization across both fields of study. As defined, the layouts clearly allow for a range of interaction that is at once enormous and daunting. Any proposed confluence requires, therefore, a keen sense of procedure. First, the actual design of the exercise should be set forth: explicit identification of the areas of interest that are to be brought together from each field of study. Second, the driving rationale underlying such an exercise should be disclosed: pointed exposition of the objectives behind such bringing together. Lastly, the actual mode of correlation in carrying out such an exercise should be unpacked: explicit account of the ways in which and the angles from which such bringing together will be accomplished. In sum, any proposed confluence requires a properly articulated exposition of the concrete problematic under consideration—its what, why, and how— and a properly activated account of and engagement with the scholarly literature regarding such a problematic.

Here is a word, then, about the present study. As an exercise in minority biblical criticism, the study singles out the following components for mutual engagement: on the part of Biblical Studies, the interpretive practices at work among biblical critics from minority groups; on the part of Racial-Ethnic Studies, the set of formations and relations involving such groups within the United States of America (U.S.). Its rationale is to examine what such practices may have in common in the light of the traditional practices forged and followed by biblical critics from the dominant group. Its mode of correlation involves, as detailed below, a focus on the rhetorical dynamics at work in such practices. To summarize, the study seeks to determine whether and how minority criticism can be differentiated from dominant criticism in interpretation.

Minority Biblical Criticism: Overview

As a variation within the conjunction of Biblical Studies and Racial-Ethnic Studies, minority criticism can itself proceed in manifold directions. From the perspective of Biblical Studies, such criticism may focus on any of the constitutive components of the discipline itself. It may thus address, individually or in combination, the ancient texts and contexts directly, the modern and postmodern interpretations of the ancient texts and contexts (within their sociocultural contexts), and the flesh-and-blood interpreters behind such interpretations (within their sociocultural contexts). Such criticism may also proceed outside the academic-scholarly tradition of reading and focus on any of the other major reading traditions of the Bible, its readings and readers and their respective contexts, whether in the realm of religion and theology, or in society and culture at large. The realm of possibilities is thus considerable. From the standpoint of Minority Studies, such criticism may focus on individual minority groups, on any combination of such groups, or on all minority groups as a whole. Such criticism may further address any number of issues related to the process of minoritization and its effects, namely, the resultant set of dominant-minority formations. The range of possibilities is thus similarly considerable. In effect, any of the various dimensions of Minority Studies may be brought to bear upon any of the different dimensions of Biblical Studies. Needless to say, this is quite a tall order, again, and with no recourse but to press ahead, if the desired confluence is to avoid undertheorization and impressionism.

Any proposed venture in minority biblical criticism demands, therefore, a sharp sense of procedure as well: blueprint of overall design, disclosure of driving rationale, and exposition of actual mode of correlation. In sum, any such exercise requires proper formulation of the specific problematic under discussion—its what, why, and how—and proper activation of the pertinent scholarly literature having to do with such a problematic, not only by way of historical trajectory, but also by way of critical dialogue.

Again, a word about the present study is in order. As an exercise in the poetics of minority biblical criticism, the study seeks to analyze the rhetorical dynamics utilized by minority critics in the United States, taken as a whole, in interpretation. Its focus in this regard is twofold: how the biblical texts and contexts are approached, and how established approaches on the part of dominant criticism are evaluated. The rationale for such a study is to highlight, classify, and unpack such moves and techniques in order to establish the differences between minority and dominant practices of analysis and argumentation. The mode of correlation involves the identification of major strategies and supporting tactics, as well as a theorization of such practices in terms of rhetorical aims and ideological agenda. To summarize, the study seeks to surface and explain the formal features of analysis and argumentation, the moves and techniques, deployed by minority critics in the face of dominant criticism and its ways.

Studying the Poetics of Minority Biblical Criticism: Why?

A crucial point remains: Why undertake such a study in the poetics of minority biblical criticism at all? Why seek to determine whether and how the practices of minority criticism differ from those of dominant criticism in interpretation? Why seek to surface and explain the formal features of emplacement and argumentation deployed by minority critics in the face of dominant criticism and its ways? This is not the place to develop the proper and detailed response that such a query deserves and demands; for now, a brief statement of ideological agenda must suffice.

In the lives of minority groups and subjects, I would argue, there is a desire for self-assertion and self-introjection, in thought as well as in practice, given the policies of silencing and censure as well as erasure and remolding that invariably govern their reality and experience in and from the outside. There is a desire, in effect, to break through the gaze-patrol of dominant culture and society. This desire is, or can be, sometimes pursued; is, or must be, sometimes repressed. Regardless, it is always fraught with uncertainty and fear. Minority criticism in general, and minority biblical criticism in particular, are no exceptions in this regard. Any critical exercise, therefore, that sets out to foreground the work and practices of minority groups and subjects constitutes a move in self-assertion and self-introjection. In its resolve to do so with respect to the practices of biblical interpretation among minority critics, the present study represents a concrete expression of such a desire.

Indeed, minority groups and subjects form part of a dialectical relation in which they find themselves cast as Other to Self, within the context of a (nation-)state, so that the opposites in question are best conceived and characterized as "minoritized" and "dominantized," that is, as constructed unequal formations and relations of power. Consequently, any move toward self-assertion and self-introjection constitutes an attempt to break through the dialectic itself and, in so doing, to conjure up alternative visions of the (nation-)state itself, as well as of the formations and relations of population groups within it. Any such move also embodies an attempt to move beyond all ways of thinking and doing under the (nation-)state, since such a dialectical process permeates and molds the whole of the material matrix and the whole of discursive production—all of society as well as all of culture—of the (nation-)state. Again, minority criticism in general, and minority biblical criticism in particular, prove no exceptions in this regard. Any critical exercise, therefore, that sets out to expose and critique the dialectic in place constitutes a move toward self-assertion and self-interjection and hence toward sociocultural breakthrough and conjuring-up. In its resolve to examine the poetics of minority criticism in relation to those of dominant criticism, the present study, I would submit, represents a concrete embodiment of such dialectical moving-beyond.

Repertoire: Strategies and Tactics

The rhetorical dynamics of minority biblical criticism will be approached, as indicated above, in terms of major strategies and supporting tactics. A repertoire of four primary strategies can be readily outlined. These I would name and summarize as follows: (1) Interpretive Contextualization, the deliberate puncturing of the traditional norms of objectivity and universality in research by way of a foundational foregrounding of the social and cultural contexts in criticism. (2) Border Transgressionism, the pointed expansion of the received boundaries, the discursive demarcations, of the field of study through the integration of heretofore unrelated concerns, material, or resources. (3) Interruptive Stocktaking, the self-conscious problematization of the established grounds and practices of criticism itself by way of rethinking and revisioning. (4) Discursive Cross-fertilization, the explicit turn to interdisciplinary inquiry through the invocation and interlacing of previously unrelated fields of study. A number of comments are in order regarding this proposed fourfold outline.

To begin with, these strategies are advanced as neither self-evident nor indispensable. They represent, rather, taxonomic constructions based on long acquaintance and sustained engagement with the critical production of minority scholars. As such, this system of classification is viewed as subject to replacement, partially or completely, by a different one altogether, should such a system be deemed more appropriate or useful. This is not to say that these strategies are unimportant, however. Quite to the contrary. While the system itself, as presently configured, is dispensable, room would have to be found for such strategies within any other system proposed.

Second, these strategies are in no way presented as self-contained and independent—mutually exclusive formations, as it were, unique unto themselves. They are seen, rather, as interrelated and interdependent, and hence deployable in a variety of combinations. Generally, to be sure, a particular strategy is adopted in any one study as the leading point of entry in the process of interpretation, while other strategies are drawn upon for support and development. Theoretically, however, there is no reason why more than one strategy cannot be activated jointly in approximately balanced fashion.

Third, each strategy is envisioned as encompassing a variety of secondary tactics. Theoretically, such tactics could be listed independently, as primary strategies in their own right, thereby yielding a system of classification involving a much greater number of strategies. As group formations, however, they are set forth as different ways of shoring up and putting into effect the driving rhetorical objectives and ideological points of the strategy in question. As in the case of the primary strategies, these tactics are also conceived as neither self-evident and irreplaceable, nor self-contained and independent. The given group formations are thus seen as subject to replacement, whether partly or fully, in light of a better outline. They are also viewed as interrelated and interdependent and hence as deployable in combination, not only within a particular strategy but also across strategies as well.

Lastly, this system of classification is by no means advanced as exhaustive, at either level, but rather as subject to ongoing revision in various directions. Several such possibilities come to mind. Expansion would represent one such development: further primary strategies or secondary tactics may be identified and incorporated accordingly. Nomenclature may undergo similar alteration as well: more accurate descriptors may be suggested for any particular strategy or tactic. Rearrangement would constitute another such development: secondary tactics may be transferred from one strategy to another or even designated, in light of prominent usage, as a primary strategy altogether. In all such cases, the system of classification would not be replaced but rather modified.

In sum, the proposed fourfold system of classification is put forward as but a first step, a working model, toward a taxonomy of minority poetics. In what follows, I shall expand on each major strategy and supporting tactic in a similarly initial attempt at theorization. Such theorization will touch on such aspects of rhetorical dynamics as formal features, strategic programs, and ideological slants.

Interpretive Contextualization: Puncturing Objectivity and Universality

A first major strategy in minority criticism consists in foregrounding context at the level of consumption alongside its continued pursuit at the level of production. Such a project of contextualization encompasses, following the overarching character of the concept of context itself, a twofold angle of inquiry, both highly interrelated and interdependent. On the one side, it involves critical analysis of social-cultural location, and thus a focus on material matrix as well as on discursive production in any given framework of inquiry. On the other side, it entails critical examination of ideological-political agenda, and hence a focus on any number of axes—in individual or intersecting fashion—involving differential relations of power within a given framework of inquiry. This strategy brings to bear, therefore, a twofold sense of placement and positioning on both the world of composition *and* the world of reception. While in theory the task of contextualization emerges as quite comprehensive, in practice a particular dimension or set of dimensions may be highlighted for analysis.

This strategy minority criticism adopts, directly or indirectly, in the face of and in reaction to dominant criticism. In so doing, it counters a received model of scholarship in which the task of contextualization is to be pursued resolutely with regard to the past, the world of production, but to be avoided with unyielding determination with respect to the present, the world of consumption. Minority criticism regards such a simultaneous opening and drawing of a critical curtain of analysis—shedding all contextual light possible on writings and writers of antiquity, while cutting off any such light on readings and readers of modernity and postmodernity—as utterly contradictory and ultimately self-deconstructing. In effect, so the argument goes, if the compositions and authors of ancient times require decipherment in context for proper understanding and recovery, why should the same principle not apply to receptions and lectors in modern and postmodern times?

This policy of critical silence on reception has yielded two basic postures in dominant criticism. The first one may be described as active and principled adherence. This represents the traditional position on scientific research: it is based on claims to abstraction from the realities of society and culture and impartiality in the webs of ideology and politics. Within this posture, the critic is a reader who transcends circumstances and interests in interpretation. The second posture may be characterized as passive and pragmatic subscription.

This constitutes a contemporary twist, at once undermining and supportive, on the traditional position: while questioning in principle any claim to ideological-political neutrality or social-cultural transcendence, it opts for reticence, absolute or overriding, in practice. Within this posture, the critic is a reader who is keenly aware of unshakable insertion in circumstances and interests, but who fails to follow through, for whatever reason, on the ramifications of such insertion in interpretation. Either way, whether by rejection on theoretical grounds or by bracketing in actual usage, the gaze uncast by dominant criticism upon itself emerges as paramount for minority criticism. Thus, it sets out, publicly and deliberately, to cast such a gaze upon itself—to construct itself and to theorize such construction of itself.

In thus relativizing itself in relation to the established model of inquiry, minority criticism might, at first, appear as mortally undoing itself. This, however, is a question of perspective. Such is, no doubt, the perception and judgment of dominant criticism. Its reaction will range from outright dismissal to effective marginalization, from a characterization of the whole enterprise as fatally biased and flawed to a classification of all such work as of interest and benefit only to the group(s) in question, but not to mainstream criticism. From this point of view, minority critics are readers who not only prove unable to transcend particularity in circumstances and interests but actually take delight in such an exposed sense of localism and slantism. From its own perspective, however, minority criticism sees itself as ultimately relativizing, and hence mortally undoing, dominant criticism. It regards its emphasis on location and agenda in interpretation as applicable to and inescapable in all situations, not only at the periphery but also at the center. From this point of view, dominant critics are readers who both deceive themselves into believing in their ability to transcend particularity in circumstances and interests and take great pride in such a mystified sense of universality and objectivity. Furthermore, dominant critics who acknowledge such mystification, who have no qualms in surrendering it in principle, but who fail to integrate such a move into their own critical work, confirm the collapse of any possibility of transcendence of particulars as a theoretical foundation, but nonetheless keep the system in place through silence.

What minority criticism does through this first primary strategy is to extend, logically, the principle of contextualization—the dictum that a cultural product from another time or place has to be situated and positioned within its own context of production. This dictum, it argues, applies to any cultural product in any time or place, including itself. As such, contextualization is relevant to both the realm of composition, the texts and authors that it studies, and the realm of consumption, all readings and readers of such texts and authors. This is so, it would add, even when a claim to the contrary has been lodged by the interpretive tradition. In fact, for minority criticism, any such claim to universality and objectivity emerges as itself subject to contextualization, localized and ideological.

In so doing, minority criticism may proceed in two different directions. It may argue that it is only through such placement and positioning in context at both levels that correct understanding and recovery can take place. From this perspective, particularity in reception is seen as leading to a more stable and precise analysis of the past. Here, objectivism is achieved via localism and slantism. It may argue instead that what such dual contextualization yields is broader understanding and retrieval through a surfacing of both multiple views (readings and readers) and multiple conflicts in such views (among readings and readers). From this perspective, particularity in reception is viewed as leading to a thoroughly unstable and varied analysis of the past. In this case, objectivism is compromised altogether. In the end, therefore, minority criticism can work with a revisioned goal of historical reconstruction or with an envisioned sense of historical construction in mind.

This first primary strategy of rupturing the universal-objective optic in criticism may be seen as encompassing a variety of supporting tactics. These I would classify as follows: (1) Relentless Denuding/Investing; (2) Appealing to Contextual Enlightenment; and (3) Retrieving the Religious-Theological.

Relentless Denuding/Investing

A first supporting tactic in interpretive contextualization involves intensive critical gazing on dominant criticism in an attempt to step behind the screen of critical silence tightly drawn on its circumstances and interests by its foundational principles of universality and objectivity. This move sets out, therefore, in deliberate and sustained fashion, to cut through such self-imposed concealment, whether by principled adherence or pragmatic subscription, by rummaging around and ferreting out the submerged location and agenda of dominant critics. The tactic may be seen as a variation, highly ironic, on the classic exclamation of exposé captured in Hans Christian Andersen's fairy tale of 1837, "The Emperor's New Suit." It is ironic insofar as the problem highlighted by minority criticism lies not with a claim to magnificent clothing that is actually invisible, materially non-existent and thus revelatory of stark nakedness, but rather with a claim to magnificent clothing that bestows invisibility, materially existent and hence revelatory of full clothing.

The plot of the story is worth recalling in this regard. An emperor whose overriding passion in life is for the acquisition and display of new clothes is taken in by two swindlers newly arrived in his great imperial city. They claim to be weavers and to produce cloth of the finest quality imaginable, not only most beautiful but also invisible to anyone unfit for office or in mind. The emperor commissions a suit of such cloth for himself in order to ascertain who are those unworthy of holding office or lacking in intelligence throughout the empire. During the weaving process, neither his trusted agents nor the emperor himself and his attendants, while unable to see the cloth, are willing to say so in public, afraid of being branded incompetent or stupid; instead, they shower high praise on the suit in-the-making. In fact, the emperor is urged by his courtiers to wear it in a procession for all the citizenry to admire. As he does so, the crowds respond at first with adulation, until a little child blurts out, "But he has nothing on at all." Gradually, the crowd joins in such a revelation. The emperor, though beset by inner doubt, decides to go through with the procession, while his attendants comport themselves with even greater dignity in the face of such public reaction.

Similarly, when confronted by the self-imputed invisibility supposedly bestowed through scientific methodology, a suit of interpretive clothes designed to neutralize the particularities of sociocultural circumstances and ideological-political interests and grant neutrality and transcendence, minority criticism cries out that dominant criticism is clothed to the hilt. Not only does the new suit fail to grant invisibility to its wearers, for their circumstances and interests remain palpably visible, but also the suit itself, its cloth and cut, comes across as quite visible, highly reflective of its own circumstances and interests. Such epistemic denuding on the part of minority criticism may or may not lead to a corresponding investing. On the one hand, the exposé may stop with the moment of unmasking as such: the realization and proclamation that such claimed scientific invisibility is imaginary. On the other hand, the exposé may go on, past this initial moment of conscientization, to full demystification: the surfacing of circumstances and interests impinging upon both wearers and suit.

Appealing to Contextual Enlightenment

A second supporting tactic in interpretive contextualization is the use of context at the level of reception, the world of the critic, as point of entry into and mode of development at the level of composition, the world of the text. This move begins, therefore, with the curtain of critical silence raised, the set of circumstances and interests underlying interpretation highlighted, and the principles of universality and objectivity replaced by localism and slantism. This move seeks direct insight from the critic's own location, by way of the material matrix or the discursive production or both, and agenda, in terms of the ideological and political webs at work, in order to render the text and its context more comprehensible and more effective. For this secondary tactic, therefore, it is not the mantle of invisibility but the surfacing of visibility in consumption that renders production visible.

Such a claim may but need not be totalizing in nature. The move could certainly argue that, without such contextualized light-shedding, the meaning and impact of the text in context would remain altogether elusive. The reading in question would be presented as requiring privileged access and yielding a privileged rendition. For the most part, however, the move tends to relativize. It argues for distinctive and significant insight into the text in context as a result of such contextualized light-shedding, without excluding similar such insights from other locations and agendas. As a result, a contextual reading is advanced as special or even unique, but such distinctiveness or uniqueness would not be denied of other readings in their own right. There would be no claim of privilege in access or rendition. From this perspective, any such claim would be seen as highly ironic, insofar as it would duplicate the exclusivist character of scientific reading in reverse, with privilege bestowed not on the objectivist and universalist perspective of scientific research, but on the experiential and interested perspective of individual critics.

Retrieving the Religious-Theological

A third supporting tactic of interpretive contextualization consists in the recovery and accentuation of the religious and theological dimension at the level of reception. This move represents an exercise in focalization with regard to the previous two tactics, the mission of denuding or investing vis-à-vis dominant criticism as well as the appeal to contextual enlightenment on the part of minority criticism. In both respects, the angle of theological beliefs and religious practices is viewed as so salient, even crucial, that it is distinguished in its own right and pursued with determination. Its background is clear. The curtain of critical silence that dominant criticism drew on location and agenda included, in paradigmatic fashion, the world of religion and theology. This angle of inquiry was pursued in earnest at the level of composition, overriding all other social and cultural angles and yielding a world saturated with conflict—God and gods; people of God and peoples of other gods; orthodoxies and heresies, upholders and deviants, within the people of God. Such conflict, however, while raging at the level of reception, was presumed transcended through scientific research and methodology.

Such silence represents a direct result of the project of liberation undertaken by traditional historical criticism in the nineteenth century. The interpretation of the Bible was to be wrested away from the domain of the church, with its use of Scripture as a timeless warrant for unproblematic appropriation in church dogma and life, and to be entrusted to the realm of the academy, with its approach to Scripture as a time-bound remnant in need of decipherment before any such application. In rummaging around the site of interpretation, however,

minority criticism leaves no stone unturned, including religious-theological formations and relations. This move is often presented as a
process of liberation in reverse: a turning away in biblical interpretation from the position of standard sanitization in dominant criticism
toward a stance of full retrieval in matters religious-theological. In
so doing, minority criticism sets out to perform in its analysis of the
past what it carries out in its analysis of the present, viewing religious-
theological frameworks just as significant and influential for reception
as for production. This tactic may proceed, at either level, by way of
detailed delineation or by way of critical engagement.

Border Transgressionism: Expanding the Area of Studies

A second major strategy in minority criticism is to call into question,
push aside, and move past the established borders of the discipline.
The élan behind this project of transgressionism is best captured by
way of comparison with the first strategy, and toward this end extending the metaphor of the curtain of analysis may prove helpful. The
driving aim of this strategy is not, as in the case of the first one, to
open the curtain on reception so that the same amount of light sought
for the object of study may be shed on the agent of study. This goal is,
in fact, taken for granted and integrated into the undertaking. Interpretive contextualization does not vanish from sight, therefore; to
the contrary, it is presupposed and continued. The aim, rather, is to
replace the system of lighting itself. This change may be implemented
in two ways: first, in terms of power: allowing light to reach farther
than before, so that it covers areas previously out of range; second, in
terms of installation: casting light from new angles, so that it brings
out surfaces and details previously unnoticed. In both regards, such
change brings about, inevitably, a reconceptualization of the discipline
as traditionally delimited, given the dismantling of old borders and
the marking of new ones.

Minority criticism also carries out this strategy, directly or indirectly, in the light of and in opposition to dominant criticism. It takes
on the received set of delimitations placed upon interpretation, evalu-
ates them as insufficient or inappropriate, and advances an alternative

and corrective set. In so doing, minority criticism invariably invokes the rhetorics and politics of exclusion and inclusion. On the one hand, a charge of exclusionism is lodged against the entrenched dominant tradition of scholarship, insofar as the omission(s) and silence(s) in question are said to work to the distinct advantage of the dominant voices and to the definite detriment of the Other. On the other hand, a banner of inclusionism is lifted on behalf of the emerging minority tradition of scholarship, given its turn to and foregrounding of such Others, so that their voices are taken into full consideration and allowed to speak. This strategy allows minority criticism to relativize the ways in which the discipline has been traditionally configured and exercised; such ways are found wanting and in need of transgression and expansion.

Such transgressionism, as already intimated, may occur at either the level of composition, through expansion of the set parameters of the critical embrace, or at the level of reception, through expansion of the operative modalities of critical approach. The strategy may thus involve the object of study—the reach or scope of the discipline. This is accomplished through the incorporation of material altogether bypassed or effectively marginalized up to this point by the lens of analysis. The strategy may also affect the mode of inquiry—the approach or framework of the discipline. This is secured through a transformation of method and theory in the lens of analysis itself.

This second primary strategy of expanding disciplinary borders in criticism reveals a number of supportive tactics. These I would characterize as follows: (1) Breaking Spatial-Temporal Models; (2) Heightening the Discourse; and (3) Desacralizing the Text.

Breaking Spatial-Temporal Models

A first supporting tactic adopted in border transgressionism is to call for a redrawing of the geographical and historical boundaries of the field. Two such moves can be readily distinguished. The first concerns the given spatial borders of antiquity as the proper context for biblical antiquity and research. The argument here is that the field as envisioned approaches the biblical texts as more closely related to an unacknowledged vision of Europe. Dominant criticism is viewed as embracing the texts as ultimately and fundamentally part of the Greek and Roman foundations of the West, separating them thereby from other areas and religions of contact and influence, such as the sociocultural frameworks of Africa or the religious-theological frameworks of Hinduism and Buddhism. The second move involves the set temporal borders of antiquity as the sole focus for biblical antiquity and research. The argument here is that the field as visualized examines only the remains of antiquity. Dominant criticism is seen as leaving out of consideration thereby the representations of antiquity and its remains, that is, the interpretations of the biblical texts and contexts and the interpreters behind such interpretations in modernity and postmodernity.

Through the first expansion, minority criticism portrays dominant scholarship as highly gravitational in aim. In so doing, it muddles the spatial or geographical constructions of antiquity by exposing their strong Western pull and raising the possibility of alternative contextualizations within antiquity itself. Through the second expansion, minority criticism depicts dominant scholarship as highly constructive in nature. In the process, it muddles any notion of antiquity as a temporal or historical reconstruction and exposes all criticism as a creative exercise in representation. While the first move stretches the discipline in largely cross-cultural fashion, away from an implicit European or Western center of gravity, the second does so in mostly transhistorical fashion, away from an explicit distantiation of antiquity as objectification.

Heightening the Discourse

A second supporting tactic followed in border transgressionism is to press for a revisioning of the methodological-theoretical repertoire informing and guiding the field. This move entails a turn toward interdisciplinary engagement and can proceed in various directions. In so doing, it follows the example of dominant criticism itself, given its earlier turn from traditional Historical Studies to Literary Studies and Social Studies since the mid-1970s, but along a different path altogether, full of complex twists and turns. Key in this regard is a recourse to the optic of minority discourse, with its focus on the problematic of minoritization and its corresponding set of dominant-minority constructions and relations. This turn can be pursued concretely and broadly. To exemplify such a range of options, I take critics from the three largest minority groups in the United States: African Americans, Asian Americans, and Latino/a Americans.

To begin with, African American, Asian American, and Latino/a American critics can turn, respectively, to African American, Asian American, and Latino/a American Studies for grounding and direction. These areas of study emerged explosively in the crucible of the 1960s, established solid footholds through the 1970s, and developed in variegated and convoluted fashion since the 1980s. They provide ample material not only for the critical task as such but also for all sociocultural dimensions and examinations of the groups in question. In addition, African American, Asian American, and Latino/a American critics can also refer to the other areas of studies besides their own. In other words, an African American critic can establish an ongoing conversation with Asian American and Latino/a American Studies, and so on, *mutatis mutandis*. Thereby, a highly comparative optic can be established between and among the various groups—their past trajectories and present realities, their social matrices and cultural productions—for mutual refinement and support, especially given the parallel appearance, establishment, and maturation of these areas of studies.

Further, African American, Asian American, and Latino/a American critics can turn, beyond a collective consideration of their own areas of studies, to dialogue with other minority groups and discourse within the country, such as, for example, Native American criticism and Native American Studies. Such amplification of the critical optic yields even greater refinement and support for all these areas of studies, individually as well as collectively. Lastly, African American, Asian American, and Latino/a American critics can further embark, beyond their areas of studies, to a more abstract consideration of Minority Studies as such. At this level, the problematic of minoritization would be pursued comprehensively, going beyond the national borders of the United States to analyze dominant-minority relations and formations across (nation-)states. The result is a highly sophisticated grasp of the problematic cross-culturally and transhistorically.

Desacralizing the Text

A third supporting tactic from border transgressionism is to call for a refashioning of the critic's attitude toward the text in the process of interpretation. This move may be seen as a direct reaction to what is by far the predominant position of dominant scholarship regarding proper critical demeanor. In effect, it is the role of the critic to extract and lay bare the findings of scholarly research without any sort of engagement with or evaluation of such findings, least of all perhaps of a religious-theological nature, given the screen of silence imposed on all such aspects of interpretation for the sake of objectivity and universality. This move may thus be seen as well as a direct result of the strategy of recovering and accentuating religious-theological frameworks previously delineated under the umbrella of interpretive contextualization.

Minority criticism may thus call for open and pointed dialogue with the text, its readings and readers, providing in the process a set of social-cultural principles and commitments toward such a conversation and hence a set of criteria for engagement and evaluation. In so doing, minority criticism also may surface the religious-theological dimensions of interpretation, raising thereby the problematic of standing within the Christian tradition, with a sense of the biblical texts as not only past and distant but also living and lived, and thus a felt need to address the ramifications of texts and interpretations alike in the light of its own sociocultural location and ideological-political agenda. This tactic moves the critical task beyond the traditional etiquette of textual sacrality, no involvement with the text on either principled or pragmatic grounds, toward a posture of textual desacralization, involvement with the text regardless of outcome, that is, whether by way of affirmation or critique.

Interruptive Stocktaking: Problematizing Criticism

A third major strategy for minority criticism consists in calling for critical conscientization, interrupting thereby the standard process of interpretation by turning criticism upon itself in a quest for self-awareness and self-reflection. This project of stocktaking addresses the identity and role of the critic as critic and thus involves considered reflection on personal as well as professional dimensions of criticism. The strategy is very much, therefore, in the spirit of interpretive contextualization, but it is differentiated in its own right as a result of its focalization on a specific dimension of contextualization, the craft of criticism. A further extension of the metaphor involving the curtain of critical analysis may again prove helpful. As in the case of the first strategy, the driving aim of this strategy remains the opening of the curtain on reception so that light may reach the agent of study. Such shedding of light, however, is carried out by way of spotlighting, focusing on criticism as embodied, as theorized and practiced, by the critic.

This strategy minority criticism again unfolds, directly or indirectly, in the face of and in reaction to dominant criticism. As such, it counters the established vision of critical status and task according to which the critic is assigned a twofold dimension: first, as indispensable medium, at once retriever and guarantor, between the past and the present, production and reception; second, as unflinching crusader, part of a collective and cumulative quest for the "truth," bound by exemplary disciplinary ideals of detachment and disengagement and unencumbered by sociocultural ties and ideological-political interests. Such interventionism aims to develop an alternative vision of critical status and task.

Such conscientization moves in two directions, which are by no means mutually exclusive. It may veer toward questions of critical identity—background and motivation. Thus, rather than engage in unreflective and mimetic criticism, the critic pauses to ponder who she or he is as a critic, whence and why she or he does what she or he does as a critic. It may also favor questions of critical role—procedure and objective. Instead of pursuing criticism in abstract terms, therefore, the critic halts to reflect on what it is that she or he does, how and to what end she or he does what she or he does as a critic. Both lines of inquiry are closely interwoven. While the first path of intervention lays the ground for a circumscription of the critical task, the second path builds on such foundations of critical identity. In the end, regardless of emphasis, criticism takes on a different hue. It ceases to be a fairly straightforward academic process, impersonal and self-evident, yielding progressive scholarly evidence under a sense of joint critical endeavor. It becomes instead a highly convoluted scholarly discussion, immersed in differential relations and discursive frameworks of all sorts, yielding tensive and conflicting positions through critical engagement on and from all sides.

This third primary strategy of problematizing interpretation through stocktaking may again be seen as encompassing a variety of supporting tactics. These I would designate as follows: (1) Taking a Personal Turn; (2) Taking a Cultural Turn; and (3) Taking a Global Turn.

Taking a Personal Turn

A tactic deployed in interruptive stocktaking amounts to a focalization of the strategy of contextual enlightenment, delineated earlier under the banner of interpretive contextualization, through personalization of the analysis of social location and ideological stance. This involves a shift—or, perhaps better, a tilt—from a more collectivist to a more individualist focus on material matrix and cultural production. Minority critics come to regard and to approach their identity and role as critics not only as members of minority groups but also as distinct members within such groups: in terms of location, different from other members, despite the similarities of membership, within the groups as constructed; in terms of agenda, espousing particular variations of visions and aims, within the overall spectrum of group aims and visions. Minority critics seek to expose and theorize such differences and particularities by foregrounding personal realities and experiences.

Thus, for example, in some respects and for some occasions, a Latino/a American critic may concentrate on the Latino/a contingent as a group, or on a particular national-origins segment within this group (say, Mexican American or Dominican American); in other respects and for other occasions, such a critic may emphasize instead a specific trajectory, problematic, or position within the Latino/a formation in general, the national-origins segment in question, or, indeed, any other subgroup within them. Such a move would demand close attention to matters autobiographical across the board—not simply by way of enumeration, but rather with theorization in mind. Such a move would lead to critical dialogue with other members of the various groups in question: critical comparison regarding trajectories, problematics, or positions. Such a move would further sanction a call for self-analysis on the part of all critics, minority or dominant. To that extent, this tactical procedure would tear apart even more radically the curtain of analysis drawn around the critical task in traditional criticism, extending it from the realm of production to the realm of consumption.

Taking a Cultural Turn

Another tactic invoked in interruptive stocktaking is to intensify the strategy of breaking spatial-temporal models, outlined earlier under the mantle of border transgressionism, by moving from the level of historiographical construction (a sense of the remains as represented) to that of disciplinary construction (a sense of the plurality of traditions of representation). This entails not just moving beyond received geographical and historical confines of the discipline, therefore, but actually stepping outside such delimitations altogether by fashioning a more comprehensive vision of the discipline as discipline. Thus, minority critics come to regard their role as critics as much too constrictive, given their professional venue in the realm of the academy and its traditional focus on scholarly discourse—trajectories, paradigms, and disputations. Consequently, they begin to push instead for a vision of their task as taking in, beyond much-needed methodological and theoretical amplification within scholarly discourse, interpretive amplification as well: attention to and analysis of readings and readers of the biblical texts outside the academy. In so doing, minority critics press—from within the academy and without abandoning the academic-scholarly tradition—for sustained and rigorous analysis of other traditions of interpretation, both within and outside of the religious realm.

In the process, minority criticism effects a twofold break: first, with dominant criticism, given its exclusive devotion to scholarly interpretation; second, with itself, as it moves beyond its own demand for contextualization at the level of interpretation within the discipline. The result is also twofold. First, a broadly comparative analysis of the reception of the biblical texts within any given sociocultural context: placing scholarly interpretation alongside invocations of the texts across society and culture—from popular and devotional appropriations to social and cultural renditions (economics, politics, literature, the visual arts, film).

Second, a similarly broad comparative analysis of the consumption of the biblical texts within the religious-theological framework in question: placing academic interpretation alongside the deployment of the texts across churches and practices—from dogmatic and theological formulations (doctrine, ethics) to institutional and liturgical appeals (polity, worship). This tactical procedure ultimately transforms the biblical critic from a strictly disciplinary practitioner into a cultural observer, with interest in and responsibility for the myriad of incarnations and uses thrust onto the biblical texts.

Taking a Global Turn

Yet another tactic employed in interruptive stocktaking lies in shifting the tactic of heightening the discourse, earlier set forth under the banner of border transgressionism as well, from engagement with Minority Studies to interaction with Postcolonial Studies. This involves a projection of minority criticism onto the global scene through the insertion of criticism into geopolitical formations and trajectories, with a focus on imperial center and colonial peripheries and hence on imperial-colonial frameworks and relations. In this process, minority critics come to regard the categories "dominant" and "minority" as too limiting, given their emergence and signification within the parameters of a (nation-)state, where they reflect internal processes of ethnicization and realization at work. Minority critics thus reach beyond political formations and approach such categories in geopolitical dimensions, with a view of the (nation-)states in question as global powers and dependencies and of foreign affairs in terms of imperial-colonial constructions and relations.

Such expansion—involving perceptions, evaluations, and attitudes of the Other as global—has an impact on all domains of the critical task. To begin with, minority critics come to see their own reality and experience in the country as a result of underlying geopolitical forces and movements, which have a bearing on their material matrix and their cultural production. In effect, African American,

Asian American, and Latino/a American critics begin to address their provenance, their passage, and their situation in the country in terms of their origins in or descent from Africa, Asia, and Latin America. In so doing, they further problematize the character of their country as a global power, not only a superpower but the hyperpower, and of its management of foreign affairs in terms of imperial-colonial constructions and relations. In addition, minority critics transfer the power of such geopolitical forces and movements onto the biblical texts and contexts, foregrounding their production within a variety of ancient imperial-colonial frameworks. Lastly, minority critics extend the influence of geopolitical forces and movements onto the dominant tradition of interpretation and its practitioners, given its historical development and continued operation within a variety of imperial-colonial frameworks in both modernity and postmodernity. Throughout, therefore, minority criticism approaches what transpires locally in dominant-minority relations and constructions of race-ethnicity in terms of what transpires translocally in postcolonial relations and constructions of geopolitical relations and constructions.

Discursive Cross-fertilization: Taking the Interdisciplinary Turn

A fourth major strategy in minority criticism is to pursue sustained and systematic critical dialogue with areas of studies and discursive frameworks that have to do with the problematic of identity beyond the formations and relations of race–ethnicity in general and dominant–minority in particular. Such a project of interdisciplinary cross-fertilization consists in bringing out the convoluted and conflicted nature of identity operative in minority groups (and ultimately in dominant groups as well) and thus represents a deliberate move away from any type of racial-ethnic essentialism in the construction of such groups. This strategy is applied to both the level of composition (the world of antiquity) and the level of reception (the world of modernity and postmodernity). As such, it may be viewed as an exercise in focalization within a dual process of textual and interpretive contextualization, in which the various differential axes of identity are activated and examined from the optic of minority formations and relations.

Recourse to the curtain of critical analysis as explanatory metaphor may prove helpful yet again. The driving aim of this strategy is
similar to that of the second strategy, border transgressionism. The
goal is not to draw back the curtain on reception, shedding light on the
agent of study. Such a step is taken for granted and fully incorporated:
both the object and agent of study should receive equal treatment in
this regard. The goal, rather, is to ensure that, within this lighting
system, installation allows the light cast from the minority fixture to
coordinate and merge with the light from other ideological-political
fixtures, so that the surfaces and details of minority formations and
relations emerge as fully and clearly as possible.

Minority criticism adopts this strategy, directly or indirectly, in
the light of and in opposition to dominant criticism. As such, it sets
itself apart from received attitudes toward interdisciplinary engagement in the various umbrella models at work in dominant scholarship.
This distantiation takes place in different ways. Thus, for example,
minority criticism distinguishes itself from traditional historical criticism insofar as it seeks interaction with areas of study regarded as
having a direct and crucial bearing on all aspects of Biblical Studies.
In so doing, it underlines the stance of isolationism endemic in historical criticism, given historical criticism's reluctance to engage critically
developments within the allied discipline of Historical Studies. From
their perspective, minority critics find it hard to understand how historical critics can avoid conversation with the trajectories and debates
occurring in recent and contemporary historiography.

Similarly, minority criticism differentiates itself from literary criticism and sociocultural criticism insofar as it seeks interaction with
areas of study that surface and address differential relations of power
in society and culture, viewed as having a constant and key impact on
all dimensions of Biblical Studies. In so doing, it accentuates the sense
of innocence that often marks such criticisms, given their eschewal
of power relations affecting identity as they engage their respective
allied disciplines in the Human or Social Sciences. From their perspective, minority critics find it difficult to comprehend how literary
or sociocultural critics can pursue analysis of the material matrix or
the discursive production without explicit attention to developments
and discussions in ideological studies.

Minority recourse to this strategy has already been noted in two respects: first, with regard to the tactic of heightening the discourse, within the second strategy of expanding the area of studies; second, with respect to the tactic of taking a global turn, under the third strategy of problematizing criticism. In the first case, the turn of minority critics to Minority Studies was described: casting concerns and interests onto the wider net, long-established and highly complex, of the minority problematic. Here, the task of criticism is related not only to the primary issue of dominant-minority relations and formations but also to a set of concepts directly linked to it: ways of irruption—causes, channels, consequences of migration; ways of settling—borderlands, diaspora, exile; and ways of insertion—dominant processes of minoritization and minority reactions to dominantization.

This task may be pursued along various lines of inquiry: from a focus on a specific group; through consideration, partial or full, of various such groups; to inquiry regarding minority groups in general, beyond the ambit of any one (nation-)state. In the second case, the appeal to Postcolonial Studies on the part of minority critics was explained: viewing concerns and interests against the broader canvas, recent in origin but no less complex, of the geopolitical problematic. Here, the task of criticism is associated not only with the crucial issue of imperial-colonial relations, but also with a closely related set of concepts: imperial expansionism—designs and discourses; colonial subordination—reactions and options; and imperial-colonial rubbings—ambivalence, ambiguity, hybridity. Both of these interdisciplinary tactics could have been classified just as readily under the present strategy, for they constitute exercises in discursive cross-fertilization. To my mind, however, they seem more appropriately situated, more pointed, within their assigned strategies.

A number of other such ideological-political frameworks can be readily mentioned as well. Three of these emerge as primary, given their prominence in the academy: Materialist Studies, Feminist Studies, and Queer Studies. Thus, minority critics may latch their concerns and interests onto such nets as the following: the problematic of political economy, with its focus on the formations and relations of social class; the gender problematic, with its central issue of male-female formations and relations; and the problematic of sexuality, with its focus on the formations and relations of sexual orientation. In each case, moreover, the task of criticism involves not only the primary issue of such relations and formations but also the concepts directly associated with such issues. Various other frameworks, not as well known, readily suggest themselves, such as Disability Studies and Trauma Studies, all of which may be called upon by minority critics for fruitful interdisciplinary engagement. Lastly, a traditional framework may also be reactivated on a different key altogether, namely, Religious Studies, an area of studies that has always involved unequal relations of power among its various formations, both within and among such formations.

This fourth primary strategy of interdisciplinary cross-fertilization again reveals a variety of supporting tactics. These I would classify as follows: (1) Tandem Engagement; (2) Multiple Engagement; and (3) Intersectional Engagement.

Tandem Engagement

As in the previously delineated confluence of minority biblical criticism with Minority Studies and Postcolonial Studies, a similar bringing together may be undertaken with such fields as Materialist Studies, Feminist Studies, and Queer Studies, or with other less prominent fields. This tactic involves a projection of minority criticism onto a variety of realms: economics, through insertion into the problematic of political economy, with a focus on the dynamics of wealth and poverty and hence on class formations and relations; feminism, through insertion into the problematic of gender, with a focus on the constructions of man and woman and thus on male-female formations and relations; and sexuality, through insertion into the problematic of orientation, with a focus on constructions of gay and lesbian as well as transvestite and transgendered and hence on straight-queer formations and relations. Such expansion—involving perceptions, evaluations, and attitudes of the Other—applies to all domains of the critical task, from composition to reception.

Any such interdisciplinary confluence in tandem demands, as already argued with respect to the problematic of minoritization or that of geopolitics, a rigorous sense of procedure. This requires, it will be recalled, close attention to the overall design, the driving rationale, and the mode of correlation of the exercise in cross-fertilization envisioned. The areas of interest in both fields have to be identified; the objectives behind the proposed conjunction must be outlined; and the ways and angles of execution must be set forth. Again, an exposition of the specific problematic under consideration—the what, why, how—is essential, duly set within the scholarly discussion in question.

Combined Engagement

Such interdisciplinary ventures may also be pursued in multiple fashion. This tactic brings together two such areas of study at once, yielding a variety of possible combinations. Thus, for example, minority critics may begin with the heightened awareness provided by Minority Studies and move on to the global turn signified by Postcolonial Studies; or proceed instead to a similar economic, gender, or sexuality turn represented by Materialist Studies, Gender Studies, and Queer Studies, respectively; or undertake a turn to somatic or psychological impairment signified by Disability Studies and Trauma Studies, respectively. There is also no reason why the problematic of minoritization need serve as the point of departure in such cross-fertilization, or even be included at all in the combination. Needless to say, such multiplication and correlation of theoretical frameworks renders any exercise in multiple cross-fertilization much more difficult and calls for a sense of procedure that is, in turn, much more sophisticated. Further, such a move applies to all sectors of the critical task, production and consumption alike.

Intersectional Engagement

Ultimately, such interdisciplinary conversations may lead minority critics to pursue the ideal of intersectionality—the crisscrossing of manifold such constructions and relations of identity at once. Minority critics may thus, for example, press for invoking, simultaneously, Minority Studies along with Postcolonial Studies and Feminist Studies; or even attempt to include Materialist Studies and Queer Studies as well—all in relation to Biblical Studies. Such a move would prove extremely challenging, given its demand for enormous theoretical sophistication and methodological savvy. Such a move would also signify a certain return to individualism, but an individualism now reconceptualized and reformulated on a radically different key—a sociocultural and ideological-political variation of individualism altogether, in which varying and shifting notions of centers and peripheries in identity take place at any one time and at all times. Such a move, lastly, would be considered applicable in both the sociocultural contexts of antiquity, the world of composition, and those of modernity and postmodernity, the world of interpretation.

Concluding Comments

This analysis of the rhetorical dynamics at work in minority biblical criticism within the United States, detailed as it is, remains, as characterized from the beginning, simply a working model, an initial move, toward a taxonomy of minority poetics. Much work remains to be done. Various lines of development immediately suggest themselves: concretization; globalization; universalization; and intersectionality.

A move toward concretization is, to my mind, of the essence. The taxonomy, like any formalist exposition of a system of classification, stands as a rather abstract apparatus—a skeletal framework, as it were, without body mass of any sort. Sustained appeal to and analysis of examples of the actual mechanics displayed by minority critics in their work, both by way of primary strategies and supporting tactics, would provide the missing body mass and would prove most insightful. Such documentary evidence would expose the fabric of rhetorical procedures employed in particular instances of critical emplacement and argumentation and explain how they are combined and to what effect. Such use of examples, moreover, should be derived, throughout, from critics who represent a variety of minority groups within the country. Such comparative evidence would bring out the widespread and multidimensional deployment of these procedures across the spectrum of minority critics. Future work on the poetics of minority criticism must thus involve, to my mind, attention to both dynamics and mechanics at once: continued theorization of the procedures alongside sustained exemplification and explanation of such procedures.

A globalizing outlook is, in my opinion, quite necessary as well. The taxonomy has as its basis, as specified from the start, the work of interpretation carried out by minority critics within the United States. An internationalist focus thus constitutes a most desirable goal in this regard. Close attention to and analysis of minority criticism outside the United States, both in the rest of the West and throughout the non-Western world, would not only expand the database of rhetorical mechanics, but also fine-tune the repertoire of rhetorical dynamics. Such a focus is especially desirable, if not indispensable, today, in the light of ongoing and massive global migration. Such migration, due in large part to the spread and consequences of global capitalism, has certainly affected the United States, as the constantly updated demographic figures and projections show in ever sharper relief. Its effects nowadays, however, have an impact on Europe as well as on all regions and (nation-)states outside the West. This upturn in migration generates a corresponding increase in processes of minoritization, yielding a greater and sharper net of dominant-minority formations and relations throughout the world. Consequently, future work on minority poetics cannot do, in my opinion, without a proper global consciousness.

A universalizing framework proves no less imperative. The taxonomy reflects the work carried out by minority critics in the realm of biblical interpretation. Biblical scholarship, however, constitutes but one area in which minority critics work. To put it differently, minority critics address the range of literary and cultural production of any country, so that biblical interpretation represents but one area of activity within such production. A close investigation of minority poetics in other realms of cultural production in general and literary production in particular, as compiled and theorized by minority scholars in such fields, would prove most valuable. Such work would lend minority biblical critics broad comparative insight into the resources and practices of minority scholars outside the field, leading, on the one hand, toward greater theorization and sharper activation of rhetorical procedures in their own work and, on the other hand, toward the incorporation of biblical interpretation into the work of minority scholarship at large. In effect, future work on minority poetics should,

I believe, integrate itself as fully as possible into the overall work of minority criticism and poetics outside biblical interpretation.

A move toward intersectional comparison is, I would argue, quite crucial as well. The taxonomy surfaces the rhetorical procedures fielded by one angle of vision, ethnic-racial minority criticism, within ideological criticism and its analysis of differential power in society and culture. Given the variety of angles of vision within ideological criticism, a comparative examination of these procedures with their counterparts in other lines of inquiry would prove most useful. Such work would establish how critics laboring under other differential axes of identity formations and relations carry out the work of biblical interpretation, would reveal similarities and differences between the rhetorical procedures adopted in such other lines of inquiry and those outlined in racial-ethnic minority criticism, and would serve as a foundation not only for the forging of critical alliances with such critics but also for critical integration among racial-ethnic minority critics who also lay claim to membership in such other groups and discourses. Future work on minority poetics should, in my view, secure and maintain a close dialogue with the rhetorical strategies and tactics developed by biblical critics active in feminist and materialist, in queer and postcolonial, and in other such circles of unequal power, in the fact of dominant criticism.

A final point is in order. The objective behind the identification and theorization of a taxonomy of rhetorical procedures was advanced earlier from a variety of perspectives. First, from the general confluence of Biblical Studies and Racial-Ethnic Studies, the exercise was presented as an attempt to determine whether and how the emergent practices of minority criticism can be differentiated from the traditional practices of dominant criticism. Second, from the particular configuration of minority biblical criticism as such, the exercise was described as an attempt to foreground and theorize the formal features of critical analysis on the part of minority critics vis-à-vis those required by dominant critics. Lastly, from the reality and experience of minority critics as "minoritized" within a dialectical process involving the (nation-)state, the exercise was defined as an ideological move toward self-assertion and self-introjection as well as in breaking-through and conjuring-up.

By way of conclusion, I should like to harp on this third point. The present study does represent, in many ways, a formalist exercise, insofar as it sets out to name, order, and describe the rhetorical strategies and tactics at work in minority criticism. The study, however, is also pointedly ideological in character.

In fact, it is so in various ways. First, insofar as, in the process of highlighting, classifying, and unpacking strategies and tactics, the rhetorical aims and ideological agenda of such moves and techniques were considered throughout. Second, because any critical exercise involving differential power relations in society and culture cannot, even if it so wished, avoid the question of politics, writ large. Any such exercise is always undertaken with a purpose, directly or indirectly, within the set of given formations and relations. Third, this formalist exercise in particular has indeed been explicitly placed at the service of an ideological program. Consequently, exposing and critiquing the dominant-minority dialectic in the field of biblical interpretation are important elements of this exercise. As such, it is very much an exercise in self-assertion and self-introjection and thus in moving-beyond. It seeks to participate in the ongoing development of voices and visages of our own among racial-ethnic minorities in the United States. Such conscientization regarding strategies and tactics, their activation and ramifications, will, it is my hope, serve in furthering the work of minority empowerment not only within the discipline and the profession of biblical criticism, but in a broad range of academic disciplines as well.

Index

dominant: critics, 289, 291, 310;
    scholarship, 296, 298, 304
Domitian, 77
dominant criticism, 283-85, 288-
    90, 292-96, 299, 301, 304, 310
Douglass, Frederick, 22, 259-78

early Christian studies: discipline
    of, 1-2, 4-5, 16, 18, 20, 159, 163,
    165, 168, 171, 179, 187, 189 n94
Eikones (Pseudo-Lucian), 69-71
Egypt: in ancient times, 35, 88, 92,
    268; as symbol of Britain, 264,
    269; as symbol of United States,
    265
emancipatory: discourses, 16; bib-
    lical studies, 13; movements,
    13-14, 17
Enlightenment, 96, 180, 224
Epictetus, 129, 150-51
eschatology, 245
essentialism, 6, 130 n1, 142 n36,
    281, 303
ethnē, 88, 94-95, 97-98, 111, 116,
    132, 139-40, 242
ethnic construction, 130-31, 133-
    34, 139 n23,154
ethnic reasoning, 19, 79-80, 101,
    103, 113, 115, 123, 125 n60
ethnicity, 1-7, 9-10, 19-21, 48, 53,
    63-65, 69, 71-72, 74, 77-84,
    85 n13, 87, 90-91, 96, 101-4,
    106, 115, 118-20, 122, 125, 127,
    130-33, 134 n10, 136, 145, 160,
    162, 164-65, 168, 171, 174, 176,
    178, 187, 190, 195, 235-36, 239,
    240-43, 245, 257-58, 278, 280-
    82, 303
ethno-Religion, 83
ethnos, 12, 14, 19, 20, 23, 82-84,
    92-93, 96-98, 116-117, 118, 126,
    129, 130, 132, 135, 150, 159,
    162, 163, 178-79, 181, 241-42,
    248, 282
ethos, 115
Europe: nationalism of, 195; racism
    in, 96, 219, 224, 227

Exodus: story of, 263, 265, 267-68,
    271, 277
Ezra, 85 n13

fascism, 188, 196
feminism: black feminism, 42;
    critical feminism, 5, 28, 306;
    Jewish feminism, 2 n5
flaventis, 37, 39
foreignness, 133
fuscus, 31-32

Galatians, 151, 161, 182 n72, 273
gender, 2-10, 13-14, 18-20, 27,
    29-31, 33, 37, 41, 49, 51-54,
    59-60, 62, 64-65, 69, 77-78,
    87, 91, 101, 103-4, 106, 119-25,
    127, 133, 154, 159, 162-63, 165,
    167-68, 171-72, 176, 178, 182,
    186-87, 191, 193, 198, 205, 220,
    230, 238, 278, 305-7
genos, 20, 82, 92, 95-97, 159, 162-
    63, 178-79, 181, 184
genocide, 167, 196, 219
Gentile(s), 19, 117, 129, 132, 134,
    135, 139, 140-42, 144-45, 147-
    54, 183, 226, 251, 254
Germanness, 220
Godwyn, Morgan, 272-73
Greco-Roman world, 98,
Greek: ethnicity, 72, 74; *paideia*,
    53, 59, 70, 73
Greek Slave, statue of, 51-60, 75, 78
Grundmann, Walter, 215 n15, 220-
    23, 228

Hasmoneans, 83, 241
haunting, 20, 22, 65 n41, 159, 164-
    71, 177, 180, 187-88, 260-61,
    266
heirs, *See* Abraham.
Hellenism: Judaism/Hellenism
    dichotomy, 83, 91, 97-98, 242;
    philosophical tradition in, 81,
    151; statuary in, 53, 71, 73, 76
heterosexism, 8, 10, 14, 22, 169,
    171-72